Joshua M.

הילר בן אודרס

MW00651619

Tefillah for Success in Observing the
Mitzvos of Interpersonal Relationships

יְהִי רָצוֹן מִלְּפָנֶיךָ אֵל רַחוּם וְחַנּוּן שֶׁתִּתֶּן בְּלִבִּי לִשְׁמֹר תּוֹרָתְךָ הַקְּדוֹשָׁה. וּלְפִי שֶׁלֹּא מָצָאתָ לָנוּ כְּלִי מַחֲזִיק בְּרָכָה אֶלָּא הַשָּׁלוֹם, לָכֵן יְהִי רָצוֹן מִלְּפָנֶיךָ, מֶלֶךְ שֶׁהַשָּׁלוֹם שֶׁלּוֹ, שֶׁתַּעַזְרֵנִי הַיּוֹם וּבְכָל יוֹם לְהִתְאַמֵּץ וּלְהִתְחַזֵּק בְּמִצְוֹתֶיךָ וּבִפְרָט בַּמִּצְוֹת שֶׁבֵּין הָאָדָם לַחֲבֵרוֹ, וְנִחְיֶה בְּאַהֲבָה וְאַחֲוָה וְשָׁלוֹם וְרֵעוּת, וְיֵעָשׂוּ כֻלָּם אֲגֻדָּה אַחַת לַעֲשׂוֹת רְצוֹנְךָ בְּלֵבָב שָׁלֵם.

רִבּוֹנוֹ שֶׁל עוֹלָם! הָאֵר עֵינַי בְּתוֹרָתֶךָ וְתֵן בְּלִבִּי לְהָבִין וּלְהַשְׂכִּיל לִשְׁמֹעַ לִלְמֹד וּלְלַמֵּד לִשְׁמֹר וְלַעֲשׂוֹת וּלְקַיֵּם אֶת כָּל הַמִּצְוֹת וּבִפְרָט הַמִּצְוֹת שֶׁבֵּין הָאָדָם לַחֲבֵרוֹ בְּכָל דִּקְדּוּקֵיהֶן כַּדִּין, וְאַף לִפְנִים מִשּׁוּרַת הַדִּין, עִם כָּל אַחַי בְּנֵי יִשְׂרָאֵל. שֶׁלֹּא אֶגְרֹם לָהֶם לַחְשְׁדֵנִי בַּמֶּה שֶׁאֵין בִּי וְלֹא אֶחְשֹׁד אֲנִי אוֹתָם לַשָּׁוְא וְאָדוֹן כָּל אֶחָד מֵהֶם לְכַף זְכוּת. וְתַצִּילֵנִי מֵחֶמְדָּה וְתַאֲוָה, שִׂנְאָה נְקִימָה וּנְטִירָה, הוֹנָאַת דְּבָרִים וּמַחֲלֹקֶת, הַכָּאָה וּקְלָלָה. וְתִשְׁמְרֵנִי מִלָּשׁוֹן הָרַע וּרְכִילוּת, דְּבַר שֶׁקֶר וּגְנֵבַת דַּעַת, לֵיצָנוּת גַּאֲוָה וָכַעַס. וּכְשֶׁתְּבוֹא לְיָדִי מִצְוַת תּוֹכָחָה הָיֶה עִם פִּי וְאַקִּימֶנָּה בְּדַרְכֵי נֹעַם וּבְנַחַת, שֶׁלֹּא אֶכָּשֵׁל בְּהַלְבָּנַת פָּנִים וְשֶׁלֹּא אֶתְכַּבֵּד בְּקָלוֹן חֲבֵרִי. אָבִי שֶׁבַּשָּׁמַיִם, עָזְרֵנִי נָא שֶׁלֹּא לַעֲמֹד עַל דַּם רֵעִי רַק אֶשְׁתַּדֵּל לְהַצִּילָם מִכָּל הֶפְסֵד בְּגוּפָם וּבְמָמוֹנָם, וְשֶׁלֹּא אַכְשִׁיל שׁוּם אָדָם בְּאִסּוּר וְלֹא אַשִּׂיא לַחֲבֵרִי עֵצָה שֶׁאֵינָהּ הוֹגֶנֶת לָהֶם. וְתֵן בִּי הַכֹּחַ שֶׁלֹּא לְהַחֲנִיף לְעוֹבְרֵי עֲבֵרָה בְּעֵינֵיהֶם אוֹ בְּעֵינֵי אֲחֵרִים. זַכֵּנִי לַעֲבֹר עַל מִדּוֹתַי וְלִמְחֹל לְמִי שֶׁחָטָא כְּנֶגְדִּי, וְלִקַבֵּל כָּל אָדָם בְּסֵבֶר פָּנִים יָפוֹת וְלִשְׁאֹל בְּשָׁלוֹם כָּל אָדָם כָּרָאוּי. טַהֵר לִבִּי לְעָבְדְּךָ בֶּאֱמֶת לָלֶכֶת בִּדְרָכֶיךָ בְּמִדּוֹת הַחֶסֶד וְהָרַחֲמִים, וְלֶאֱהֹב אֶת הָרַע כָּמוֹנִי וְלַעְזֹר בְּכָל צְרָכָיו: בְּהַכְנָסַת אוֹרְחִים, בְּהַכְנָסַת חָתָן וְכַלָּה, בְּבִקּוּר חוֹלִים, בְּחֶסֶד שֶׁל אֱמֶת וּבְנִחוּם אֲבֵלִים. וְלָשֵׂאת בְּעוֹל עִם כָּל אֶחָד מִיִּשְׂרָאֵל. חַזְּקֵנִי נָא לְכַבֵּד הוֹרִים וּמוֹרִים, חַכְמֵי יִשְׂרָאֵל וְכֹהֲנִים. וְאַף בִּמְקוֹם שֶׁלֹּא נֶאֶמְרוּ אִסּוּרִים אֵלּוּ, כְּגוֹן לְשׁוֹן הָרַע בְּבֵרוּרֵי שִׁדּוּכִים אוֹ מַשָּׂא וּמַתָּן, הַכָּאַת בָּנִים וְתַלְמִידִים לְשֵׁם חִנּוּךְ וְשִׂנְאַת הָרְשָׁעִים, תִּשְׁמְרֵנִי מִלַּעֲשׂוֹת יוֹתֵר מִן הַצֹּרֶךְ וְלַעֲמֹד בְּכָל הַתְּנָאִים הָאֲמוּרִים בַּדָּבָר.

וּבִזְכוּת קִיּוּם מִצְוֹת אֵלּוּ תַּשְׁרֶה תַּשְׁרֶה שְׁכִינָתְךָ בְּתוֹכֵנוּ, וְתָחִישׁ גְּאֻלָּתֵנוּ וְתִבְנֶה בֵּית מִקְדָּשֵׁנוּ וּתְפָאֲרֵנוּ בִּמְהֵרָה בְּיָמֵינוּ, אָמֵן.

(If one is not able to say the entire tefillah,
he may recite only the first and last paragraphs.)

The Code
OF Jewish
Conduct

Avoiding Falsehood • Sheker L'to'eles • Avoiding Deceit • Love Your Fellowman as Yourself • Walk
Special Situations • Honoring Parents • Honoring Torah Scholars and the Elderly • Honoring Kohan
eeting Others • Striking • Do Not Curse • Hurting with Speech • Putting to Shame • Saving Your Fello
Coveting the Possessions of Others • Your Brother, Your Friend, A Member of Your People, Your Eq
soling the Mourners • Chasan V'Kallah • Hospitality to Guests • Loshon Hora and Rechilus L'To'eles I
Revenge • Do Not Bear a Grudge • Laws of Asking Forgiveness • Avoiding Strife • Pursuing Peace •
h of Children • Torah Education for Girls • Flattery of a Sinner • Causing Another to Sin/Giving Ba
ve Your Fellowman as Yourself • Walk in Hashem's Ways • Visiting the Sick • Attending to the Dec
holars and the Elderly • Honoring Kohanim • Judge Your Fellow With Righteousness • Do Not Hate
eech • Putting to Shame • Saving Your Fellow Jew's Person or Property • The Obligation to Give R
Your Friend, A Member of Your People, Your Equal • Avoiding Falsehood • Sheker L'to'eles • Avoi
tality to Guests • Loshon Hora and Rechilus L'To'eles in Special Situations • Honoring Parents • Hor
sking Forgiveness • Avoiding Strife • Pursuing Peace • Greeting Others • Striking • Do Not Curse •
lattery of a Sinner • Causing Another to Sin/Giving Bad Advice Coveting the Possessions of Others
m's Ways • Visiting the Sick • Attending to the Deceased • Consoling the Mourners • Chasan V'Kall
dge Your Fellow With Righteousness • Do Not Hate • Do not Take Revenge • Do Not Bear a Grudge
w's Person or Property • The Obligation to Give Rebuke • Chinuch of Children • Torah Education fo
• Avoiding Falsehood • Sheker L'to'eles • Avoiding Deceit • Love Your Fellowman as Yourself • Walk
Special Situations • Honoring Parents • Honoring Torah Scholars and the Elderly • Honoring Kohan
eeting Others • Striking • Do Not Curse • Hurting with Speech • Putting to Shame • Saving Your Fello
Coveting the Possessions of Others • Your Brother, Your Friend, A Member of Your People, Your Eo
soling the Mourners • Chasan V'Kallah • Hospitality to Guests • Loshon Hora and Rechilus L'To'eles
Revenge • Do Not Bear a Grudge • Laws of Asking Forgiveness • Avoiding Strife • Pursuing Peace •
h of Children • Torah Education for Girls • Flattery of a Sinner • Causing Another to Sin/Giving Ba
ve Your Fellowman as Yourself • Walk in Hashem's Ways • Visiting the Sick • Attending to the De
holars and the Elderly • Honoring Kohanim • Judge Your Fellow With Righteousness • Do Not Hat
eech • Putting to Shame • Saving Your Fellow Jew's Person or Property • The Obligation to Give F
; Your Friend, A Member of Your People, Your Equal • Avoiding Falsehood • Sheker L'to'eles • Avo
tality to Guests • Loshon Hora and Rechilus L'To'eles in Special Situations • Honoring Parents • Hor
sking Forgiveness • Avoiding Strife • Pursuing Peace • Greeting Others • Striking • Do Not Curse •
lattery of a Sinner • Causing Another to Sin/Giving Bad Advice Coveting the Possessions of Others •
m's Ways • Visiting the Sick • Attending to the Deceased • Consoling the Mourners • Chasan V'Kal
dge Your Fellow With Righteousness • Do Not Hate • Do not Take Revenge • Do Not Bear a Grudge
w's Person or Property • The Obligation to Give Rebuke • Chinuch of Children • Torah Education fo
• Avoiding Falsehood • Sheker L'to'eles • Avoiding Deceit • Love Your Fellowman as Yourself • Wal

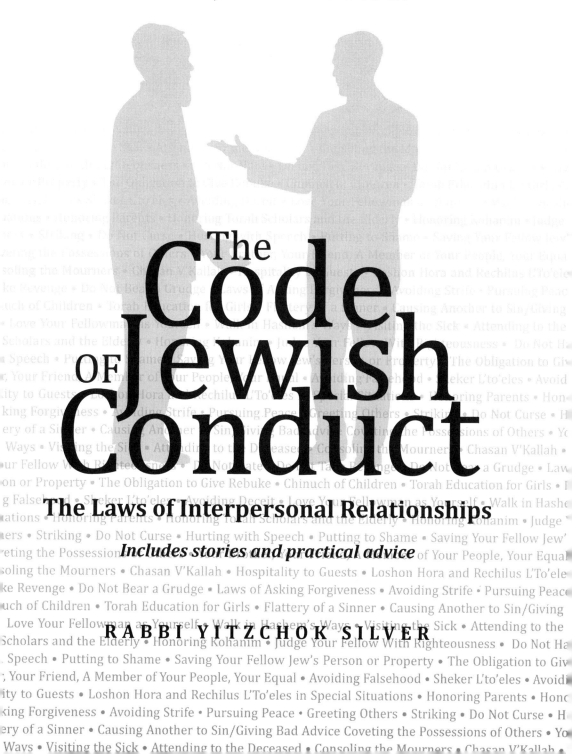

THE ROSENBERG EDITION

ספר משפטי השלום - הלכות בין אדם לחבירו

The Code of Jewish Conduct

The Laws of Interpersonal Relationships

Includes stories and practical advice

RABBI YITZCHOK SILVER

TRANSLATED BY:
Rabbi M. Silver
Mr. and Mrs. D. Broch

ADAPTED BY:
Mrs. D. Reichel

EDITED BY:
Mrs. S.C. Mizrachi

PAGE LAYOUT AND DESIGN:
Mrs. E. Chachamtzedek

COVER DESIGN:
Mrs. Z. Thumim

DISTRIBUTED BY:
Israel Bookshop Publications
501 Prospect Street
Lakewood, NJ 08701

Tel: (732) 901-3009
Fax: (732) 901-4012
www.israelbookshoppublications.com
info@israelbookshoppublications.com

לינת הצדק
CENTER FOR
JEWISH VALUES
המרכז ללימוד ההלכות שבין אדם לחבירו

6 Grossberg St. Jerusalem, Israel
4001 Fallstaff Rd. Baltimore, MD 21215
(443)270-9410   info@jvalues.com

Printed in the United States of America

בס"ד

שמואל קמנצקי
Rabbi S. Kamenetsky

2018 Upland Way
Philadelphia, Pa 19131

Home: 215-473-2798
Study: 215-473-1212

11 Tammuz 5768

Hilchos Bein Adam L'Chavero, the Torah laws governing inter-personal relations, are relevant to nearly every facet of daily life. However, while the concepts are familiar, many of the Halachos for practical observance are rarely studied, and remain unclear.

Linas HaTzedek: The Center for Jewish Values was established with the goal of making these Halachos accessible to the public. Under its auspices, Sefer Mishpatei HaShalom was written by Rabbi Yitzchak Silver. It presents the Halachos of Bein Adam L'Chavero in a clear and concise fashion. Over the past two years, this sefer has been extremely well received. It has become a basic and crucial sefer and has opened a window to the Torah's directives regarding these vital Mitzvos for thousands of people.

I am therefore happy to hear that the sefer will now appear in English, entitle "The Code of Jewish Conduct." This book is ideal for independent study, as resource material, and as a textbook in schools. It will raise the awareness of Bein Adam L'Chavero in the English-speaking public of all ages, making these Halachos and their observance come to life.

The Beis HaMikdash was destroyed due to Sinas Chinam. Strengthening Bein Adam L'Chavero will surely hasten the coming of the Geula, b'mehera b'yamenu.

Letter of Blessing from Hagaon Hagadol
Harav Mattisyahu Chaim Salomon *shlit"a*

Lakewood, New Jersey

Thursday, *parashas Toledos* 5768

To my dear friend, the *ga'on* Harav Yitzchak Silver, *shlit"a*,

I was extremely pleased to receive the *sefer Mishpetei Hashalom*. The material is clearly explained, and it guides the reader directly along the correct path in fulfilling the *mitzvos* of relating to other people. The style is smooth and easy to read. I am confident that many people will be inspired to fulfill the 4 of relating to others in a fair and just manner, which is, according to the Ramban, the fulfillment of the 4 of being holy.

Now you are about to publish an English translation of the book for the benefit of those who might not understand the Hebrew version. This is certainly a worthy project and will bring merit to many more people. As *Chazal* have taught, one who brings merit to the masses will shine forever in *Shamayim* like the stars.

I extend my blessings to you. May you continue to produce *sefarim* of true Torah content for the public's benefit.

Best wishes to you always,

אמצ' חיים סלומן

Mattisyahu Chaim Salomon

---

* *The above is a translation of the original Hebrew letter of blessing.*

RABBI YAAKOV HILLEL

Rosh Yeshivat

Hevrat Ahavat Shalom

45 Arzey Habira St. Jerusalem

יעקב משה הלל

ראש ישיבת

חברת אהבת שלום

רח' ארזי הבירה 45 ירושלים

בס"ד

3 Tammuz 5768

Harav Yitzchak Silver, author of *Kitzur Mishpetei Hashalom*, has asked me to comment on his *sefer*.

I have not known Rav Silver personally until now, but his reputation has preceded him. I see how others have praised his diligence in Torah study and his expertise in expressing *halachah* in a clear manner. He has now authored a *sefer* about the *mitzvos* of one's relations with other Jews, a *sefer* that is most useful and necessary. In it he has invested his talent in clarifying the *halachos* and codifying them in an orderly fashion. He has based this latest volume on his previous work, *Mishpetei Hashalom*, in which he explained in great depth and breadth the sources of each *halachah* and the opinions of the earlier as well as the later *poskim*. In every section of this book he has brought important points that testify to his mastery of the material.

Besides being a scholarly work, it is also a practical one. It includes much guidance and advice that people will find very necessary for their daily lives. In particular, this last volume, containing the halachos without the lengthy Talmudic discussions behind them, will enable the reader to become familiar with many subjects that are not at all well-known in our times. This is a wonderful merit for the masses.

I extend my blessings to the author that he continue to study and teach Torah and provide our people with more such useful *sefarim*. May he merit to magnify the Torah's brightness in the world. May G-d grant him success and protect him from stumbling, *amen*.

I attach my signature in honor of the Torah and those who study it,

---

* *The above is a translation of the original Hebrew approbation.*

הרב ישראל גנס

רח' פנים מאירת 2
קרית מטרסדורף, ירושלים 94423
טלפון 5371782

בס״ד ...נ.י.סן...תשס״ז..........

A manuscript of the important book *Kitzur Mishpetei Hashalom* was brought before me. This book is based on the work *Mishpetei Hashalom*, which already merited the approbations of *gedolei Yisrael* and has been distributed in the thousands and tens of thousands, earning resounding approval, with Hashem's help.

The author, Hagaon Rabbi Yitzchak Silver *shlit"a* did well by investing his concentrated energies into this crucial area, since this condensed version enables young boys and seminary girls to learn the matters related to *mitzvos bein adam lechaveiro,* which form an inseparable part of our sacred Torah, and are relevant to each and every one of us in our everyday lives.

In view of the importance of the book, which is presented in an eminently organized and crystal-clear fashion, all I can add is my *brachah* that the author should continue to produce more and more texts for the benefit of *Klal Yisrael* and the enhancement of Hashem's Name in the world.

Yisroel Ganz

---

* *The above is a translation of the original Hebrew approbation.*

Rabbi Yitzchak Berkovits

Sanhedria HaMurchevet 113/27

Jerusalem, Israel 97707

02-5813847

יצחק שמואל הלוי ברקוביץ

ראש רשת כוללים לינת הצדק

סנהדרי׳ה המורחבת 113/27

ירושלם ת״ו

Menachem Av 5768

Mitzvos bein adam lechaveiro account for the majority of mitzvos which apply today. However, even the Torah observant public is often unaware of the particulars of these Halachos and their applications. A major factor contributing to this incongruity is the lack of comprehensive seforim dealing with these important topics.

As a Rosh Kollel in the Linas Hatzedek Network of *bein adam lechaveiro* Kollelim, Rabbi Yitzchok Silver is an expert in all areas of *hilchos bein adam lechaveiro*. Rabbi Silver has organized and compiled many of these Halachos into an extensive, and user-friendly sefer. The original Hebrew edition of this sefer has been tremendously successful and has changed the lives of all who have studied it.

Becoming an expert in *hilchos bein adam lechaveiro* is a process, and an exercise in self-improvement. Though this sefer can not provide all-encompassing rules and decisions pertaining to every single scenario, it does give the reader/student the tools to gain a fundamental understanding of the concepts involved.

I sincerely hope that this sefer will become a means of enhancing the learning and observance of *hilchos bein adam lechaveiro* throughout *Klal Yisrael.*

Yitzchak Berkovits

---

* *The above is a translation of the original Hebrew approbation.*

EXCERPTS FROM APPROBATIONS FOR
MISHPETEI HASHALOM*

All of the *mitzvos bein adam lechaveiro* are principally Torah-based *halachos*, not extra pious behavior or ethical conduct... One must learn and delve into the *halachah* of what is permitted and what is prohibited... Anyone who makes a regular habit of learning these *halachos* will certainly gain much benefit... The study of these *halachos* should be instilled among the general public...

(Hagaon Rabbi Michel Yehuda Lefkovitz, *shlit"a*)

*

...A veritable treasure in all matters *bein adam lechaveiro*, both the positive acts of "Love your neighbor" and the avoidance of negative *middos* and common prohibitions, encompassing all aspects of a Jew's daily life... in a clear and illuminating manner. The erudition and depth of understanding of the author are evident...

(Hagaon Rabbi Chaim Pinchas Scheinberg, *shlit"a*)

*

...These commonly occurring *mitzvos* apply in all places, at all times, both for men and women. The *Mishnah Berurah* wrote "...There are many *mitzvos* that are not cited in the Shulchan Aruch and yet are found in the books enumerating the *mitzvos*... Every person should learn them and become familiar with them, and only in this way will he be able to properly fulfill them."

(Hagaon Rabbi Aryeh Leib Finkel, *shlit"a*)

*

---

* *All of the excerpts were translated from the original Hebrew approbations.*

This book contains a collection of *halachos* and clarification of laws, in issues between man and his Creator, and between man and his fellow ... and these matters are of the utmost significance in life....

(Hagaon Rav Yaakov Perlow, *shlit"a*, the Novominsker Rebbe)

*

...The author has grown in Torah in our yeshivah for decades... Hashem granted him exceptional success in reaching lofty levels of clear understanding and breadth of knowledge. The author's presentation is exceptionally clear... his *yiras Shamayim*, personal conduct and manner befit a *talmid chacham*... May his words enter the hearts of his readers... and increase *kevod Shamayim* and *kevod haTorah*.

(Hagaon Rabbi Nosson Tzvi Finkel, *shlit"a*)

*

The esteemed, brilliant author, who is himself "pure silver," intended his work to be only for the sake of Heaven, to increase peace and exalted fellowship in the eyes of G-d and man.

(Hagaon Rav Moshe Halberstam, *zt"l*)

*

The author presents each individual issue with astounding clarity ... in all its minute details. He developed this work based on the words of *Chazal*, *Rishonim* and *Acharonim* ... with vast knowledge and a balanced Torah approach, all in clear, straightforward style.... It is a great light which will lighten up the darkness of our times.

(Hagaon Rav Menachem Mendel Fuchs, *shlit"a*)

*

...This book is a necessity for our time and is invaluable... This is what destroyed our *Beis Hamikdash* and burned our sanctuary, and it still dances among us... How urgent it is to instill these *mitzvos* among all groups of the people.

(Rabbi Asher Zelig Weiss, *shlit"a*)

Contents

Contents

Contents

לזכרון עולם בהיכל השם

לעילוי נשמות

ר' **אריה יהודה** ב"ר יצחק ז"ל
וזוגתו מרת **אדל** ב"ר ראובן ע"ה
ראזענבערג

אשר היו לאות ולדוגמא בחביבות
קיום מצוות שבין אדם לחבירו,
ומצאו חן ושכל טוב
בעיני אלוקים ואדם,
אהובים למעלה ונחמדים למטה,
תפארת לו מן האדם
אשר שם שמים התאהב
על ידיהם כל ימיהם

יהי זכרם ברוך

ת.נ.צ.ב.ה.

הישר באדם

איש נעים הליכות

צנוע ומעלי אשר

התהדר בקיום ההלכות

השייכות בין בני אדם

לזכרון עולם

ד״ר שלמה ב״ר יעקב פרנצלאו ז״ל

נלב״ע י״ג אדר תשס״א

ת.נ.צ.ב.ה.

לזכרון עולם בהיכל השם

לע"נ

ר' **משה** ב"ר **שלמה אהרן** ז"ל
נלב"ע י"א מרחשון תשס"ח

נדבת בנו

ר' **יוסף יצחק קזרנובסקי**
ומשפחתו

לזכרון עולם בהיכל השם

Foreword

- ❐ You only want to buy a can of soda, but all the customers in the supermarket checkout line have full carts. May you cut the line?

- ❐ What "inside" information can you reveal about your roommate for *shidduch* purposes?

- ❐ Are lies ever permissible?

- ❐ Under what circumstances — if any — may computer software be duplicated?

THESE QUESTIONS ARE NOT matters of opinion, nor are they merely thought provoking questions. There are clear Torah guidelines dictating the exact response to each of the scenarios mentioned above, and every other interpersonal interaction.

Yet, many of us cannot answer these questions.

In fact, *hilchos bein adam lechaveiro*, the Torah laws which govern interpersonal relations, comprise more than half of the *mitzvos* that apply today. They are relevant to nearly every facet of daily life. These Halachos include business ethics, relationships, and family life, and range from honesty to *tzedakah*, from *lashon hara* to copyright laws.

However, while the concepts are familiar, many of the *halachos* for practical observance are rarely studied, and therefore, remain unclear.

Linas HaTzedek: The Center for Jewish Values was founded in 5761/2001 to fill this void. The organization is responsible for a wide array of programs, publications and activities that bring *hilchos bein adam lechaveiro* alive to the wider public.

Our flagship program is the Linas HaTzedek Kollel Network, an international group of *kollelim* which study *bein adam lechaveiro* in depth. Following a unique, structured curriculum, the *kollelim* educate *Talmidei chachamim* to become authorities in the *halachos* of *hilchos bein adam lechaveiro*.

The Center for Jewish Values has published and produced varied resource materials, including reference books, teachers' guides, tapes and videos in both Hebrew and English. Additionally, the Center organizes *shiurim* and learning programs in dozens of settings across the globe.

We are privileged that **Rabbi Yitzchak Berkovits**, a world-renowned expert on *bein adam lechaveiro*, serves as Dean and Rosh haKollelim. Rabbi Berkovits' masterful and systematic compilation of *hilchos bein adam lechaveiro* serves as the basis for all Center for Jewish Values projects.

Under Rabbi Berkovits' insightful leadership, a new generation of Torah scholars, laymen and students are gaining an awareness of these *halachos* and their proper application in all facets of daily life.

*   *   *

Rabbi Yitzchok Silver is a *dayan* and a *moreh horaah* for students in the Mirrer Yeshiva in Jerusalem. Rabbi Silver was a member of the first Linas HaTzedek Kollel. Today, Rabbi Silver serves as a Rosh Kollel in the Linas HaTzedek Kollelim. He is also a much sought-after lecturer on *hilchos bein adam lechaveiro*.

Under the auspices of the Center for Jewish Values, Rabbi Silver authored the *Mishpatei HaShalom* series. This Hebrew language series summarizes and encapsulates many areas of *hilchos bein adam lechaveiro* and their practical application. To date, tens of thousands of copies of these *sefarim* are in circulation, and their popularity continues to grow. However, until today, the impact of these books has been limited to Hebrew speakers.

The Center for Jewish Values is proud to participate in the publication of *The Code of Jewish Conduct*. This *sefer* will make *hilchos bein adam lechaveiro* accessible to the English-speaking public. It will serve as another valuable tool in the effort to raise the awareness and knowledge of *hilchos bein adam lechaveiro*.

The Center for Jewish Values is constantly developing new formats to promote the awareness of *hilchos bein adam lechaveiro*. We welcome proposals for effective usage of this *sefer*, as well as new ideas for advancing the dissemination of *hilchos bein adam lechaveiro*.

Foreword

It is my sincere hope that the learning and practice of *mitzvos bein adam lechaveiro* will serve to bring the Jewish People closer to one another. And together, may we soon merit the *geulah sheleimah*.

Paysach Freedman, Director
Linas HaTzedek: The Center for Jewish Values
Menachem Av 5768
Jerusalem

יזכור א' נשמת אמי מורתי

הצדקת **יטלא** עליה השלום

בת החבר רבי **שמעון** בלומנטהל ז"ל

סילבר

עלתה השמימה באשמורת הבוקר ו' בסיון תשס"ח

בעת קבלת התורה

יראת שמים טהורה היא חכמתה, ואמונתה איתנה כסל**ע**

טוב עינה ומידותיה היו למופת, ובתבונתה השכילה אל ד**ל**

לשונה שמרה מכל משמר, ובזולתה לא הטילה גנאי ודופ**י**

אהובה לשמים ולבריות, תמימה ותמה בכל דרכיה ומעשי**ה**

סדין עשתה ותמכור, ובמעט שבמעט כל ימיה הסתפק**ה**

יושר וצדק היו נר לרגליה, וגדולי החכמים זכתה לשמ**ש**

לבה חש ברגשי הבריות, בשעות צער ובעיתות שמחה וגי**ל**

ביתה פתוח לרווחה בפני כל, ונפשות רבות במחיצתה התנחמ**ו**

ראתה את העוה"ז כפרוזדור לטרקלין, ולא נהנתה ממנו כלו**ם**

תהא נשמתה צרורה בצרור החיים

Preface

הודו לה׳ כי טוב כי לעולם חסדו

I AM GRATEFUL TO *Hakadosh Baruch Hu* for enabling me to present this *sefer* to *Klal Yisrael*.

The Code of Jewish Conduct is an abridged English-language version of my original Hebrew *sefarim*, entitled *Mishpetei Hashalom* and *Emes Knei*. They are scholarly works, with sources and explanations, presenting the *halachos* of over fifty *mitzvos bein adam lechaveiro*.

These very practical *sefarim* were the fruit of in-depth *shiurim* delivered to many groups across Israel, mainly under the auspices of Linas HaTzedek: The Center for Jewish Values, headed by Rabbis Yitzchak Berkovits and Paysach Freedman. Both of these men inspired me to write this *sefer*, which organizes the *halachos* in a manner that is palatable to layman and scholar alike. I offer them my heartfelt thanks.

The aim of these *sefarim* is to make people aware of the fact that *mitzvos bein adam lechaveiro* have clear halachic guidelines, and are not simply manifestations of extra piousness. It is my hope that these *sefarim* will encourage the study of these somewhat neglected areas.

With Hashem's help, the Hebrew versions of *Mishpetei Hashalom* (including an abridged version, *Kitzur Mishpetei Hashalom*, which made these *halachos* available to an even broader public) succeeded far beyond anyone's dreams. They have filled a vacuum, as it seems, of a general lack of books dealing with these topics. In the two years since its publication, over 35,000 copies of these books have been sold, and the results have been extraordinary.

The *sefarim* have made deep inroads in many *chinuch* and *kiruv* establishments, for men and women, boys and girls, all over the world. It is now common for people everywhere to use these *sefarim* in learning sessions with friends or relatives, in public forums or on an individual basis, on all levels.

It became evident that there was a need to share all this with the English-speaking public. The translation of these *sefarim* was in the works for about three years. My dear father, who was the first translator for this project, spared no effort, combining his vast Torah knowledge with his renowned language expertise to produce a true masterpiece. With sound advice in each and every relevant area, his painstaking work established the high standards that have been applied throughout the continuation of this project.

Many thanks are due to *Hamodia* newspaper for publishing major portions of these *sefarim* in the paper's daily *halachah* column, both in the United States and in Israel.

The inspiration and support of a very special family from Switzerland has advanced this project on many levels. Their perseverance is a lesson in itself. It was they who introduced the *sefer* to *Hamodia* and to Pirchei of America, making it available to a much wider audience than ever before. They have been a strong driving force in this translation as well. Hashem will surely repay them for their exceptional deeds.

I would like to take this opportunity to thank a loyal and close friend who has encouraged and assisted me in many aspects of this project — and particularly for recently introducing to me to a wonderful group of precious individuals from the Johannesburg community. They joined forces and undertook a major part of the financial burden of this translation and publication, foreseeing the massive worldwide effect it would have in all sectors of our society. May the merit of all those who learn and live by these *mitzvos* stand by them forever.

I also wish to thank the Bikur Cholim Gemilas Chassadim Trust of Manchester for their substantial assistance in all of my Hebrew publications, particularly the *Kitzur Mishpetei Hashalom*. They have been instrumental in vastly increasing its distribution, particularly within educational systems throughout Eretz Yisrael. May their efforts be a true *ilui neshamah* for Efrayim, *z"l*, ben Reb David *Hakohen*, *shlit"a*, and Brachah, *a"h*, bas Reb David, *Hy"v*, along with the *neshamos* of the other departed members of their families.

Others who have been tremendously supportive of these projects are Mr. and Mrs. Jonathan Faith; my nephew, Y.Z. Schleider; my loyal *talmid* Ari Sanger; and Rabbi Chanoch Ludmir of Yerushalayim. They have all earned my deepest gratitude. May this work be an _ilui neshamah_ for Yaakov Yisrael, _z"l_, ben Chanoch Henich, _shlit"a_. Additionally, there are a number of other special individuals who were instrumental in many ways to the success of this project, who, for one reason or another, preferred not to be mentioned. My heartfelt thanks go to each and every one of them. May Hashem reward them abundantly.

I wish to thank the many Rabbanim and _talmidei chachamim_ who have given of their precious time and abilities to ensure the success of this project. In particular, Rabbi Yehudah Heimowitz oversaw various stages of the preparation of this work.

I am humbly indebted to my parents for their endless self-sacrifice on my behalf. They spared neither effort nor resources to be _mechanech_ me and all my siblings in the _derech haTorah_. May this _sefer_ be an _ilui neshamah_ for my mother, Yitte'le (Henriette) bas Hechover R' Shimon, who passed away this year on the first night of Shavuos. May _Hakadosh Baruch Hu_ bless my father, Rabbi Menachem Manelei (Emanuel) Silver, with many long years of good health and _nachas_ from his entire family.

My deepest appreciation goes to my most dedicated family, who has been my lifelong support and endless source of _nachas_ on every level. May _Hakadosh Baruch Hu_ reward you manifold for all that you have given and continue to give and share with me.

*   *   *

The Code of Jewish Conduct has been divided into daily learning portions, for those who are interested in studying it in this fashion. This system was instituted after experiencing an unexpected phenomenon: after distributing over 9,000 copies of _Kitzur Mishpetei Hashalom_, we test-ran a version of the Hebrew book divided into daily learning portions. Ever since that time, almost no one has been interested in the earlier edition that is not divided into daily portions! (It should be noted that the division covers only a regular year. When there are variations in the number of days in Kislev and Teves, the reader may need to combine two portions to stay in line with the learning schedule. During a leap year, when an additional month of Adar is added, the reader should carry on into Nisan and realize that he will be a month behind.)

Following the daily program, *The Code of Jewish Conduct* takes a full year to complete. Therefore, we have clearly marked three possible tracks to follow, giving people a chance to start at any of three points throughout the year. In fact, however, anyone can start whenever he/she wants, at the beginning of any chapter or even in mid chapter, at a new heading. Most of the chapters stand on their own; their content is not dependent on that of previous chapters. Indeed, even after finishing the entire *sefer*, it would be wise to review it, starting again at any point. Through regular review of the material, one will internalize these *halachos* and the fine character traits that inevitably follow.

It would have been wonderful to have been able to include all the sources for each and every *halachah*. Originally, there were many suggestions for possible ways to structure the book. However, the final decision was that it would have been impossible to include everything, as there is simply too much material for one book. Therefore, it was decided to cite the chapter and section numbers of the original Hebrew *sefarim Mishpetei Hashalom* and *Emes Knei*. The more advanced reader will be able to look up more information and do his own research in the sources cited.

May this book help instill the awareness of *mitzvos bein adam lechaveiro* in people's lives and characters, thereby increasing harmony in interpersonal relationships.

Rabbi Yitzchok Silver
17 Menachem Av 5768
Yerushalayim

VOLUME I

Introduction

IN A WORLD FRAUGHT with dissension and in a generation nurtured on the philosophy of "looking out for number one," the Jewish people stand apart in their goal of fostering peace and achieving unity with their fellow Jews. We seek to merge our hearts as one, to create of our nation a unified body "to do the Will of Hashem of one accord."

How can this lofty objective be achieved?

The answer to this question lies, first and foremost, in the words of the Vilna Gaon, who asserts that all service of Hashem is contingent on the degree to which we perfect our *middos*, our character traits. *Middos* are the garment of the soul and the basis for perfecting man and uniting mankind. Fine-tuning those *middos* forms man's core purpose in this world.

1 Elul	1 Teves	1 Iyar

Mitzvos — the Channel for Perfecting Middos

THE PRIMARY CHANNEL through which we can perfect our *middos* lies in the *mitzvos*, both positive and negative. When we do Hashem's Will by performing *mitzvos* — any *mitzvos* — the built-in benefit is perfection of character. The average person may find it difficult to grasp how *mitzvos* such as taking the *lulav*, affixing a *mezuzah* to the doorpost or erecting a fence to surround our roof will affect our *middos*. But when it comes to *mitzvos bein adam lechaveiro* — *mitzvos* between man and his fellow man — anyone can understand how keeping them heightens our sensitivity to others and polishes our character.

When we do *mitzvos bein adam lechaveiro* time and time again, being particular about all their *halachos* and fine details, they will affect our essence and turn us into people of refined character. With each act of kindness we perform for our fellow Jews, we emulate Hashem's ways and forge a bond with Him. The world outside of *Klal Yisrael* also fosters an element of brotherhood within each family, city and national unit. However, these acts are often fueled, at least in part, by motives of

1

self-interest — perhaps to gain a favor in return or to feed one's pride. In contrast, each act of kindness that a Jew does for his fellow, without expecting any human reward, performed because his Creator commanded it, is an act of *kedushah* and of drawing closer to God.

Bona Fide FOR MANY GENERATIONS, a large portion of the *mitzvos*
Mitzvos *bein adam lechaveiro* were, in a sense, left by the wayside in *halachic* sources. While a few of these *mitzvos* are well-organized and arranged in the *Shulchan Aruch*, many of them are not fully represented there, and their details remained scattered throughout *Shas* and *poskim*. It was only a century ago that the Chofetz Chaim, *zt"l*, delved deeply into these matters and emerged with the pure, crystal-clear presentation of the *halachos* for a number of these neglected *mitzvos*, such as *hilchos lashon hara* — the laws of forbidden speech in all of its forms — as well as the obligations of *tzedakah* and *gemilus chassadim*.

Nevertheless, regarding a number of these *mitzvos*, the Chofetz Chaim wrote only a few brief words in the preface to his work. As a result, many fine, upstanding people live under the mistaken impression that these *mitzvos* are no more than "admirable conduct," good habits that are not dictated by *halachah*, but are, rather, a form of "extra credit" — a superior *mussar* level or a sign of *chassidus*.

In fact, these are actual, bona fide *mitzvos*, complete with an entire system of *dinim* and *halachos*, obligations and prohibitions, just like any other *mitzvah* given to *Am Yisrael* — and, yes, with their own *chumros* and *hiddurim* — optional stringencies and enhancements, as well. The principles that apply to *mitzvos bein adam laMakom* — such as the obligation to give up our possessions rather than violate them, or the obligation to fulfill them with conscious intent — apply equally to these *mitzvos*.

2 Elul	2 Teves	2 Iyar

Among the THE *MITZVOS BEIN adam lechaveiro* are even more sig-
Precious Few nificant in our times than they were thousands of years ago. Now, when we do not have the *Beis Hamikdash*, and we have no king, *navi* or *kohen gadol*, we are left with only about

two hundred applicable *mitzvos* from the full gamut of 613 *mitzvos*. Many of these apply only to individuals, such as *kohanim*, or are carried out only once, or only a handful of times during one's lifetime, such as *bris milah* and *pidyon haben*. Some are *mitzvos hateluyos ba'Aretz, mitzvos* that can be done only in Eretz Yisrael and are not relevant outside of the Land. Then, of course, there are many positive *mitzvos* that are time-related, from which women are exempt.

In contrast, the overwhelming majority of the *mitzvos bein adam lechaveiro* apply to men and women (and to children, too, as an aspect of *chinuch*), both in Eretz Yisrael and outside the Land, at all times. We encounter challenges in this area in almost every situation involving other people, all day, every day. Though there may have been those who have blurred the details of the *mitzvos* through the ages, the essence of these *mitzvos* never left our midst; they were engraved in the heart and concealed deep within the soul of every Jew throughout the generations.

Even Jews who have strayed far from Torah are considered the most benevolent individuals in the world at large, because these *mitzvos* continued to pulsate within them, though they were perceived as intellectual imperatives rather than as Hashem's command.

However, when we do a kindness for another Jew, it is not sufficient to do it to satisfy our desire to help him out; we have to do the kindness because Hashem commanded it, and we must have in mind that we are acting for the sake of the *mitzvah*. Thus, we certainly cannot suffice with "doing good things" or "having a Jewish heart"; we have a strong obligation to become thoroughly familiar with these *mitzvos* and understand well how to apply them to the situations that come up constantly in our everyday lives.

Gaining Clarity AS WE HAVE mentioned, many people mistakenly regard the *mitzvos bein adam lechaveiro* as if they were "nice habits" rather than actual obligations. Consequently, there are many who fail to follow the *halachos* properly. This stems, in part, from an ignorance of the obligations and specific *dinim* that apply to these *mitzvos*. Part of the problem, however, lies in an ignorance of the *heteirim* — the allowances within *halachah*. Without knowledge of these *heteirim*,

Introduction

people are led to think erroneously that it is impossible to manage in life while keeping these *halachos* properly.

This is in fact a common strategy of the *yetzer hara* — to deter us from keeping the basic *halachah* through the trick of making it appear insurmountable. The *yetzer hara* fabricates its own, extra prohibitions, and then when a person fails to meet these imaginary requirements, he feels like a hopeless *rasha* and is easily led to violate real prohibitions.

Furthermore, when we are not familiar with the legitimate *heteirim*, we may see respected *talmidei chachamim* who seem quite often to be employing leniencies, which are actually fully permissible, although to the uneducated observer they may appear to be a *chillul Hashem* — a desecration of Hashem's Name. As a result, the impact of these *mitzvos* is diluted, *chas veshalom*.

Therefore, it is not enough to have a superficial knowledge of these obligations; we also have to know where there is room to apply a *heter*, often with a Rav's guidance.

The basic premise for most of these *heteirim*, as Harav Elchanan Wasserman wrote, is that all of the prohibitions *bein adam lechaveiro* were meant to apply only in a case where they would cause unnecessary destruction, and not where the "prohibited" act would have a positive, constructive purpose. For example, *lashon hara* and *rechilus* may be said, in keeping with certain conditions, when the goal is constructive; hurtful words can be used if the purpose is justified rebuke.

But these *heteirim* for a constructive purpose are also delineated clearly in *halachah*. Never may anyone decide for himself which constructive purpose lifts the prohibition and which does not. For example, stealing someone else's property is never permitted for any constructive purpose. Even in the event that we are allowed to save ourselves in a time of mortal danger by taking someone else's money or property, we are still required to repay him afterwards.

Moreover, special care must be employed when dealing with situations in which there is an aspect of benefit for the person utilizing the *heter* of *to'eles*, since in many cases his judgment may be colored by his self-interest, and his act will therefore be a violation of a Torah prohibition.

The Joy of
Self-Control
UNITY IS NOT possible without perfection of character; perfection of one's _middos_ can be accomplished only through _mitzvah_-observance; and proper fulfillment of _mitzvos bein adam lechaveiro_ cannot be achieved without full, clear knowledge of the detailed _halachos_.

But knowledge of these _halachos_ has an added advantage. When we learn the details of the _mitzvos bein adam lechaveiro_ and keep them, we will benefit from the dividends of our actions in this world and will still have the principal left in the World to Come. As we exercise personal discipline and learn to let our minds rule our emotions, we will find ourselves enjoying a peaceful life, filled with calmness and joy, and untainted by anger and jealousy.

Doubts and pangs of conscience will not plague us, since we will know we are doing what is right in each situation. For example, when we meticulously observe the _mitzvos_ of "_lo sikom_" — "do not take revenge" and "_lo sitor_" — "do not bear a grudge," we will know how and when we are permitted to keep a safe distance from another person. At the same time, we will know what our obligations are in terms of continuing to cheerfully do _chessed_ even for someone who aggravated us and hurt us time and again. By subjecting ourselves to the rule of _halachah_, we will not only succeed in "swallowing our words"; we will learn to restrain ourselves even from feeling unpleasant feelings toward others.

Thus, not only is the general goal of bringing peace to the world accomplished through these _mitzvos_; the individual himself is transformed into one who is "strong — who subdues his personal inclination," who is a master of self-control.

Peace — a
Primary Value
THE GOAL OF peace accomplished through proper observance of _mitzvos bein adam lechaveiro_ is an invaluable objective in itself. Hashem holds peace to be so dear that He allows His Holy Name to be erased in the case of the _sotah_ — the wife suspected of unfaithfulness — for the sake of making peace between man and his wife. Peace is so great that the entire Torah was given for the purpose of bringing peace to the world, as the _passuk_

states (*Mishlei* 3:17), "Its ways are ways of pleasantness and all of its pathways are peace."

The purpose of the *mitzvos bein adam lechaveiro* is to restore us to the recognition that we are "as one man, with one heart." The *sefarim hakedoshim* write that Hashem is One and His Name is One, and therefore His *Shechinah* can rest only in a place of unity. May we be *zocheh* to be among those who bring peace to Hashem's world and restore the *Shechinah* to its rightful dwelling place.

We are delighted to present the reader with this unique work on the *halachos* of *mitzvos bein adam lechaveiro*, in the hope that we may serve as a vehicle to help restore these vital *halachos* to the consciousness of every Jew. This is an adapted translation of the original *sefarim*, *Mishpetei Hashalom* and *Emes Kenei*, two scholarly yet practical works, written in Hebrew. An abridged Hebrew version of these works, including vowels and with accompanying stories, has also been published for the broader public. Over thirty-five thousand of these books have been distributed during the past two years.

This volume of *The Code of Jewish Conduct*, prepared expecially for the English-speaking public, makes these important *halachos* of unity and interpersonal relationships more accessible. The book offers a clear overview of the *halachos* for the average reader in a flowing, readable form, interspersed with true-to-life anecdotes that demonstrate how the *halachos* apply in our daily struggles and common encounters. We hope and pray that this book will make the details of the *mitzvos bein adam lechaveiro* readily available and easily understood, and that it will enhance peace in our midst, bringing the *ge'ulah* closer.

There are some *halachos* that have been omitted from this *sefer*. The Hebrew volume includes extensive footnotes, for the scholarly reader, elaborating on the varying opinions regarding certain *halachos*. In this volume we have attempted to keep the style clear and concise, for the benefit of the average reader.

> This book has been written as a book of *halachah* rather than as a *mussar* work; nevertheless, it is intended to be used as a source for learning, not as decisive *pesak halachah*. It is recommended that readers learn through the subject, down to the source of each *halachah*, and then, when necessary, ask a Rav for direction.

⚜ 1 ⚜

בצדק תשפוט עמיתך
Judge Your Fellow with Righteousness

| 4 Elul | 4 Teves | 4 Iyar |

Judging Your Fellow Is Judging Yourself The imposing marble walls compound your feeling of nervousness as you pace up and down the halls, waiting your turn to plead your case. True, it is only a $200 speeding ticket that you have come to contest, but the atmosphere is fraught with tension. A young fellow rushing down the hall lands squarely on your toe, and to his mumbled "Excuse me," you respond vehemently, "Why don't you watch where you're going?"

"I'm sorry," the young man retorts. "I didn't mean it. Do you think I did it on purpose?"

"Well, if you would have been more careful it wouldn't have happened."

Moments after that unpleasant exchange, the door opens and you are called in to stand before the judge. Humbly, you begin your plea: "I know I was traveling above the speed limit, but you have to understand..." The words get caught in your throat as you look up and see the judge glaring at you from his seat on the platform; seated next to him is that fellow you just encountered in the hall.

"That's my son," the judge explains. "Now, what were you saying?"

"No point in continuing," you realize. "He's going to judge me as harshly as I judged his son — and rightly so."

EVERY TIME WE judge our fellow Jew, there is a Father in Heaven watching to see how exacting that judgment will be. Accordingly, "Whoever

7

judges his fellow favorably will be judged favorably in *Shamayim*"
(*Shabbos* 127b).

Addressing the Dayan THE TORAH COMMANDS us to "judge your fellow with righteousness." In its more limited application, this *mitzvah* is addressed to *dayanim* and refers to certain specific guidelines the *dayan* must follow in order to ensure fair judgment. For example, the *dayan* must relate to the two claimants as though they were of equal status, not leaving one standing while the other is permitted to sit, not telling one to keep his case short while allowing the other to speak at length. If one party is made to feel less important, it is likely that he will be unable to present his points with confidence and clarity, and this may lead the *dayan* to an incorrect ruling.

Another aspect of this *mitzvah* as it relates to *dayanim* is the special regard a *dayan* is required to accord *talmidei chachamim* who come to *beis din* for a judgment.

(The *mitzvah* is also interpreted as a command that anyone who is qualified to judge — should do so.) (*Mishpetei Hashalom* 1:1–4)

5 Elul	5 Teves	5 Iyar

Judging Favorably MOST OF US are not authorized to be *dayanim* in *beis din*. But the truth is, we are passing judgment all the time. Any time we see someone performing a questionable act, our judgmental antennae go up, and in our minds we rule "guilty" or "not guilty." In this second, broader application of the *mitzvah*, the Torah delineates how we are expected to exercise that judgment, depending on the case and on the nature of the person we are observing.

The basic rule is: In general, any time we see a Jew doing something that could be construed as either a positive or a negative act, we are obligated to give him the benefit of the doubt and judge him favorably in our minds, rather than suspecting him of being guilty of committing an *aveirah*.

Note that this *mitzvah* addresses our thought process. Even if we have not said or done anything based on our negative evaluation of the person, once we have judged him negatively *in our minds*, we have violated this *mitzvah* of the Torah and will be liable to punishment, as per the Gemara's warning: "One who suspects the innocent will suffer physical punishment" (*Shabbos* 97a). (*Mishpetei Hashalom* 1:5–6, 8–9)

Who Did It? THE REQUIREMENT TO give the benefit of the doubt is not a blanket statement, applicable equally for all people and in all situations. The *halachah* will differ depending on who is doing the act we have observed — a *tzaddik*, a *rasha*, or someone in between — and to what extent the act appears to lean in the direction of *zechus* or *chovah* — innocent or guilty. This is not showing "favoritism"; rather, it is "judging with righteousness" — according to the way the person has proven that he conducts himself in general.

> On your way to shul one morning, you notice your neighbor, Rav Shulman, a fine *talmid chacham* and *tzaddik*, looking around furtively and then pulling out a different neighbor's newspaper from his mailbox and walking off with it — rather suspicious, by all accounts. The judgmental gears start turning — but you stop them in their tracks.

Rav Shulman falls into the *halachic* category of "tzaddik." For such a person, the *halachah* tells us: Even if you saw him clearly doing an *aveirah* at night, do not harbor any doubts about him the next day, because he will certainly have done *teshuvah* by then.

What if the act was *not* clearly an *aveirah*, but it leans strongly in that direction? As long as there may be some far-fetched explanation for what you observed — perhaps he was forced to act in that way, or had positive intentions you are not aware of — then even if the possibility is rather remote, you are obligated to judge the *tzaddik* favorably. (*Mishpetei Hashalom* 1:7)

6 Elul	6 Teves	6 Iyar

The Wicked — According to His Wickedness Nimrod is not the kind of person you'd want to meet in a dark alley. A truly "bad egg," his deeds are consistently negative and his cynical attitude indicates that his *yiras Shamayim* is probably nonexistent. One day, as you stand by the bus stop, you see Nimrod saunter over and help an old man carry some of his numerous packages. *It's more likely that he intends* *to run off with the merchandise than that he wants to perform a chessed,* you think to yourself.

ARE YOU GUILTY of violating the *mitzvah* of judging with righteousness?

A person who is a notorious *rasha*, or whose deeds are more often bad than good, or someone who has shown himself to be totally devoid of *yiras Shamayim*, is to be judged according to the model he himself has created: Even if you see him doing something that appears to be a good deed, if there is any possibility that his intentions are really malicious — as in the case cited above — then you should judge him negatively and assume that either he was really doing something negative, or that his deed was done only to garner honor and he did not really mean well.

Chazal add that if the *rasha* is also a *meisis* — someone who leads other Jews astray — then it is prohibited ever to judge him favorably. (*Mishpetei Hashalom* 1:10)

Mr. Average   MOST PEOPLE DO not fall into either of these categories. They may not be exemplary *tzaddikim*, but on the other hand, they certainly do not qualify as notorious *reshaim*. The average person, who tries to avoid *aveiros* but at times slips up, is to be judged in accordance with the following guidelines:

If the action in question leans toward a positive interpretation, or if both sides seem to be about equal, the Torah obligates us to judge the person favorably and give him the benefit of the doubt. If the action seems more likely to be negative, but not definitely so, we ought to suspend judgment and leave the matter in doubt rather than judge the person negatively. However, *middas chassidus* (a worthy approach) would be to judge him favorably even in such a case. (*Mishpetei Hashalom* 1:11)

7 Elul	7 Teves	7 Iyar

What About a Stranger?   THE RULES ABOVE would apply in regard to someone you know. But what if you see someone you never met before doing a questionable act? If you do not know the person, and the nature of the deed is unclear, then *min haTorah* there is no *obligation* to judge him favorably. Here too, however, *middas chassidus* would urge you to judge him favorably.

Nevertheless, the Torah allows us to protect our legitimate interests. At times, when dealing with a stranger there is a risk of damage or monetary loss if we are too trusting of his actions. In such cases, *Chazal* advise, "Respect him and suspect him" — treat the person cordially, but exercise caution. Even so, a person should not give verbal expression to his suspicions; he should keep them to himself.

> Yanky was out riding his new bike when a boy he did not recognize from the neighborhood stopped him and asked, "Can I have a turn on your bike? I'll just take a ten-minute spin and then bring it right back." Yanky hesitated. He was generous by nature, and the boy looked okay, but... Finally, Yanky said, "Sorry, I have to be home in a few minutes. I can't lend the bike out now."

Yanky did not judge the boy outright to be a bicycle thief, but since he had to consider a potential loss, he was, wisely, cautious, and respectfully maintained his distance.

Even in a case of someone we *do* know and would ordinarily be obligated to judge favorably — if the situation is one in which the doubtful action might lead to harm or damage to oneself or others, then *halachah* permits us to harbor suspicion in order to protect ourselves. (*Mishpetei Hashalom* 1:12)

CHART SUMMARY

Person \ Action Appears	Good	Doubtful	Bad
Tzaddik	Judge favorably	Judge favorably	Judge favorably
Rasha	Judge unfavorably	Judge unfavorably	Judge unfavorably
Average	*Min haTorah* — Judge favorably	*Min haTorah* — Judge favorably	*Min haTorah* — leave in doubt, but *middas chassidus* to judge favorably
Stranger	*Middas chassidus* always to judge favorably		

Who Is Obligated? THE OBLIGATION TO judge favorably is incumbent on every Jew — man or woman — at all times, and in respect to every Jew — man, woman, child or adult (excluding resha'im, who have forfeited the title of amisecha, and excluding akum. Although there is no Torah commandment not to suspect an akum, nevertheless, it is neither ethical nor healthy to be suspicious of anyone, and it can cause a breakdown of one's fine character traits. Only when there would be a good reason to hate someone would it be permitted, but even then it must be in a controlled, intellectual manner, not an exaggerated blind, emotional hatred. Certainly, one must be careful never to make a chillul Hashem, especially when community relations are at stake and animosity could result.

One should strive constantly to maintain peaceful relations with everyone and to live in harmony with all. Extra care should be taken in one's relationships with people of power, such as politicians or one's boss, and with one's neighbors or business partners, with whom one interacts frequently).

This means that when your mother-in-law sends over soup every week, over your protests, you should *not* interpret it to mean that she is criticizing your cooking; you should evaluate her action as a selfless act of chessed. And when the neighbor passes by for the third time without responding to your "Hello," you may not judge him to be a snob; you should assume he is preoccupied with something, and perhaps offer him your help.

Children should be trained in this mitzvah from an early age. How do we train them to do a mitzvah that is performed essentially in one's mind? Simply *think out loud*. When you observe someone doing a questionable act in the presence of your child, say what is going on in your mind: "Hmm … at first it looked like that boy just pushed ahead to get on the bus before the other boys, but then I noticed that his little brother got separated from him, and he had to get on quickly to look after his brother." Another thing you can do is to describe imaginary situations and help the children practice using favorable judgment. (Mishpetei Hashalom 1:13–15, 17)

Rebuke Remains an Obligation   THE CHOFETZ CHAIM points out that even when we are obligated to give a person the benefit of the doubt, that does not excuse us from our obligation to rebuke a person who has acted in a questionable way, when the circumstances require it. For instance, if you see your child running through the flower patch on his way to the school bus, you may assume that he did not mean to cause damage; he was merely oblivious to his route. Yet you still must admonish him to be more careful in the future and, when necessary, help him correct the damage he has caused.

If it is necessary to investigate what really happened, for the purpose of carrying out the *mitzvah* of soft-spoken rebuke effectively, we should do so. (However, it is unclear whether this obligation applies to anyone other than one's close family members.) (*Mishpetei Hashalom* 1:18, footnote 9)

Sorry — My Mistake   Daniel saw Yisrael pulling a paper from his pocket during the math test and immediately assumed he was cheating, without giving him the benefit of the doubt. Later, word got out that Yisrael had indeed been punished by the teacher for cheating on the test. Daniel felt vindicated — his suspicions had been justified! Or had they?

IF WE JUDGE someone negatively in a case where *halachah* would require us to judge him favorably, then even if he turns out to be guilty of wrongdoing, it would appear that *we* are still guilty of violating the *mitzvah*. And the opposite is also true: If we judge someone favorably as required, and when the truth emerges we learn that the person really *was* guilty, we can rest assured that we fulfilled the *mitzvah* properly, regardless of the reality of the situation. (*Mishpetei Hashalom* 1:16)

The Up-Side of Being Under Suspicion   NO ONE LIKES to be erroneously suspected of wrongdoing. But *Chazal* reveal to us that the extreme discomfort of such a situation may be worthwhile, since the victim will be well rewarded: "Let my portion be with those who are suspected of something they have not done" (*Shabbos* 118b).

These words of *Chazal* are comforting to the victim who was suspected, but they do not exonerate the one who wrongly suspects. He is still obligated to conciliate the person he suspected, and even to go a step further by giving him a hearty blessing. However, if he never expressed his suspicions but only harbored them in his mind, or even if he expressed them but the person he suspected did not find out about them, then he should *not* ask his forgiveness (since he will simply cause the victim unnecessary aggravation). (*Mishpetei Hashalom* 1:19)

10 Elul	10 Teves	10 Iyar

Keep Your Display Window Clean   Mr. Schwartz stopped by the grocery store every morning after *davening*, took a loaf of bread from the box outside without paying, and rushed home. Actually, every *Rosh Chodesh* he would pay for all the loaves he would take that month, and this saved him time waiting in line. But Shimon didn't know about that arrangement, and each time he saw Mr. Schwartz walking off with the bread, he had to make a concerted effort to judge him favorably.

UP TO THIS point, we have clarified the obligations of the person who *observes* the wrongdoing. But the person who is doing an act in public has an obligation of his own — to avoid doing things that will rouse the suspicion of others. *Chazal* say that it is our responsibility to make sure we appear blameless in people's eyes, just as we must be blameless in the Eyes of Hashem, as the *passuk* states, "You shall be blameless before Hashem and Yisrael" (*Bamidbar* 32, 22). Several examples of this principle are found in the Gemara and *poskim*, and other cases are cited where we are prohibited to act in certain ways because of *maris ayin* — the way others will view our actions. Therefore, when it is necessary to act in public in a manner that is likely to rouse suspicion, we should give those around us an explanation for our actions.

Ordinarily, we are advised not to publicize our sins — they are to remain between us and Hashem. However, in a case where someone else is under suspicion for having committed a wrong for which *I* am responsible, the proper thing to do would be to admit one's sin in order to clear the other person of suspicion. The Gemara tells of great people who admitted to wrongdoing even when they were *not* to blame, in order to save the true culprit from shame. (*Mishpetei Hashalom* 1:20–21)

Judge My Children Favorably   REMEMBER THE UNCOMFORTABLE incident at the judge's bench, which opened our chapter? Imagine if your reaction to the toe-crushing pain had been different: "That's all right. I'm sure you're rushing to somewhere important, and you never meant to cause harm. It could happen to anyone." Surely his father, the judge, would have given you a much warmer welcome, knowing that you gave his careless son the benefit of the doubt.

There are times when we have no choice but to publicly denigrate someone who is violating the Torah, for the constructive purpose of warning others against such behavior, or to cause the sinner to regret his ways. Still, we should take care not to denigrate these wrongdoers in our *tefillah*, because Hashem — like every father — loves those who speak in defense of His children, even the errant ones. (*Mishpetei Hashalom* 1:22)

In summary: The *mitzvah* of "judging with righteousness" obliges us to judge questionable actions of others favorably, in keeping with the guidelines of *halachah*, which take into consideration the person in question, the circumstances and the risk of damage. At the same time, we should conduct ourselves in ways that will not rouse the suspicion of others.

"Whoever judges his fellow favorably will be judged favorably in Shamayim" (*Shabbos* 127b).

→ **2** ←

לא תשנא
Do Not Hate

It Is the   When the Friedmans moved into Shimon's building,
Thought That   Shimon tried to make the new family feel welcome. He
Counts ...   was a bit surprised at Mr. Friedman's cool response, but it
                   did not daunt him; he continued to make friendly over-
tures, offering his help and advice freely.

After a few days Shimon began to feel increasingly uncomfortable. Not
only was the new neighbor unresponsive, for some reason it seemed he
was holding a grudge against Shimon. Not only did he not respond to Shimon's greetings, it seemed Mr. Friedman was going out of his way to annoy
him. Shimon sensed feelings of animosity growing within him, but with
enormous effort he managed to restrain himself and did not say a word,
keeping his burgeoning feelings of antagonism locked tightly inside.

"It isn't easy," Shimon told himself, "but at least I'm doing the right thing
by holding in my feelings..."

SHIMON'S INTENTIONS MAY have been admirable, but the Torah is
specific in its requirements, and Shimon may well have violated its injunction.

The Torah commands us: "Do not hate your brother in your *heart*"
(*Vayikra* 19:17); that means that even if we do not do or say a word

16

against our fellow Jew, if we harbor hatred in our hearts when it is prohibited to do so, we have violated this _mitzvas lo saaseh_ — no matter how hard we may be working to restrain ourselves. (_Mishpetei Hashalom_ 2:1, 4)

The Obligation —
Who and to
Whom?

THE _MITZVAH_ OF _lo sisna_ is incumbent on men and women alike, at all times and in all places. Children should be trained in this _mitzvah_ from a young age. We should certainly not do the opposite, and try to drag children into our own hostilities by urging them to dislike those we consider our enemies. (If a parent does this, it is forbidden for the child to obey him, as in any case where a parent tells his child to violate a _mitzvah_.) The best way to train our children is by example. Phrases like "I can't stand so and so," and other such hostile expressions should never be heard in our homes, especially in the children's presence.

Jews come in all stripes and types. The basic _mitzvah_ forbids us to hate "your brother" — this means any Jew, even an _am ha'aretz_. (While there is no _issur_ to harbor such feelings against an _akum_, it is not ethical to hate anyone, Jew or non-Jew, as it can destroy relationships and can harm one's own character traits. Moreover, one must be careful never to make a _chillul Hashem_; one should strive constantly to maintain peaceful relations with everyone.) There are specific exceptions that apply to various levels of sinners, as well as in cases where someone threatens to harm us. Hatred toward a child is always forbidden, even in a case where the child commits serious _aveiros_, since he is not yet fully responsible for his actions, nor is he fully obligated to keep the _mitzvos_. (_Mishpetei Hashalom_ 2:2, 3)

12 Elul	12 Teves	12 Iyar

What Is Worse —
Hidden or Exposed
Animosity?

One day, Shimon was surprised to come across the _halachah_ that hatred in the heart is the basic prohibition of _lo sisna_. "Well," he figured, "if that is the case, then I was wrong to hold in my feelings. I would do better getting the hostility out of my system."

> The next time Shimon bumped into Mr. Friedman, he stopped him in the hallway and launched into a long, irate tirade about all the wrongs Mr. Friedman had done to him from the day that he moved in. By the time Shimon finished, they were no longer hidden rivals; they were outright enemies.

TRUE, WE ARE not allowed to harbor hatred in our hearts. In addition to the *issur* of *lo sisna*, feeling *sinah*, hatred, in one's heart for a Jew (without *halachic* justification) constitutes a violation of the *mitzvah* to love our fellow Jew (*Vayikra* 19:19). However, if we release that hatred in an unharnessed manner and express it by striking a person, whether physically or with words, or even deny him a favor because of our hatred, then according to many *poskim* we are all the more guilty of transgressing the *issur* of *lo sisna*, in addition to whatever other *aveiros* we committed along the way (such as *lashon hara* and other *aveiros*).

On the other hand, in the case of a *baal aveirah* whom we are allowed to hate (as we will discuss later in this chapter), according to some opinions we are not permitted to hate him secretly while making an outward show of friendliness to him. Rather, we *should* show him our hatred openly.

So, what are we to do — show hatred or keep it under wraps? The answer emerges when we note how the *issur* of *lo sisna* is linked to the *mitzvah* that follows in the same *passuk* — the obligation to rebuke our fellow Jew. If someone does us a bad turn, the Torah advises us, we should *not* pretend to be his friend while hating him in our heart. Instead, we should go over to the fellow and tell him our grievances — privately, so as not to embarrass him, and in a pleasant tone of voice: "Tell me, why did you do X to me?"

If this "rebuke" is presented properly, one of two things will likely happen: Either we will find out that he was justified in what he did, or he will admit his mistake and apologize, and we will be able to forgive him. Either way, the hatred will be effectively drained and peace will be restored.

But we must proceed with great caution, because a wrong word or tone may initiate a full-blown feud, as in the case of Shimon. Sometimes the person may be better approached through a letter or an emissary; in many cases it is best to seek rabbinical advice before proceeding.

Sometimes, when the risks appear too great and the chances of success too slim, the best choice is to forgo the *tochachah* and instead work on uprooting the hatred by forgiving the person completely in our hearts.

According to the Chofetz Chaim and others, once we have informed the individual of the reason for our hatred and brought the issue out into the open, we are no longer liable for violating the *mitzvah* of *lo sisna*. Of course, until things are patched up we would still be guilty of other transgressions, if, for example, we spoke *lashon hara* or if we held a grudge. But, as the Chofetz Chaim states, "hatred in the heart is the most potent of all" — both because of its intensity and because the object of someone's hatred is unaware of the other's feelings and cannot defend himself. (*Mishpetei Hashalom* 2:4–7)

13 Elul	13 Teves	13 Iyar

The Measure of Sinah   WHAT IS THE minimum measure of the violation of *lo sisna*? The *halachah* gives us a number of specifics: If we don't greet someone because of our feelings of anger or animosity (not because we were daydreaming or in the middle of *davening*), we have violated the *issur*. If the person is someone we generally speak to regularly and we do not speak with him for three days because of our feelings toward him, then halachically, that constitutes *sinah*, which, for example, would disqualify us from acting as a *dayan* in *beis din* in a case involving that person.

We derive additional parameters for *lo sisna* from a *passuk* cited in the Torah's discussion of the *rotzei'ach beshogeg*, the unintentional murderer: "He is not his enemy and does not seek to do him harm" (*Bamidbar* 35:23). Implied here is that scheming to cause harm to another Jew falls into the category of *sinah*. Another not uncommon indication of *sinah* is when we rejoice in someone's misfortune because of hostile feelings between us. (*Mishpetei Hashalom* 1:8–9)

No Excuse for Hatred   Ever since the unsuccessful attempt at *tochachah*, the relationship between Shimon and Mr. Friedman continued to deteriorate. Shimon's friend Yossi attempted to smooth out the kinks in the relationship, but he was up against a brick wall. Shimon was convinced

that he was not at fault. "Look, I tried to clear the air, and Friedman didn't let up on his animosity. If he can't stand me and my family, then I have a green light to hate him too."

OUR GUT REACTION when we experience hostile feelings being radiated toward us may be to reflect them right back. But the Torah expects us to overcome gut feelings. According to some opinions, even if Mr. Friedman hates Shimon or his family, this does not place him in the category of *rasha*; therefore, it is still prohibited for Shimon to hate Mr. Friedman. It isn't easy to abide by this requirement, but by meeting the challenge, Shimon will succeed in overcoming his natural, base instincts. More often than not he will gain something else as well: if he consistently responds to the hatred with expressions of love, most likely he will eventually melt his opponent's icy front and they will make peace with one another.

Needless to say, envy of another's success (in social relationships, for example), or rivalry (such as in business) does not give anyone license to act or feel *sinah* toward the other person. Since it is common for people of the same profession to feel antagonism toward one another, we should be especially careful in this regard. (*Mishpetei Hashalom* 2:10–11)

14 Elul	14 Teves	14 Iyar

But — You
May Keep Your
Distance

"All right, all right," Shimon concedes. "I admit I was wrong in the way I handled my feelings toward Mr. Friedman. What now? I suppose I ought to change my seat in shul and sit next to him, or invite him out to dinner, even though I can't even carry on a proper conversation with him; we think differently on every topic." Not necessarily, Shimon …

WHILE WE MAY not hate someone who rubs us the wrong way, we do not have an obligation to be his best friend. Therefore, when people differ in their opinions or *hashkafos* on life (as we often find among different religious circles, political factions or families), or when another person's physical defect, habits or actions are repugnant to us (even if it is only due to our own hypersensitivity), then there is nothing wrong with keeping our interactions with that person to a minimum, as long

as we are not doing it because of underlying feelings of *sinah*.

At times, keeping a certain distance may even be recommended, as it will help us retain a sense of mutual respect. However, we should always be careful to nurture feelings of love for the person, even if certain aspects of his behavior, personality or lifestyle are not to our liking, so as to avoid violating the *mitzvah* of *ve'ahavta lerei'acha kamocha* (see chapter 18).

Similarly, we may avoid a person's company for the simple reason that we find it to be a waste of time, or because we are not on the same wavelength, or because we don't want to have to tolerate his bad *middos*. Certainly we may keep our distance if we don't want to learn from his ways or from his poor character, as long as we are careful to avoid doing anything that would fall into the category of revenge or bearing a grudge. Even if we have no particular reason at all, other than the fact that we don't enjoy being with him, we are not obligated to maintain a friendship — but we must meticulously avoid any feelings of *sinah*. (*Mishpetei Hashalom* 2:12–13)

"Fear of Hashem Is Hatred of Evil" (Mishlei 8:13) AS WE MENTIONED earlier, while the general rule is that we may not hate a fellow Jew, there are certain categories of people who, because of their reprehensible conduct, lose their status as someone we are forbidden to hate. If we personally see someone violate an *issur* that everyone knows is prohibited (such as committing an immoral act or eating food that is obviously nonkosher) we are permitted, and even obligated (*midivrei Kaballah*) to despise him. If two kosher witnesses saw him sin and testified against him in *beis din*, then *everyone* is permitted to hate him.

According to the Rambam, this applies only if the offender was warned beforehand that the act he is about to do is forbidden and if we are certain that he has not yet done *teshuvah*. The *Sefer Hachinuch* maintains that the *halachah* would apply only if we gave him *tochachah* again and again and he refused to listen.

Even if a person has, unfortunately, fallen into the category of "sinner" that warrants our feeling *sinah* toward him and keeping our distance from him, that does not give anyone *carte blanche* to act in any way he wants against the offender. In most cases it is still prohibited to speak *lashon hara* about him and to rouse *sinah* against him in others; nor are we allowed to cause him any harm, just as is the case with any other Jew. (*Mishpetei Hashalom* 2:14–15)

15 Elul	15 Teves	15 Iyar

Helping Your Sonei — Two Opinions Shimon was on his way home one day when he saw two familiar faces at the bus stop, both of whom had just gotten off the bus. One of them was his not-so-friendly neighbor Mr. Friedman, who was struggling with a large, unwieldy package that was about to fall. The other was his old friend Pinchas, trying to lift half a dozen bags laden with fruits and vegetables. *Hmm*, he thought, *I can only help one of them. Who will it be?* Not an easy decision!

THE GEMARA PRESENTS a situation similar to Shimon's dilemma when it discusses the *mitzvos* of helping one person who is having trouble loading packages onto his donkey and another who is struggling with unloading his donkey's burden. In general, when faced with a choice between the two, the *mitzvah* of unloading would take precedence, since there is an issue of *tzaar baalei chaim* for the donkey that has collapsed under its load. However, the Gemara tells us, if the one who needs help unloading his donkey is a friend, and the one who needs help loading his donkey is an enemy, then we are to give precedence to helping the *sonei* — the enemy — load his donkey, so as to exercise control over our *yetzer*, which prods us to ignore the needs of the enemy. The same would apply in all *mitzvos* of *chessed* when a similar choice presents itself.

The question that arises is: If we are talking about the kind of person whom it is a *mitzvah* to despise (i.e., the *baal aveirah* described above), then what is the point of overcoming our *yetzer* — and even at the cost of *tzaar baalei chaim*? After all, we are *supposed* to hate him.

Some authorities explain that the Gemara is not referring to a *rasha* as defined by *halachah*, but rather to a person toward whom we feel *sinah* without halachic justification. Certainly, in such a case we would have to give precedence to the *sonei* in order to bend our *yetzer*. But when it comes to a legitimate *sonei* — a *rasha* whom we are supposed to hate, we should *not* give precedence to him when that would entail *tzaar baalei chaim*. Nevertheless, according to all opinions we are still required to help him load his donkey afterward — or to help him out in any other case where we would be required to help a fellow Jew. (*Mishpetei Hashalom* 2:16–18)

| 16 Elul | 16 Teves | 16 Iyar |

The Limits of **Sinas Resha'im** OTHER *POSKIM* DIFFER and say that the Gemara's case *does* in fact refer to the *rasha* whom we are halachically obliged to despise. Nevertheless, even regarding *him* we should control our *yetzer* and give the *sonei* precedence. Why should that be? A number of explanations are offered, and each one sharpens our understanding of the issue:

1. The *mitzvah* to hate a *rasha* is specifically because of his *aveiros*. However, any added antagonism that we feel as a result of the *rasha* hating us in return is not legitimate. In order to control that *sinah*, we are advised to "bend the *yetzer*" and give the *sonei* precedence.

2. Others explain that the *mitzvah* is purely to despise the *aveirah*, not to harbor a personal hatred (as we see in the story of Rabbi Meir's wife Bruriah, who suggested that her husband pray that the *sins* be decimated, not the *sinners* [*Brachos* 10b]).

3. Another view is that the *mitzvah* to hate the *rasha* is limited to a case where he violated *mitzvos bein adam laMakom*. If he violated *mitzvos bein adam lechaveiro*, we are obligated to control our *yetzer* and refrain from any feelings of *sinah*.

4. Finally, some explain that *sinah* is warranted only if the offender sinned by actively doing a wrong. If he merely failed to do something he should have done, then it is not a *mitzvah* to hate him, although we are permitted to do so, and in such a case we *are* advised to "bend the *yetzer*" and give him precedence.

All of these explanations point in one direction: When our father is not treated with the proper respect, we instinctively feel animosity toward the one who has wronged him. Similarly, *sinah*, even when

required, is meant to be a specific reaction to the wrong that has been actively perpetrated against *kevod Shamayim*, the honor of our Father, Hashem. The challenge is to keep that warranted *sinah* from spilling over into forbidden hatred. (*Mishpetei Hashalom* 2:19–21)

| 17 Elul | 17 Teves | 17 Iyar |

Hating Those Who Hate Hashem ALL OF THE above is true regarding a *rasha*, a sinner, as long as he is still a believer. But *kofrim*, *minim* and *apikorsim* — who do not believe in any one of the thirteen principles of faith — and the *meisis umeidi'ach* — who incites other Jews to leave a Torah way of life — fall into another category altogether. (These various types of sinners will be defined extensively in Chapter 18.) Regarding such people, it is a *mitzvah* to hate them, to argue with them and to frustrate their plans. Even if their life is in peril we should not save them from danger. These instructions are absolute; there is no element of "bending the *yetzer*" involved here.

Since there is no obligation of *tochachah* toward nonbelievers (or toward people who have fallen so low that, given the choice between equally priced kosher and nonkosher food of similar quality, they will choose the nonkosher food), we are permitted to hate them even without first giving them *tochachah*. Although there are certain leniencies regarding our relationship to a nonbeliever who is a *tinok shenishba* (a concept that will be defined at length in Chapter 18), it would appear that in a case where there is a risk that he will incite other Jews to *apikorsus*, these leniencies would not apply. One should seek rabbinical advice in this delicate area.

But remember — these severe injunctions are addressed exclusively to the nonbelievers and *meisisim* mentioned above. If a Jew believes in the thirteen principles of faith, even if he is known to be a *rasha* who eats *treife* food to indulge his desires — we may hate him, but he is not excluded from *Klal Yisrael*. All the other obligations we have toward a fellow Jew apply to him as well — to support him with *tzedakah* funds, to ransom him if necessary, to return his lost item and to do any other favor the Torah commands us to do for our fellow Jew. (*Mishpetei Hashalom* 2:22–24)

At What Cost?   SOMETIMES WE ARE in the unpleasant position of having to interact on a regular basis with people who would fall into one of the categories mentioned in this chapter. We may not want to carry on a conversation with a _rasha_, but if he's our boss — what are we to do?

Even though there is a _mitzvah_ to hate the _rasha_, if we have a specific, genuine benefit from him, financial or otherwise, or if we think that remaining in his company might afford us the opportunity to draw him back to _Yiddishkeit_, then we are not required to distance ourselves from him, as long as he at least believes in the basic principles of faith.

If the person in question is a _kofer_, the _mitzvah_ to hate him and keep our distance from him is much more severe. Even so, we may not have to actually quit our job for this purpose, since a person is generally not expected to give up his livelihood in order to carry out a _mitzvas aseh_. Still, we have to be on our guard not to have more to do with him than is absolutely necessary, because heretical ideas tend to have a strong magnetic attraction. Certainly we should not try to curry his favor or imply in any way that we condone his ideas. (_Mishpetei Hashalom_ 2:28–29)

Have We Met the   "You won't believe what I saw last week. I was in the
Conditions?   city on business, and when I passed by this fancy _treife_ restaurant, who should I see sitting at the table with a sumptuous meal before him but your own neighbor, Friedman," Shmerel the rumor-monger whispered to Shimon one day after _minyan_.

"Hmm … thanks for the information," Shimon responded. _Aha_, he thought to himself smugly, _now I'm free to consider that despicable fellow a rasha, with all the_ halachos _that go along with it._

Not so fast, Shimon …

THE CHOFETZ CHAIM enumerates seven conditions for speaking _lashon hara leto'eles_, some of which are prerequisites to permitting _sinas resha'im_:

1. We have to have seen the wicked act ourselves or have checked out carefully that the report is indeed true, or it must be a universally

known fact that the person commits this *aveirah*. (We may not jump to conclusions merely on the basis of *lashon hara* we heard and were not allowed to believe.)

2. We must consider very carefully whether what he did was really an *aveirah* according to *halachah*.

3. Where applicable, we are required to rebuke him, and then only if he did not do *teshuvah* is he a candidate for the title *rasha*.

4. Even after all of the above conditions have been met, we have to be sure that we will not cause him more damage than he deserves according to *din Torah*, and we have to continue doing all the *mitzvos* of *chessed* for him as the Torah requires us to do for any other Jew. (*Mishpetei Hashalom* 2:27)

| 19 Elul | 19 Teves | 19 Iyar |

The Gravity of the Sin of Sinas Chinam As the Three Weeks drew near, Shimon heard a few *drashos* that addressed the severity of the *aveirah* of *sinas chinam*. He began to feel pangs of conscience when he thought about his relationship with Mr. Friedman, but he quickly silenced them: "Oh, I'm not guilty of *sinas chinam* — that's groundless hatred. I have good reason to feel toward him as I do ..."

HATRED OF ANY person who is not an *apikores* or a *baal aveirah*, and who does not seek our harm, constitutes *sinas chinam*. Any other reason for *sinah* is not halachically justified.

Chazal tell us that the severity of *sinas chinam* is equivalent to the three paramount *aveiros* — *avodah zarah*, *gilui arayos* and *shefichus damim* — idol worship, immoral acts and murder. At the time of the second *Beis Hamikdash* the Jews were immersed in Torah, *mitzvos* and *gemilus chassadim*, yet the *Beis Hamikdash* was destroyed because of the *sinas chinam* that existed among *Bnei Yisrael*.

The pernicious effects of *sinas chinam* are felt on a personal level, too, and are terrifying. *Chazal* say that as a result of *sinas chinam* a person will have strife in his home, his wife will miscarry and his children will die young.

The impact of _sinas chinam_ on _shalom bayis_ can be devastating. We have to be especially careful to avoid any hostility between spouses, since _sinah_ can lead one to act in an irrational manner and can even destroy the Torah observance in the home. Children of a union that is fraught with _sinah_ ("_bnei senuah_") may be born spiritually handicapped, with innate bad character traits and tendencies that can easily lead them astray unless they put forth a concerted effort to improve themselves.

(Nevertheless, if a woman behaves indecently, in a way that arouses suspicions about her morality, one is permitted to hate her and should try to separate from her. If it was proven that she committed an immoral act or violated _das Moshe_ or _das Yehudis_, then one is obligated to divorce her.) (_Mishpetei Hashalom_ 2:32–35)

**Auxiliary Effects**   WHAT BEGINS AS a small feeling of hatred in the
**of Sinah**   heart may easily mushroom into a torrent of devastating _aveiros_: seeking the person's harm; rejoicing at his misfortune; damaging property; informing; and even murdering. In the introduction to his _sefer_, the Chofetz Chaim enumerates a large number of _mitzvos aseh_ and _lo saaseh_ that one might violate when speaking _lashon hara_.

The same can be said of a person who hates his fellow Jew. He may simultaneously violate any number of the following _issurim_: taking revenge or holding a grudge; flattering the _rasha_; speaking and believing _lashon hara_ and _rechilus_; misleading people with bad advice (_lifnei iveir_ ...); _machlokes_; striking; cursing; and publicly shaming another Jew. Among the _mitzvos aseh_ he is likely to violate are the obligations to love his fellow man, to rebuke and to judge favorably. If the _sinah_ is directed toward a _talmid chacham_, his Rav, a parent or older sibling, a _kohen_, orphan, widow or _ger tzedek_, he will be guilty of even more violations.

Sinah is like a termite that steadily erodes the _nefesh_ and can easily lead to a breakdown of one's entire Torah observance; any rational person recognizes it to be the lowliest, most repulsive _middah_. (_Mishpetei Hashalom_ 2:36–37)

So What Should We Do with Our Feelings? Shimon is frustrated. He has no doubt that one of his neighbors hates him, and he cannot deny the reciprocal feelings in his own heart, but whatever he does to deal with the situation seems to entrench him more deeply in prohibited *sinah*. What practical guidance can we offer him?

THE FIRST THING to do when we sense that someone hates us is to try to discover the reasons for his feelings. At times this is best done indirectly, through a third party. Once the reasons are clear we can apologize and clear the air. If matters are not so open-and-shut, we should go to a Rav or even to a mutual friend to hear both sides and settle matters between us and, if necessary, take the issue to a *din Torah* before a proper *beis din*, where all the uncertainties will be ironed out.

When these approaches are not practical, the other alternative is to accept the fact that the aggravation we are going through is a *gezeirah* from *Shamayim* and that the other person is no more than an agent for bringing it about. We wouldn't slap the mailman for bringing us an electric bill; nor should we explode at the other fellow for being the *shaliach*, the emissary, for our pain.

Granted, the other fellow may be guilty of violating the *issur* of *lo sisna*, and it is naturally difficult to love someone who hates us. Still, according to many opinions we are not allowed to hate him and certainly not to cause him any harm or even to refrain from doing him any favor the Torah would require us to do for another Jew. It is important to realize that if the Torah demands such behavior of us, then it is within our power to act in this way.

(The exception to this rule would be if we are absolutely certain that this person wants to cause us physical, emotional or financial harm, even though we have not done him any wrong. In such a case, as well as in the instance of a *talmid chacham* who is belittled, a different *halachah* would apply. See chapter 3, on the laws of revenge and grudge-bearing.) (*Mishpetei Hashalom* 2:30–31)

In summary: The *mitzvah* of *lo sisna* prohibits us from hating any Jew in our heart, with the exception of certain categories of sinners, some of whom we are permitted to hate but must otherwise treat like any other Jew; and others — *kofrim* — who are in an even more severe category. The Torah delineates what constitutes *sinah* and advises us regarding how to deal with our negative feelings in acceptable ways. *Sinas chinam* is dangerous and destructive, and it can lead to a breakdown of family and social harmony, as well as of general Torah observance.

*"Hatred stirs up quarrels, but love covers
all offenses" (Mishlei 10:12).*

*"Who is strong? He who conquers
his yetzer" (Avos 4:1).*

*"Hashem will give His nation might; Hashem will bless
His nation with peace" (Tehillim 29:11).*

⇥ **3** ⇤

לא תקום ולא תטור

Do Not Take Revenge and Do Not Bear a Grudge

A Natural Reaction — but Not Enough for Us   "Shira, could you lend me your *Chumash* notebook, fast!" Dina begged, just moments before the bell was to ring. "Mrs. Green said she was going to quiz us today on yesterday's lesson, and I completely forgot to review — and now I can't find my notebook."

"That's your problem. You're such a scatterbrain. Don't expect me to come to your rescue," Shira replied, too lazy to pull her notebook out of her bag. Dina, disappointed, had no time to ask anyone else. She resigned herself to getting a low grade on the quiz.

Two days later, Shira sidled over to Dina after class. "Uh … Dina, I heard you put together a really great outline of everything we need to know for the history final. Do you think I could just borrow it for this recess? You know how awful I am in history …"

If this conversation had taken place anywhere else but in a Torah-true environment, there would be little doubt as to what Dina's reply would have been. What could be more natural than to answer, "What nerve! When I needed your notebook, you wouldn't lift a finger to help me! Forget it — you won't get my outline now or ever!" At the very best, the response

30

might have been toned down to a snide, "Sure, no problem. I'm not like some people who think only of themselves and don't want to share their notes. Here, take it …"

HASHEM IS WELL aware of the pain a person feels when he has been hurt, and the sweet pleasure that comes with getting back at the one who hurt us. Nevertheless, the Torah commands us, "Do not take revenge" (*Vayikra* 19:18). Hashem expects us to summon our inner strength, rise above our natural reactions, and resist the urge to pay tit for tat.

In fact, not only does the Torah tell us not to take revenge; it goes on to command us, "Do not bear a grudge" (ibid.) — to erase the memory of what happened from our heart, to wipe away hard feelings and, at the next opportunity, to treat the other fellow as if nothing ever happened. Impossible? Not for us! If the Torah demands such conduct, then it may be a challenge but it is definitely within our reach.

An Important Formula for Peace and Harmony
THE TWO *MITZVOS* of *lo sikom*, "Do not take revenge," and *lo sitor*, "Do not bear a grudge," are twin *mitzvos* that are elementary to creating and maintaining a peaceful, unified society. It is prohibited for us to do someone a bad turn in return for what he did to us, or even to bear a grudge in our heart against the other person. Consequently, we may not refrain from giving him *tzedakah* when necessary or doing him a favor wholeheartedly, despite the fact that he treated us badly.

If someone owes us money or compensation of some sort, then we are not expected to forget about his debt — but we should not harbor a grudge because of it; instead, if he does not pay up we should simply take the case to a proper *beis din* and get what he owes us in accordance with *din Torah*.

When revenge and grudges are taken out of the social picture, then arguments and *machlokes* within the Jewish community are greatly reduced. Love, peace and a feeling of brotherhood prevail, and we can really be unified "as one man" — as Hashem wants us to be. (*Mishpetei Hashalom* 3:1)

To Whom Do These Mitzvos Apply? FOR SOME PEOPLE, refraining from vengefulness and from holding on to hard feelings is not so difficult with close relatives, but is much harder when it comes to more distant acquaintances. For others, the opposite is the case. However, the *halachah* does not distinguish between personality types: The *mitzvos* apply at all times and places, and to men and women, in their relationships with those as close as a spouse and as distant as a stranger.

There are some exceptions, however. There is no *issur* of *nekimah* (revenge) or *netirah* (bearing a grudge) toward *akum*, although it is neither ethical nor healthy to take revenge on or bear a grudge toward anyone. One should always strive to maintain peaceful relations and to live in harmony with everyone. These *issurim* do not apply to a *meisis*, an *apikorus*, an informer, or certain categories of sinners (i.e., a *mumar letei'avon*, who sins for his pleasure, and someone who sins intentionally all the time and does not repent). (Regarding a *tinok shenishba*, see ch. 18.)

Although the above exceptions exist, great care should be exercised in using the *heter* toward people in these categories. If they are currently in positions of power and could potentially do harm, then it is not wise to incite them, even when the *halachah* permits it. (*Mishpetei Hashalom* 3:2–3)

From a Young Age CHILDREN SHOULD BE trained in this *mitzvah* as much as their ability to understand it permits. In this particular *mitzvah*, *chinuch* requires a rather delicate balance. Children, especially boys, do get into fights. While *nekimah* is prohibited, the child is permitted to protect himself and should be taught to do so when he is being abused by other children. However, he should also be taught that he may strike out or speak up only to protect himself from further blows in the midst of conflict, but not in order to get back at the other fellow.

The child can be shown how at times he might accomplish his purpose more effectively by using the strategy of "buying a friend" —

offering the bully a candy or even a small gift to win him over. (*Mishpetei Hashalom* 3:2)

What if He Owes Me Money? AS WE MENTIONED earlier, the *halachah* does not deny us the right to claim money that is owed to us. That is why we have a full volume in the *Shulchan Aruch* on *halachos* relating to monetary matters — the *Choshen Mishpat*. Everyone is responsible to pay up his loans, to return what he took unlawfully, and to pay for damage he caused. Anything we do — within the bounds of Torah law — to acquire what is rightfully ours or to prevent a future loss, whether we arrange it between ourselves or take it to a *beis din* for a ruling, does not fall into the category of *nekimah* and *netirah*.

Nevertheless, when a negligible loss is involved, we should try to act *lifnim mishuras hadin* — to bend ourselves and be yielding, rather than to fight over every penny. After all, as *Chazal* say, one of the reasons Yerushalayim was destroyed was that people were *too* exacting in the *din*. (*Mishpetei Hashalom* 3:4)

A Definition of Nekimah WHAT IS *NEKIMAH*? On Sunday Reuven requests of Shimon, "Lend me your drill," and Shimon refuses. The next day Shimon knocks at Reuven's door and asks, "Could you lend me your lawn mower?" "Oh, no," Reuven replies. "You didn't lend me your drill; I won't lend you my lawn mower."

The Torah does not *require* anyone to lend any particular item to someone else. There are a dozen legitimate reasons why we might not want to lend our lawn mower — we might think we'll need it today, or we may be afraid it will be damaged — and that being the case, we are entitled to refuse. (Even if we refuse just because of plain stinginess, then at worst we're lacking in our fulfillment of the *mitzvah* of loving our fellow man.)

However, the moment our refusal flows from a desire for revenge, that same "no" renders us guilty of violating the *mitzvah* of *lo sikom*. (*Mishpetei Hashalom* 3:6–7)

A Definition of Netirah LET'S RETURN TO the two neighbors, Reuven and Shimon. In this scenario, when Shimon asks for the lawn mower, Reuven rises above his urge to take revenge and says, "Yes, you can use the lawn mower. Even though you wouldn't lend me your drill, I won't follow suit."

Reuven may have thought that he rose above his feelings, but his words reveal that he is still nursing a grudge against Reuven; consequently, his gallant agreement to lend the lawn mower is a violation of *lo sitor*. Even had he kept his thoughts to himself and not said a word, he still would have violated the *mitzvah* by bearing a grudge in his heart.

Granted, wiping out of one's heart all memory of the bad turn someone did us is not a simple matter. At times it can be extremely difficult to erase every trace of hard feelings. Consider the case of a person who suffered permanent injury from an accident caused by someone else's negligence. The paralysis he must cope with on a daily basis does not allow him to erase all memory of the facts. Nevertheless, every person who suffers at the hands of another *can* rub out the hostile feelings that dwell in his heart against the one who hurt him. (Judging favorably can be a useful tool to help us accomplish this purpose.) (*Mishpetei Hashalom* 3:8)

Protecting Yourself Dassy has been sitting next to Isabel in class for a few weeks, and she can't take it anymore. Isabel pinches her and bothers her in any number of ways. Besides, she still owes Dassy the $10 that Dassy lent her on the class trip two months ago.

Dassy wants to ask the teacher to change her seat, or to help her cope with her difficulties in dealing with Isabel. But wait, would that be considered *netirah*, bearing a grudge against Isabel because of all the problems she has been causing her?

DISTANCING OURSELVES FROM a person or refraining from helping him, just because of something bad he did to us, *would* be considered *netirah*. But at the same time, we do not have to sit idly by and continue being that person's punching bag. If our purpose in staying away from a bad neighbor who has caused us problems is to avoid further suffering, as in

Dassy's case, or in order to protect ourselves from his negative influence, then we are permitted and entitled to do so, as long as we make every effort to prevent feelings of *netirah* from creeping into our hearts. Also, we have to make sure our motives are clear to others, so that no one will be misled into thinking that we are acting out of *netirah*. (See chapter 1, "You shall be blameless …") (*Mishpetei Hashalom* 3:9)

---

25 Elul ⬛ 25 Teves ⬛ 25 Iyar

Personal Pain: Dassy did not know what to do. Until now she had
Two Approaches tried hard to resist harboring bad feelings for Isabel
because of the money Isabel owed her and because
of the pencils Isabel took from her desk without permission. But today
at recess, Isabel got up in front of the class and did a cruel parody of all
of Dassy's expressions. The whole class was laughing — at Dassy! She felt
awful and did not know what to do with her pain.

First ACCORDING TO SOME opinions, the *issurim* of *nekimah* and
Opinion *netirah* apply only when lending items, or in other monetary
matters. However, in cases where someone has offended us
personally — by insulting or shaming us in public, or by causing us
bodily harm, as might happen in the course of an argument — the *issur* does not apply. It would be *middas chassidus* — praiseworthy conduct — to overlook the offense and to take the attitude that it was our own sins that brought about the incident, but according to the letter of the law, in this case we would be permitted to retain hard feelings in our hearts.

Chazal tell us that "any *talmid chacham* who does not take revenge and bear a grudge like a snake is not a *talmid chacham*." Having learned of the severity of the *mitzvos* of *lo sikom* and *lo sitor*, we might find these words somewhat puzzling. However, according to this opinion, *Chazal* are referring here to matters of personal offense. The *talmid chacham*, who is not just a private citizen but a representative of *kavod haTorah*, should keep a mental record of the personal offense (and if someone else comes forward to take revenge on his behalf, he should remain silent and allow justice to be done).

All of this holds true only until the offender comes to conciliate him. Once he comes to apologize, the *talmid chacham* should be quick to forgive and forget. (*Mishpetei Hashalom* 3:10–11)

Second Opinion NOT ALL *POSKIM* agree that an exception should be made for personal offense. Some opinions (among them the Chofetz Chaim) are stringent and say that even in a case where we are emotionally abused or physically hurt, the *issurim* of *nekimah* and *netirah* still apply. According to this view, we have to keep in mind that whatever the nature of the pain inflicted, nothing in this world is important enough to warrant our taking revenge. In any case, though an individual may have been the direct trigger of our pain, the true cause is our *aveiros*; the other fellow is not a cause but merely the tool to bring about what we needed to experience.

As for the *talmid chacham*, according to this view it would be only in a case of public humiliation that it would be prohibited for him to let the matter go. Once the offense is in the public eye, our concern is for the honor of Torah that has been violated rather than for his personal pain. In fact, if the *talmid chacham* forgives a public offense, then he himself is also held liable for tolerating the desecration of the honor of Torah. On the contrary, he should "take revenge and bear a grudge like a snake" — until the offender comes to apologize. Then he can resume his soft demeanor, forgive him and drop the matter.

> "I'm not really a *talmid chacham* of such caliber. I learn all day, and I give a *shiur* here and there. But *Chazal* couldn't have been speaking about me when they made that statement."

Although humility is a fine *middah*, in this case the person might have the responsibilities of a *talmid chacham*, whether he thinks of himself as such or not. A *talmid chacham* is defined as anyone who has reached such a level of knowledge and leadership qualities that his community has an obligation to honor him. Naturally, this is a very relative definition, and if in doubt we should seek counsel to determine our status. (*Mishpetei Hashalom* 3:12–14)

Referring Our Case to Din Shamayim SOMETIMES, WHEN SOMEONE has been badly hurt by another person, he may be so enraged that he is tempted to turn to *din Shamayim* — to demand that Heavenly justice be visited upon the perpetrator. But just as a father is displeased when one child comes to demand that his brother be punished, so does Hashem frown upon this practice among His children. Similarly, we should not pray that Hashem punish the person who wronged us.

In *maseches Shabbos*, we learn that someone who causes his friend to be punished is not admitted in to the company of Hashem. In fact, *Chazal* say that someone who refers his case to *din Shamayim* is punished even before the offender is punished.

This is the case when there is recourse to justice in a human *beis din*. However, if that opportunity does not exist in the community, or if the offender was called to *din Torah* and refused to abide by the ruling of the *dayanim*, then we may take the case to *din Shamayim*. According to some opinions, however, even that is permitted only if the offender was warned in advance. Practically speaking, even where calling upon *din Shamayim* was halachically permitted, the *Chachamim* were wary of doing so. (*Mishpetei Hashalom* 3:16)

In the Heat of the Moment Little Shimmy worked all afternoon building a huge creation from his construction set. He looked forward to showing the edifice to his father when he came home later that evening.

At six o'clock Shimmy's older brother Nosson came home from school in a miserable mood. Without a word he threw down his briefcase, walked over to the play corner where Shimmy was putting the finishing touches on his creation and, with one well-placed kick, knocked the whole thing down. In an instantaneous response, Shimmy gave his brother a punch and a kick, and a scratch for good measure. Hearing screams, Mrs. Schwartz came running and sized up the situation in a moment. Now she was in a quandary. Should she say anything to Shimmy? Nosson certainly deserved a talking to for his thoughtless act. Shimmy's response was rather violent, but considering the circumstances …

לא תקום ולא תטור את בני עמך

MRS. SCHWARTZ IS correct in sensing that Shimmy's reaction is not a violation of the *issurim* of *nekimah* and *netirah*. These two *issurim* do not apply at the time when the offense is being committed. If a bully starts hitting us, we are permitted to hit back — not only to protect ourselves, but even right after he stops, as long as we are still all worked up or, as the *passuk* defines it, "hot-hearted." This is true not only in a case of physical abuse, but also when we have been insulted or shamed.

Consequently, the *Shulchan Aruch* rules that in a case where compensation is due, the one who started the fight — and not the one who fought back — must pay the penalty. The Torah recognizes human nature; a person cannot be expected to stand by while someone is assailing him with hurtful words. Therefore, the Torah does not command us to be silent as a stone in the face of attack. As Mrs. Schwartz sensed, Shimmy did what any normal human being would do, and his actions are not a violation of *lo sikom*.

The exception to this rule is when it was the person's parents who hurt him. In that case, whether or not we feel the parent is justified in his or her hurtful or humiliating words or painful actions, we are commanded to keep quiet and not answer back at all. (*Mishpetei Hashalom* 3:17)

28 Elul	28 Teves	28 Iyar

Rising above Human Nature A TALMID CHACHAM who finds himself the target of abuse, though permitted to respond, should try to do so in a pleasant tone, without an extreme outburst of anger.

Some people of great spiritual stature find the inner strength to restrain themselves completely, even when permitted to respond, as they are concerned that otherwise they might lose control and become too angry. Naturally, this lofty level is not one that can be demanded of everyone, but a person who has worked on himself to reach this level is very beloved by Hashem: "Those who are insulted and do not insult, who hear their humiliation and do not respond, it is of them that the *passuk* speaks when it says, 'Those who love Him shall be like the rising sun in its glory.'" (*Mishpetei Hashalom* 3:17)

Revenge for a ACCORDING TO SOME opinions, in a case where justice
Constructive cannot be served by *beis din*, an act of revenge may be
Purpose permissible if it is *leto'eles* — for a constructive purpose.
According to this view we would be permitted to strike
or humiliate the offender, even in public, in order to ensure that he will
not repeat the offense against ourselves or against others. However, utilizing this *heter* is like playing with fire, since we have to be so extremely
careful to eliminate any trace of resentment about what was done in the
past and to focus our intentions purely on future improvement.

Since the matter is so complex, and a minute detail can change the
halachah drastically, we should never rely on this *heter* without receiving a clear ruling from the local Rabbanim.

Even in the rare case where revenge for a constructive purpose
would be permissible, certain conditions have to be met first (as in the
case of *lashon hara leto'eles*):

- If there is another way to accomplish the same purpose, we must
  try that alternative first.
- If we can give the offender *tochachah* and perhaps prevent him
  from a repeat offense in that way, then the *heter* may not be employed.
- We have to either have seen the offense ourselves, or be absolutely
  certain that it really took place and that there is no reasonable
  explanation for it.
- Finally, we must examine the matter closely to confirm that the
  act is really considered an offense according to *din Torah*.
- Assuming all the above conditions have been met (and that we
  have received a ruling from our Rav), we still have to be careful
  not to strike or humiliate the offender any more than is absolutely
  necessary to accomplish the purpose.

At times, *halachah* permits us to listen to *rechilus* for a constructive
purpose. Although we are not permitted to believe what we hear, we *are*
allowed to exercise caution based on what we have heard. Naturally, our
conduct toward the person is likely to change somewhat as a result of
this caution. For example, whereas previously we might have lent him

large amounts of money freely, we might not want to do so now without demanding guarantors. Such changes in conduct are not considered violations of the *issur* of *nekimah*. (*Mishpetei Hashalom* 3:5, 18–20)

> **In summary:** The *mitzvos* of *lo sikom* and *lo sitor* prohibit us from taking revenge against someone who has wronged us physically, monetarily or verbally, as well as from bearing a grudge against him in our heart. Exceptions exist, according to some opinions, in cases of personal offense, when a *talmid chacham* is the victim, and — on rare occasions — when there is constructive benefit. These *issurim* do not apply in the "heat of the moment."

"When a person is maavir al midosav — when he lets offenses pass and is forgiving — he will be forgiven for all his sins" (Yuma 87b).

⟿ 4 ⟾

דיני מחילה
Laws of Asking Forgiveness

Laws of Mechilah — Asking Forgiveness — When Miriam began high school, she felt a sincere desire to make a fresh start, as a new person. She knew that in the past she hadn't been too careful (to put it mildly) in her interpersonal relationships. Her sharp sense of humor was often used to put down other girls in public, and her careless attitude toward others' possessions led her to borrow items far more frequently than she returned them.

"I'm going to turn over a new leaf," Miriam resolved. "From now on I will measure every word carefully before I speak. I'll post a list on my closet door of every item I borrow, no matter how small, and it will stare me in the face until the item is returned or the money paid back."

Miriam felt pure — as if she had wiped away her past and was starting the year with a sparkling-clean slate.

Good luck, Miriam, but you've forgotten one important thing…

YOM KIPPUR DOES not atone for sins *bein adam lechaveiro* — against other people — unless and until we appease the victim and ask his forgiveness. Similarly, if we owe someone money, then all the *teshuvah* in the world — including sincere regret and heartfelt *viduy* — will not clear our slate until we have repaid our debt.

41

For some people, compensating for damage they have done and re-paying a debt are relatively easy; it is apologizing that they find so difficult. Nevertheless, when we have done an *aveirah bein adam lechaveiro*, such as stealing or injuring another person, even if we have already paid for any physical or monetary damage we have caused, we are still obligated to ask *mechilah*. Certainly in a case of cursing or verbally offending another person, the *aveirah* is not removed from our record until we have conciliated the victim and asked his forgiveness. (*Mishpetei Hashalom* 3:21–22)

Obligations of the Offender IDEALLY, THE OFFENDER should appease the victim and personally ask his forgiveness. However, if this is extremely difficult, or if we know that our efforts are likely to be more successful if they are carried out by an intermediary, then we may do so through an agent.

We should not give up if our apology does not elicit immediate results. We are obligated to make three separate attempts to appease the other person, and we should be accompanied by three people and should use a different approach each time. If we have done this, and if we have paid the victim any monetary compensation we owe him (according to *halachah*) for the shame or pain he suffered at our hands — and the person still refuses to forgive us — then we are not obligated to press the matter any further. At that point we should declare in the presence of ten Jews that we have asked the person for *mechilah*, making it clear that we have done our part.

If, however, the victim is a teacher who taught us Torah, even if he is not our *rebbe muvhak*, our primary mentor, then our obligation is greater; we must go back to him again and again until he agrees to forgive us. (*Mishpetei Hashalom* 3:24–26)

1 Tishrei	1 Shvat	1 Sivan

Obligations of the Victim THE RAMBAM WRITES that the victim should not be cruel and withhold his forgiveness; this is not the Jewish way. Rather, once the offender comes to ask his *mechilah* and pleads with him once and then again, then as long as he

feels assured that the offender has genuinely repented and regrets his wrongdoing, he should forgive him. "The quicker he forgives, the more praiseworthy he is; the Sages approve of him."

According to some opinions, even though we are not permitted to harbor a grudge or take revenge by doing to the other person what he did to us, the basic _halachah_ does not require us to forgive him in every case.

One of the exceptions to the general obligation to be quick to forgive is a case where someone has been _motzi sheim ra_ — spread false reports to sully our reputation. This is a wrong that is almost impossible to correct. In such a case, we do not have to forgive the offense, although it is an act of _chassidus_ to do so nevertheless.

There is, however, no obligation to forgive the offender until he has done _teshuvah_ for his act and has come to appease us and ask our forgiveness. Certainly, if he persists in his aggressive behavior, we would not be expected to forgive him, nor must we forgive him in a case where we know that his attitude is flippant: "I'll offend him and he will forgive me." (Even Hashem does not forgive the person who says, "I'll sin and then do _teshuvah_…")

If outstanding financial claims remain between us and the offender when he approaches us, we can mention them at that time, so that there will be no implication that we are forgiving the debts he still owes us, and we can take the opportunity to encourage him to pay the debt sooner. (_Mishpetei Hashalom_ 3:23, 27–28, 30)

2 Tishrei	2 Shvat	2 Sivan

"For His Own Good" Shmuel was the class troublemaker. If there was some prank to be played, Shmuel was the one to do it. A good-natured fellow, afterwards he would always come over to the teacher cheerfully to apologize, and then go right back to his antics the next day.

One day, after stopping up the sink and flooding the classroom, Shmuel went blithely over to the teacher and asked his forgiveness. After all, there was a class trip the next day and he didn't want to miss it. This time the teacher was firm. "No, I do not forgive you, and you can forget about

> participating in the trip." Shmuel couldn't believe his ears.
>
> Later that day, he came over to the teacher again, cheerful as always, but again his teacher refused to forgive him. Why was the teacher being so cruel? Doesn't the Rambam say that you should be quick to forgive?

THE TEACHER WAS well aware of the Rambam's statement. However, one is justified in withholding *mechilah* when it is for the benefit of the asker, so that he will not make a habit of his misbehavior, or for the benefit of the one who is being asked to forgive, if he thinks that he may suffer damage if he forgives the offender quickly or easily. Nevertheless, when he senses that the offender is genuinely sincere, he should relent and forgive him. (*Mishpetei Hashalom* 3:29)

> That afternoon, the teacher received a phone call from Shmuel. The happy, carefree tone was gone; it was clear that now he truly regretted his behavior and was bent on changing himself. With a sigh of relief, the teacher graciously forgave him.

Tar'omes — Harboring a Complaint IN A NUMBER of places in Gemara, we find that although the offended party has no rightful claim to monetary compensation, he may have a right to *tar'omes* — to retain a complaint, until the other person either conciliates him or makes some form of reparation. This is the ruling of the *Shulchan Aruch* in certain specific cases — which implies that, other than in these cases, we are not permitted to harbor a complaint against another person. (*Mishpetei Hashalom* 3:31)

In summary: *Aveiros bein adam lechaveiro* cannot be atoned for until the victim is appeased and has given his forgiveness. When someone is in the position of being a victim, he should be quick to forgive, unless there is a justifiable reason to postpone his forgiveness. In a few, specific cases, *tar'omes* — harboring a complaint — is permissible even where there is no justified claim for monetary compensation, until the victim is adequately conciliated.

⇥ 5 ⇤

מחלוקת
Machlokes — Avoiding Strife and Pursuing Peace

3 Tishrei	3 Shvat	3 Sivan

Lighting the Fire or Keeping It Aflame — Both Guilty! Adina Berger couldn't even remember how the rift started between her and her downstairs neighbor, Shaindy Weiss. Was it when she heard Shaindy bawling out Moishy for dropping a candy wrapper in the hallway? Or perhaps it was when the Weiss family was doing renovations, and it became impossible for Adina to get the baby to sleep for her afternoon nap. Maybe it was when they heard that Mr. Weiss had a hand in sabotaging her husband's job prospect. Regardless of what it was that started the fight, the conflict remained in full force.

"It's not my fault, though," Adina assured herself. "I definitely did not fire the opening volley. Once Shaindy threw the wrench into our relationship, I had no choice but to respond to her in kind. I'm certainly not the one who has to take the first step toward reconciliation. She's the one who started it; let her patch things up. I refuse to come crawling to her on my knees!"

Adina's assumption is mistaken. It makes no difference whether she started the conflagration or kept it going; either way, she's playing with fire!

45

THE *MITZVAS LO SAASEH* prohibiting us from engaging in *machlokes*, quarelling, is based on the *passuk*: "He shall not be like Korach and his congregation" (*Bamidbar* 17:5). Some opinions explain this *mitzvah* to be primarily a prohibition to raise objections to the *kehunah* being awarded to the descendants of Aharon, as the context implies. *Chazal* tell us, however, that anyone who supports a *machlokes* also violates this *mitzvah*. This includes both a person who instigates a fight between two people and one who furthers the conflict.

The word "*machlokes*" has acquired multiple meanings in Jewish speech and literature through the millennia: disagreement, dissension, dispute, argument, argumentativeness, divisiveness, strife, fighting, feud, conflict, contentiousness, factiousness, insurgency, rebellion and open warfare. Since there is no one English word that carries all that meaning, in most cases we will leave the Hebrew word "*machlokes*" untranslated.

The punishment for *machlokes* is the most severe of all. A human *beis din* punishes a child only from the age of thirteen; the Heavenly Court punishes only from the age of twenty. Yet in the case of the *machlokes* of Korach, even nursing infants were swallowed up in the ground. There is no doubt that *machlokes* is one of the most destructive forces that exist in social relationships. (*Mishpetei Hashalom* 4:1)

4 Tishrei	4 Shvat	4 Sivan

No One Is Excluded MEN AND WOMEN alike are obligated in the *mitzvah* of avoiding *machlokes*, which applies in all places and at all times. Children should be taught from a young age to steer clear of fights and should be guided to avoid associating with *baalei machlokes*. Certainly, parents should never involve children in their own *machlokes* or command their children to support them against an "enemy." If a parent does this, the child should not obey him in this matter. On the contrary, children should do everything in their power to put an end to the *machlokes* in which the parent is snarled, even if it entails a great investment of time or effort; by doing so they will fulfill the words of the *passuk*, "Seek peace and pursue it" (*Tehillim* 34:15). (*Mishpetei Hashalom* 4:20–21)

Resolving Disputes WHEN TWO PEOPLE have a disagreement, their
Peacefully goal should be to resolve their differences.
Unfortunately, the method they most commonly
use to achieve that goal — fighting it out — will virtually never result in
a peaceful resolution.

As soon as two individuals see that they are unable to reach an understanding and accommodate each other on their own, they should
go to a third party, someone who is acceptable to both of them, to help
negotiate a compromise. The third party might be a Rav, a mutual friend
or a fellow businessman. If this option is not available, or if their efforts
are unsuccessful, their next step should be to go to a *din Torah*, as the
Torah advises, "When there is an argument between people, let them
come to judgment" (*Devarim* 25:1), in keeping with the many detailed
halachos on the subject as presented at the beginning of *Shulchan Aruch
Choshen Mishpat*. (*Mishpetei Hashalom* 4:2)

5 Tishrei	5 Shvat	5 Sivan

Keeping a Safe MACHLOKES SEEMS TO have a magnetic attraction,
Distance pulling in people who would seem to have no personal interest in the disagreement. The Torah warns
us, "Do not follow the many to do evil" (*Shemos* 23:2); we are enjoined
not to support or encourage sinners, nor to join with those who approve of their wrongdoings. The Torah advises us not to associate with
resha'im in worldly matters — not even for the purpose of doing a *mitzvah*; how much more should we take precautions not to get involved in
their *machlokes*.

One way in which we express our wholehearted disapproval of
machlokes is by withholding official honors from people who are involved in *machlokes*. We are even allowed to speak *lashon hara* about
baalei machlokes (when the conditions permitting *lashon hara leto'eles*
have been met), if this will be effective in defusing the fight. *Machlokes*
is such a dangerous phenomenon that some opinions permit speaking
lashon hara about *baalei machlokes* even without having a specific constructive purpose.

However, we must be very sure that these methods will not lead to

the opposite of our desired goal, by intensifying the quarrel instead of quelling it.

The one time we are allowed to engage actively in *machlokes* is when dealing with *resha'im*. Even then, we should be very careful not to employ *azus*—brazen arrogance. The goal should be to put a stop to their wickedness and to prevent others from being drawn after them. At the same time, we have to be careful not to go so far as to persecute them, since there is an immutable principle that Hashem favors the *nirdaf*—the one who is persecuted—even if the persecutor is a *tzaddik* and the victim is a *rasha*. (*Mishpetei Hashalom* 4:6–9)

> **Peace—** "Rabbi Sheinberger, I'm happy to see you here on our
> **at Any Price** block. I wanted to tell you how appalled I was at how
> Steinfeld acted and at the way he tried to round up sup-
> port to oppose the Rabbi's new *takanah*—"
>
> "Please, Reb Leibel, I'm happy to see you too, but let's not get side-tracked, getting into things we shouldn't be saying."
>
> "Oh, that's right. So tell me, Rabbi, what brings you to our parts?"
>
> "I'm on my way to Reb Hershel Steinfeld, to patch things up."
>
> "What?! The Rav is going to that no-good—I mean, that fellow? Isn't that beneath the *kavod* of the Rav?
>
> "Is my *kavod* any more sacred than Moshe Rabbeinu's was…?"

EVEN A HIGHLY esteemed person should forgo his own honor if this will help defuse a *machlokes*—as Moshe Rabbenu did, when he went personally to Korach to give him the opportunity to back down and avoid the tragic conclusion of the *machlokes* he had begun.

The *gemara* in *Gittin* enumerates eighteen *takanos* instituted by the *Chachamim*, "*mipnei tikun ha'olam*"—to ensure social order; and many of them are intended specifically to promote peace, with Jews and non-Jews alike. Among these are: order of precedence in the allotment of *aliyos laTorah*, distribution of water from a limited supply, greeting *akum* and supporting their poor along with the Jewish needy, and other *takanos*.

Another *halachah* that shows us the significance of keeping peace is the Rambam's ruling that when a person's financial resources are limited, buying Shabbos candles take precedence over buying Chanukah candles or wine for Kiddush. Light in the house promotes *shalom bayis*, and *shalom* is paramount. We know how precious *shalom bayis* is in Hashem's Eyes; He allowed His Holy Name to be erased in the case of a *sotah*, a woman suspected of disloyalty, for the sake of making peace between husband and wife.

"Peace is so great that the entire Torah was given in order to bring peace to the world, as it says (*Mishlei* 3:17), 'Its ways are ways of pleasantness and all its paths are peace.'" (*Mishpetei Hashalom*, 4:10–11)

6 Tishrei	6 Shvat	6 Sivan

Forgoing Even a Mitzvah   Reb Shloime stepped solemnly up to the *amud*. This was the Shabbos before his father's *yahrtzeit* and, as the only son, he was always particular to arrange with the *gabbai* in advance to be the *chazzan* for *Mussaf*, as is the *minhag*.

Just before he began, an unfamiliar visitor in the shul elbowed his way to the *amud* and not-so-gently nudged him aside. "I need to *daven* today. My grandfather's *yahrtzeit*, you know." Reb Shloime began to explain politely that his obligation gave him halachic precedence, but it soon became clear from the other man's rising tones that this newcomer was not interested in details of *halachah*. He wanted the *amud*, and that was that.

Reb Shloime quickly stepped down. In response to the *gabbai's* questioning gesture, he whispered, "Keeping *shalom* is a greater *zechus* for my father than *davening* at the *amud* — don't you agree?"

EVEN WHEN IT means forfeiting a *mitzvah*, more refined people withdraw and forgo the privilege in order to avoid *machlokes*. This is true even in a case such as Reb Shloime's, where the other fellow will probably not be as worthy a representative for the *tzibbur*; nevertheless, it is still preferable to give in. (*Mishpetei Hashalom* 4:12)

Nothing More Precious Than Peace   NOT ONLY SHOULD a *mitzvah* at times be forfeited in favor of peace, Hashem even allows us to bend the truth when necessary for the sake of *shalom*. *Chazal* describe to us how Aharon Hakohen would alter the facts somewhat in order to make peace between two people who were at odds, and Hashem Himself changed Sarah Imeinu's words from "My

husband is old" to "I am old," in order to avoid any possibility of adversely affecting *shalom bayis*.

When we are confronted by someone who is looking for a fight, we may have the perfect response at the tip of our tongue — but we know that saying it will only fan the fires. It is important to keep in mind the words of *Chazal*: "The entire world exists only in the merit of the person who restrains his words at the time of a quarrel" (*Chullin* 89a). Some opinions even hold that there is a special *issur* to respond in the heat of an argument. The destruction engendered by *machlokes* is so great that we should be as fearful of it as we are of leaping flames. (*Mishpetei Hashalom* 4:17–18)

| 7 Tishrei | 7 Shvat | 7 Sivan |

For the Sake of Heaven — or Is It? A MACHLOKES THAT is *lesheim Shamayim* — for the purpose of reaching the truth, for everyone's benefit — "will endure"; that is, the two sides will remain friends and both will be blessed with long life. However, a *machlokes* that is not really *lesheim Shamayim*, but is meant only to tear down another person's viewpoint and gain personal benefit and status — will not endure. Moreover, the disputant will find it difficult to do *teshuvah* and may end up, *chas veshalom*, like Korach.

Unfortunately, there are many *machlokos* that "masquerade" as being *lesheim Shamayim* when in fact they are far from fitting that definition. The benchmark is whether the *machlokes* limits itself to the specific issue on which the sides disagree, while on a personal level the two sides remain loving friends, as was the case with *Beis Hillel* and *Beis Shammai*. If a *machlokes* leads to personal enmity, that is proof that the *machlokes* was not *lesheim Shamayim* to begin with. (*Mishpetei Hashalom* 4:13)

Torah Disputes THE ONE TYPE of argument that gives pleasure to Hashem is a heated battle between two people in the course of Torah study. We are even allowed to question our rebbe's words (and perhaps even to disagree with him, if we have clear proofs for our opposing view). However, we have to be extremely careful to retain a tone of high respect. *Chazal* spoke strongly against a person who defies his rebbe, complains against him or challenges the purity of his motives.

In any case, we are not permitted to learn just in order to "look for trouble" and undermine the rebbe's words; *Chazal* say that a student who does so is better off never having been born. We should certainly never scoff at the words of the *Chachamim*, since that is tantamount to *apikorsus*, heresy.

Occasionally, we may catch a rebbe or parent making a mistake. In such a case, we have to choose our words with care to preserve their respect, making the point in a gentle way, such as, "What does the Torah mean when it says…?" Never should we contradict them outright; and even if we agree with them, we should never be so presumptuous as to express our approval openly: "I agree with the rebbe/father." (*Mishpetei Hashalom* 4:14)

8 Tishrei	8 Shvat	8 Sivan

Respect for Colleagues   ALTHOUGH A SPECIAL measure of respect must be accorded our teachers, we must also exercise great care in dealing with our colleagues in a respectful manner, even when we are "fighting out" a Talmudic point. Tens of thousands of *talmidim* of Rabbi Akiva died because they were lacking — on their lofty level — in mutual respect.

When both learning partners are truly seeking the truth, then they will listen to one another and always conclude their battle on a peaceful and loving note: "*Talmidei chachamim* increase peace in the world."

The same principle applies in all other areas, not only learning. No two people are just the same. Each of us has his own opinions and *hashkafos*. Nevertheless, we can allow people their differences and still maintain a respectful and loving relationship, steering clear of arguments and *machlokes*. (*Mishpetei Hashalom* 4:15–16)

Lo Sisgodedu   THE *MITZVAH* OF *lo sisgodedu* (which literally means that we should not cut ourselves in grief) includes the *issur* of creating factions within a community, breaking it into separate groups. Within each city, the *beis din* can decide how *halachos*

on any particular issue are to be applied and establish the local *minhag* of the community.

Practically speaking, the prevalent opinion is that two different *batei din* may have different customs within the same city; the *issur*, according to this more accepted view, is to have two opposing rulings within one *beis din.* (*Mishpetei Hashalom* 4:3)

| 9 Tishrei | 9 Shvat | 9 Sivan |

On the Road   WHEN SOMEONE TRAVELS from his home town to another town with differing customs, how should he conduct himself — according to the *minhagim* of his native town or according to those of the host community?

If his move is a permanent one, then he should follow the local custom. If he is a temporary resident of the new place, he should adopt the stringencies of the host town while unobtrusively continuing to observe the stringencies of his native town. But when being more stringent than the locals, one should be careful to hide one's stringencies, since flaunting one's extra *chumros* in a place where they are not practiced can easily cause friction.

Extreme care should be exercised not to diverge from the local custom, since this can easily lead to *machlokes.* Exceptions may apply in cases where one is far away from the Jewish neighborhood and will not be observed by other Jews, in which case he may be permitted to carry on according to his native custom.

Even in a case where the local custom is to prohibit something that is absolutely permissible, we are still not allowed to conduct ourselves in the permissible manner in front of those who prohibited the practice. (The many details of these *halachos* are enumerated in *Shulchan Aruch Yoreh Dei'ah* 214.)

When a girl gets married, she often encounters differences between the *minhagim* she grew up with and the *minhagim* of her spouse. The rule is that the wife accepts all of her husband's customs — whether they are more stringent or less stringent than her previous *minhagim.* However, many opinions make an exception in customs relating to the special *mitzvos* of the woman — such as, for example, candle-lighting — and rule that in these areas the woman retains the *minhag* of her mother, and the husband accepts the change. (*Mishpetei Hashalom* 4:4–5)

These rules do not extend to *chumros* (extra stringencies) that her husband has taken on, which are neither obligations nor *customs*. It is generally accepted that the husband does not impose his *chumros* on his wife, unless she understands the implications fully and wishes to accept them of her own accord.

10 Tishrei	10 Shvat	10 Sivan

Classic Examples IN OUR MOBILE generation, the *halachos* regarding differing *minhagim* are very relevant. A classic example is the question of whether to observe one day of Yom Tov or two days, for visitors to or from Eretz Yisrael. Other examples include foods that may be eaten in some places on Pesach and not in others, or the status of *erev Pesach* — in some places people are allowed to perform *melachos* until noon, while in other places they conduct themselves with the stringencies of *chol hamo'ed* the entire day.

In communities that include families of different origins, there may be no fixed practice in certain areas of *minhag*, and presumably, retaining different customs in these areas will not result in *machlokes*. Hence, whereas in a strongly chassidic town a hundred years ago, it may have been unheard-of for a visitor to eat *gebroktz* — matzah or matzah meal that has come in contact with water — today, in most religious communities that include Jews of many backgrounds, we find some families eating *gebroktz* and others not, without any *machlokes* being generated. The same applies in mixed Ashkenazi/Sefardi areas, where the Sefardi families eat *kitniyos* — such as rice and legumes — on Pesach, and the Ashkenazim do not.

Auxiliary Effects of Machlokes AS WE POINTED out in our discussion of the *mitzvah* of *lo sisna*, and it applies to *machlokes* as well, a violation of the *issur* generally brings with it violations of many other *mitzvos*, such as the positive *mitzvos* of loving your fellow man, following in Hashem's ways, judging favorably, staying away from falsehood (a fight inevitably involves exaggerations

and even outright lies), and also the *mitzvah* of *vedibarta bam* — *bittul Torah*. (How many hours of Torah learning are lost as people process and re-process the details of a local *machlokes*?)

In addition, there are many *mitzvos lo saaseh* that are trampled by the *baal machlokes*, such as following the many to do evil, and bringing about a *chillul Hashem*, causing others to sin, violating the various *issurim* involved in *lashon hara* and *rechilus*, cursing or striking others, stealing (e.g., *machlokes* may cloud a person's judgment and lead him to withhold payment from someone to whom he owes money), cheating, delaying payment of a worker's wages, failing to support the needy, shaming others, taking revenge, bearing a grudge, hating someone in one's heart, and degrading the honor of a *talmid chacham*. (*Mishpetei Hashalom* 4:19)

11 Tishrei	11 Shvat	11 Sivan

Practical Tips to Avoid Machlokes   ONCE A SMALL incident flares up into an argument, and from there into a full-blown *machlokes*, it is very hard to close the floodgates and avoid being swept away by one's emotions. But if we employ some of the following tips, we can avoid getting into a *machlokes* in the first place, or end a budding *machlokes* before it has a chance to develop into a major conflict:

1. If you are involved in an unpleasant situation with your friend, try not to discuss it with your spouse. Not everyone is blessed with a spouse like the wife of On ben Peles, who managed to save him from being sucked into Korach's *machlokes*; some spouses may tend to react more like Korach's wife and fan the fire all the more.

2. Be prepared to swallow your pride and give in, even when you know you're right — and certainly when there's a chance the other fellow might be justified.

3. Stay away from bad company — specifically people who like to get together and poke fun at others.

4. Avoid speaking, hearing and believing any form of *lashon hara* or *rechilus*.

5. Never shame people, in public or in private, or hurt them with your words, even "as a joke."

6. Make a point of always showing others respect — no matter how they speak to you.

7. To avoid confrontations, keep your distance from people who do not like you, no matter what their reasons.

8. Don't be overly exacting, even in matters of Torah and *mitzvos* — and certainly in other areas — if it is likely to make you tense, melancholy or irritable.

9. Avoid falling prey to the *middos* of jealousy, anger and irritability; this enables you to remain rational and not be overcome by your emotions when things don't go your way. When you are in control of yourself, you can remember that whatever happens to you is from Hashem; the other person is just an emissary in Hashem's plan, so there is no point in picking a fight with him.

10. Foster the precious *middah* of *vatranus* — yielding. People are greatly mistaken when they think that giving in is a sign of weakness. The very opposite is true: The weak person is the one who can't control himself, who is afraid to back off from his position for the sake of peace, and who allows his bad *middos* to overcome his rational thinking and force him to prolong the *machlokes*.

11. Do not make the mistake of thinking that once a *machlokes* is under way, there is no way to stop the avalanche. Not so! If you are strong enough to swallow your pride, there is always a way to nip the conflict in the bud, or at least to prevent it from developing into a bigger conflict.

12. An important safeguard is to find a Rav who understands and cares about you, one you feel you can turn to for truly objective advice that you will be willing to follow. No one can see his own faults clearly, and there is no substitute for a reliable, objective advisor. (*Mishpetei Hashalom* 4, footnotes 28–31)

If we would only recognize the potentially fatal destructive forces that *machlokes* can engender, we would have little trouble keeping our

head out of the lion's mouth. As the Rambam writes in his famous letter to his son: "I have seen children blackened, families cut off, villages crumbled … respected ones degraded — all because of *machlokes*. Prophets prophesied and *Chachamim* philosophized and will continue to speak of the evils of *machlokes*, and yet will never finish saying all there is to say.… Keep away from it and from all who support it, lest you be decimated in their sin." (*Mishpetei Hashalom* 4, footnotes 28–31)

In summary: The *mitzvah* of "He shall not be like Korach and his congregation" requires us to avoid stirring up a fight or supporting an existing one. *Machlokes* is extremely volatile and leads one to many other *aveiros*; we should go to any lengths to preserve or restore peace, including bending the truth where necessary and squelching our pride. The only acceptable *machlokes* is one that is *lesheim Shamayim*, a *machlokes* for the sake of seeking the truth in Torah, which does not result in personal antagonism.

"Rabbi Shimon ben Chalafta said, 'The only vessel Hashem could find that could contain brachah for Yisrael was shalom, as it says, "Hashem will give strength to His people, Hashem will bless His nation with peace" (Tehillim 29:11)'" (Uktzin 3:12).

~≡ 6 ≡~

שאלת שלום
Greeting Others

Hashem's Name "That's the twentieth customer to walk in to the store
— A Heartfelt this morning without so much as a nod of the head,"
Greeting Meir the grocer pondered as he rang up Mr. Diamond's
items and handed him his change. "Nobody has time
for anybody these days."

A cheerful voice woke him from his reverie. "*Shalom aleichem*, Reb Meir!
How are you feeling this fine morning?"

"Rabbi Singer, I knew it was you before I even looked up! I can always
depend on you for a proper greeting to brighten my day — and you always beat me to the draw, too," Meir said with a smile that lasted for the
rest of the morning.

SHE'EILAS SHALOM IS usually translated as "greeting," but it actually
means inquiring about someone's well-being. The Gemara usually refers
to greeting someone with the word "*Shalom*," which is one of the Names
of Hashem, as Rashi explains (*Shabbos* 10b), Gidon called Hashem
"Shalom" (*Shoftim* 6:24). Thus, when we use the term "greeting" in our
context, we refer to this aspect as well — that by saying *shalom* we are
giving the other person a blessing that Hashem help him.

The power of a warm greeting of *shalom* cannot be overestimated.

Chazal actually instituted a *takanah* that people should greet their friends and inquire after their well-being using the word *"shalom"* — one of the divine Names of Hashem. Using the word *"shalom"* to honor our fellow man is not considered disrespectful to Hashem's Name; we can even use *shalom* in greeting non-Jews. To a *talmid chacham*, we show our esteem by doubling our *shalom* (*"Shalom, shalom"*). (*Mishpetei Hashalom* 4:22)

**Taking
First Place**

When the Jewish camp "Yachlifu Ko'ach" arrived at the Swiss mountain village resort, Mr. Buch, a respected member of the Zurich community who was visiting at that same time, had a few gentle words with the camp's Rav.

"In the course of my work, I come in contact with a lot of gentiles from around here. The local custom in these mountain villages is to warmly greet anyone you pass and offer assistance graciously when necessary. I am sorry to tell you that some of these gentiles have claimed that the reason they despise Jews is that the visiting Jewish tourists do not bother to return their greetings.

"Perhaps where you come from, people are not accustomed to saying 'Gut Shabbos' to every Jew they meet in the street, and certainly not to gentile strangers. But," he added in a gentle but insistent tone, "even the *malachim* who came to visit Avraham Avinu changed their habits to adapt to the local custom."

The camp Rav appreciated this tactfully worded rebuke and shared the message of the importance of a warm and friendly greeting to everyone — including non-Jews — with his eager campers.

At the end of that summer he was pleased to overhear some local villagers speaking among themselves: "What a fine group of boys the Jews sent here this time — polite and friendly. It was a pleasure to have them."

"*Baruch Hashem*," the Rav thought with satisfaction. "A true *Kiddush Hashem*!"

EVERY MORNING WE pass our neighbor on the way to work, and each time, he gives us a warm greeting. If that is the case, we must try to give him our *shalom* first — "Seek peace and pursue it" (*Tehillim* 34). In any case, we must be sure to respond to his greeting; if someone gives us *shalom* and we do not respond in kind, we are considered *gazlanim* — robbers. In contrast, when we bless our friend with a warm greeting, we are blessed from *Shamayim*.

אהבת שלום

But we should not limit our greetings to old friends and close neighbors. *Chazal* say that we should be the first to greet *everyone*. Rabbi Yochanan ben Zakai was known for being the first to receive everyone he met — even non-Jews — with a warm greeting (*Mishpetei Hashalom* 4:23–24). Shammai Hazaken as well — though he was often mistakenly perceived as a grim, serious personality, due to his stringencies in *halachah* — was actually very particular to greet everyone *beseiver panim yafos* — with a warm smile.

13 Tishrei	13 Shvat	13 Sivan

Put on a Happy Face   MUMBLING THE WORD "*shalom*" with a grumpy face does not achieve the purpose of increasing love and goodwill among people. *Chazal* say that we should greet everyone with a pleasant countenance (*Avos* 1:15). They add that showing a friend a white, toothy smile does more for him than offering him a nourishing drink of white, frothy milk. In fact, as we find in *Avos DeRabbi Nosson* (13:4), if we give someone all the gifts in the world with a sour face, it is as if we gave him nothing; but if we greet him with a warm smile, then even if we have given him nothing tangible, it is as if we gave him all the gifts in the world.

People who are blessed with a good sense of humor have countless priceless opportunities to cheer up those who are feeling sad; or they can use their skills to bring rivals back together by lightening the atmosphere with a good joke. (This is the complete opposite of what some people do — using the gift of humor to mock others and create *machlokes*.)

Greeting others is so vital that at times it is permissible to greet another or to respond to his greeting even in the middle of *Krias Shema* (under certain circumstances, and subject to numerous details, as explained in *Shulchan Aruch Orach Chaim* 66). (*Mishpetei Hashalom* 4:25–26)

Auxiliary Effects   IT IS WORTH noting that greeting someone is the big key to many of the other *mitzvos bein adam lechaveiro*, and to success in interpersonal relationships. Silence sometimes breeds suspicion between people; these feelings will melt away with a warm greeting. It is much more difficult to hit, curse, speak or listen to

lashon hara, or even hurt with words, someone whom we greet regularly. Moreover, it is much more difficult to give pleasant reproof and expect the recipient to feel it's for his own good if you don't even greet him when you see him.

The effects of *she'eilas shalom* can be compared to a garment: two pieces of material are useless until they're sewn together as a garment. A greeting is like the thread that "sews people together" to build warm, productive relationships. Generally, *ve'ahavta lerei'acha kamocha* and all the *mitzvos* associated with it thrive and progress much more smoothly between people who greet each other.

14 Tishrei	14 Shvat	14 Sivan

Exceptions to the Rule THERE ARE CERTAIN places and times when our obligation to give *shalom* is limited. Since *shalom* is a divine Name of Hashem, it is forbidden to use it in any place where we could not say other *devarim shebikedushah* — words of Torah and *tefillah* — such as in the *mikveh* or in places where there is excrement lying around. When writing the word "*shalom*" in a letter or other paper that is likely to be discarded later, one should leave out a letter of the word *shalom,* so that Hashem's Name will not be disgraced.

In the morning, before *Shacharis,* you may not go to your friend's door to give him *shalom,* but if you meet him, you may tell him "Good morning." (Details regarding exceptions and qualifications to this practice are listed in *Shulchan Aruch Orach Chaim* 89.)

Mourners should not greet anyone during the week of *shivah.* (*Minhagim* vary regarding the Shabbos of the *shivah.*) The same rule applies on Tishah B'Av, when we are all mourners. However, if an ignorant Jew meets you and greets you, you should respond in a serious, quiet tone, and preferably explain to him that it is forbidden to give a greeting on this day.

Chazal said that men should not give *shalom* to women; however, many contemporary *poskim* have permitted a simple greeting, since it is considered basic manners and does not imply any degree of familiarity. Similarly, a man may ask the woman's husband how his wife is doing but should not send her regards. However, this all depends very much on the *minhag hamakom*, and therefore each person should follow the ruling of his Rav in this matter.

A Joyful   A PERSON WHO sees his friend after not having seen or heard
Reunion   from him for thirty days makes the *brachah* of *sheheche-*
            yanu. If twelve months have elapsed, the *brachah* that he
is to recite is an even more powerful one — *mechayei hameisim*. Saying
either of these *brachos* is contingent on the friend's being especially
dear to him, so that he derives great joy in seeing him. (Nowadays, with
so many advancements in travel and communication, this *brachah* is
recited only rarely.) At times, when the bond between two people is
very warm, one may even recite the *brachah* of *hagomel* when his friend
survives a danger. These *halachos* demonstrate how deeply our feelings
could and should be for the other person.

A Substantial   SO GREAT IS the power of greeting others, that the
Commodity   words of greeting can be considered as an article of
            substance being given to the recipients. Therefore,
someone who is not accustomed to greeting his friend would not be
allowed to begin doing so when he owes him a debt, as this greeting
would seem to constitute payment of interest on the loan.

In summary: In order to promote peace and goodwill, the *Chachamim* made a *takanah* obligating us to greet others with "*shalom,*"
Hashem's Name, and to inquire after their welfare. One should try
to be the first to greet others and to do everything possible to cheer
and encourage them. Certain circumstances preclude giving *shalom*,
such as the time (before *davening*), the person (an *avel*), or the place
(an unclean one). In certain instances we recite a special *brachah*
upon seeing a friend whom we haven't seen in a long time.

⊸ **7** ⊸

לא יוסיף – הכאה
Striking

| 15 Tishrei | 15 Shvat | 15 Sivan |

Hands Off! When Shaya came up to his dormitory room after lunch, he was appalled to find his roommate, Noson, sitting on his — Shaya's — bed and rummaging through the pile of private papers he had left there that morning. Spontaneously, he stepped over to Noson, slapped him on the face and grabbed the papers out of his hand. Stunned by Shaya's reaction, Noson guiltily mumbled an apology and beat a hasty retreat from the room.

While Noson was out and Shaya had begun to calm down, Dovid, the soft-spoken third occupant of the room, came over to Shaya and said quietly, "You must have been pretty upset to find Noson going through your things. But you know, we just came across the *gemara* yesterday that talks about how serious an *aveirah* it is to hit or even raise your hand against another Jew. I know you're upset, but maybe you should go over to Noson and ask his *mechilah*; you don't want an *aveirah* like that on your record."

THE SOURCE OF the Torah *issur* against hitting another Jew is a *passuk* that actually deals with the *malkos* — lashes — administered by *beis din* when someone is guilty of certain offenses: "Forty [times] he shall strike him; *lo yosif lehakoso* — he shall not strike him again, *pen yosif* ... — lest he add more [strikes] than these ... and your brother will be humiliated before you."

62

The offender here is a *rasha* who violated a *mitzvas lo saaseh* before witnesses after having been duly warned. Nevertheless, he is not given more than thirty-nine lashes (or whatever number the *beis din* determines he can tolerate). The moment he has gotten his due, he regains the title of "brother"; at that point, if the *beis din* adds even one more lash, the *dayanim* are guilty of violating the *issur* of "*lo yosif.*" (*Mishpetei Hashalom* 5:1–2)

Striking IF THE TORAH warns us against adding even one stroke
Another Jew to a sinner who deserves lashes, then certainly if we
strike a Jew who never deserved lashes in the first place,
we violate the *issur* of *lo yosif.* Although striking an *akum* does not constitute a violation of this *mitzvah*, one must be extremely careful in this area, as it is morally wrong to strike anyone without a compelling reason, and it could certainly cause a *chillul Hashem.* According to some authorities, striking a *rasha* is also not a violation of this *mitzvah.*

The Rambam states that we are forbidden to injure any Jew — even oneself. It is also prohibited to strike any Jew — young or old, man or woman, or one who is mentally unstable — even without causing injury. This *mitzvah* is incumbent on all Jews, men and women, in all places and at all times.

Children should also be trained in this *mitzvah* as soon as they have reached the stage of being able to understand it. Small children who cannot yet express themselves are quick to punch and kick as a means of acquiring what they want or showing their frustration. However, even young children can gradually be given the tools to express their feelings and needs verbally, and can be rewarded for restraining themselves from physical aggression. (*Mishpetei Hashalom* 5:3–4, 6)

16 Tishrei   *16 Shvat*   *16 Sivan*

Raising a STRIKING ANOTHER JEW is so severe that the Gemara tells
Hand us (*Sanhedrin* 58b): "A person who raises his hand against
another Jew, even though he did not actually hit him, is
considered a *rasha*"; he can be categorized halachically as a *rasha* and is disqualified from giving testimony in *beis din* until he does *teshuvah.*

According to some opinions, anyone who strikes another person is automatically subject to a *cherem* — excommunication (a form of banning) — imposed by *Chachamim* many generations ago, and this *cherem* would have to be officially annulled before he could be counted as part of a *minyan*. However, as soon as he agrees to follow the ruling of *beis din*, the *cherem* should be lifted, even if the victim is not yet agreeable.

Even someone who strikes another unintentionally must pay the victim the necessary payments, where they apply, and also must ask him *mechilah* and conciliate him. Some say this does not include an incident of *ones* — a case where the incident was not merely unintended or careless; it was *completely* out of the person's control. However, someone who is drunk, for example, would be responsible if he caused damage or struck someone, since his own actions brought him to this situation of loss of control. (*Mishpetei Hashalom* 5:5, 9)

Power of Sanhedrin and "Beis Din Musmach" — IN THE TIMES of the Sanhedrin, as well as in the generations when the *Chachamim* had *semichah* — authorization to judge cases of corporal and capital punishment and to assign monetary fines (not to be confused with what is called *semichah* today, which is a much more limited rabbinical ordination), the *beis din* used its authority to apply the severe punitive measures cited in the Torah for people who strike others. For example, one who struck a parent, causing even the most minimal injury, was subject to the death penalty; one who struck any Jew, even without causing injury, was punished with *malkos*.

If injury was incurred, then the person was required to pay the victim compensation, which consisted of five components: *nezek* — the amount by which the value of the victim was reduced (were he to be sold as a slave); *tzaar* — compensation for the pain suffered; *ripui* — medical costs incurred; *sheves* — loss of earnings while he was incapacitated; and *boshes* — damages for the embarrassment suffered.

Today, the executive power of *beis din* is more limited. The *poskim* differ on the question of whether in our times the *beis din* can demand that the offender pay for medical expenses and compensate the victim for loss of earnings. In practice, *beis din* can impose a monetary fine according to their assessment of the circumstances, and they can order the offender to placate the victim. In any case, even after payment has been made, the offender has to ask the victim's *mechilah*. (*Mishpetei Hashalom* 5:8)

Corporal Punishment in Beis Din

TODAY THE SECULAR world looks askance at any physical measures taken by those in positions of authority, even, for example, when applied in the questioning of dangerous terrorists. In earlier generations, however, when the prevailing government granted *beis din* civil powers, corporal punishment was permitted and used effectively by *beis din* in several areas:

If a person did not obey an order of the *beis din*, he could be pressured strongly to do so, using various physical measures. A *beis din musmach* in Eretz Yisrael could administer thirty-nine *malkos* to someone who violated a *mitzvas lo saaseh* and could even exceed that amount, if necessary, to force someone to carry out a *mitzvas aseh* that is not unduly expensive (such as making *tzitzis* for his garment), if he was told to do so and refused to comply.

In certain urgent cases, when specific *aveiros* are spreading out of control, then, theoretically, the *Gadol hador* or *shivah tovei ha'ir* (a halachically elected committee of respected laymen) who are acting purely *lesheim Shamayim* can order that violators be given corporal punishment even without halachically valid testimony, in order to stem the evil tide. However, this is a very delicate matter, and there are many issues that need to be considered before taking action in such a case (see *Shulchan Aruch Choshen Mishpat* 2). (*Mishpetei Hashalom* 5:10–12)

The Din of Rodef and Its Applications

When Michael joined the Civilian Patrol in his neighborhood, after several violent incidents which prompted this police-supported project, he never thought he would actually need to do anything with the weapon that was put in his hand after he had been given careful training in its use.

His late-night monthly shift started off rather quietly. Then, at about 1 a.m., he spotted a teenager running breathlessly across the park, with a brawny young man wielding a knife close at his heels. "Stop!" he shouted,

running in their direction. The pursuer turned around for a moment and then resumed his pace, closing in on his intended victim. "Stop or I'll shoot!" Michael cried. When there was no response, he aimed at the pursuer's legs and pulled the trigger.

The next day Michael was at his Rabbi's house, in tears. "I feel terrible. I heard that the injury I caused may prevent the man from ever walking again. And someone told me that they're from our community — both the boy and the pursuer. How can I live with myself?"

The Rabbi reassured Michael: "You may have saved the boy's life. You did the right thing — just what the *halachah* required you to do."

WHEN A PERSON is a *rodef* — pursuing someone to kill him, or attempting to forcibly take a woman who is forbidden to him — then even if the *rodef* is a minor, every Jew is required to do whatever is necessary to save the *nirdaf* — the pursued, even if that entails dismembering a limb of the *rodef*. If even that will not be enough to ensure the safety of the intended victim, then one may kill the *rodef*, even though he did not yet actually commit the intended crime. (If he has already committed the crime, then one may *not* harm him, but he may be tried in *beis din*, with proper testimony, and then punished.)

Even though taking a matter to secular courts is generally a serious *issur*, there are cases when it is necessary and permissible to summon the police to prevent someone from striking or molesting others, especially children. However, where there is no urgency and the matter can wait a bit, a Rav should be consulted before doing so.

Another application of the *din* of *rodef* is in the case of an expectant mother whose unborn child endangers the mother's life. In such a case, the fetus is considered a *rodef*, and the life of the mother takes precedence, even if saving the mother means that the unborn child will die. (*Mishpetei Hashalom* 5:14)

| 18 Tishrei | 18 Shvat | 18 Sivan |

Self-Defense WHEN REUVEN STARTS hitting Shimon, then Shimon is allowed to hit him back to defend himself, or even just as an instinctive response in the heat of the moment (but not at a later point, once he has cooled off; that would be considered a violation of both *lo yosif* and *lo sikom*, taking revenge). The same applies to curses and insults, as evident from the *halachah* stating that someone who starts a round of insults is fined by *beis din*, but the one who responds is not. As we explained earlier, in chapter 3, one cannot be expected to sit by like a stone while he is being insulted; the *halachah* recognizes this aspect of human nature. Still, even though one is permitted to answer back, the *talmid chacham* should respond softly; certain people who have reached even loftier levels may succeed in restraining themselves from responding altogether — gaining them the status of those who "love Hashem" (see chapter 3).

According to some opinions, the *heter* is restricted to striking back in self-defense. If, on the other hand, someone hits back in the heat of the moment, when it is not necessary for his own protection, he will not be held liable for the payments, but the act itself is not permitted.

When it is a parent who is dealing the blows, whether verbal or physical, the *heter* of responding in self-defense does not apply. In that case, even if the son is a respected personage, seated in his finest garments at the head of an important gathering, and his parents come in and rip his clothing, hit him on the head and spit in his face, he should not demean them; he should remain silent and respect the King of kings Who commanded him to do so. (*Mishpetei Hashalom* 5:15–16)

| 19 Tishrei | 19 Shvat | 19 Sivan |

Protecting Your Property Mr. Helman was standing at the ledge near the bank machine, filling out deposit slips and endorsing checks. Suddenly, from the corner of his eye he noticed a fellow sliding his hand over, pulling out one of the signed checks from the pile and sliding it into his own pocket. "Hey, give that back," he shouted as the fellow rushed away.

Mr. Helman did not give up. He chased the scoundrel down the block, caught him by his collar and demanded the check. When the fellow refused to cooperate, he shook him hard and didn't let go until the thief shoved the check in his hand and disappeared down an alleyway. *What chutzpah!* Mr. Helman thought.

But was he allowed to utilize force in order to retrieve his check?

IN CERTAIN CASES, when a person's property is endangered, he is allowed to strike another person to protect what belongs to him. For example, if an intruder comes onto your property without permission, you are allowed to forcibly remove him. If you strike him unnecessarily, though, the *halachah* would require that you compensate him. But if he absolutely refuses to budge and his presence is a serious disturbance, you are even allowed to injure him if necessary in order to get him out.

Similarly, if you have reasonable grounds to suspect an employee of dishonesty, you may terminate his employment before the time originally agreed upon, and if he refuses to leave, you are permitted to strike him until he agrees to go.

In certain cases you are allowed to "take the law into your own hands" to protect your property or to get it back from someone who has taken it unlawfully (as in the case of Mr. Helman and his check), even if you would not lose anything by waiting until you can bring the matter to *beis din*. If necessary you are even allowed to strike a person for this purpose.

You may also employ force to prevent someone from doing an *aveirah*, if that is the only way to stop him. (*Mishpetei Hashalom* 5:17–18)

Injury by Request   IF, FOR WHATEVER reason, someone asks his friend to strike him or injure him, and the friend complies, he is still held liable to pay the "victim" compensation when applicable. If the first person stated clearly and explicitly that the other would not be liable for damages, then the one who struck him would not have to pay, but he may still be guilty of violating the *issur* of *lo yosif*.

An interesting application of this case is in self-defense training, such as karate or judo classes, or in sports such as wrestling. In each of these cases, the people involved are striking each other by mutual consent and often with the understanding that if injury would be incurred, compensation would not be demanded. Although there are different opinions on the matter, since it was not done aggressively or degradingly, the prevalent opinion is that in such a case those who strike each other would be liable for transgressing the *issur* but would not be compelled to compensate each other. (*Mishpetei Hashalom* 5:21)

Injury for Medical Purposes   ONE PLACE WHERE a great deal of pain is inflicted is in a hospital or doctor's office. Yet no one would accuse a caring doctor of violating the *issur* of *lo yosif*. Injuring and causing pain to someone for medical purposes — such as, for example, when removing a splinter, draining an abscess or even amputating a limb when necessary — is fully permissible. We do not concern ourselves with the possibility that the practitioner will cause more damage than he had to, since we assume he would treat the person as he would have treated himself if he were suffering from the same condition, and therefore the act would be permissible under the principle of "loving your neighbor as yourself" — we are forbidden to do to others only that which we would not want others to do to us.

However, one's child should not administer any medical treatment that might cause even very minimal injury, even unintentionally, to his or her parent (since this borders too closely on intentional injury to a parent, which would make the offender liable for a death penalty). That is, however, only the case if there is someone else available who can perform the necessary service. If there is no one else available, and the parent is suffering, then the child is permitted to administer any treatment a qualified expert would deem necessary — even if the parent objects.

There are differing opinions as to whether someone may undergo plastic surgery for purely cosmetic reasons, since, according to the Rambam and others, we are not allowed to injure even ourselves. The question is whether the cosmetic surgery would fall into the category of permitted medical treatment or that of unnecessary injury. A Rav should be consulted. (*Mishpetei Hashalom* 5:22–23)

In the Home   TRADITIONALLY, WOMEN IN the Jewish world have been held in high esteem. The Torah obligates a man to honor his wife even more than he honors himself. Unfortunately, there have always been those who have ignored this principle and thought it permissible to strike their wives. This is not a Jewish practice and is not befitting any Jewish husband.

לא תוסיף — הכאה

The fact is that someone who strikes his wife violates the *issur* of *lo yosif*, just as he does when he strikes any Jew. Furthermore, if he makes a habit of striking his wife, *beis din* is empowered to punish him, to use means of coercion, to put him in *cherem*, or to require him to take an oath that he will not repeat the offense. If he persists and does not obey the *beis din*, some authorities say that he can be forced to divorce her. (*Mishpetei Hashalom* 5:29)

21 Tishrei	21 Shvat	21 Sivan

Striking Students and Children   IN MODERN TIMES, hitting children at home and in school has "gone out of style." In some places a parent can even be arrested for slapping his own child. In Jewish life, striking children within the limits of *halachah* has its place in *chinuch*. We will first cite the *halachic* guidelines and then expound a bit on the subject, including applications to today's generation.

Walking a Fine Line   JUST AS THE agent of *beis din* performs a *mitzvah* when he strikes a deserving offender, so does the father who strikes his son, or the teacher who strikes his student, as long as there is indeed an offense to justify his action. However, someone who hits his son for no reason at all is guilty of a grave sin.

The intent of the parent or teacher determines whether the act is a *mitzvah* or not. If he strikes the child for the sake of *tochachah*, and sincerely intends it for his welfare and future success, then the act is a *mitzvah*. If he strikes the child for any other reason, he violates the *issur* of *lo yosif*; if he does so for a personal reason, as from anger about something the child did to him in the past, he violates the *issur* of *lo sikom* as well.

Therefore, a parent or teacher should never strike a child when he, the authority figure, is overcome with anger. Nor should he administer many strokes at one time, but only a little and only occasionally. (If one hits a child often, it will lose its effectiveness in any case.)

In a school where the rebbe is permitted to strike the child for *chinuch* purposes, he should never hit the student with violence, nor with a stick, but only with a small strap at most. If he injures the student he has to pay compensation. During the period of the three weeks between Shivah Asar B'Tammuz and Tishah B'Av, he should not strike the students at all. (*Mishpetei Hashalom* 5:24–25, 28)

22 Tishrei	22 Shvat	22 Sivan

Too Big/ A PARENT WHO strikes his grown child is in danger of
Too Small violating the *issur* of *lifnei iveir*, causing another to sin, since the child may not be able to resist the urge to raise his hand back at his parent or to curse him — both of which are offenses that incur the death penalty. Or the child might answer back in a disrespectful manner, violating the *mitzvos* of honoring and fearing his parents.

How old is too old for a spanking? The Gemara cites differing opinions, and many later authorities rule that the answer depends very much on the nature of the child and his particular rate of development. The moment a slap will cause more harm than good, one should think twice before using it.

A young child should be dealt with gently as much as possible, with words of *mussar* that he can understand and accept. In the past, fathers who hit their small children excessively were put into *nidui* — excommunication. (*Mishpetei Hashalom* 5:26)

The Ideal WHEN PARENTS AND children have a comfortable, lov-
Relationship ing relationship, then an occasional slap is accepted and effective. In general, a father should not be too strict in demanding his children's honor, so that he should not bring them to a violation of *kibbud av*. Rather, he should have, as the saying goes, "one blind eye and one deaf ear" — ignoring small things when possible. "A father may waive his honor" (*Yoreh Dei'ah* 240:19).

It is important for a parent to show his child that he is listening to him, taking him seriously and respecting his opinions. If he does so, it will be easier for the child to respect what the parent has to tell him. As they grow older, a father should relate to his sons as if they were brothers, and they should show one another mutual respect (see *Rashi* on

Bereishis 31:46). If a father and son do not get along well when learning together, it is preferable that they not learn together (the father can hire someone to learn with his son in his place), and instead preserve their positive relationship. (*Mishpetei Hashalom* 5:27)

23 Tishrei	23 Shvat	23 Sivan

Conditions for Constructive Striking WHENEVER STRIKING IS permissible for a constructive purpose, the conditions outlined by the Chofetz Chaim in *hilchos lashon hara* must first be met: We should have a constructive intent and not act out of *sinah* or *nekamah*; we must be certain that what was done was a wrongdoing; we must be certain that there is no alternative method of correction; and we should be careful not to strike any more or any stronger than is absolutely necessary to make our point. (*Mishpetei Hashalom* 5:28)

The Torah View on Striking Children USING CORPORAL PUNISHMENT in child-raising and education is a controversial subject nowadays. In early sources we find that Jewish tradition approved of its use and disapproved of those who refrained from it.

In *sefer Mishlei*, Shlomo Hamelech speaks often of the value of using the rod when necessary: "Foolishness is tied to the child's heart, but the rod of *mussar* will drive it away from him" (*Mishlei* 22:15); "Do not deny a child *mussar* … strike him with a rod, and you will save him from death" (*Mishlei* 23:13–14).

The Malbim comments on the *passuk*, "One who spares the rod, hates his son" (*Mishlei* 13:24): If you spare the rod because you cannot bear to see the child's pain, you are indulging in self-love at your child's expense.

Although we cannot judge our great ancestors, we can learn from the fact that the Midrash criticizes some of the greatest *tzaddikim* for not being strict enough with their sons: Avraham with Yishmael, Yitzchak with Esav, and David Hamelech with his sons Avshalom and Adoniyahu.

Striking with Wisdom   ALTHOUGH THE BASIC Torah view is that striking has its place in *chinuch*, this is a tool that needs to be used with wisdom. The child must get a strong message that the slap is being administered for the best of motives, out of love and understanding, and for the express purpose of putting him on the right path for the future.

Some children have a difficult nature and will rebel if handled at all harshly — especially nowadays, when the youth have difficulty coping with any pressures in life, and when "chutzpah is rampant." The child's individual nature must be taken into account before using one's hands to discipline. On the other hand, some children are actually waiting for a smack from a parent to set down clear limits and show them that the parent cares about what they do. At times the child may be setting a bad example to siblings or classmates by his behavior, and we may have to deal with his conduct harshly in order to prevent others from being influenced and getting out of hand. Much depends on the child's age, place in the family and social circle, and on his personal nature. The rule is: "Rear a child according to his way" (*Mishlei* 22:6).

Apologize or Explain When Necessary   AT TIMES A child may be scolded — or slapped — in error. Suspecting a child unjustly is a serious offense and can leave deep scars on a child's tender soul. In such instances it is vital that the parent or teacher apologize and appease the victim. Otherwise, he may grow up thinking that he will be punished no matter what he does, right or wrong, and then future punishments will be ineffective. At all times it is important that the child understand exactly why he is being hit. If he mistakenly deems the punishment unnecessary and walks off feeling disgruntled, the whole effect of the punishment is lost. At the same time, the parents' explanation can be stern and should not be apologetic.

24 Tishrei	24 Shvat	24 Sivan

Less Is Better   NEEDLESS TO SAY, physical punishment is not the first option. The lion's share of the child's education and training should be based on the parents and teachers setting proper

examples — simply acting right. Sometimes they can supplement this by explaining the practice and warmly encouraging the children to follow suit.

"Scolding penetrates an understanding person more deeply than a hundred beatings penetrate a fool" (*Mishlei* 17:10). Well-worded verbal *mussar* is often preferable to and more effective than hitting. Teachers and educators today tend to rely more on explaining and reasoning with a child, according to his level. Sometimes even raising one's voice is considered counterproductive.

When it comes to punishment, the less necessary, the better. For a child who has a good relationship with his parents and/or teachers, seeing a truly disappointed expression will work just as well as or even better than physical punishment. Partial withdrawal of privileges or rewards is another means of correction. And encouraging positive behavior by praise or prizes is far better than threats or actual punishment.

Still, there will be times when it may be necessary to use physical punishment in response to gross misconduct — such as disrespect for *tashmishei kedushah* (sacred objects), lying, or relating to younger siblings or weaker friends with undue cruelty. When physical punishment is reserved for such situations, it is much more effective.

Disciplining the Special Child   AS WE MENTIONED, the *issur* of *lo yosif* applies regarding someone who is mentally or emotionally challenged as well. At times, however, it will be necessary to physically restrain such an individual, in whatever manner is possible, in order to prevent him from damaging or injuring others. Many children with mental and/or emotional challenges do not derive much educational benefit from being hit.

Still, on occasion one may need to strike such a child for the immediate purpose of getting him to do what he must do, or stopping him from doing something he should not be doing, for his own benefit and/or protection — not for the *mitzvah* of *chinuch*, but rather to carry out the obligation of *ve'ahavta lerei'acha kamocha*.

When in doubt as to the particular status of a special child, a Rav should be consulted. (*Mishpetei Hashalom* 5:footnotes 33–41, 7:36, 9:19–21)

In summary: The *issur* of *lo yosif* prohibits us to strike another Jew. Even raising a hand is forbidden. The *beis din* has authority at times to use physical force. Some exceptional situations that warrant striking are in self-defense, pursuing a *rodef*, protecting one's property and preventing someone from sinning. Striking a child for *chinuch* purposes can be a positive tool in the Jewish view, when utilized properly and within strict limitations.

לא תוסיף – הכאה

◦⇒ 8 ⇐◦

איסור קללה
Do Not Curse

25 Tishrei	25 Shvat	25 Sivan

The Power of a Word   A recent arrival at the local day school, Ronny was doing quite well making the adjustment from public school. The double workload of Jewish and secular studies did not daunt him, nor did the new dress requirements. Still, there were some habits that he had brought with him from his old junior high that he never would have guessed would be a problem.

One day, as Ronny sat at his desk putting his notes in order, another boy rushed by and carelessly knocked over the pile of papers, strewing them in every direction. Instinctively, Ronny reacted as he would have in his old school — cursing his classmate with a stream of maledictions, as if he wanted to bring down all the scourges of *Shamayim* on that boy's head.

To Ronny's surprise, Rabbi Belfer, who had just walked into class and heard his tirade, gently pulled him outside the classroom. "Ronny, I understand that this way of speaking was the norm in public school, but it is absolutely taboo here."

"But I didn't do a thing to him; it was just words …" Ronny said in his own defense.

"If we would only know the power of the words that come from our mouths, we would choose them as if we were picking out diamonds," Rabbi Belfer sighed, putting his arm around Ronny and walking him back into the class.

איסור קללה

THE TORAH ABSOLUTELY forbids us to curse any Jew — man or woman, child or adult, or even oneself, with or without using Hashem's Name. True, a curse is just "words"; however, as we shall see, our words wield great power, whether for good or for bad. The seriousness of this _mitzvah_, which is incumbent on men and women, in every place and at every time, can be seen by the fact that the violator is given _malkos_, lashes, even though the act is "just words."

Children should be trained from their earliest years to speak in a positive manner and not to use any language that resembles a curse. As in most _mitzvos_, the strongest _chinuch_ is a positive example. Children will speak in ways that they hear us speak, rather than as we _tell_ them to speak. (_Mishpetei Hashalom_ 6:1, 18)

Levels of Severity   WHILE WE MAY not curse any Jew in any way, various factors determine the severity of the offense and, consequently, the punishment for which one would be held liable. Some of these factors are: whether or not one used Hashem's Name (this includes a divine Name, a substitute such as "Hashem," and a word that designates Hashem in any language), and whether the offense was committed in the presence of witnesses and after the offender was warned.

If the curse was pronounced with Hashem's Name, in the presence of witnesses and after a warning, the offender would be held liable in _beis din_ for lashes for having violated the _mitzvah_ of "Do not curse a deaf person." (_Mishpetei Hashalom_ 6:1)

26 Tishrei	26 Shvat	26 Sivan

A Dayan, Parent and Nasi   IF THE OFFENDER cursed a _dayan_, a judge in _beis din_, an additional _issur_ would be violated: "Do not curse a judge." (The reasoning behind the separate _issur_ regarding a _dayan_ is in order to prevent the judge from being intimidated by the thought that the person he is judging might curse him. According to many opinions, however, this _issur_ applies only to a _dayan_ with "genuine _semichah_," i.e., _semichah_ accorded through an unbroken line reaching back to Moshe Rabbeinu, which we do not have today.)

A son or daughter who curses a parent using one of the seven Names of Hashem, which, according to *halachah*, may never be erased, violates another, even more serious *issur* and is punishable by death through *sekilah* — stoning — even if the curse was uttered after the parent passed away. If one of these Names of Hashem is not used, the punishment would be *malkos*. Someone who curses a *nasi* — the head of *Sanhedrin* or a Jewish king — violates a an additional, separate *issur*, as the *passuk* states, "Do not curse a *nasi* among your people." (A prince who curses his father can therefore incur four sets of *malkos*, as the Rambam points out.)

Even though a *dayan* or *nasi* is permitted — and even advised — to forgo his honor in many instances, he may not overlook a curse. Similarly, if an ordinary person chooses to forgive a curse, the offender is still liable to be punished with *malkos*. (However, if the offender was put into *nidui*, excommunication, the *beis din* may absolve him from the *nidui* if they determine that doing so will not detract from Hashem's honor.) (*Mishpetei Hashalom* 6:1, 3–5)

Why a "Deaf Person"? ALTHOUGH THE WORDING of the *passuk* that informs us of the basic prohibition to curse is: "Do not curse a deaf person," this does not mean to imply that it is prohibited to curse only those who are hearing-impaired. The wording of this *passuk* teaches us that we may not curse *even* someone who does not hear us and therefore will not suffer mental anguish after having heard the curse. The *issur* applies all the more to one who curses a person who *does* hear us and can be hurt by our words.

On a practical level, this means that we violate this *issur* even if the object of the curse is not present and will never know what we said. In addition, someone who curses a person who had died has violated this *issur* (although he would not be punished with *malkos*).

There are people who would never curse an individual, certainly not to his face, but who feel free to curse a group, a community, the inhabitants of a particular town, or even all of *Klal Yisrael*. They are deeply mistaken in this matter, since cursing a group is also a violation of this *issur*, and, as the Rambam states, the offender can never do complete *teshuvah*, since there is no specific individual from whom he can ask *mechilah*. (*Mishpetei Hashalom* 6:2, 6, 10)

What Constitutes a Curse? AS WE HAVE mentioned, cursing a Jew even without using Hashem's Name is prohibited, even though the offender would not be punished with _malkos_. If we hear someone using Hashem's Name and sense that he is about to express a curse, we should stop him in mid-sentence, even though it appears that we are causing him to be _motzi Sheim Shamayim levatalah_ — to utter Hashem's Name in vain — because the _issur_ of cursing a Jew is even more severe.

The term "_arur_" — "Cursed be ..." — constitutes a curse when used to express the thought that someone should be "_arur_ — cursed" by Hashem. Sometimes, however, the language of _arur_ is used as part of an oath: "May I be _arur_ if I do not ...," and in that context it might not be included in the _issur_.

> "You're leaving my employ and opening your own insurance office, after all I did for you? Hashem shouldn't give you a drop of _hatzlachah_, you ungrateful wretch."

Cursing indirectly, by implication, such as by saying, "May he not be blessed by Hashem," is prohibited, even though it is not punishable by _malkos_. As in the above example, this can occur between business rivals; one should be careful to avoid any such language. (_Mishpetei Hashalom_ 6:7–9)

Cursing One's Husband THIS _ISSUR_ IS generally observed meticulously among the Jewish people, who are careful not to utter a curse.

Therefore, if a Jewish woman habitually violates the _issur_ and curses her husband in his presence or in the presence of his son, for no justifiable reason; or if she curses her father-in-law in the presence of her husband or his son, this is considered a breach of _das yehudis_ — the way a Jewish woman must conduct herself in accordance with _halachah_.

In certain cases this would render her liable to be divorced and to forfeit part of her _kesubah_, the settlement owed to her through the marriage contract.

However, if the curse is uttered as a spontaneous response to physical or verbal abuse on her husband's part, the woman would not lose her financial due, since the words were uttered under duress. (*Mishpetei Hashalom* 6:11)

28 Tishrei	28 Shvat	28 Sivan

Exceptions to the Rule THERE IS NO *issur* of cursing an *akum*; nevertheless, it is ethically wrong to curse anyone, and it is a crass reflection of bad character traits. Certainly, one must be careful never to make a *chillul Hashem* or to cause animosity on any level. One should strive constantly to maintain peaceful relations with everyone.

As is the case regarding other *mitzvos* we have discussed, the *issur* to curse applies to Jews who conduct themselves as Jews. Therefore, we would be allowed to curse a *rasha*, as long as he has not yet done *teshuvah*. (Regarding a Jew who falls into the category of *tinok shenishba*, see chapter 18.)

In certain cases the *beis din* is permitted to curse those who refuse to obey their rulings and sinners who refuse to accept *tochachah*, rebuke. The same is true in any specific case where *Chazal* deemed a curse to be a constructive tool for the sake of the general good.

A classic application of this is regarding the curse known as *mi shepara* — "He Who punished," which is used in a situation such as the following: Reuven agrees to sell something to Shimon and has even accepted payment, but Shimon has not yet made a *kinyan*, a *halachic* acquisition. At that point, one of them backs out of the deal. Even though the *halachah* allows him to do so, this action is not in keeping with the standards of Jewish business ethics. The *beis din* can summon him and, after fair warning, curse him with the words, "He Who punished the generation of the Flood … shall punish those who do not keep their word." The constructive purpose of this curse is to deter people from conducting themselves in this unethical manner. (*Mishpetei Hashalom* 6:12–14)

Referring an   AS WE DISCUSSED in chapter 3, turning to _din_
Offender to Din _Shamayim_ — demanding that Heavenly justice be
Shamayim   visited upon an offender — is greatly frowned upon,
and _Chazal_ say that someone who does so is punished even before the offender is punished.

However, where there is no recourse to justice in a human _beis din_,
or if the offender refuses to abide by the ruling of the _dayanim_, then a
person may declare that _din Shamayim_ be meted out to the offender,
although according to some opinions this is permitted only if he had
warned the offender in advance. In any case, the _Chachamim_ were wary
of using this _heter_.

The Gemara relates several incidents involving _Chachamim_ who
considered dealing with troublesome people by asking that Heavenly
punishment be brought upon them and were advised against this approach:

A heretic was giving Rabbi Yehoshua ben Levi a lot of trouble, and
Rabbi Yehoshua ben Levi planned to curse him, but when he did not
manage to do so, he concluded that this was not the recommended way
to deal with the heretic, as _Mishlei_ (17:26) states, "For a righteous man
to punish is also not good" (_Brachos_ 7a).

In another incident, Mar Ukba asked Rabbi Elazar if he was allowed
to inform on someone who was causing him serious trouble, and Rabbi
Elazar responded with the _passuk_ from _Tehillim_ (39:2), "I will fasten a
muzzle to my mouth even when the wicked one is in my presence."

When matters became intolerable, Mar Ukba presented the question again, and Rabbi Elazar again answered by quoting _Tehillim_ (37:7),
"Be silent [and leave it] to Hashem, and wait patiently for Him," and
he interpreted it as: "Go to the _beis medrash_ morning and evening to
daven or to learn Torah, and they [the problems] will come to an end of
their own accord [without your intervention]," and that is exactly what
happened (_Gittin_ 7a).

On the other hand, there were occasions where the _Chachamim_ approved of putting someone in _nidui_ — which can sometimes have the

same effect as a curse. They did this either to coerce the person to mend his ways or to protect the rest of the community from harm, but never for the sake of revenge. (*Mishpetei Hashalom* 6:15)

Special Situations between Father and Son

SOMETIMES THE *BEIS din* will require a person to take an oath using language that involves cursing himself if it turns out that he is swearing falsely. A son who takes his father to *beis din* for judgment is not allowed to require his father to take an oath like this. Such an oath looks too similar to the serious *issur* of cursing a parent. However, the son is allowed to request that the *beis din* require his father to take a standard oath, which does not include any curse. Under no circumstances may he bring his father to an embarrassing situation; doing so would bring upon him the Torah's curse: "Cursed is the one who brings his father and mother into contempt."

A *ger tzedek* — a convert to Judaism — is not considered halachically to be related to his biological parent. Nevertheless, there is a Rabbinical prohibition for a *ger* to curse his father, so that people should not think that when he converted, his level of *kedushah* dropped (i.e., that he became less restricted in his behavior than he was before). However, even if his parents converted as well, a child who was conceived before his parents converted to Judaism would not be guilty of a Torah violation if he cursed his parents, though he would still be guilty of the *issur* of cursing.

A *shtuki* — a child whose father's identity is uncertain — must not curse his mother, but this *issur* does not apply to his [supposed] father.

If a Jew is born of a Jewish father and a non-Jewish mother, he is not held liable for cursing his father.

A *mamzer* — a child born of a forbidden relationship — should not curse his father, even if his father has not yet done *teshuvah*. However, if he does curse his father, he is not held liable for doing so. (*Mishpetei Hashalom* 6:16–17)

| 1 Cheshvan | 1 Adar | 1 Tammuz |

Watch Your Words   "Don't climb up that ladder! You'll break your leg!" the anxious mother called out to her mischievous five year old. A minute later the child lay sprawled on the floor; an X-ray at the hospital confirmed a fracture in his leg.

"I'm late. I'm going to miss that bus, I know it," Miriam said to herself. In the end, she managed to get to the bus stop on time; but the bus had left a minute early.

ONE OBVIOUS REASON it is prohibited to curse is to prevent the ill will that would result if the person who was cursed would hear about it. The Rambam wrote that the reason for this *issur* is to serve to protect the spiritual state of the one uttering the curse — that he should not accustom himself to losing his temper or taking revenge. (Rambam does not mention anything about the possible damage to the one he is cursing, implying that the curse itself does not actually cause harm.)

The *Sefer Hachinuch* differs with the Rambam, pointing out that all nations and cultures are concerned about the effects that an ordinary person's curse can have. Words have power, and by prohibiting us from uttering a curse, the Torah is preventing us from causing harm to another person. "A promise has been given to the lips" (*Mo'eid Katan* 18a) — when Hashem breathed "a speaking spirit" (*Targum Unkelos*) into man, He gave man's words the power to affect those outside of him.

Chazal tell us that we should never even "open our mouths to the *satan*" — that is, we should never mention that something bad will happen, since by merely mentioning it — as in the examples cited earlier — we can bring the bad thing upon others or upon ourselves. This is true even when we mention it in an ambiguous or unintentional manner. The Shelah warned against threatening a child using language such as, "Be a good boy or the cat will come and get you," since some aspect of the threat may indeed materialize. The greater the spiritual level of the speaker, the more potent and immediate that effect — whether for good or for the bad; therefore, we seek out the blessings of great people, whose words have the most profound effect. (*Mishpetei Hashalom* 6:19–20)

Precautions to Avoid Unintended Damage BECAUSE OF THE potency of words, we find that in Gemara discussions, when learning with a colleague a *passuk* or *mishnah* that includes negative language written in the second person, such as, "He will strike you," the *Chachamim* would read it as though it were written in the third person: "He will strike *him*."

For the same reason, an enemy of the *baal korei* — the Torah reader — should not be given an *aliyah* when the section of the *tochachah* is being read (since it sounds as if the reader is directing the Torah curses toward his enemy). This is also the reasoning behind the custom to exchange blessings of *Shalom aleichem* — "Peace be unto you!" during *Kiddush Levanah* — for prior to that, we recite the *passuk, Tipol aleihem eimasah vafachad*, "Dread and terror shall befall them" — which, in the eyes of an onlooker, may resemble a curse.

Do not underestimate the power of even a simple person's curse, for we see that Avimelech cursed Sarah by implication (when he said, "'Let this be a covering for your eyes' — since you hid from me the fact that you were Avraham's wife and caused me this pain, may you have children whose eyes are covered over"), and as a result, her son Yitzchak lost his vision in his old age. (By the same token, the blessing of a simple person is more powerful than we might have thought.)

As we have stated, the words of a Rav are even more potent than those of a simple person. Therefore, if a Rav utters a curse, even if it is unfounded, or if a curse was uttered with a condition (and the condition was not met), it will still materialize in some form.

What if someone cursed you — is there any way to avoid the deleterious effects that have been initiated by his words? The Gemara has a suggestion, based on the experience of Rava (*Bava Basra* 153a): A woman once cursed Rava that his ship should sink. Rava wet his clothing in water, so that the curse could be considered to have taken effect in this minor way.

Similarly, if you are concerned about the effects of someone's curse, *Chazal* advise you to do some small action that is reminiscent of the curse, so that perhaps the words will have their effect in this way, and not in the more severe way in which they were intended. (*Mishpetei Hashalom* 6:21–24)

In summary: The *issur* of *lo sekalel* prohibits us from cursing another Jew. If the object of one's curse is a *dayan*, a *nasi* or a parent, the *issur* is even greater. An *akum* and a *rasha* are excluded from the *issur*. In some instances the *beis din* has authority to use a curse to impose its authority, or for the general good. Words are very potent, and even a simple person's curse or blessing has an effect. A Rav's words are even more powerful and will materialize even when said unintentionally.

"Do not curse the nation, for they are blessed"
(Bamidbar 22:12).

אסור קלל

⊷ 9 ⊷

אונאת דברים
Hurting with Speech

| 3 Cheshvan | 3 Adar | 3 Tammuz |

Sharper Than a Mr. Sol Goldman tried to slip into shul unnoticed. Ever
Sword Blade since he was accused of dishonest practices in the
bank where he worked, and word of his indictment
had reached the newspapers, he couldn't bring himself to show his face
outside his door. Although he knew he was innocent of the charges and
hoped the truth would come to light, he could not face the curious and
accusing looks of his acquaintances.

Today his wife Naomi had practically pushed him out the door. "Why
should you let people's groundless suspicions and lack of tact deprive you
of the mitzvah of hearing *Krias haTorah* in shul?" Grudgingly, he took his
tallis and *tefillin* and dragged his feet to shul, hoping no one would pay
attention to him as he sat in the back row and davened.

Hardly had he opened his *tallis* bag when he heard a booming voice
from the other end of the large room. "Well, if it isn't our old friend Sol
Goldman. I've been waiting to get some advice from you on my bank
investments. I understand you know how to make good money dealing
with the bank," he said with a smirk, while a few of his cronies tried in vain
to stifle their guffaws. By the time they looked in Mr. Goldman's direction
again he was gone. His face white with shame, he had grabbed his *tallis*
bag and rushed back home, where he would be safe from the hurtful remarks of cruel "friends."

86

"*LO SONU*—Do not aggrieve one another, and you shall fear Hashem" (*Vayikra* 25). From this *passuk Chazal* learn that, just as it is forbidden to hurt people financially by defrauding them in business relationships, so is it forbidden to hurt people with words. This is the *issur* of *ona'as devarim*. In the incident cited above, besides *ona'as devarim*, the speaker was also guilty of shaming a fellow Jew—this is forbidden because of the *issur* of *lo sisa alav cheit*, as we will discuss in chapter 10.

People sometimes mistakenly think that words are of little substance and cannot cause real harm. The popular jingle, "Sticks and stones will break my bones, but names will never hurt me" is the opposite of the Torah outlook. The Gemara states that in several ways, hurting others with words is a more severe transgression than cheating them financially. Money taken fraudulently can be returned; hurt feelings cannot always be restored. Fraud affects only the person's belongings; *ona'as devarim*—hurting with words—affects the person himself. When someone has been hurt by words and he cries out to Hashem in his pain, he is answered instantly, and punishment is meted out quickly to the offender.

> "But I didn't mean to hurt him; I said it in perfect innocence."

Since the interpretation of hurtful words often depends on the speaker's intentions, the Torah concludes the *passuk* with the words, "And you shall fear Hashem"—neither the victim nor the bystanders may know that you meant to hurt him, but Hashem knows your innermost thoughts and whether you really spoke innocently or not. Fear Him and refrain from hurtful words! (*Mishpetei Hashalom* 7:1–2)

4 Cheshvan | 4 Adar | 4 Tammuz

To Whom Does the Issur Apply?

MEN AND WOMEN alike are included in this prohibition, which is incumbent at all times and in all places, in dealing with every Jew, young and old alike. Children should be taught to be careful with their words from an early age and should be made aware of the pain that words can cause. Sometimes this is best taught when they themselves have been hurt. "How did you feel when Shimmy called you a baby? Did it hurt you deep inside, even though he didn't touch you? Now, imagine how Yankie feels when you say to him..."

When it comes to *ona'as devarim*, some people are unaware of the fact that children are people too; they also have feelings and are sensitive to hurtful words. The prohibition of *ona'as devarim* applies equally whether the words are directed to a child or an adult. This is especially important for parents and teachers to keep in mind; even when rebuke is necessary, it should always be given in the gentlest way that will be effective, and with the intention of promoting good behavior, not for the sake of hurting the child. We will elaborate on the subject of *ona'ah* in the *chinuch* of children later in this chapter.

The Chazon Ish once saw a father explode at his child for a possible transgression of *muktzeh* on Shabbos, hurting the child to the quick. The Chazon Ish commented that the child may have transgressed an *issur deRabbanan*, but the father most definitely violated an *issur de'Oraisa* of *ona'as devarim* ...

A man should be especially careful not to hurt his wife's feelings, since a woman is particularly sensitive to her husband's words, and she is easily moved to tears when she receives barbs instead of the praise and appreciation she craves. (*Mishpetei Hashalom* 7:3–6)

5 Cheshvan	5 Adar	5 Tammuz

A Broadly Inclusive Prohibition WHAT CONSTITUTES *ONA'AS DEVARIM*? The details of this prohibition are many, and often, whether or not a comment is hurtful is a very relative issue, depending how it is being said and to whom. As a general definition, we can say that any words or actions that embarrass, humiliate, hurt, frighten, cause suffering, or anger or shock another person — in other words, anything we might do that would cause the other person an unpleasant feeling — would be prohibited as *ona'as devarim*.

Note that the prohibition may be violated at times without saying a word — merely by showing an angry face or hinting at something negative using body language, or in other ways that do not use words. As long as we intend to hurt the other person, this would fall under the category of *ona'as devarim*.

Causing Disappointment or Troubling Someone THE GEMARA IN *Bava Metzia* (58b) warns us not to ask a merchant, "How much does this cost?" if we have no intention of buying the item, as that would be a violation of *ona'as devarim*. Several reasons for this have been suggested: Another person who was considering purchasing the item might overhear the exchange and conclude that if you did not buy it, the item must not be worth the price, or that perhaps something is wrong with it; if, as a result, he does not make the purchase, you will have caused the shop owner financial loss. The owner may also have lost a sincere potential customer who chose to leave the store rather than to disturb you and your negotiations.

Furthermore, the merchant himself might assume from your reaction that he is overcharging. In any case, by asking him a price when you have no intention to buy, you are causing his hopes of a sale to be disappointed and are troubling him for nothing.

Similarly, if you ask a worker how much he charges when you have no plans of hiring him, you are leading him on and raising his hopes unfairly.

What should you do if you want to compare prices on a major item or on a service? If there is any chance that you will complete the transaction, then your questions to the proprietor are legitimate and there is no *ona'as devarim* involved.

However, what if you have already completed the transaction elsewhere and, out of curiosity, or for any other reason, you want to ask about the price when you have no intention of buying? Or what if you have a similar item or service to offer and you just want to check out what price others are asking? If you make your intentions clear to the shop owner or worker before asking, then your question is legitimate and is not a violation of *ona'as devarim*. (*Mishpetei Hashalom* 7:8)

6 Cheshvan	6 Adar	6 Tammuz

Be Careful Not to Step on Toes While walking down the avenue on his way to yeshivah, Michael, a recent *baal teshuvah*, stopped alongside a store window to read some help-wanted ads that were posted on the side. Always on the alert for part-time work opportunities to help support his studies, he didn't even notice that the store was a nonkosher delicatessen.

Just then Shlomo, a sharp-tongued acquaintance of his from the shul he had started attending on Shabbos, came by and noticed Michael standing by the store.

"Hmm … smells good to you, I suppose. I'll bet you miss a hearty breakfast of bacon and eggs like you used to have, don't you?"

Michael wished he could sink into the ground; how callous could a person be?

AVOIDING *ONA'AS DEVARIM* requires developing a sensitivity to the tender points of each individual. If you are speaking to a *baal teshuvah*, do not say something like, "Remember all those *aveiros* you used to do?" If a person has a facial blemish or a physical defect, avoid mention of any related topic.

When speaking with someone who comes from a family of *geirim*, don't remind him about the misdeeds of his parents or grandparents. If a *ger* or a *baal teshuvah* comes to learn Torah, don't say, "A mouth that used to eat nonkosher foods should come to learn the Torah that was given from the Mouth of Hashem?!" (At times, however, such words may be meant as a compliment, as when one is marveling at how far this person has raised himself. As we mentioned earlier, that is why the *passuk* concludes, "And you shall fear Hashem" — Hashem knows whether your intentions are worthy or malicious.)

The same is true regarding any shortcoming or defect that exists in a person's community, family, spouse or children; the speaker should be sensitive enough to avoid mentioning that sore point when speaking with the person, or even when speaking in his presence.

When speaking with a person who is suffering from illness, has lost a child, or has undergone some other misfortune, do not say to him, as Iyov's friends said to Iyov, "Has anyone innocent ever perished…?" — implying that there must be something wrong with him if Hashem sent him such suffering. If you deem it necessary to convey such a message in order to rouse the person to *teshuvah*, it should be presented indirectly and very delicately, so as to avoid causing him pain.

One situation in which children — and many adults as well — often lack sensitivity, is when a person is ill or injured and is being carried into an ambulance. When a crowd of curious onlookers gathers around, this causes the patient and his family pain and embarrassment, and it may also hamper rescue efforts and endanger the person's life. (*Mishpetei Hashalom* 7:9–12)

| 7 Cheshvan | 7 Adar | 7 Tammuz |

No Practical Jokes, Please   While sitting in the park, Tova and her friends heard a woman bemoaning the fact that she had run out of baby formula and could not buy any now, as the stores were already closed. With a broad wink to her companions, Tova sidled over to the woman and said sweetly, "See that building over there? There's a lady named Gottlieb on the first floor who has a lending *gemach* for baby formula. You can knock there any time."

The woman thanked Tova profusely and rushed over, with her children in tow, in the direction she was shown. Meanwhile, Tova and her friends ran to the building from the other side, so as not to miss out on the "fun." Mrs. Gottlieb was a bitter old lady who was always snapping at the children of the building for one reason or another. She was also highly suspicious of strangers and easily excitable. This was the girls' chance to have some fun at her expense.

They all hid behind the bushes and tried to contain their rolling laughter while they watched the "show": The lady innocently tried to inquire about the nonexistent *gemach*, while Mrs. Gottlieb got all worked up, screaming that the woman was mistaken and that if she didn't leave right away, Mrs. Gottlieb would summon the police. Not once did Tova imagine that by orchestrating this scene she had violated a Torah prohibition...

MANY SO-CALLED "PRANKS" or "practical jokes" are actually serious violations of the prohibition of *ona'as devarim*. For example, if someone from out of town asks, "Where can I buy such and such?" we should not send him to someone who does not sell it. This is embarrassing and uncomfortable for both the buyer and the seller. At times there may also be a financial loss involved for which the offender would be held liable. Examples of this would be calling a taxi for nothing or ordering a pizza to be delivered to an address "just for fun." Making anonymous prank phone calls, an unfortunate pastime of some bored youngsters, can

אונאת דברים

cause real anguish to the recipients. And a false call to the fire department may not only cause financial loss to the person whose home they
were summoned to, but could even endanger lives if a real fire occurs
while the firefighters are out responding to the false alarm.

If someone frightens another person, such as by sneaking up behind
him and screaming or appearing beside him suddenly in a dark alley,
the offender would be liable for punishment by *dinei Shamayim*. If the
prankster also made physical contact with him at the time, such as by
grabbing onto him, blowing into his ear, pushing him or taking hold
of his clothes, then he would be liable to pay the victim compensation.
Children should be advised of this, especially around Purim-time, when
some people tend to act with a good deal less restraint.

Putting someone on the spot is also a violation of this prohibition.
For example, if someone has a question regarding a particular area of
knowledge, he should not pose his question to someone he suspects
might be ignorant of the topic. He should not ask, "What do you have
to say about this?" if it is likely that the person will have nothing to say.
Similarly, you should not ask your Rav or teacher something he may not
be well enough prepared to answer. *Chazal* were extremely careful in
this area. (At times it would be permissible for a teacher to ask a student
a question he may not know the answer to, if the purpose is to test him
or enhance his status — but not for the purpose of putting him down.)

If someone inadvertently asks a foolish question, one should be careful not to look at the asker, so as to minimize his shame as much as
possible. Some master educators were skilled in turning a silly question
around to make it sound like a brilliant query, all in order to protect the
student's honor. (*Mishpetei Hashalom* 7:13–14, 18)

8 Cheshvan	8 Adar	8 Tammuz

At the Other's   ONE EXTREMELY LOW example of *ona'as devarim* is
Expense   the tendency to belittle another person in order to ag-
grandize yourself through comparison. Someone who
makes a habit of gaining honor for himself by disgracing his friend
loses his portion in the World to Come. The prohibition is violated even
if the friend is not present, as long as the offender is lining up his good

deeds and wisdom alongside those of the other fellow for the purpose of building up his own image and belittling his friend.

If Reuven spits at Shimon, and his saliva lands on Shimon's body, Reuven must pay the required compensatory payments. If it only touched Shimon's clothing, or if Reuven shamed Shimon with words, then according to the strict law of the Gemara Reuven would not have to pay, but the *beis din* has the authority to allot whatever punishment or fine it deems appropriate, depending on the time and place. According to some opinions, such a person should be put into *nidui*, while others advise that he be given lashes. In earlier times, if one called his friend "slave," he was put into *nidui*; if he called him "*mamzer*," he was flogged; and if he called him "*rasha*," he was persecuted severely.

Even if these punishments are not meted out in most *batei din* in our times, they certainly give us a sense of the severity of causing another Jew pain or humiliation. (*Mishpetei Hashalom* 7:15, 17–18)

9 Cheshvan	9 Adar	9 Tammuz

Even by Accident   THE MAIN OBLIGATION of the prohibition of *ona'as devarim* is to refrain from intentionally saying or doing things that will shame or cause pain to another Jew. Nevertheless, we should take precautions to keep our distance from anything that might lead us to cause pain to another, even inadvertently.

In the words of *Chazal* on *sefer Shmuel*, we see the extent of the punishment Hashem exacts from someone who causes pain. Peninah, the wife of Elkanah, teased Elkanah's other wife Chanah about her childlessness, with the finest of intentions — in order to get her to pray harder for children. Yet even though she meant well, she was punished severely for the pain she caused Chanah, and she lost most of her own children.

An even more shocking example is cited in Gemara *Kesubos* (62b), which discusses how Rav Rechumi unwittingly caused his wife anxiety when he was late coming home. In her anguish she wept one solitary tear — and as a result, Rav Rechumi died in a fatal accident.

The excuse of ignorance of simple *derech eretz* and human decency is not acceptable, since everyone is responsible for being aware of what is proper behavior and for thinking before he speaks and acts, taking into account the situation, the place, the time and the people involved, so that he will not cause anyone pain, even unintentionally.

We have all seen countless instances of "thoughtless *ona'as devarim*," such as when someone opens a window on a bus on a cold day when most people would prefer it closed, or davens a very long *Shemoneh Esrei* in a spot that blocks others from taking their steps back or from sitting down. While the prohibition of *ona'as devarim* will not actually be violated unless these acts are done intentionally to hurt another person, we should certainly avoid doing them even with no intentions to hurt others. Consider some of the following common examples:

- Disturbing sleep: Waking someone up from his sleep (when he hasn't asked to be roused), and preventing someone from falling asleep by making noise, are frequent occurrences of unintentional *ona'as devarim*. Common pitfalls we should look out for are ringing a doorbell, making a phone call or honking a horn loudly at times that are generally considered sleeping-hours.

- Taking someone's turn: Pushing into a line instead of taking a place at the end of the queue causes anguish to the people who were waiting there before you. At times, actual damage is caused as well — for example, when the bus fills up and pulls out leaving behind one of the people whose place you usurped, causing him to miss an appointment, which will end up costing him money. (There are exceptions to this rule, such as a *talmid chacham* or *kohen*, who at times *should* be given precedence.)

- Health and hygiene: Smoking in the company of others, spitting in front of them, and other, similar unbecoming habits acted out publicly, can easily cause personal distress to those present. (*Mishpetei Hashalom* 7:7)

If one does violate the prohibition of *ona'as devarim*, whether intentionally or not, once the offender has placated the victim and obtained his forgiveness, he will be spared severe punishment from *Shamayim*. (*Mishpetei Hashalom* 7:16)

Exception — One Who Is Not "Amisecha"   SINCE THE TORAH prohibits *ona'ah* in regard to *amiso* — his companion in Torah and *mitzvos* — here too, as in the *mitzvos* discussed earlier, there is no prohibition of *ona'ah* — either monetary or verbal — toward an *akum*. However, we always have to be on the alert for a *chillul Hashem* that might emerge from utilizing this *heter*, as well as for any possible dangerous consequences.

As with other *mitzvos bein adam lechaveiro*, certain categories of Jews are outside the realm of *amisecha* — such as *apikorsim*, the *meisis umeidi'ach*, and any Jew who willfully rejects the authority of the Torah, even if only relative to a single *aveirah*. Regarding these Jews, we are permitted, with rabbinical guidance, to decry their misdeeds publicly and to shower them with contempt until such time as they do *teshuvah* and regain their status as "*amisecha*."

However, note that nowhere are we told that *ona'as mammon* — monetary fraud — is permitted against such Jews. Even though these people have removed themselves from the category of *amisecha*, there is always the possibility that they will have an heir who is righteous and does not deserve to be deprived of his rightful inheritance. (*Mishpetei Hashalom* 7:28–29)

"With You in Torah and Mitzvos"   RAV CHANINA THE son of Rav Idda further defined the limits of the obligation of *ona'as devarim*. He explains that when the Torah tells us "*Lo sonu ish es amiso*," this applies only to "people who are with you in Torah and *mitzvos*." The commentators disagreed about Rav Chanina's intention in this phrase:

- Some say he meant to include the *am ha'aretz* in the prohibition; though he is not learned in Torah, he is still "with you" in observing the *mitzvos*; do not cause him pain.

- Others interpret it as limiting the prohibition to *yerei Hashem*, as opposed to those who are habitual sinners, even if it is only one *aveirah* that they deliberately transgress.

Another angle is presented by the Rama when he quotes a puzzling *midrash* cited by the Nimukei Yosef, which states: "If someone verbally abuses you (literally, 'yourself'), you are permitted to verbally abuse him," explaining that this person is not called *amisecha*. Here too, there are varying interpretations of this exception:

◻ Some say that the *midrash* is actually referring to the *baal aveirah* — the habitual sinner mentioned above.

◻ Others say that if a person abuses you, you are indeed allowed to abuse him, either because by virtue of his conduct he excludes himself from the title of *amisecha*, or in order to protect yourself from damage that he may cause you, or as a permitted natural reaction at the time of a heated exchange, when the Torah does not demand that you sit like a stone and remain silent (though, as we have mentioned before, *middas chassidus* would be to restrain oneself and tolerate the insults without responding).

◻ Others explain that we are referring here to someone who verbally abuses *himself*. Since he does not have self-respect, he is not deserving of respect from others. As this is not a normal way for civilized people to act, he exempts himself from the title of *amisecha*. (Later *poskim* were *machmir* in this situation and did not allow *ona'as devarim* toward such a person.) (*Mishpetei Hashalom* 7:30–35)

11 Cheshvan	11 Adar	11 Tammuz

Parents and Teachers Binyamin was so busy fiddling around with the paper airplanes he had made during recess that he did not even notice the rebbe's approach until he was standing right next to his desk.

"Have you landed in our local airport yet, Captain Binyamin Shechter?" the rebbe said quietly, with a stern face. "I expect you to be with us one hundred percent; leave your flying to recess time." Binyamin turned a bright red. No one had heard the rebbe's comment, but Binyamin was still wounded by the sharp words. Mumbling an apology, he stuffed the papers in his briefcase and focused on the words of the *Chumash*.

אונאת דברים

IF A TEACHER sees that his students are slacking off in their learning, he is not only permitted but obligated to make a show of anger and make them feel ashamed, the purpose being to sharpen their minds and induce them to try harder and maximize their learning potential. Some say that even if the students are not slacking, the teacher can use such tactics to keep them on their toes. (This would explain a number of instances in the Gemara where one *Chacham* uses rather sharp language toward another who has asked an irrelevant question, such as "It seems he has no brains," or "He doesn't seem to have learned any Gemara.")

A teacher should show a student anger or speak to him sharply only when the teacher honestly thinks that the student is not trying as hard as he can. However, if the student is trying but does not understand the material because it is too difficult for him, then the teacher should not use biting remarks but should rather be patient and explain the subject again and again, until it becomes clear. Regarding this, we learn in *Pirkei Avos* (2:6): "The shamefaced pupil cannot learn, and the impatient teacher cannot teach." (*Mishpetei Hashalom* 7:36)

Special Situations: ALTHOUGH WE HAVE to be careful not to hurt
The Ger   any Jew, there are certain categories of people
who are especially sensitive, and toward them the Torah applies an additional prohibition of *onaah*.

The *ger*, a convert to Judaism, is often alone, without any family, and in a new, strange and challenging situation. He is unaware of established customs and is easily taken advantage of. The Torah advises us to be especially careful not to hurt *geirim* with words, nor to oppress or distress either them personally or their property: "Do not hurt or oppress a *ger*" (*Shemos* 22:20).

The Gemara asserts that *onaah* of a *ger* constitutes a violation of three *mitzvos lo saaseh*, and oppressing him violates another three. The Torah warns us in no less than thirty-six places (some say in forty-six) not to mistreat a *ger*. This is in addition to the basic prohibition of *onaah* toward any Jew. Note that regarding a *ger*, there is no limitation of "*amisecha*"; hence, we may not oppress even a *ger* who is not "with you in Torah and *mitzvos*." (*Mishpetei Hashalom* 7:37)

Special Situations: Widows and Orphans

ANOTHER HIGHLY VULNERABLE category of people is that of widows and orphans. Even if they are not financially strapped, the widow and orphan feel depressed and helpless, and are likely at a loss to demand their rights, as the Torah says: "Do not afflict the widow and orphan" (*Shemos* 22:21). (The *Mechilta* interprets this *passuk* as referring also to keeping people waiting when they have come for judgment — "*inui hadin.*") In afflicting a widow or orphan, one thus violates an additional prohibition, besides the basic prohibition of afflicting any Jew.

When talking to widows or orphans, we should be careful to speak gently and respectfully. Anyone who teases them, angers them, causes them pain, takes advantage of them or causes them financial loss — and certainly if he strikes or curses them — violates this prohibition. The punishment for such conduct is frightening indeed: "I shall become angry and kill you by the sword, and your wives will become widows, and your children, orphans" (*Shemos* 22:23).

The prohibition is violated only if the oppressor is doing so for his own benefit. In certain cases, however, a teacher must be harsh with a student who is an orphan in order to teach him Torah or a profession, or to correct his conduct. In such a case, the teacher's actions would be permitted; still, he should not treat him on a par with other children, but rather should favor him and treat him with extra compassion and respect. (Regarding striking, see end of chapter 7.)

These extra precautions in *ona'ah* apply to a child who has lost either his father or his mother. The orphan retains his status until he is old enough to look after his own affairs like any other adult, without having to rely on someone else to look after him and care for him.

A widow is defined as any woman — young or old — who has lost her husband. Even if many years have passed since her husband's death, as long as she has not remarried she retains that status, since she still tends to be easily depressed and unable to stand up for herself.

For widows and orphans, as for *geirim*, there is no mention of "*amisecha*"; therefore, even if they are not *mitzvah*-observant, the pro-

hibition still applies (and that is certainly the case regarding an orphaned child, who is not yet obligated in the *mitzvos* at all). (*Mishpetei Hashalom* 7:38–41)

13 Cheshvan	13 Adar	13 Tammuz

Employer Pressure ONE AREA WHERE it is common for one Jew to put undue pressure on another is in an employer/employee situation.

According to one opinion, there is a specific prohibition to make a fellow Jew work for us like a slave, based on the *passuk*, "With your brethren, the Children of Israel — a man with his brother — do not subjugate him through hard labor" (*Vayikra* 25:46).

According to this opinion, if as an employer our work relationship is such that the employee is afraid of what we might do to him, or if he is afraid or ashamed to refuse any request of ours, then we are not permitted to order him to do any personal service for us, large or small (such as to boil us a cup of water or to buy us something in a shop), unless it is clear that he is willing and amenable to the request. (Shimshon, who judged the nation loyally for twenty-two years, was lame in both legs, yet he was careful not even to ask someone to pass him his stick. Similar stories are told of present-day *Gedolim* who are exceedingly careful not to ask those around them for personal favors unless absolutely necessary.)

Similarly, we must be careful not to impose *avodas perech* — open-ended or unnecessary tasks — on our Jewish workers or family members. For example, we should not ask a worker to peel potatoes without telling him how many or until what time. When making a request of a family member, even if it is a *devar mitzvah*, we should always do so gently and politely, so that he will carry out the request willingly.

Other opinions maintain that the prohibition of "Do not subjugate" applies only in the case of an *eved Ivri* (a Jew who has sold himself, or has been sold by *beis din*, as a slave) but not to a free man, who always has the option to refuse to work for us and will obey us only if he chooses to do so.

A Jew who does not behave correctly may be pressed into any kind of service. (*Mishpetei Hashalom* 7:42–43)

In summary: With the prohibition of *lo sonu* — *ona'as devarim* — the Torah forbids us to hurt another Jew, young or old, with our words or actions. (Financial damage is a separate prohibition.) Included in this *mitzvah* are a wide range of actions and painful comments that in some way cause discomfort to others. Sensitivity is required to determine what is considered *ona'ah* to each person. Even unintentional *ona'ah* can have disastrous results. Exceptions to the application of *ona'ah* include *akum*, *apikorsim* and *baalei aveirah*. At times a parent or teacher may use hurtful words for a constructive purpose. Special care must be exercised not to hurt or oppress *geirim*, widows or orphans.

ונאת דברים

⇒ 10 ⇐

הלבנת פנים
Putting to Shame

Turning   Mrs. Tzipora Eidelman will never forget her niece Dina's wed-
Colors   ding — not because of the thrill of seeing her dear niece
married, nor because of the elegant surroundings. The aspect
that remains vivid in her mind is how awful she felt when a fancy, obviously very expensive crystal glass slipped out of her hand and crashed to
the floor. All eyes turned in her direction, and to add to her embarrassment, her cousin announced in a loud voice, "Oh, we always used to call
Tzipora 'butterfingers.' A family meal never went by without her breaking
something."

Her face turned from bright red to ivory white, but Tzipora couldn't help
noticing gratefully that at one table, not a single head turned in her direction. It was the "Rebbetzins' table." Those refined women understood that
no matter who dropped the glass, her embarrassment would certainly be
much greater if they would look at her — so they restrained their natural
curiosity and continued talking as if nothing had happened.

ACCORDING TO MOST opinions, there is a Torah obligation not to shame
another Jew; however, the source of the *issur* is a matter of debate among
the *poskim*. Some say that the *issur* derives from the conclusion of the
passuk requiring us to give *tochachah*: "Reprove your fellow, *and do
not bear sin because of him*" (*Vayikra* 19:17). The Gemara (*Arachin* 16b)

101

explains this: Correct him if you see him doing wrong, but if you think you can do so even if this means putting him to shame, "do not bear sin because of him." Even when you must rebuke him, be careful not to shame him while doing so.

According to other opinions, the *issur* of *halbanas panim* — shaming another Jew (literally, making his face turn pale) — is derived from the prohibition of *lo sonu* — that one may not hurt another Jew — discussed in the last chapter. In fact, we will find that the two are closely related. However, due to the gravity of this *issur* and the many details involved, we have devoted a chapter to this *issur* alone. (*Mishpetei Hashalom* 7:20)

Supremacy of Human Dignity　ONE OF *BNEI YISRAEL'S* outstanding qualities is *baishanus*, and the Torah is very meticulous about protecting a Jew from shame. We see how strongly the Torah values *kavod habrios* — human dignity — by the fact that at times the preservation of *kavod habrios* pushes aside even certain Rabbinic prohibitions, even though these prohibitions are based on the Torah obligation of *lo tasur* — "Do not stray to the right or the left from what they [the *Chachamim*] tell you" (*Devarim* 17:11). The *Chachamim* were even willing to forgo their own honor (by allowing the rules they instituted to be disregarded) in specific cases where human dignity was at stake. The following are a few examples:

- If you discover while in the street that you are wearing a garment that contains *shaatnez deRabbanan*, you do not have to shame yourself by removing it on the spot; you may wait until you get to a more private place.

- If one of the *tzitziyos* on your *tallis* becomes *pasul* on Shabbos, so that continuing to wear the *tallis* would be considered carrying the remaining strings, then, if the area is considered a *karmelis*, where carrying is forbidden only *deRabbanan*, you would not be obligated to remove the *tallis* in the street.

- *Kohanim* are permitted to pass through places where there are certain types of *tumas meis mideRabbanan* in order to show respect to a mourner.

- Certain objects that are *muktzeh* (a Rabbinical *issur*) may be

handled if necessary for personal hygiene in the bathroom on Shabbos.

Even the dignity of a simple thief is taken into consideration in the Torah: One who steals and then sells or slaughters an ox has to pay back the equivalent of five oxen; one who steals and then sells or slaughters a sheep, and therefore has to suffer shame carrying the beast on his shoulders through the streets, has to repay only four times the value. (*Mishpetei Hashalom* 7:19)

| 15 Cheshvan | 15 Adar | 15 Tammuz |

Cautious Rebuke AS WE HAVE mentioned, according to some opinions, the source of the *issur* of shaming another Jew is derived from the *passuk* obliging us to reprove someone who is doing wrong, but to be careful not to shame him in the process. Therefore, we should not reprove the wrongdoer in public, since this would cause him embarrassment. Even when rebuking privately, we should not come down hard on him but should rather choose our words carefully, so as not to embarrass him.

This rule applies in matters of *bein adam lechaveiro*. However, when the offense involved is in matters involving *divrei Shamayim* — between Man and Hashem — if *tochachah* in a private setting was not effective, then, as we see from the *nevi'im*, the offender should be publicly humiliated and his sin publicized. He should be abused to his face, treated with contempt and cursed — until he repents. Obviously, this is a matter for Rabbanim to decide and not for a layman to do.

(In practice, we find that the *nevi'im* gave strong *tochachah* for matters involving *mitzvos bein adam lechaveiro* as well. In the Gemara we find that certain offenses *bein adam lechaveiro* are publicized and punished publicly, such as in the case of a man who refuses to provide for his children.) (*Mishpetei Hashalom* 7:21–22)

Public Shaming — to Be Avoided at Any Cost PUBLICLY SHAMING ANOTHER Jew is tantamount to shedding blood (since when one is embarrassed, the blood is literally drained from the victim's face). If someone makes a habit of this despicable

behavior, he goes down to the depths of *Gehinnom* and has no portion in *Olam Haba*.

Chazal say that "One should rather let himself be thrown into a fiery furnace than expose another person to public shame." They learn this from the incident of Tamar (the daughter-in-law of Yehudah), who was suspected of immoral behavior and, as the daughter of a *kohen*, was sentenced to death by fire. As she was being set alight, she sent a message to her father-in-law hinting that he might choose to admit his part in the incident and thereby prove her innocence. If, however, he would not have come forward, she would not have shamed him by giving him away, even though she would have been consigned to the flames.

Midrash Tanchuma cites a similar example (on *Bereishis* 45:1): Yosef ordered everyone out of his chambers before revealing himself to his brothers, to spare them from shame. By doing so he was risking his life, since at that point Yehudah was furious and ready to attack him. Nevertheless, he preferred to risk being killed rather than to embarrass his brothers in public.

Why do we consider death preferable to embarrassing someone publicly? One approach (espoused by the Rashbatz) is that the momentary pain of death is far less agonizing than the anguish of lifelong shame. Rabbeinu Yonah takes this a step further, saying that even the pain experienced briefly at the moment of embarrassment may be worse than death. The *Sefer Chassidim* adds that, given the choice, the victim might well choose to die rather than suffer the embarrassment. (*Mishpetei Hashalom* 7:24)

16 Cheshvan	16 Adar	16 Tammuz

Equal to the Three Worst Sins FROM *CHAZAL'S* STATEMENT that it is better to throw oneself into the fire than to publicly shame another person, it would appear that the *issur* of *halbanas panim* is on a par with the three most serious sins — *gilui arayos* (adultery), *shefichus damim* (murder) and *avodah zarah* (idolatry) — for which the rule is *yeihareig ve'al yaavor* — one should allow oneself to be killed rather than violate them. In practice, is this rule applicable to *halbanas panim* as well?

Some opinions (such as that of *Tosafos*) imply that this is literally the case. Rabbeinu Yonah, too, suggests that *halbanas panim* is a minor form of homicide, since it causes the blood to drain from the victim's face, and thus is parallel to a minor infraction of any of the other serious sins. Just as one may not use the wood from an *asheirah* — a tree used as *avodah zarah* — even if someone may die if it is not used (although this is not actual idolatry, but rather an auxiliary form of it), so would *halbanas panim* be forbidden even if the alternative is death.

On the other hand, according to other opinions, the statement of *Chazal* was meant figuratively, to stress the severity of the *issur*, but the aspect of *yeihareig ve'al yaavor* was not meant to be carried out in practice. The Pre Megadim understood that it is permissible, but not obligatory, to choose death over shaming someone.

An additional indication of the severity of *halbanas panim*, cited by the Gemara (*Bava Metzia* 59a), is that while an adulterer is punished by death, afterwards he is granted his share in *Olam Haba*, whereas one who embarrasses another Jew loses his portion in *Olam Haba*.

From all of these sources we can see that even though humiliating someone in public does not necessarily require one to pay compensation, as causing monetary damage would, it is still an extremely serious sin. Moreover, one who abuses and shames an entire community is nothing short of a fool, an arrogant boor and a *rasha* (as stated in *Choshen Mishpat*). (*Mishpetei Hashalom* 7:23–24)

17 Cheshvan	17 Adar	17 Tammuz

Name-Calling "Hey, Shorty Schwartz, please pass the salt," a voice called from the opposite end of the table in the yeshivah dining room. Shimon Schwartz tried to hide his wince, putting on a blank face as he dutifully passed the salt. The other fellow didn't mean to embarrass him. Some boys were so used to calling him Shorty that they didn't even remember his first name. You'd think after years of hearing the nickname, Shimon would be used to it. But what could he do? His diminutive height was and remains a sore point, and each time he hears it, the nickname stings again.

Calling people by an insulting nickname is a practice to be strictly

avoided. Even if the person is used to being called by that name and is no longer hurt by it (which, as in the case of Shimon Schwartz, is not always as it seems), if one's intent is to embarrass him, it is forbidden to do so, and the name-caller loses his portion in *Olam Haba*. It is an admirable practice to avoid using a nickname even when there is *no* intent to put the person to shame. One Sage, when asked how he had merited living to a ripe old age, attributed it to the fact that he had never called anyone by a nickname, even if it was not derogatory.

Sometimes, when people sit together and "kid around," for example, at a Purim *seudah*, they may direct barbs and "good-natured" insults at one of those who are present. The people involved may find this practice rather entertaining, and the butt of the jokes may repress his feelings and laugh along with them, claiming that he is not offended. But while he laughs externally, in his heart he is crying.

A number of different serious *issurim* are violated in such a scenario: *ona'as devarim*, seeking honor at another's expense, rejoicing at someone's misfortune, and *halbanas panim*, to name a few. Participating in a gathering of this kind is strictly forbidden. If you find yourself in such a situation, you have a responsibility to object and to rebuke the participants, using your good sense to find a way to do so effectively. (*Mishpetei Hashalom* 7:25)

18 Cheshvan	18 Adar	18 Tammuz

Degrading Epithets IN CERTAIN CASES, the *beis din* used to impose fines on people who shamed another Jew by calling him an openly degrading name, such as *mamzer*, *rasha*, or *passul*. Other cases of people who would be fined in this way include those who say to someone that he "lies like a *mamzer*," or who announce, "*I* am not a sinner" or "*I* am not a criminal," with the unspoken implication: "… like *you* are…"

If a person is *motzi sheim ra* — spreads false information to defame another Jew — in addition to the other *issurim* involved, this is also a violation of the *issur* to shame another publicly. (Details are expounded in *Shulchan Aruch Choshen Mishpat* 420:38.)

Since a *talmid chacham* ought to be regarded with even greater

respect than a less learned Jew, someone who treats a _talmid chacham_ with contempt is punished more severely. If he degrades the _talmid chacham_, even if it is only verbally and not in his presence, the _beis din_ would put him into _nidui_, not to be lifted until he duly apologized to the _talmid chacham_ and conciliated him. If the offender degraded the _talmid chacham_ after the latter's death, the _nidui_ would be lifted only after the offender did _teshuvah._

At one time, a heavy monetary penalty of a pound of gold was imposed on someone who treated a certain level of _talmid chacham_ with contempt. Although today there are no _talmidei chachamim_ of such rank, the _dayanim_ of the _beis din_ are entitled to impose a fine on the offender as they see fit.

The circumstances in which _halbanas panim_ takes place can at times intensify the violation. Extreme care should be taken not to shame any person in front of a _talmid chacham_, nor in shul, and certainly not before a _sefer Torah_. In this context, we should be careful when correcting the _chazzan_ or _baal korei_ when he makes a mistake, so as to minimize their embarrassment as much as possible. In _Perek Chelek_ we are told that someone who shames his friend in the presence of a _talmid chacham_ is considered an _apikorus_ and loses his portion in _Olam Haba_. (_Mishpetei Hashalom_ 7:26–28)

In summary: _Halbanas Panim_, the _issur_ of shaming another Jew, derives either from the _passuk_, "_Lo tisa alav cheit_" or from the _issur_ of _onaas devarim_. The Torah is extremely careful to preserve human dignity. Consequently, there are certain leniencies in Rabbinic _issurim_ where _kavod habrios_ is involved. Correspondingly, the punishment for causing _halbanas panim_ is severe. Some opinions put this _issur_ on a par, figuratively or in practice, with the three supreme _aveiros_, for which the rule is "_yeihareig veal yaavor_." Nicknames are to be avoided. Where the honor of a _talmid chacham_ is involved, the _halachah_ is even more strict.

⇒ 11 ⇒

לא תעמד על דם רעך
Saving Our Fellow Jew's Life or Property

Don't Stand Idly By! "Help! Help!" A shriek resounded from the dining room of the day camp.

Penina, the head counselor, came running. "What happened?"

"Little Chanie Scherman — a bone in the fish — stuck in her throat — she can't catch her breath! Help!" Mimi, her counselor, rambled hysterically.

Penina took out her cell phone immediately and called Hatzolah, and she tried to calm Chanie until help arrived.

Mimi noticed her friend Tzippy standing off to the side, watching the drama. "Tzippy, you just finished an advanced first-aid course. You know what to do. Save her!"

Tzippy squirmed and tried to avoid eye contact. "You know I hate to be in the center of things. And I'm not sure I remember exactly what to do. And besides, Hatzolah will be here soon…"

Mimi grabbed her and pushed her toward the child, whose lips were starting to turn blue. "You got a perfect mark on that course. You certainly know what to do better than anyone here. You can't just stand there and do nothing. Get to work!"

108

MIMI IS CORRECT; that is precisely what the Torah tells us. When a fellow Jew is in danger, anyone who is in a position to save him is required to do so, as the *passuk* states, *Lo saamod al dam rei'echa*, "Do not stand aside while your fellow's blood is shed" (*Vayikra* 19, 16).

Therefore, if we see a Jew drowning, or being attacked by armed robbers or a wild animal, we may not turn away; we are obligated to rescue him if we can. Similarly, if we hear that violent people — *akum*, informers or others — are plotting against him or setting up a trap to ensnare him, we must inform him of what we have heard. (*Mishpetei Hashalom* 8:1–2)

Definite Danger vs. Potential Danger

IF RUNNING INTO our neighbor's home to save him from armed robbers will pose a clear danger to us, then we are not obligated (and, according to most opinions, not allowed) to do so.

But what if the danger to us is a *safek* — a potential danger, but not a definite danger? For example, pulling an injured man from a mangled car after an accident might involve some risk, since the fuel in the engine might ignite at any moment. But the injured man is definitely in mortal danger if he is left there.

According to some opinions, in such a situation we are obligated to take that chance and save the person who is clearly in danger. However, the majority of *poskim* disagree and say that there is no such obligation. Nevertheless, we have to weigh each situation carefully and not inflate every minor concern into a "possible danger" in order to free ourselves of the obligation to act on behalf of a fellow Jew. (*Mishpetei Hashalom* 8:3)

20 Cheshvan   20 Adar   20 Tammuz

Rescue That Costs Money

Kalman came running to the lifeguard at the separate beach. "My friend is out there; he swam out too far, and I think he's going under!"

"Look, fellow, the black flags are up, and your friend should have known better than to disobey the rules. I'm not responsible for reckless swimmers," the bronze lifeguard replied lazily.

"But he's drowning!" The lifeguard did not react, but merely continued puffing on his cigarette.

"Here's a hundred dollars. Will that do it?" Kalman begged. Suddenly the lifeguard came to life. Stuffing the green bill into his drawer, he jumped down to his rescue skiff and was at the struggling swimmer's side in moments.

IN ADDITION TO being obligated to save a fellow Jew through our physical efforts, we are obligated to spend our money, when necessary, in order to do so. This might involve hiring others to do the rescue work (as in Kalman's case), or paying off the *akum* or some violent people to prevent them from doing harm, and so on.

If the individual who is saved has the financial means, he must subsequently repay the rescuer for any expenses he incurred in the process. The same applies if Reuven redeemed his friend Shimon who was taken captive — *pidyon shevuyim*; if Shimon has the money, he is obligated to repay Reuven for the ransom money immediately upon his release. Even if Shimon feels he is exempt from payment for some reason, or has a monetary claim against Reuven for a different matter, he must first pay him the sum of the ransom money and only afterward litigate in *beis din*.

If Reuven runs after Shimon's pursuer in order to save Shimon, and while running he damages property belonging either to the pursuer or to anyone else, he is not obligated to pay damages. *Chazal* instituted this rule so that people would not be deterred from taking action to rescue others due to fear of having to pay for potential damages. (*Mishpetei Hashalom* 8:4–6)

21 Cheshvan	21 Adar	21 Tammuz

To Whom Does the Obligation Apply? THE OBLIGATION TO save a fellow Jew applies to men and women, in all places and at all times. If we see someone in danger and do not save him, we violate the positive *mitzvah* of "*Lo saamod al dam rei'echa.*" (If the person is a captive and we pass up an opportunity to redeem him, we violate several additional prohibitions, such as tightening our fist from helping

those in need, allowing someone to be subjected to grueling labor without intervening, not saving those being led to death, and other, similar transgressions, as explained in _Shulchan Aruch, Yoreh Dei'ah_ 252.)

The _mitzvah_ obligates us to save Jewish men, women and children, including the elderly, the ill and the mentally unstable. Although we are not obligated halachically to save an _akum_, we should not ignore his plight and certainly in a case of risk of _chillul Hashem_ or hostile relations we should help him to the best of our abilities.

We are not permitted to save a _mumar lehachis_, an _apikores_, a _min_, a _meisis_, or informers, until they have done _teshuvah_. As for the _mumar letei'avon_ (the one who sins for the sake of his own pleasure), the _poskim_ differ on the question of whether we are _permitted_ or _obligated_ to save him. There is no obligation to save a persistent sinner — that is, someone who indulges in sin regularly and without regrets. (The many laws and guidelines pertaining to each of these categories are addressed in chapter 18.)

Even if a Jew does not want to be saved and shouts, "Do not save me!" we are still obligated to save him. If, for example, he does not want to give up an opportunity to die _al kiddush Hashem_, we still overrule his request and save him. However, if he has a valid reason for wanting not to be saved (such as a desire to die _al kiddush Hashem_), then he does not have to repay any expenses incurred by the one who saved him against his will.

Although opinions differ, it seems that one _is_ obligated to save a person who is trying to commit suicide, certainly when he is mentally or emotionally unstable and therefore less responsible for his actions. (_Mishpetei Hashalom_ 8:7–8, 12–13)

22 Cheshvan	22 Adar	22 Tammuz

Saving Others from Financial Loss When Mrs. Ringel returned home from the grocery store, she was surprised to see her husband at home eating breakfast. "Didn't you say that this morning at eight o'clock was the _din Torah_ of Katz, and that they asked you to give testimony on their behalf?"

"Yes, they asked me, but I have a busy day at the office today. I'm not

in the mood to waste an hour or two at the *beis din*. He'll manage without me."

"I thought you said your testimony could help him retrieve his money
from the contractor. Maybe you should ask the Rav if you're allowed to sit
this one out …?"

ACCORDING TO SOME opinions, the *mitzvah* of *lo saamod* includes the
issur to withhold testimony, if doing so will cause a monetary loss to
another Jew.

Any time we are able to save a person from monetary loss and do not
do so, it would be a violation of this *mitzvah*. For example, our neighbor
has gone on a two-week vacation, and we notice that he left the garden
sprinkler on. Left as is, not only will he have to pay for the large amount
of water wasted, his garden might be damaged as well. According to
this opinion, we would be obligated to follow up the problem and figure
out a way to get the water turned off or put on a timer. If we shrug our
shoulders and look the other way, we may be violating the *issur* of *lo
saamod*.

(Even according to those who do not consider this a violation of *lo
saamod*, we still have the *mitzvah* of *ve'ahavta lerei'acha kamocha*, which
requires us to care about the possessions of our fellow Jew as we would
care about our own, and the *mitzvah* of *hashavas aveidah* — returning
a lost object to its owner.)

According to some opinions, we are obligated to make an effort to
save others even from worry and anguish. For example, a husband who
knows that his wife is easily worried should make sure to call her whenever he will be slightly delayed in coming home, before she has a chance
to agonize over the reason for his delay. (*Mishpetei Hashalom* 8:9–10)

The Greatest   SOME *POSKIM* INFER that if we are obligated to save
Rescue Effort   someone from physical danger, then we are certainly
obligated to rescue him from spiritual peril, thereby
saving him in body and soul. According to these opinions, the obligation to save our fellow Jew from doing an *aveirah* is included in the
mitzvah of *lo saamod*. (This would be in addition to the basic obligation
of rebuke, as we shall discuss in chapter 12.) (*Mishpetei Hashalom* 8:11)

In summary: The *issur* of "*Lo saamod al dam rei'echa*" prohibits us from standing idly by when a fellow Jew is in danger and we are in a position to save him from that danger. This includes both exerting oneself physically and, when necessary, spending money to save him. If saving the other person will definitely place the rescuer in danger, there is no obligation to save him; when the danger to the rescuer is not certain, opinions differ as to his obligation. According to many opinions, the *mitzvah* includes doing whatever is possible to save someone's property. Some also say this *mitzvah* includes a responsibility to save another Jew from transgressing.

לא תעמוד על דם רעך

·≈ 12 ≈·

הוכיח תוכיח את עמיתך
The Obligation to Give Rebuke

Speak Up!   "Last *motzaei Shabbos* my high school rebbe gave a talk to the *bachurim* from last year's group," Naftali reported, as he sat around the yeshivah dining-room table with his *yeshivah gedolah* friends. "Besides hearing the rebbe, it was a great chance to see my old friends — sort of a reunion. You wouldn't believe what Shimmy Stern told me about Daniel Weinstein—"

Yehuda Rosenberg felt his "antennae" go up. Ever since he started learning *hilchos shemiras halashon* with his *chavrusa* for a few minutes a day, he had become sensitive to the warning signs of an upcoming bit of *lashon hara*. In a fraction of a second, the various possibilities went through his mind: He could find some excuse and just get up and leave. That would save him from hearing the probably-prohibited words that were about to be said — and it would be the easiest solution.

Easiest, perhaps, but not the best, he confessed to himself. It would be much harder to speak up, but if he really cared about Naftali and the other boys, that was the right thing to do.

"Hey, Naftali," Yehuda interrupted him, "you wouldn't believe it — that's exactly the *halachah* we got to today in *sefer Chofetz Chaim* — about meeting somebody from your hometown and the dangers of asking about what everyone is up to, without a constructive purpose. It's so easy to get

114

pulled into _lashon hara_ at reunions like that. So what did your rebbe talk about …?"

THE TORAH TELLS us: _Hochei'ach tochiach es amisecha_ — "Reprove your fellow Jew" (_Vayikra_ 19:17). If we see a Jew transgressing a _mitzvah_ — _bein adam laMakom_ (toward Hashem) or _bein adam lechaveiro_ (toward man) — we have a responsibility to give him _tochachah_ (rebuke) — to inform him that he is transgressing, so that he will correct his actions.

This obligation of _hochei'ach tochiach_ is incumbent on men and women, in all places and at all times. (At times there may be an obligation to train children in this _mitzvah_ as well, if they are particularly mature; however, in many cases young children do not really have the tact that we shall see is necessary in order to give _tochachah_ properly.)

In addition to the responsibility every individual has to rebuke his fellow Jew when necessary, the Rambam ruled that "Every community should appoint a Rav, who is both a _yerei Shamayim_ and well-liked by the people, so that he can speak to the _kehillah_ and help them correct their ways," much as the prophets did in their times. (_Mishpetei Hashalom_ 9:1, 3)

| 24 Cheshvan | 24 Adar | 24 Tammuz |

What Does the Obligation Include? THE _MITZVAH_ OF _tochachah_ is not only to rebuke someone after the fact; it also includes the obligation to stop a Jew who intends to sin from carrying out his intent. _Chazal_ expand the obligation, maintaining that we should offer reproof for improper behavior even when no specific Torah _issur_ is at stake. Even if we see someone violating a _mitzvah_ unintentionally — because of a lack of knowledge or out of forgetfulness — the _mitzvah_ of _tochachah_ would require us to advise him of his mistake or remind him of the _halachah_, so as to keep him from continuing or repeating his error.

You might wonder: What happened to our all-important _mitzvah_ of judging others favorably? Why should we immediately assume that the person is transgressing? Maybe the act is not what it appears to be; perhaps he is justified in doing what he is doing.

True, in your heart you should certainly judge the person favorably. However, this does not give you license to sit back and let him carry on with his action that is a possible sin. Rather, you should question him diplomatically, and if you find that he indeed transgressed, you should give him *tochachah*. (*Mishpetei Hashalom* 9:2–3)

Getting the Message MANY PEOPLE MISTAKENLY perceive *tochachah* as a negative thing. Actually, we should be happy to receive *tochachah* and should love those who offer it. In fact, if a person has a number of friends, some of whom flatter him and others who rebuke him when necessary, he should favor the latter; those are the friends who really care about him and his future.

When possible, a person should try to live near his mentor, so that he can benefit from his *tochachah* — but only on condition that he accepts that rebuke.

According to some opinions, receiving *tochachah* willingly is a fulfillment of the obligation to "circumcise your heart" (*Devarim* 10). In contrast, someone who rejects *tochachah* violates the *issur* of "Do not be stiff-necked" (ibid).

The attitude we adopt toward *tochachah* may affect the obligation of those around us, since, according to some, the *mitzvah* to reprove is relevant only toward someone who will be pleased to hear the *tochachah*. If the recipient will respond with hatred and possibly revenge, then the other person is free of the obligation to rebuke.

A person who hates *tochachah* is actually harming himself. By refusing to hear the words of *mochichim*, those who rebuke him, he blocks off options for *teshuvah* and remains mired in his sins, since in his self-imposed ignorance, he does not even see them as wrong. (*Mishpetei Hashalom* 9:4, 6)

25 Cheshvan	25 Adar	25 Tammuz

Different Types of Aveiros When the Reisner parents went away for a few days, their daughters, Mindy and Sarah, thoroughly enjoyed spending time at their cousins' home — except for one uncomfortable incident.

On Shabbos morning, as they dressed for shul, the girls were shocked to see their cousin Leah standing in her room brushing her hair with a regular, hard-bristled brush.

"Say something, Mindy," Sarah whispered to her older sister. "You know that's *assur* on Shabbos."

"Why don't *you* say something?" Mindy retorted.

"You're older than me," Sarah insisted.

"Well ... I think if she had done something to you or me, you know — *bein adam lechaveiro* — then I would have to speak up. But this is between her and Hashem. It's not our business," Mindy rationalized — mistakenly.

IN BOTH CATEGORIES of *mitzvos* — those between man and his fellow man, and those between man and Hashem — the *mitzvah* of *tochachah* applies. In the case of *bein adam lechaveiro*, if one person wrongs another, the wronged party should not hold in his anger and foster hatred toward the wrongdoer; that is the way of the *resha'im*, and is a violation of the *halachah* of *lo sisna*.

Instead, he should inform the other person of his dissatisfaction, and say, "Why did you do such and such and sin against me in this way?" This open rebuke gives the person a chance to explain himself if applicable, and to apologize if necessary, clearing the air and restoring peace between them.

In the case of a transgression *bein adam laMakom*, we have an equal obligation to speak up, since every Jew should feel responsible not only for his own spiritual success but for that of other Jews as well. Therefore, if we see another Jew sinning against Hashem or slipping off the *derech*, we are obligated to explain to him what he is doing wrong and to help him get back onto the right path.

The extent of our obligation can be seen from the following *halachah*: A person who is capable of protesting against wrongdoing and does not do so is held responsible and is heavenly punished for that *aveirah*, even if he himself is a complete *tzaddik*. For example, if he can object to a transgression that was committed in his household, in his city or even in the entire world (if he is a person of repute whose words are widely heeded), and he remains silent — he will be held accountable for those sins! (*Mishpetei Hashalom* 9:9–10, 18)

Limits of the **EVEN THOUGH WE** have an obligation to protest against
Obligation those who transgress, we are not required to spend
money on fulfilling this *mitzvah*. Therefore, in a case
where voicing rebuke would endanger one's physical security or one's
property, we are exempt from speaking up.

Needless to say, if the sinner is known to be physically violent and
there is a risk that he will try to kill or even strike anyone who reproves
him, there is no obligation to give *tochachah*.

We are not required to rebuke a non-Jew who violates one of the
Seven Noachide Laws. If a Jew has thrown off the yoke of Torah completely — for example, if he is *mechallel Shabbos* publicly or eats *treife*
food *lehachis* — he removes himself from the *halachic* category of *amisecha* (your fellow), and we are no longer obligated to rebuke him even
about something that is written explicitly in the Torah.

Nevertheless, sometimes there is an obligation to speak up even in
the case of such a sinner, either in order to protest the *chillul Hashem*
caused by his actions or to prevent others from being drawn after his
ways. This is especially important in a situation where remaining silent
might be interpreted as agreement with the wrongdoing — "If so-and-so
didn't say anything, it must be all right."

Often, peaceful demonstrations are organized for this reason
even when no practical results are expected to emerge from them; in
such a situation the protest serves to express our own disapproval of
the sin and to discourage others from being pulled in that direction.
Furthermore, we *are* obligated to try as much as possible to stop others
from sinning.

Today, when many sinners have not intentionally rejected the way
of Torah but are merely ignorant of their heritage, or misinformed (and
may well be considered in the category of *tinok shenishba*; see chapter
18), there certainly is great merit in introducing them to the *mitzvos*
and allowing them to taste of the Torah's nectar; in many cases, that is
all the "rebuke" they will need in order to begin a process of correcting
their ways. (*Mishpetei Hashalom* 9:7–8, 26–27)

The Parameters YOU HAVE POINTED out someone's sin once …
of the Mitzvah twice … three times, and he continues to transgress. How much *tochachah* is enough to fulfill your
obligation? *Chazal* derive the answer to this question from the *passuk*
"*Hochei'ach tochiach es amisecha*," which we have cited earlier: From the
word "*hochei'ach*" they infer that you should rebuke him even a hundred
times or more if necessary; from the word "*tochiach*" they learn that you
should rebuke even someone who is greater than you. This includes a
student's rebuking his Rav (even for transgressing a Rabbinical prohibition) and a child's rebuking his parent.

Giving *tochachah* to your superior is a delicate matter and demands
tact to ensure that one does not violate the requirements of respect.
Therefore, in such situations one should certainly not say outright, "You
violated a *mitzvah* of the Torah!" Instead, one may ask gently, "Father,
doesn't it say such and such in the Torah?" or, "Rebbe, didn't you teach
us such and such?" In this way the parent or teacher will get the message
on his own but will not have to be embarrassed.

When *Chazal* told us to rebuke even a hundred times, they meant
that there is no maximum limit. However, if the recipient of *tochachah*
becomes upset, then one should stop earlier. Some say you must continue
to rebuke until the offender strikes you. Others say to go on only until
he curses you. A third opinion maintains that you should stop when
the sinner gets angry and reprimands you. Beyond this point, "just as
there is a *mitzvah* to say something that will be accepted, so there is a
mitzvah to refrain from saying something that will be ignored," and
therefore, at that point you should abandon your efforts. (However, bear
in mind that each time a person commits a different *aveirah*, there is a
new obligation to give *tochachah*.) (*Mishpetei Hashalom* 9:11–12)

Stopping a Sin As Mimi and Estie walked down the avenue, they glanced
in Progress into a restaurant and noticed their friends Shulamis and
Adina eating a sandwich at one of the tables. "Say, isn't

that the restaurant that was listed in yesterday's newspaper as having lost its *hechsher*?" Mimi asked, suddenly remembering.

Glancing at the name on the storefront, Estie nodded. "Yes, you're right."

"So let's go in and tell them. I'm sure they didn't hear about it; otherwise they wouldn't be in there." Mimi headed toward the entrance.

"Oh, come on. We'll tell them tomorrow. You're not going to go in now and make a scene, are you?" Estie shuddered.

"What are you talking about? Wait till tomorrow?! They said the place was actually selling **treife** cold cuts. I'm stopping them right now!"

WHEN WE SEE someone in the midst of doing an *aveirah*, we have a *mitzvah* to stop them, and at times even to restrain them forcibly. For example, if you see your friend wearing a jacket or even pants that you know have *shaatnez*, and he ignores your verbal protest, you are required to tear the garment off of him, and if the *shaatnez* is of a type that is a Torah prohibition, then you should do so even on a public street.

If the offender is your Rav, you should do so anyway, since the honor of the Rav cannot come at the expense of a *chillul Hashem*. If damage was caused to the garment while you are pulling it off, no compensation needs to be paid.

Of course, when time will not be lost, it is best to do so in as private a place as possible to avoid embarrassing the person. If the sin is clearly being done unintentionally, then you can wait until the sinner is out of the public eye and then inform him discreetly of his sin.

Even though ordinarily we do not even think about *devarim shebike-dushah* (sacred things) in an unclean place, we are permitted to speak of such matters and even to discuss it using *Lashon Hakodesh* and rab-binical terminology in the bathroom, in order to stop someone from doing an *aveirah*.

Similarly, one should do anything possible to remove potential stumbling blocks in order to prevent people from sinning. For example, if you notice a flyer on the floor with an immodest picture, don't just turn away and leave it there for someone else to see as well. Take the trouble to bend down, crumple it up and throw it into the nearest trash can. (*Mishpetei Hashalom* 9:13)

Tochachah — A UNFORTUNATELY, MANY PEOPLE perceive *tochachah*
Loving Message — at least when it is directed against them — as a
critical, negative form of speech, perhaps even an
attack. It is true that some people rebuke harshly, using humiliating
words and not explaining how the person can improve. Obviously, their
words will not achieve the desired results. However, when *tochachah* is
given properly and with the right intentions, this negative perception of
tochachah could not be further from the truth.

Rebuking in public is limited to situations when there is an urgent
need to stop a person from committing a sin. The immediacy of the matter justifies the shame that the offender will suffer. In general, however,
we have to be very careful not to embarrass the offender when giving
tochachah, as we learn from the conclusion of the *passuk* of *hochei'ach
tochiach*: "*Velo tisa alav cheit* — and do not bear a sin because of him"
(explained by Rashi to mean, "You will be sinning if you embarrass
him").

Therefore, we should not speak to the offender harshly and should
not reprove him in front of other people. Rather, we should speak to
him privately, using pleasant, gentle language, reminding him all the
time that we have only his interests in mind — that he should merit a
good portion in the Next World.

In giving *tochachah*, the wise person chooses gentle, conciliatory
words that will draw the person to the Torah, as Aharon Hakohen did.
Ideally, along with the rebuke he should offer guidance in how to correct the transgression.

The mode of rebuke should match the subject. If the wrongdoer is
of soft character, a soft approach should be used; if he is tough, then a
more forceful approach may be necessary. When *tochachah* is given to a
well-respected person or in front of a public audience (not all of whom
are guilty), we should only hint at the sins committed and not state
them explicitly, so that our words will be accepted. Nowadays, the most
effective way to ease in the rebuke painlessly is often to "sugarcoat it"
with a good joke.

An important prerequisite before we give *tochachah* is to check ourselves to make sure we are not guilty of the same sin. People have a tendency to notice the faults of others while being blind to their own. If an honest examination reveals that we too are lacking in this area, we should correct our own deeds before rebuking others on the same point. Aside from the moral imperative involved, this is advised from a practical standpoint; no one is likely to accept *tochachah* offered hypocritically. A typical response to such *tochachah* would be, "Look who's talking…" (*Mishpetei Hashalom* 9:5, 14 and footnote 1)

1 Kislev	1 Nisan	1 Av

Additional Guidelines   THE RULES OF rebuking privately apply when a sin has been committed privately. However, when the transgression was done in public, we should rebuke the offender on the spot, so as to avoid a *chillul Hashem*.

When one person has been wronged by another, the wronged party should reprove the offender privately, as many as a hundred times, as we mentioned, or until the offender strikes him. If he prefers not to rebuke — either because the offender is a simpleton or is of unsound mind, or for any other reason — he may choose instead to forgive the wrongdoer wholeheartedly. This is even considered *middas chassidus* — an act on a higher spiritual level. Once the person does so, he no longer has an obligation to give *tochachah*, since in matters *bein adam lechaveiro*, the whole function of the *mitzvah* of rebuke is to prevent animosity between the two, and once a person has forgiven the one who wronged him, there is no danger of ill will.

However, in the case of *divrei Shamayim* — sins against Hashem — even if the sin was done in private, if the offender does not repent after being rebuked privately, he should be shamed publicly and his sin publicized. The local Rabbanim should curse and humiliate him to his face; but this must be done with the constructive purpose of getting the sinner to do *teshuvah*, or preventing a *chillul Hashem*, as the prophets did in their time. These measures should be continued until the person repents. (*Mishpetei Hashalom* 9: 15–17)

A Special Responsibility to Household Members ALTHOUGH, AS WE said, the *mitzvah* of rebuke is incumbent upon us regarding any Jew who has sinned, the head of a household carries an extra measure of responsibility toward his family members. As the Rambam and *Shulchan Aruch* state: "Anyone who is not careful to keep track of his wife and children — to warn them against sin and to know where they are going, what they are doing and what they are exposed to — is considered a sinner."

If a person becomes aware of a problem of some kind in his home, he should rebuke the offender gently and pleasantly, as we described above. Never should *tochachah* be given when one is upset and angry, nor should it flow from extreme zealousness or personal resentment. In any case, rebuke given under such circumstances will not achieve its purpose; if we want our words to be well-received, they should be delivered in the softest manner possible.

In general, the atmosphere in the home should be one of mutual love and respect. As *Chazal* said, "A person should not impose excessive fear in his home; his interaction with his wife should be pleasant, without any anger or aggravation." Besides the intrinsic importance of *shalom bayis*, it is an unfortunate fact of life that lack of harmony in the home is one of the primary causes of children going off the *derech*. (*Mishpetei Hashalom* 9:19)

2 Kislev	2 Nisan	2 Av

The Rebellious Child RAISING A CHILD who is rebellious against the Torah is an awesome challenge. In most cases, however, the child can be gradually drawn back to a Torah path with the magnetic power of unconditional love. While the child is deeply entrenched in his rebellion, the parents should temporarily not make an issue over spiritual matters, but should limit their demands to minimal standards of *derech eretz*. However, great care must be taken that the other members of the family not be negatively influenced.

At times, often because of a fear of this negative influence, parents of a rebellious child are faced with the agonizing decision of whether or not to send the child out of the house. Banishing the child should be avoided if at all possible. As long as he remains in the home, enveloped by his parents' love and patience, the chances are that his rebellion will exhaust itself and he will get back on track. If, however, we send him off on his own into the alluring outside world, he could be lost to *Yiddishkeit* forever.

Moreover, sending him away does not always resolve the problem of his influence on his siblings; sometimes it can actually aggravate the situation, as the contact between them will be less regulated and out of the parents' control. At times, persuasion from his position "on the outside" can be even more destructive than it is from within the home. Of course, each case must be judged and treated according to its particular circumstances, with the guidance of a competent Rav. (*Mishpetei Hashalom* 9:20)

Accentuate the Positive ALTHOUGH THERE IS no guarantee that anyone will be spared the pain of rebellious children, we can take measures to reduce the risks. We have already mentioned that *shalom bayis* is an important factor in producing well-adjusted children. The *chachamim* of our times stress that constant criticism is an almost-certain formula for breeding resentfulness, and that in our sensitive generation, picking on a child for every small deviation can lead to rebellion and, *chas veshalom*, his leaving the path of Torah.

When rebuking one's child is necessary, it should be well-cushioned by plenty of compliments. The best approach is to gloss over failures and "catch" the child in his successful moments. Then we can comment sincerely on his achievements and positive points, thereby encouraging and strengthening him.

Even when there is a need to "lay down the law" in our home in matters concerning Torah prohibitions, we should do so in a pleasant tone. On the few occasions when we must display anger in order to stress the gravity of the violation, it should be feigned anger, not genuine anger. *Chazal* compare a person who explodes in true anger and loses control to an idol-worshipper; under such conditions he certainly cannot expect to educate his family in spiritual values. (*Mishpetei Hashalom* 9:21)

Better to Remain Mr. Eisenberg and his neighbor Mr. Rosenfeld were
in Error on their way to shul one Shabbos afternoon, when
they passed a group of teenagers, most of them with
bushy hair and small *yarmulkes* perched on top. Apparently, these boys
were "on the fringe." They were sitting on a bench and talking animatedly.
As they approached, Mr. Eisenberg saw one of the boys pull a comb out
of his pocket and run it through his hair.

"I think we should say something," Mr. Eisenberg said. "Maybe they don't
know or don't remember that you're not allowed to use a comb on Shabbos."

"A lost cause," Mr. Rosenfeld asserted. "They won't listen anyway, so you
don't have to tell them."

"First of all, if this is a case of a Torah *issur*, then I'd have to speak up anyway. And second, who says they won't listen? I'm willing to give it a try."

True to his word, Mr. Eisenberg apprached them and started a friendly,
casual conversation with the boys. Before long he had persuaded the offender to discard his comb and had invited the whole group to his house
for *seudah shelishis*.

IN CERTAIN SITUATIONS, when it is absolutely certain that the offender
will not accept the rebuke, we are told to refrain from giving *tochachah*,
adopting the approach that "it is preferable that they transgress unintentionally than that they do so with full knowledge," as well as the
principle we have mentioned earlier that "just as there is a *mitzvah* to
say something that will be heard, so there is a *mitzvah* to refrain from
saying something that will be ignored."

But we should not be too quick to assume that the *tochachah* will
fall on deaf ears. Sometimes the situation is not so clear-cut; it may be
our own fear or embarrassment that had led us to a wrong assumption.
Trust in Hashem that He will put the right words in your mouth, keep
in mind how great your reward will be if you help a sinner do *teshuvah*,
and go ahead with your efforts.

The nature of the transgression will also determine whether we employ the principle of its being "preferable to transgress unintentionally."
If the violation is of an *issur* that is not stated explicitly in the Torah,
then if the person is transgressing unintentionally and we are certain

that he will not accept the *tochachah*, we are advised not to rebuke him. The same applies in the case of a Torah *issur* in which the public has assumed the unfortunate custom of being lenient in the prohibition. Sometimes, however, there is an obligation to voice our objection even in such a case, if it is necessary so that others should not learn from their ways.

If there is a doubt as to whether the *tochachah* will be accepted (as in the case Mr. Eisenberg encountered), then we should rebuke the transgressor anyway, even if the violation is of a Rabbinical prohibition. Likewise, in a case where the offender is transgressing two sins, and the *tochachah* will certainly not succeed in deterring him completely from both, we should still rebuke him so as to prevent him as much as possible from sinning.

If the offender is fully aware of the *issur* and is violating it intentionally, then the principle of its being "preferable to transgress unintentionally" obviously would not apply. In that case, even if we are certain that he will not accept our rebuke (and therefore we would not be held accountable were we to remain silent), there is still a *mitzvah* to speak up.

In the case of the intentional offender who will definitely not accept our *tochachah*, we should rebuke him in a private setting, even a hundred times, or until he strikes us (or curses us), as we discussed earlier. However, we should rebuke him in public only once. (*Mishpetei Hashalom* 9:22–25)

4 Kislev	4 Nisan	4 Av

Auxiliary Mitzvos Connected to Rebuke IN ADDITION TO the basic *mitzvah* of *hochei'ach tochiach*, we fulfill many other *mitzvos* and basic Torah values when we encourage a sinner to improve his ways. Among the *mitzvos* are: Do not stand aside while your brother's blood is shed; *kiddush Hashem*; love of Hashem; and returning a lost object. Finally, encouraging others to do what is right is the essence of the principle of *Kol Yisrael areivim...* — that all Jews are responsible for one another. (We will elaborate on each of these below.)

Even in certain cases where we would be exempt from the *mitzvah* of *tochachah*, we might still be obligated to rebuke because of one of these other *mitzvos*.

- **Kiddush Hashem:** The *mitzvah* of "I will be sanctified among *Bnei Yisrael*" (*Vayikra* 22:32) includes, according to some opinions, a command to sanctify Hashem's Name by publicizing true *emunah* in the world, such as by rebuking sinners.

- **Loving Hashem:** The Sifri includes in this *mitzvah*, "To bring others to love Hashem, as did Avraham Avinu. Our great love and appreciation of Hashem should compel us to seek out even the *kofrim* and the ignorant and to help them acquire knowledge of the truth and of the ways in which to serve Hashem properly."

- **Returning a lost object:** Some say that when we see people erring and transgressing the Torah, we "cannot ignore them," but must try to help them return to Hashem, just as we are required to return any lost object to its owner.

- **Kol Yisroel areivim zeh lazeh:** From the time of the giving of the Torah at Mt. Sinai, every Jew became responsible for his fellow Jew's Torah observance. Therefore, when one person sins openly (even if only in front of his wife and children), and those who see him sinning are capable of protesting and they refrain from doing so, they are held accountable for the sin. (*Mishpetei Hashalom* 9:28–32)

5 Kislev	5 Nisan	5 Av

Bringing Our Brothers Back THE CHILDREN AND grandchildren of heretics, who have been misled by their parents and educated and raised in a life of heresy, are considered to be in the category of *tinok shenishba* (literally, a child raised in captivity). Even if these individuals subsequently hear that they are Jews and have an opportunity to be in contact with Jews and the Jewish faith, they are considered *anoos* — their sins are completely unintentional and beyond their control.

Therefore, these unaffiliated Jews are not rejected as *resha'im*; rather, they should be drawn gently to Torah in a pleasant, peaceful way, until they do *teshuvah*. We have a special interest in their spiritual success. Because of our *arvus*, responsibility for one another (as explained above), we are held responsible collectively for each other's shortcomings. That is why we find, for example, in *sefer Yehoshua* (7:11), in the case of Achan, that Hashem said, "*Chata Yisrael* — All of Israel sinned," when in fact only one Jew transgressed.

Our Torah observance is so closely linked to that of our fellow Jews that one Jew can make a *brachah* on behalf of another to fulfill a Torah obligation such as Kiddush, even if he himself has already fulfilled his obligation.

For the same reason, at times it is preferable for a person to fulfill a *mitzvah* in more of a minimal form, without stringencies, if doing so will enable another Jew to fulfill the *mitzvah* as well. Some suggest that it is even permissible for a man to mention Torah subjects in front of immodestly dressed women, although it would ordinarily be forbidden for a man to do so, if this will enable the women to learn Torah and come closer to Judaism.

Among the *brachos* pronounced by the *kohanim* at Har Gerizim was, "Blessed is he who upholds all the words of the Torah to do them." This statement obligates anyone who is capable of strengthening Torah observance in the face of those who seek to uproot it to do his part — whether by founding yeshivos, speaking publicly to draw the people to *Yiddishkeit*, or thwarting the plots of those who seek to undermine Torah observance.

No one is exempt from this requirement, not even a *tzaddik gamur* who already learns and teaches and observes all the *mitzvos*, positive and negative; he still carries a responsibility to promote the Torah observance of the *klal*. (*Mishpetei Hashalom* 9:33–34)

In summary: The *mitzvah* of *tochachah* requires us to rebuke our fellow Jew when we see him transgressing or in order to prevent him from a sin he is about to commit. The rebuke must be given gently, in a manner that will be accepted by the listener. We do not have to rebuke certain *resha'im* who are no longer considered *amisecha*. The parameters of rebuke are until the person hits, or curses, or reprimands angrily. In certain specific cases, we are exempt from giving rebuke, such as when there is no violation of a Torah command and we are sure the rebuke will not be accepted. A special responsibility rests on the head of the household to supervise and, when necessary, gently rebuke the members of his family. One who rebukes also fulfills several other *mitzvos*, and in particular, the principle of every Jew's being responsible for every other Jew in Torah observance.

"Whoever rebukes his friend for the sake of Heaven merits his portion from Hashem and is given a touch of grace" (Tamid 28a).

"To those who give rebuke shall be delight, and a blessing of good shall come upon them" (Mishlei 24).

הוכח תוכיח את עמיתך

⋙ 13 ⋘

חינוך הקטנים
Chinuch of Children

| 6 Kislev | 6 Nisan | 6 Av |

More Than It was an uncomfortable moment for the family and guests
"Education" at the Landau Shabbos table when 5–year-old Yitzy went
into his room and turned on the light so he could find
something he needed. To their surprise, Mr. Landau did not say a word to
Yitzy, neither publicly nor privately. Tuning in to their unspoken question,
Mr. Landau explained, "He's still little; I don't want him to suffer scars from
undue criticism at this tender age."

A few minutes later Yitzy was running after his little brother and
bumped into an expensive vase, knocking it to the floor. Sparks flew as
Mr. Landau lashed out at the child for his carelessness.

No one said a word to Mr. Landau; they were too polite. But it was clear
to them that the *chinuch* that would remain with Yitzy was that *hilchos
Shabbos* are of secondary importance; valuable vases are far more significant.

A PARENT IS obligated to provide his child with *chinuch* — a word that is
often inadequately translated as "education," but it means far more than
a simple transfer of information. *Chinuch* means setting the groundwork
for the child's future fulfillment of Torah and *mitzvos* by giving him a
proper start in each one of the *mitzvos* when he is developmentally ready
for it, according to *halachic* standards.

130

As we will see, _halachah_ provides guidelines for these obligations in many areas; the guidance of a Rav is necessary, at times, to rule on particular questions vis-a-vis a specific child. In any case, the attitude we convey to our children regarding the gravity of Torah and _mitzvos_, and the example we set for them, are the mainstays of a proper _chinuch_.

Two Specific Mitzvos TWO _MITZVOS_ IN the Torah relate directly to the obligation of a father to be _mechanech_ his children: First, the father is obligated to teach his son Torah, as the _passuk_ states, "And you shall teach your children" (_Devarim_ 11:19). This _mitzvah_ includes hiring a tutor to teach the child when necessary. Mothers also share in this _mitzvah_; by bringing their children to the rebbe and encouraging them to learn, mothers earn their place in _Olam Haba_.

The second _mitzvah_ is a father's obligation to relate the story of _yetzias Mitzrayim_ to his son each year on Seder night, as the Torah states, "And you shall relate it to your son on that day" (_Shemos_ 13:8).

These are the only two specific Torah obligations; however, there is a general Rabbinic obligation to be _mechanech_ one's children in Torah and _mitzvos_, and this has always been the focus of a Jewish parent's hopes and dreams. The Shel"a writes that parents should accustom their children to _devarim shebikdushah_ and should be _mechanech_ them in _yiras Shamayim_ and good _middos_. He adds that parents should make a point of doing _mitzvos_ in the presence of their children, so they can demonstrate and explain how they should be done. The Chofetz Chaim exhorts us in the _Mishnah Berurah_ (347:10) that parents should have a prayer on their lips constantly that their children will grow up to be _talmidei chachamim_, _tzaddikim_ and _baalei middos_. (_Mishpetei Hashalom_ 9:35)

7 Kislev	7 Nisan	7 Av

Age of Chinuch for Positive Mitzvos A FATHER — and, according to some opinions, a mother as well — must teach his child to perform positive _mitzvos_ when the child reaches what is referred to as the "age of _chinuch_." The "age of _chinuch_" is the point at which he achieves an awareness of the _mitzvah_. Naturally, there can be no clear-cut age-chart for this awareness; the age will depend on the child's development and how bright and sensitive he is, as well as on the particular *mitzvah* in question.

For example, a child who understands the concept of Shabbos should hear Kiddush and Havdalah. The child who is capable of donning a *tallis katan* properly should begin wearing *tzitzis*. This rule applies both for *mitzvos aseh* that are Torah-ordained and for Rabbinically-ordained *mitzvos*. However, there is no obligation to train a child in *mitzvos* that he will not be obligated to keep when he grows up, such as the positive, time-bound *mitzvos* for a girl. Similarly, there is no obligation to train a child in what the adult is not halachically obligated to do. (*Mishpetei Hashalom* 9:36)

Examples of Chinuch Guidelines THE HALACHIC GUIDELINES of *chinuch* for minors are scattered in numerous places throughout the Gemara and *poskim*, and are quite diverse, since there are so many different factors that determine when each child should be educated in a particular *mitzvah*. The following are a few general examples; keep in mind, however, that parents should consult a rabbinic authority often to help them apply the *halachos* in their particular situation:

◦ **Birkas Hamazon:** As soon as a child is capable, he should be taught to recite the *Birkas Hamazon* (even if he ate a piece of bread that is only the size of *kezayis*, making the requirement a Rabbinic one, and not an amount that is *kedei seviah* — fully satiating, which would make it a Torah requirement).

◦ **Arbaas Haminim:** Once a child knows how to shake a *lulav*, his father should acquire a set for him and the child should be encouraged to shake it each day of Sukkos.

◦ **Sukkah:** A boy who is mature enough to understand the concept of Sukkos and old enough to manage without his mother should be introduced to eating all meals in the sukkah as adults do, and he can begin to sleep in the sukkah as well.

◦ **Yom Kippur:** A child should abstain from washing and from wearing leather shoes on Yom Kippur, but he may eat and drink. As children mature, if they are physically healthy they can begin

to fast for a few hours into the morning. A strong, healthy twelve-year-old boy or eleven-year-old girl may fast the whole day.

| 8 Kislev | 8 Nisan | 8 Av |

- ❑ *Kiddush and Havdalah*: Even though a child should be trained to hear Kiddush and Havdalah, he may eat beforehand.
- ❑ *Waiting Between Meat and Milk*: Some opinions maintain that a child need not wait the full amount of time between eating meat and milk. According to these authorities, a *brachah acharonah* and a one-hour wait is sufficient.
- ❑ *Aveilus* (**mourning**): The laws of mourning are limited for a child, but he *should* tear *keriah* and say Kaddish for a deceased parent. On days of public mourning (such as Tishah B'Av), the child should be taught to abide by the relevant *halachos*.
- ❑ *Nedarim* and *Shevuos* (**oaths and swearing**): Children should be strongly discouraged from making any oath. If a child does swear to do something, then if there is no serious suffering involved in keeping his word, he should be compelled to do so, so that he will not get into the habit of swearing. When the child is within a year of bar- or bas-mitzvah, his or her *nedarim* are binding, and a Rav should be consulted.
- ❑ *Krias Shema*: The age at which a child should be taught to recite *Krias Shema* is a matter of discussion among the *Rishonim*. Rabbeinu Tam maintains that there is no need for the child to do so until he reaches the age of *chinuch*. Rashi holds that even when he has reached the age of *chinuch*, the child cannot yet be trained in this *mitzvah*, because young children often go to sleep before it is time for the *Krias Shema* of *Maariv* and are not up early enough to say *Krias Shema* of *Shacharis*. Nevertheless, from the moment a child begins to speak he should be taught to say the first *passuk* of *Krias Shema* (even if he will not say it at the ordained times).

It is advisable to follow the view of Rabbeinu Tam when possible and train the child who is capable to read *Shema* with its *brachos* at the proper time. Even if *tefillah* in school is later than

חינוך הבנים

the prescribed time, the father can tell the boys to say *Shema* before going to school.

◻ **Shemoneh Esrei**: According to all opinions, a parent must teach his child to say the *Shemoneh Esrei* of *Shacharis* and *Minchah* once the child reaches the age of *chinuch* and is able to manage saying the entire *tefillah*. However, the child should not be allowed to suffer; he is allowed to eat and drink in the morning even before *davening*. (*Mishpetei Hashalom* 9:37–38)

9 Kislev	9 Nisan	9 Av

Chinuch for Mitzvos Lo Saaseh WHEN IT COMES to *mitzvos lo saaseh* — negative commandments, both Torah — and Rabbinic prohibitions, the child should be trained not to violate the *mitzvah* as soon as he is old enough to grasp the concept that the act or food is prohibited, even before he reaches the age of *chinuch*. Therefore, if a father sees his child transgressing an *issur*, he should scold him and prevent him from doing so (as opposed to Mr. Landau's response to his child, in the anecdote related above).

If the child is so young that he cannot even understand when told that something is *assur*, then neither the father nor *beis din* is required to stop him from violating the prohibition, whether he is violating a law of Shabbos, eating a forbidden food or transgressing in any other way.

Nevertheless, even though there is no actual responsibility to stop him from violating the *issur*, we should still prevent him from eating foods that are prohibited, as such foods can have a spiritually harmful effect and can imbue him with bad characteristics. (*Mishpetei Hashalom* 9:39–40)

For Himself or for Others When it was time to put the children to sleep on Friday night, Mrs. Landau said in a mournful tone, "How will I ever get the boys to sleep with the light on in their room?" Rivka'le, the bright, alert two-year-old, started running to the boys' room with a chair in hand, obviously intending to climb up and flip the light back off. "No, Rivka'le!" everyone shouted, catching her just in time.

When a small child is violating a prohibition for his own pleasure, then we do not have to stop him. But if he is clearly doing it for an adult's benefit, knowing that the adult wants the act performed (as in the case of Rivka'le), then he *should* be stopped.

According to some opinions, when the child is violating a Rabbinic *issur* clearly for his own benefit, then even if he has reached the age of *chinuch*, we do not have to stop him. (*Mishpetei Hashalom* 9:41)

10 Kislev	10 Nisan	10 Av

Halachic Leniencies for Children   IN CERTAIN CASES the *halachah* permits children to do an act that would be prohibited for an adult. For example, a child may take a haircut on *chol hamo'ed* and may blow the *shofar* on Rosh Hashanah even after he has fulfilled his obligation of hearing the *tekios*.

The *halachah* at times provides leniencies for adults as well, when the purpose is for a child's *chinuch*. For example, an adult may say a *brachah* with Hashem's Name, for or with the child when only the child is eating the food. He may also say Kiddush or make Havdalah for the child even after he has fulfilled his own obligation. (*Mishpetei Hashalom* 9:42)

Preventing a Child of Chinuch-Age from Violating Issurim   You notice a group of eight-year-olds in the yard plucking leaves from the tree on Shabbos. After a quick look, you are relieved to see that your son is not among them. Do you still have to speak up, or can you ignore them in good conscience?

A difference of opinion exists as to who is responsible for preventing a child of *chinuch*-age from violating an *issur*. According to the *Shulchan Aruch*, if, for example, a child eats nonkosher food on his own, then his father has to stop him, but others do not have to stop him. However, the Rema maintains that anyone who sees the child eating the forbidden food has an obligation to stop him.

In practice, when a Torah prohibition is involved, we are *machmir* and rule according to the Rema, and when the *issur* is *deRabbanan*, we

rule according to the opinion of the *Shulchan Aruch*.

Therefore, if we see a gentile offering a Jewish child forbidden food, if the food is prohibited by the Torah, we would all be obligated to protest. If, however, the food is prohibited *mideRabbanan*, then only the child's father would have to stop him.

If the child's father does not do his duty in preventing his child from violating a Torah prohibition, *beis din* has the right to step in and compel the father to do so. This is not the case with Rabbinical prohibitions.

(The laws of striking children can be found in chapter 7; also, see chapter 7 for many insights regarding the *chinuch* of children. The subject of *ona'as devarim* as it relates to *chinuch* can be found in chapter 9.) (*Mishpetei Hashalom*, 9:43–44, 46)

11 Kislev	11 Nisan	11 Av

Chinuch in Violations of Issurim Bein Adam Lechaveiro

IF A FATHER hears his young child speaking *lashon hara*, he should stop him and scold him, to prevent the child from repeating the offense. The same is true for violations of all the *mitzvos bein adam lechaveiro* — *machlokes*, lying, cursing others, and so on.

Besides our obligation to educate the child in these areas, when we do so we give him a great gift. Once a negative habit has become ingrained in a person from his childhood, it is very difficult for him to change his ways later; this forbidden manner of speech and conduct is almost perceived by him as permissible. On the other hand, when we train a child early on to speak positively, avoid falsehood and deal kindly with those around him, he will find it much easier to maintain these habits in the future.

In communities where the *beis din* is invested with full power to lay down the law, if a child stole or caused damage, then *beis din* has an obligation to strike him so that he will not make a habit of such practices. The same applies if a child injured or embarrassed someone, or if he transgressed any other *mitzvos bein adam lechaveiro* — the *beis* _din_ has a responsibility to step in and stop the child so that he will not cause further damage. (_Mishpetei Hashalom_ 9:45, 50)

Causing Children to Violate an Issur — UNTIL NOW WE have been discussing cases where a child is violating a prohibition on his own. An adult is certainly not permitted to intentionally cause a child to violate an _issur_ — even a child who is too young to understand the violation. We learn this _halachah_ from various _pesukim_ (on subjects such as forbidden blood and _tumas kohanim_) that clearly imply that adults may not feed a child forbidden food or command a child to do an _aveirah_. In fact, we should not even give a small child forbidden food to hold or play with if there is a risk that he might put it in his mouth. This _halachah_ applies equally to Torah prohibitions and Rabbinic _issurim_.

A common application of this _halachah_ is in dealing with a child who is a _kohen_ and is subject to the various stringencies of _kohanim_. A child _kohen_ — even an infant in the cradle — may not be taken into a place of _tumah_, nor may the child be commanded to enter such a place. However, if he went in on his own, we do not have to take him out.

When the wife of a _kohen_ is due to give birth, she may go to a hospital (which is considered a place of _tumah_ since there are liable to be _niftarim_ or _nefalim_ there), even thought there is a possibility that she will give birth to a boy. If she knows in advance that the baby is definitely male, then she should consult a Rav as to how to proceed.

12 Kislev	12 Nisan	12 Av

We certainly should not accustom a child to violate _issurim_ of Shabbos and Yom Tov, not even a _shevus_ (a kind of Rabbinic prohibition), and not even in a case where we would be allowed to hint to an _akum_ to do the _issur_ — such as carrying a key to the door through a _karmelis_ (an area where carrying is prohibited only by Rabbinical injunction) for the purpose of a _mitzvah_.

In cases of medical need, however, the principle of not causing the child to violate a prohibition is sometimes suspended. For example, the father can tell a gentile to give a child _chametz_ to eat on Pesach, if the child needs it for health reasons. The parent himself can bathe a small child on Yom Kippur if necessary. (*Mishpetei Hashalom* 9: 47–49)

Older Children THE OBLIGATION OF *chinuch* is incumbent on a parent only until the child is of bar- or bas-mitzvah age. (This is the reason the father of a bar-mitzvah boy makes the *brachah* "*Baruch shepetarani ...*" — up until now, the father was responsible if the child sinned since, in a sense, it reflected his inadequate *chinuch*; now the child is responsible for himself.)

Nevertheless, the *mitzvah* of giving *tochachah* in all of its details is still applicable, especially for a parent. Since the parent's words are generally valued by his children, and he is in a strong position to correct them, the principle of "He who is capable of protesting sin and does not is held accountable for the other person's sin" is particularly relevant.

From the standpoint of the child, if the father commands him to violate any *mitzvah* — *aseh* or *lo saaseh*, *de'Oraisa* or *deRabbanan* — he should not listen to him. Similarly, in all matters of *ruchniyus*, if someone feels that he will learn more successfully in a certain school or yeshivah, and his father objects for some minor reason, he does not have to listen to his father.

Likewise, if he wishes to marry and his father protests the match, he can choose not to listen to his father. However, when the parents are *yerei'ei Shamayim* and their attitudes are based on Torah, in most cases the child would be well-advised to heed their advice, since their intentions are genuinely for his own good, and being older, they have more life experience.

If a parent instructs his child not to speak with someone or to withhold his forgiveness from that person, the child can go ahead and make peace with the other fellow immediately, disregarding his father's instructions. (Other laws of *kibbud av va'em* will be discussed in Volume II, chapter 32.) (*Mishpetei Hashalom* 9:51–53)

In summary: Parents have an obligation to educate their children in Torah and *mitzvos*, at the stage when they are ready for each *mitzvah*. The *halachah* distinguishes between children who have reached the age of *chinuch* and those who have not, and recommends specific standards regarding *mitzvos aseh* and *mitzvos lo saaseh*. In certain cases, only the father must stop his child from sinning; in others, *beis din* and, at times, any Jew would share in that responsibility. Even in cases where we are not obligated to stop a small child from violating an *issur*, we still would not be permitted to cause him to sin. Once a child is bar- or bas-mitzvah, the parent no longer has a *mitzvah* of *chinuch*. However, all the obligations of *tochachah* still apply.

חינוך הבנים

← 14 →

כה תאמר לבית יעקב
Torah Education for Girls

| 13 Kislev | 13 Nisan | 13 Av |

Vital Role of   "Adina, do you want to come this afternoon to study with
Women   us for tomorrow's final? We're meeting at Rivky's house,"
Chaya said as she walked home with Adina after school.

"No thanks, Chaya," replied Adina. "My father doesn't believe in girls learning so much. He says I'm not a boy and I don't have to be such a *talmid chacham*. I'm planning to stay home and babysit for my nephews."

"But just tell me one thing, Adina. Did you tell your father that tomorrow's final is on *hilchos Shabbos*? I'm not sure he would say that if he knew you were studying something you really need to know…"

"SO YOU SHALL say to the 'house of Yaakov' and tell '*Bnei Yisrael*'" (*Shemos* 19:3). When Hashem was preparing to give the Torah to the Jewish nation, He instructed Moshe Rabbeinu to speak first to "*Beis Yaakov*" — the women — giving them a brief outline that they would be able to understand, and only afterward to address "*Bnei Yisrael*" — the men.

Why were the women given precedence at this crucial moment? The women of *Klal Yisrael* are the ones who lay the foundations for all future generations. When children are still young and impressionable, it is the women who set the tone for their attitude toward Torah and *mitzvos*.

140

They send them off to school with the proper attitude, keep a close eye on their progress and receive them warmly when they return home.

Mothers provide the initial motivation for small children by drawing them to Torah with encouraging words and attractive prizes so that they will want to learn and keep the Torah and not fritter away their time and talents. The women teach the children *yiras Shamayim* from their earliest childhood, and these early impressions stay with the child forever. "Educate the young child according to his way; even when he grows old, [that *chinuch*] will not leave him" (*Mishlei* 22). It is no surprise that the modest, unassuming women were given precedence at *matan Torah*; they are the primary builders of all the Torah and *yirah* that develops in the next generation. (See Rabbeinu Yonah's *Iggeres Hateshuvah*, siman 72.)

14 Kislev	14 Nisan	14 Av

Men's Obligation in Torah Learning... EVERY JEWISH MAN — even if he is impoverished, sick, old or beset by pain and difficulties — has an obligation to learn Torah. Whatever his situation, he must set aside time for Torah learning during both the day and the night, as the *passuk* states, "Delve in it day and night" (*Yehoshua* 1). If he cannot learn himself, either because he does not know how or because his difficulties do not leave him an available moment to do so, he should at least support others who are learning.

In order to properly fulfill the obligation to learn Torah, it is not enough to become proficient in the twenty-four books of the *Tanach* and the six *Sidrei Mishnah*. A Jewish man is expected to *delve* into Torah — that is, to study Gemara — so that he can understand the concepts on a deeper level, sharpen his power of deduction, compare and contrast different texts to reach the root of the matter, and utilize all the different *middos shehaTorah nidreshes bahem* — techniques by which the Torah can be expounded. He should continue to ply the sources, engaging in *pilpul* — Torah debate — with others, with the goal of achieving a thorough understanding, until he grasps the gist of each *mitzvah* with such clarity that he would be qualified to rule on matters of *issur* and *heter* for himself and others.

The man's obligation encompasses all parts of Torah, including those areas that are not relevant to him in practice. Nevertheless, there is an added value to learning with the intention of applying the knowledge, since "The deed, not the study, is the main thing" (See *Baba Kama* 17a).

...Versus Women's Obligation in Torah Learning THE WOMAN, ON the other hand, has no such all-encompassing obligation. Nevertheless, if she is motivated to study Torah she will be rewarded, just as anyone who does a *mitzvah* he is not required to do is rewarded (such as, for example, in any of the other time-related *mitzvos* for women).

However, women do have their own obligation in Torah learning; they are responsible to learn and know clearly all of the *halachos* related to the *mitzvos* in which they are obligated — which includes almost all *mitzvos lo saaseh* and all of the non-time-related positive *mitzvos*, as well as the *mitzvos deRabbanan* — so she will know how to observe the Torah's laws properly. For example, if a woman will not study *hilchos Shabbos* or *hilchos yichud*, how could she possibly avoid violating the many detailed *halachos* in these areas?

Since women do have this limited obligation in Torah learning, they must recite the *birkas haTorah* every morning as men do (*Mishnah Berurah* 47:34) and must also recite the words "For the Torah that You taught us" in *Birkas Hamazon*.

15 Kislev	15 Nisan	15 Av

Teaching Torah to Girls AS WE HAVE mentioned (ch. 13), a father has a *mitzvah de'Oraisa* to teach his son Torah. The *Sefer Chassidim* explains that even though this *mitzvah* does not include teaching Torah to daughters, the father is obligated to teach his daughter the *halachos* she needs to know in order to carry out the *mitzvos* properly. As for the statement of *Chazal* that "If anyone teaches his daughter Torah, it is as if he taught her *tiflus* (frivolity)," this refers to teaching girls Gemara in depth and Kabbalistic secrets. The learning of relevant *halachos* is not included in that statement, as we see from the time of Chizkiyahu Hamelech, when even the women

were well-versed in the complex _halachos_ of _kodshim_ and _taharos_ (_Sefer Chassidim, siman_ 313).

Why isn't in-depth Gemara study geared for women? Far from being a "put-down" to women's intelligence, as some groups and individuals have at times attempted to project, this distinction stems from a profound understanding of women's strengths vis-a-vis men's strengths. After all, _Chazal_ tell us emphatically that women were given _binah yeseirah_ — a certain insight that is greater than that which men have (_Nidah_ 45b), and therefore, for example, women can size up unfamiliar guests better than their husbands can. So we are not speaking here of women's _degree_ of intelligence but rather of the _type_ of intelligence each excels in.

The Gemara tells us (_Kiddushin_ 80b) that "The women's mind is _kallah_ ['light' or 'swift']." The Gemara means to say that women tend to think quickly, which is often a strong advantage. The danger, however, is that in their quickness of thought they might deduce things, make connections or draw conclusions when the matter is not yet fully clarified.

Chazal also state (_Menachos_ 110a) that "A woman's mind is not focused" in the way that a man's mind is. Therefore, at times she may assume she has grasped something when she still lacks a degree of understanding. For this reason, the Rambam writes (_Hilchos Talmud Torah_ 1:13), there is a concern that when it comes to in-depth learning, women might misinterpret _divrei Torah_ in ways that are not entirely logical.

Others explain the limitation as being addressed to young girls, who may spend much of their time on insignificant matters, or to the father who does not understand his daughter's way of thinking.

The Taz points out that for the _mitzvah_ of _hakhel_, in which the king had to gather the entire nation and teach the _Sefer Mishneh Torah_, his instructions were to "Gather the nation, men and women." It would appear, therefore, that the Torah itself is saying that it is clearly permitted to teach women Torah. However, as the Taz explains, at that _hakhel_ gathering the king conveyed only the simple meaning of the words, which all agree we are permitted to teach women, as opposed to in-depth explanations of _divrei Torah_, which was prohibited _lechatchilah_. This explains why the Gemara says of _hakhel_ that, "the men came to learn and the women to hear" — telling us that the women would hear the basic meaning of the material but would not be involved in the more esoteric study.

The Maharal's **THE MAHARAL** (IN his *Drush al HaTorah*) takes an
Approach entirely different stance regarding the reason women
are not obligated to engage in deep Torah study. He
portrays the male character as being inherently restless and active and,
therefore, less receptive to the tranquility and peace that characterizes
Olam Haba, which is the epitome of restfulness. Therefore, men need
to toil in Torah continuously, night and day, in order to achieve this
readiness for spiritual peace.

Women, on the other hand, are intrinsically ready for and receptive
to the tranquility of *Olam Haba*, since they were not born with this
drive for action and arousal. For this reason the intensive toiling at
Torah is not necessary to help them reach their spiritual perfection.

Nevertheless, throughout our history there have always been great
women in *Klal Yisrael*, from the time of the *Imahos*, the Matriarchs, to
our own times, some of whom were outstanding in their Torah wisdom,
such as Devorah Haneviah, Bruriah the wife of Rabbi Meir, and Yalta
the wife of Rabbi Nachman. The Vilna Gaon wrote to his wife that his
daughters should devote their Shabbosos to learning books of *mussar*
and Jewish thought. The Chasam Sofer was said to have learned the *aggados* of *Chazal* with his daughters, and Rabbi Yosef Chaim Sonnenfeld
had a regular learning session with his wife for a half-hour each day in
Shulchan Aruch Orach Chaim.

Women's Learning **IN THE EARLY** part of the twentieth century a
in Recent revolution took place in the sphere of Torah
Generations learning for women, when Sarah Schenirer initiated the Bais Yaakov movement. The Chofetz
Chaim, one of the most respected *gedolim* of the time and a keen supporter of Sara Schenirer's project, clearly explained the need presented
by the new generation:

"When *Chazal* said that someone who teaches his daughter Torah
is teaching her frivolity, their comment was meant for times when the
transmission of Torah values from father to child was extremely strong,
and virtually everyone automatically followed in his father's path.

"In our times, however, when the link to parents has become greatly weakened and it is not uncommon to find girls who do not even live in their parents' home, and especially when so many girls have accustomed themselves to learning secular subjects, there is no question that there is a great *mitzvah* to teach them *Tanach* and the teachings of *Chazal*, such as those found in *Pirkei Avos*, so as to strengthen in them our pure *emunah*. If not, they are at risk of leaving the way of Hashem completely and violating all the fundamentals of *Yiddishkeit*."

This being the Chofetz Chaim's view of the situation, it is not surprising that he issued a public letter encouraging everyone to invest all possible efforts to found more and more Bais Yaakov schools, in every city and village, to teach girls Torah, *yiras Shamayim*, *mitzvos* and *derech eretz*, "since this is a great and urgent matter in our time."

17 Kislev	17 Nisan	17 Av

Then and Now YEARS AGO, WOMEN and girls would seldom leave their house — perhaps not more than once or twice a month, in keeping with the Torah principle that "the honor of the daughter of the king is within." Women who would go out more often were looked down upon; the *Rishonim* said that there is no greater beauty for a woman than to sit in the privacy of her home.

In our times, on the other hand, the reality for many women is as Shlomo Hamelech writes in *Eishes Chayil*: "She makes linen and sells it." Many women leave their homes regularly, as the main supporters of their households, sometimes after having acquired higher education to facilitate their jobs — while their husbands occupy the *batei midrash* and fill them with sounds of Torah. As a result of this situation, secular knowledge often penetrates the homes; everywhere you turn, you cannot help but encounter facets of secular learning. Any and every form of knowledge has become readily available, to be easily absorbed by even the simplest people.

If secular knowledge has made itself "at home" in our communities, it is only right that girls and women receive at least an equal dose of Torah wisdom; "Hashem created one opposite the other." Our magnificent and sacred heritage should not take a backseat to secular education;

it is our "wisdom and insight in the eyes of all the nations." The fine girls' educational network that exists today makes these treasures available to our *bnos Yisrael*.

Even so, the *gedolei haposkim* have written that women should not be given regular classes in *mishnayos*, and certainly not in Gemara and *mefarshim*. Nor should a woman delve into *pilpulim* and in the sources and rationales for the various *mitzvos*. Even if a woman is well-versed in *halachah*, she cannot serve as a *dayan* and should not rule on questions of *issur* and *heter* for herself or others in any situation that calls for a *she'eilas Rav*.

The Woman's Reward EVEN THOUGH THE woman is not obligated to teach her son Torah, if she helps her son or husband in ways that enable them to learn, she shares in their reward. This is one of the primary areas by which a woman earns vast reward. *Chazal* say (*Brachos* 17a) that the promise Hashem gave to women exceeds that which He gave to men, as the *passuk* says, "Serene women, rise and hear My voice; trusting girls, pay heed to My word" (*Yeshayah* 32).

(This entire chapter is based on *Mishpetei Hashalom: 'Ko Somar Leveis Yaakov,'* following chapter 9.)

> **In summary:** Although the *mitzvah* of learning Torah is not an obligation for women, they are nevertheless required to learn what they need to know in order to observe the Torah properly. The same applies to the father's obligation to teach his daughters. Various reasons are given for why women are not obligated to engage in in-depth Torah learning, such as Gemara. In our times, when women go out more and are less attached to their parents' transmission of values, there is an even greater need for girls and women to be taught both necessary *halachos* and other Torah studies that will strengthen their *emunah* and *yiras Shamayim*. When women help their sons and husbands learn, they have a part both in that learning and in the reward.

⇒ 15 ⇐

איסור חנופה
Flattery of a Sinner

Flattery —
"Pledging Allegiance"
to the Sinner

Mr. Levin and Mr. Cohen were co-chairmen of their organization's annual dinner. Among their responsibilities was the job of choosing a guest of honor, preferably someone well-known worldwide who would attract many people and bring in a lot of money for the organization. "Shimon tipped me off that the Israeli government minister, Mr. X, expressed an interest in getting the honor this year," Levin said. "Do you realize how much money that would rake in for the organization? I think we should go for it."

Mr. Cohen was hesitant. "I don't know, Levin. It doesn't smell right to me." "I'm sure you know about all the damage that fellow caused the *yeshivah* community in *Eretz Yisrael* when he pushed through some laws that cut thousands of dollars from the *yeshivah* budgets. Just imagine — when we introduce him we'll have to sing his praises and rave about his dedication to the Jewish people ... it sounds a lot like *chanufah* — flattery — to me."

"You have a point there," Levin conceded. "Let's see what our alternatives are and then discuss it with the Rav."

ANYONE WHO SEES another Jew violating an *issur* and flatters him, whether with words or some gesture that indicates his approval, or even if he remains silent and does not reprove him for the sin, has transgressed

147

not only the *mitzvah* of *tochachah*, but also — according to some opinions — the prohibition of flattery, derived from the *passuk* (*Bamidbar* 35:33), "Do not sully the land with flattery." By implying that we approve of the sinner's misdeeds, our allegiance to Hashem comes under question, since a servant cannot love his master if he loves his master's enemies.

We find that *Chazal* spoke very strongly against the flatterer: "From the day that flattery gained power, judgments have been perverted and deeds have become corrupted. A flatterer brings Hashem's anger into the world, and his *tefillah* is not accepted. He is called a defiler of the land and causes the *Shechinah* to depart from the Jewish people; he brings about exile and falls to the depths of *Gehinnom*."

In addition, *Chazal* listed flatterers as one of the four groups of people who will not be admitted to the Presence of the *Shechinah* in the next world. They also warned that someone who flatters the *rasha* will end up falling into his hands or into the hands of his descendants. (*Mishpetei Hashalom* 10:1–2)

19 Kislev	19 Nisan	19 Av

Better to Remain Silent Than to Show Agreement
"I'm sure he wouldn't have listened to me if I had rebuked him, so what could I have done other than go along with him?"

Even when you are certain that your *tochachah* will not be accepted, that does not justify giving the sinner a pat on the back. You always have the option to keep quiet. Although you might feel uncomfortable about not saying a good word, keep in mind that according to some opinions, flattering a wrongdoer may be prohibited even when you are not merely uncomfortable but are in actual danger.

Consider the incident with King Agrippas, who appropriated the monarchy although according to *halachah* he was not entitled to rule, because of his lineage. *Chazal* say that when the people who had assembled in the courtyard of the *Beis Hamikdash* flattered the king and indicated that he had their support, they deserved to be wiped out, *chas veshalom*. Even though they acted out of fear of the ruler, their fear of Hashem should have been stronger. (*Mishpetei Hashalom* 10:3–4)

When There Is a Risk of Personal Danger THE INCIDENT AT the time of King Agrippas seems to imply that even when there is a risk of personal danger we should not flatter the _resha'im_; but there are three different opinions on this matter: According to Rabbeinu Yonah, when the sin is done in public and it may cause a _chillul Hashem_, we are indeed required to show disapproval even if it endangers us, since the Torah commands us, "Do not fear anyone [in judgment]" (_Devarim_ 1:17). Some limit this requirement to a case where our actions would imply that the deed was not prohibited.

The opinion of Tosafos is that in the case of Agrippas, there was no definite danger in withholding approval; therefore the Jews were at fault for their flattery. However, when there is definite danger, you may express approval of the sinner in order to save your life, since this is not a matter of _yeihareig ve'al yaavor_, where one would be required to face death rather than transgress. Tosafos derive this rule from an incident cited in _maseches Nedarim_ (22a): The Sage Ulla was traveling to Eretz Yisrael, and he was joined by two violent men who were headed in the same direction. On the way, one of the men killed the other and then turned to Ulla and asked if he had done the right thing. Fearing for his own safety, Ulla answered, "Yes."

Later, when Ulla came to his teacher, Rabbi Yochanan, he asked him if he had been guilty of supporting a sinner. "You saved your life," his teacher reassured him, and that is what one is supposed to do under such circumstances.

A third opinion maintains that the Jewish people's transgression was that they catered to Agrippas in order not lose his favor. However, had they felt a real fear for their safety, there would have been nothing wrong with their remaining silent. (_Mishpetei Hashalom_ 10:5)

20 Kislev	20 Nisan	20 Av

Honoring Resha'im GENERALLY, WE SHOULD not praise or honor _resha'im_ — not in their presence and not in their absence. Moreover, we should avoid their company and refrain from awarding them any position of honor or leadership in the community.

Nevertheless, the _halachah_ recognizes the constraints we sometimes

encounter when dealing with *resha'im*. Therefore, when such people are in power and are enjoying a period of success and we are not in a position to subdue them, then we are permitted to show them respect to the same degree that we may show respect to potentially violent people, out of fear of what they might do to us.

Chazal conceded that we are "permitted to flatter the wicked in this world." However, while we may praise them if necessary for their beauty, intelligence, talent or the like, we should not honor them in any way that may be interpreted as approval of their transgressions; doing so would fall under the category of prohibited flattery.

A situation that arises frequently is when a person who is guilty of certain sins committed in public comes to shul expecting to be granted the traditional shul honors. For example, a supporter of a certain *yeshivah*, who is a *kohen* married to a divorcee (a halachically prohibited marriage) and who shaves with a razor, may show up in the *yeshivah* for his righteous grandfather's *yahrtzeit*. While he should not be honored with the first *aliyah laTorah* (a privilege given to a kosher *kohen*), he can be given the lesser honor of opening the *aron kodesh*. As long as his transgression of shaving with a razor is not discussed, there is no need to protest the sin or rebuke him about it, since such *tochachah* will be damaging and certainly will have no effect. While the *hanhalah* of the yeshivah should be careful not to praise him in a way that would imply approval of this transgression, they can certainly praise his grandfather highly and mention that in the righteous grandfather's merit, his grandson is a supporter of Torah. (*Mishpetei Hashalom* 10:6)

---

21 Kislev   21 Nisan   21 Av

Different Categories of Flattery

IN *SHAAREI TESHUVAH*, Rabbeinu Yonah lists nine different categories of *chanufah*:

1. **One who sees another sin and does not rebuke him** — Because he is lax in defending the truth, the offender will not regret what he has done and will likely repeat the offense. This is even more serious if the sin was done in public, since it is perceived as a show of contempt for the Torah's authority.

2. **One who praises a *rasha*, even not in the *rasha*'s presence** — Such a person is counted among those who "Forsake the Torah and praise the *rasha*" (*Mishlei* 28:4). Even when he finds it necessary to mention some good aspect of the *rasha*, he should make sure to mention a bad point as well, so that the listeners should not consider the offender a *tzaddik*.

3. **One who praises the *rasha* to his face** — This person causes the *rasha* to take pride in his ways so that he will not repent. David Hamelech said of such flattery: "Hashem will cut off all lips of smooth talk [i.e., flattery]." Some people flatter powerful people so that those people will give them honor and raise their position, but *Chazal* said that someone who flatters another for the sake of gaining honor will end up parting from him in disgrace.

4. **One who associates with the *rasha*** — To the *tzaddik*, "the despicable is repulsive" (*Tehillim* 15). Some say that we may not even look at a *rasha*. By joining up with the *rasha*, a person indicates that, to some degree, he too is a *rasha* at heart, for "birds of a feather flock together." Many roads may lead to the death of such a person; one way or another, his punishment will catch up with him.

5. **One who appoints a person who is unworthy or dishonest as a *dayan* or teacher** — If as a result of his support, the community relies on the unworthy candidate, then the one who appointed him is considered to be on the same level as someone who planted an *asheirah* (a tree of *avodah zarah*). And if there was a *talmid chacham* in the same place, then he is like someone who planted an *asheirah* next to the *mizbei'ach*. Hashem will punish such a person.

6. **One who is in a position to object to sin and does not** — is held responsible for that sin.

22 Kislev	22 Nisan	22 Av

7. **One who is uncertain about whether his *tochachah* will be accepted** — is also held responsible for the sin if he did not at least attempt to give *tochachah*.

8. **One who is certain that his *tochachah* will not be accepted** — is still obligated to speak up so that people will not think that he approves of the transgression. For this same reason, if there is an assemblage of *reshai'im*, one should leave them, so people will not think he is one of them.

9. **One who shows honor to *resha'im* because of their wealth** — If he shows them no more honor than he would any other wealthy person, such honor is permissible if the *resha'im* are in a position of power (as mentioned earlier). However, one should not praise them or speak well of them to others. (*Mishpetei Hashalom* 10, note to 6)

Permitted Flattery FLATTERY THAT IS prohibited includes: praising *resha'im* or wickedness, praising someone in a way that will cause him to sin or will reinforce his error, "buttering up" someone so that he will trust you and you can then deceive him, and praising your child or other relative when he or she is doing wrong.

But there are times when flattery can be used for constructive purposes. In such cases flattery is not only permissible but is even considered a *mitzvah*. For example, we may flatter our spouse in order to promote *shalom bayis*, and flatter our students and colleagues to smooth the way for them to accept our *tochachah* and, as a result, improve their *mitzvah* observance and Torah study. Flattering a rebbe to get him to teach us Torah is also clearly for a positive purpose. It is also permitted to flatter a creditor to stop him from exerting pressure on us, and to flatter the rich, even if it is purely for the sake of gaining benefit from them.

However, as a general rule it is advisable to stay away from flattery. In fact, even though we may praise a person lavishly when he is not present, we should avoid praising him too much in his presence, even if we mean every word we say, because to others our words may appear to be empty flattery.

A habit related to flattery that should also be avoided is hypocrisy. The hypocrite makes a false show of being a *tzaddik* or a *talmid chacham*, when inside he is in fact far from that image. Similarly, a person should not say one thing when he means another. (*Mishpetei Hashalom* 10:7–8)

"Do Not Grant IN RELATING TO *AKUM*, the Torah exhorts us *Lo*
Them Grace" *sechonem*, "Do not grant them any grace" (*Devarim*
7:2). *Chazal* explain that this prohibition includes
not giving them gifts, and not even praising them, such as by saying,
"How beautiful this *akum* is," or any other form of compliment. The
prohibition applies even if the praise is true and deserved; if the praise
is unjustified, then the prohibition to flatter the *akum* is even clearer.
(*Mishpetei Hashalom* 10:9)

If the gift or compliment is for a constructive purpose — such as for a
boss or a worker, a business partner, a neighbor, a *Shabbos goy*, or someone with political influence — and there will be mutual benefit from the
exchange, then the gift or compliment is permitted and in some cases
encouraged. Of course, we always pray for the peace and success of the
government of the country, state and/or city where we live.

Assorted Halachos AS MENTIONED IN Chapter 2, in cases where we
Regarding Relating are permitted to hate a *rasha*, we should not hate
to Resha'im him in our hearts while putting on a show of liking him, but rather show our hatred openly.
The general rule regarding *resha'im* is to avoid them at all costs.
We should not associate with them in business or in any partnership,
not even in a joint effort for a *devar mitzvah*, so that we should not be
influenced by them in any way. It is at least as important not to associate
with people who approve of wrongdoing and with *baalei machlokes*.

Do Not Fear ... A *DAYAN* IS sometimes faced with the difficult situa-
in Judgment tion of having to deal with people who are not only
transgressors but may even be violent and aggressive.
If two claimants come before a *dayan*, one of them a hard, violent type
who does not listen to authority and the other a soft, weak person (who
will not be able to help the *dayan* if the *din* goes against the violent
character and he attacks the *dayan*), then as long as the *dayan* has not

yet heard both sides, or even if he has heard the sides but does not yet know in which direction the decision will go, he does not have to agree to rule on the case. If, on the other hand, both claimants are strong types, he must deal with their case, since even if one side attacks him the other one will come to his aid.

If the *dayan* is a public appointee and it is not so clear that there is potential damage, then he is obligated to accept the case. Also, if the *dayan* has already heard the sides and has begun to see where the wind is blowing, he must follow through with the case, since abstaining at that point would be a violation of "Do not fear anyone [in judgment]."

Some opinions maintain that in our times, we do not protest the deeds of transgressors, because there is a danger that they will report us to the secular authorities. However, in a situation where there is no real danger, and our only fear is that the violent person will harbor complaints against us, then an appointed *dayan* does not have a right to refuse to judge the case. (*Mishpetei Hashalom* 10:11–14)

In summary: When we see someone transgressing, it is forbidden for us to flatter him, since flattery implies our approval of his deeds. Even when there is a risk of danger, opinions differ regarding whether we may express our approval of them, whether we may remain silent, or whether we must speak up. Honoring *resha'im* is prohibited, with the exception of certain situations where the *resha'im* are in power and we need their goodwill, and our flattery will not be perceived as approval of their deeds. In some cases flattery may be permitted for a constructive purpose. Hypocrisy is closely related to flattery and should be avoided. There are specific *halachos* outlining how a *dayan* should deal with claimants who are potentially violent.

🔹 16 🔹

לפני עור לא תתן מכשול
Causing Another to Sin/
Giving Bad Advice

Making the
Aveirah Possible

Shmuli and Binyamin noticed a group of their friends huddled in the corner of the yard. "Hey, what are you all so busy with there?" Shmuli asked curiously.

"Dovid managed to get some great explosives for Purim — a lot stronger than the kiddy cap guns. You want to see?" Shloimie replied.

"Say, aren't those the ones Rav Braun said are *assur* to use?" Shmuli asked indignantly. "They're really dangerous, and they're so loud that some people actually had heart attacks from hearing them go off."

"Oh, don't be such a goody-goody. Nothing's going to happen. Don't you believe in a little Purim fun?" Dovid retorted. "Here, Binyamin, you want a few?"

"Wow, I would never be able to get hold of those on my own," Binyamin answered eagerly, ignoring Shmuli's words. "And my parents sure wouldn't let me have them, even if I had a place to buy them. Here, let me have a couple."

"Dovid, isn't it bad enough that you're ignoring what the Rav said? How can you go ahead and make somebody else do an *aveirah* too?" Shmuli turned around in disgust, leaving the group to digest his words.

155

"*LIFNEI IVEIR LO sitein michshol* — Do not place a stumbling block before the blind" (*Vayikra* 19:14). In addition to the plain meaning of these words, this *passuk* teaches us that we may not do anything to cause another person to sin. It is even forbidden to make it easier for him to sin. This *mitzvah* is incumbent upon men and women, at all times. The prohibition applies not only to causing a Jew to transgress but even to doing something that would enable a non-Jew to violate one of the seven *mitzvos* in which he is obligated.

Children should be trained in this *mitzvah* from a young age. It is important to instill in them — mainly by example — a feeling of genuine caring for other Jews. As they grow up, that concern for others will expand to include a hope for their spiritual success. As a result, they will do whatever they can to help others grow in their *Yiddishkeit* and certainly will not take action that might cause someone else to sin. (*Mishpetei Hashalom* 11:1, 33)

26 Kislev	26 Nisan	26 Av

Classic Examples CLASSIC EXAMPLES OF *lifnei iveir* cited in the Gemara are not handing a *nazir* a cup of wine and not giving *eiver min hachai* (meat from a live animal) to a non-Jew, if they would not otherwise have had access to these items that are forbidden to them. In both of these cases, though, we are not forcing them to sin; we are making the opportunity more readily available and are therefore responsible for causing them to stumble.

For the same reason, we are not permitted to sell weapons — or any other items that can cause damage to the general public — to an *akum*; nor may we repair such items for him. Doing so would be considered not only making it easier for him to sin but actually supporting him in the transgression — *machzik yedei ovrei aveirah*. Similarly, we may not sell such an item to a Jewish dealer who will in turn sell them to an *akum*. However, it is permissible to sell weapons to a country's armed forces, since they will use them to protect the country's Jews, among the other citizens. Those who deal in arms are advised to consult a competent *posek* in matters concerning their trade. (*Mishpetei Hashalom* 11:2-3)

***Other
Applications of
Lifnei Iveir*** WE HAVE MENTIONED the classic examples of *lifnei iveir lo sitein michshol*, but the *issur* would apply to any action that is likely to lead another person to transgress. In fact, we should not even hand a potential sinner something that belongs to *him*, if we have reason to believe he will use it for a sinful purpose. For example, we should not hand an apostate his own bag of forbidden food — even though it is his property — since it is clear that he intends to transgress and eat it. Similarly, it would be wrong to give a Jew his car keys moments before Shabbos begins, when he has stated clearly that he is planning to drive the car on Shabbos. However, we could pass such an item to a Jew whom we do not have particular reason to suspect, even if we do not know him well.

A Jew should not sell to an *akum* any item that is earmarked for use in idol worship, when we know that he will most likely use it for *avodah zarah*. However, some opinions maintain that doing so is forbidden only if the *akum* does not own any similar item and cannot buy it anywhere else. This scenario might occur if, for example, the Jew owns the only store in town that carries such items, and without buying it from this Jew, the *akum* would have no other way to obtain it. However, if a similar item could be bought elsewhere, then there is no *issur* in selling it.

However, other opinions maintain that it is prohibited to sell such items that are earmarked for use in *avodah zarah* even if they are available elsewhere. The generally accepted practice is to allow one to sell the item in this case; however, a *baal nefesh* — a person with higher aspirations — should be stringent and refrain from doing so. (*Mishpetei Hashalom* 11:4-7)

27 Kislev	27 Nisan	27 Av

***Assisting a Jewish
Sinner in His
Transgression*** IN CHAPTER 13 we mentioned that if a child is seen eating *neveilah* (meat from an animal that was not *shechted* halachically), then *beis din* is obligated to stop him. Being that we are obligated to *stop* someone — even a child — from a sin he is involved in, it follows

logically that we certainly should not *assist* him in transgressing. In fact, we have pointed out (in chapter 13) that we should not even give a small child a nonkosher item to play with if there is a chance that he will put it in his mouth and eat it. If this is the rule regarding a child, who is not fully responsible for *mitzvah* observance, then it certainly applies to an adult.

Therefore, for example, we should not give a Jew *chametz* food on *erev Pesach* close to the time when *chametz* is prohibited, if we have reason to suspect that he will eat it after the time when the prohibition takes effect.

Although the primary *issur* of *lifnei iveir* applies only when the offender would not have been able to violate the *issur* without our help, we are still forbidden to help him even in a case where he *can* violate the *issur* on his own. We derive this from the *mitzvah* of "Do not follow after the multitude to do evil" (*Shemos* 23:3), which the *Shaarei Teshuvah* explains to mean that we may not assist a sinner in any way.

If we see someone doing a prohibited act — such as tending his garden on Shabbos — we are not allowed to wish him success in his endeavor, even if we are doing so simply as an expected gesture of politeness. (*Mishpetei Hashalom* 11:8–9, 13)

Assisting the Akum or Mumar in His Sin REGARDING AN *AKUM* who can accomplish his transgression on his own, the *poskim* differ as to whether we are allowed to assist him. Some say that in such a case there is no *issur* of assisting the *akum* and that this is the case regarding assisting a *mumar* — a Jewish apostate — as well. Some extend this leniency to any Jew who is transgressing a sin *bemeizid* — intentionally. Their rationale is that the *issur* of assisting one in sinning is relevant only for people whom we would have to stop from sinning (i.e., a Jew, even a child); in the cases mentioned here — the *akum*, the *mumar* and the intentional sinner — there is no obligation to stop them and, therefore, no *issur* to help them.

Other *poskim* maintain that there is no blanket *heter* to assist anyone in sin; according to these opinions, even assisting the *akum* is permissible only to keep the peace or if it is necessary for one's *parnassah*.

Another opinion limits this *heter*, asserting that the aforementioned distinction applies only before the person has begun to violate the transgression; however, once he has actually begun the sin, it would be prohibited *mideRabbanan* to directly assist him in any way, even if he began the *aveirah* on his own. Therefore, according to all opinions, it would be forbidden to directly feed a *mumar* forbidden food, even if he would be able to take the food by himself. (*Mishpetei Hashalom* 11:10–13)

Practical Applications: Marriage-Related Matters IN ERETZ YISRAEL, where the Rabbinate has official authority over marriage laws, the accepted practice is not to authorize weddings of irreligious couples unless the *kallah* has undergone ritual purification before the wedding, even if it is clear that they will not continue to keep the laws of family purity afterward.

However, outside Eretz Yisrael the general practice is to be lenient in this area, since if we were to insist on such a condition, many couples would opt to undergo a nonreligious or even a civil marriage ceremony and would end up cutting off any connection they may have had with *Yiddishkeit*.

Some opinions permit officiating at the wedding of an irreligious couple for pay, and others permit it even when no payment in involved, following the *poskim* we cited earlier who permit assisting an intentional sinner in his transgression.

For the same reason, many permit acting as a matchmaker for irreligious Jews (so as to prevent them from marrying out of the faith), and renting them wedding halls, since the main purpose is for a permissible act. Even though we have reason to suspect that they will engage in forbidden acts as well, the *poskim* still permit renting the hall to them, since it will prevent them from opting instead for a hall that serves nonkosher food.

However, renting a hall to such people for the express purpose of forbidden conduct, such as for a "mixed-dancing evening," would be prohibited in any case. (*Mishpetei Hashalom* 11:14)

Practical Applications: Dealing in Forbidden Items   A JEW MAY not give or sell nonkosher food items to someone whom he suspects intends to eat them or to sell them to another Jew as kosher. The same applies to dealing with other forbidden articles, such as razors and shavers that the *halachah* does not permit for men's use, immodest clothing and provocative *sheitels* (wigs) or other accessories, and clothing that may contain *shaatnez* (if we suspect that the buyer will not have it checked). Another item that is forbidden to give away or sell is an *esrog murkav* — an *esrog* grown from a cross-grafted tree, which is disqualified for use for the *arbaah minim* and would be likely to cause someone to make a *brachah levatalah* and to lose out on the *mitzvah* of *arbaah minim*.

It is forbidden to buy or sell stolen goods; nor are we allowed to give the thief any assistance in stealing or marketing such items. Doing so is a serious *aveirah*, because if the thief did not have anyone to sell his goods to, he would not steal. Even if he could, theoretically, find a customer elsewhere, he will be discouraged from stealing if he encounters difficulty getting rid of the stolen goods. Therefore, by dealing with him we would be supporting the sinner and violating the *issur* of *lifnei iveir*.

Someone who publishes or markets books that should not be read because of their useless content, false ideology or rousing, romantic themes, is guilty of causing the public to sin. *Chazal* tell us that such a person will find it extremely difficult to do *teshuvah*. The same applies to one who distributes such materials to libraries, making it readily available to the public.

One should not give a non-Jew a piece of *shechted* meat in which the *gid hanasheh* (the sciatic nerve, which must be removed) is not readily noticeable, since he might pass it on to a Jew, who will eat it as kosher, not realizing that the *gid* is still there. Similarly, one should not sell an item of clothing that contains hidden *shaatnez* to a non-Jew, since he might resell it to a Jew. The same applies to selling wheat before Pesach if you know that it contains unnoticeable *chametz*. (*Mishpetei Hashalom* 11:15, 17–18, 20)

Practical Applications: Causing Chillul Shabbos ONE MAY NOT lend work tools to a Jew whom we suspect will use them on Shabbos, unless we have reason to assume he will use them for a common, permitted use (such as using a hammer to break open a coconut on Shabbos). Similarly, we should not give a Jewish tailor an article of clothing to repair if we suspect he will do the work on Shabbos.

For this reason, there are some _poskim_ who prohibit selling or renting out banquet halls, workplaces, and even houses or tools, which might potentially be used for _chillul Shabbos_, to someone whom we suspect might use them for such purposes. Other _poskim_ allow such sale or rental, as long as the following conditions are met:

- The person could easily find other sellers or renters.
- We do not offer the item or property at a lower rate than others.
- We do not offer better credit terms than others offer.
- The quality of our product is not superior to that which is available from others.
- We should specifically instruct the buyer or renter that he should not use the property or item in a way that would transgress any sin.

However, someone who is completely lenient in such matters, without meeting all the conditions, has _poskim_ on whom to rely.

We should be careful not to invite a _mechallel Shabbos_ to daven with us in shul or to join us for a Shabbos meal if we know that he will violate Shabbos in order to arrive.

Whenever possible, it is preferable not to patronize Jewish-owned establishments that are _mechallel Shabbos_, such as stores and amusement parks. Even though we are not a direct cause of _chillul Shabbos_ when we use their facilities or services during the week, nevertheless, to a certain extent we are supporting the sinner if he sees that his open violation of Shabbos does not prevent religious Jews from giving him their business. Besides the additional value of supporting the livelihood of observant Jews by using _shomer Shabbos_ stores and services, abstaining

from patronizing the other establishments can influence the owner to close his doors on Shabbos, if only to increase his religious clientele.

(Regarding hiring workers to do work that involves *issurim*, refer to *Shaarei Mishpat, Shaar Sechirus Po'alim*, 3:14) (*Mishpetei Hashalom* 11:19, 24)

1 Teves	1 Iyar	1 Elul

Practical Application: Parents and Children   AS WE HAVE mentioned in chapters 7 and 13, there are times when a parent or teacher may need to spank a child in order to guide him toward proper behavior and observance of Torah and *mitzvos*.

However, if a parent strikes his grown child, he violates the *issur* of *lifnei iveir*, since the child may not be able to resist the urge to defy the parent — or even to hit back or curse him, both of which are serious transgressions that would warrant a death penalty in the times of the *Sanhedrin*. Some say that the same applies even with a smaller child, if he is by nature the type who will defy the parent verbally or physically.

Parents should never test a child to see if he will respond in anger, even if they decide in advance that they are *mochel* (forgo) their *kavod*, unless they inform the child in advance of their *mechilah*. Otherwise, if the child indeed responds in anger, he will still need *kaparah* (atonement), because as far as he understood, he was doing an *aveirah* — speaking angrily to his parents (even though in reality, since they had been *mochel*, he did not actually transgress). Therefore, the parents will still have violated the *issur* of *lifnei iveir*.

Some opinions say that the same is true in a parallel case — giving *tzedakah* to a fraud who presents himself deceitfully as a poor man. Even if the giver is aware of the fellow's deceit and is *mochel*, deciding to give him the money anyway, that will not help the deceiver to be free of guilt, unless the giver tells him in advance that he is *mochel*. Otherwise, as far as the impostor knows, he is willfully taking money under false pretenses, which is considered theft, and therefore, despite the giver's generosity, he, the giver, will have transgressed the *issur* of *lifnei iveir*. (*Mishpetei Hashalom* 11:22–23)

Practical WHEN A WOMAN dresses immodestly or wears pro-
Applications: vocative makeup in public, she is guilty of causing
Modesty Issues men to transgress by drawing them to gaze at her
and rousing their *yetzer hara*. In doing so, she vio-
lates the *issur* of *lifnei iveir* and will be punished along with each man
who turned to look at her, since she was the one who caused him to sin.
The same applies to the use of heavy perfume, singing or dancing in the
company of men, and any other conduct that attracts men's attention.

For this reason, many *poskim* forbid women to bathe even at separate beaches or swimming pools where the lifeguard is a Jewish man,
unless they wear robes that will keep them covered modestly. (*Mishpetei
Hashalom* 11:16)

Practical Applications: IT IS FORBIDDEN to cause an *akum* to
Causing the Name of a swear in the name of his *avodah zarah*.
False Deity to Be Uttered Therefore, one should avoid making a business partnership with an *akum*, since in a
business situation he might be required to make such an oath, and the
Jewish partner would then be guilty not only of causing the name of
avodah zarah to be uttered, but also of *lifnei iveir*. However, once such
a partnership exists, and the need for an oath arises, we are permitted
to accept the oath.

Nowadays we are lenient regarding such partnerships, because the
name of *avodah zarah* is not mentioned in the format of a standard oath.
Wherever a deity is mentioned it refers to the Creator, or at worst to a
shituf (as in the case of Christians). Since, according to many *poskim*,
believing in *shituf* is not forbidden for a non-Jew, this would not be a
violation of the *issur* of *lifnei iveir*. (*Mishpetei Hashalom* 11:25)

2 Teves	2 Iyar	2 Elul

Other IF A PERSON lends or borrows money with interest,
Miscellaneous then in addition to transgressing the *issur* of dealing
Applications with interest, he is also guilty of transgressing the *issur*
of *lifnei iveir*, since the borrower and lender each play
a role in causing the other to sin. All of those involved in such a transac-

tion — the agent, the guarantors and the witnesses — without whom the loan could not have taken place, are guilty of violating *lifnei iveir*.

When a person lends out money without witnesses or a *shtar* (documentary proof) he is violating *lifnei iveir*, even if the borrower is a *talmid chacham*, since in the absence of legal proof, it might cross the borrower's mind, ever so briefly, to deny that he took the loan.

Someone who bribes a *dayan*, in addition to violating the *issur* of bribery, is also guilty of *lifnei iveir*, since he causes the *dayan* to transgress by accepting the bribe.

We may not give food to someone if we know he will not make a *brachah* before eating, or even if we are not sure if he will make a *brachah*. (Some opinions are lenient regarding a poor person whom we are feeding as a form of *tzedakah* and who might make a *brachah*.) The same rule applies regarding offering bread to someone who will not wash *netilas yadayim*. However, we do not have to cross-examine every person to whom we serve food; as long as the person is an observant Jew, we may assume that he will make the necessary *brachos*.

Care should be taken in less religious sectors when passing food around at a *kiddush*; the participants should be reminded to make the relevant *brachos*. Some people announce at *simchos*, "Hand-washing for those who want to wash." It would seem more appropriate to announce, "I'm not saying 'Hand-washing for those who want to wash,' because all must wash." If this is said in a humorous tone it will probably not offend anyone, and it may influence more people to wash.

What if we have non-Torah-observant guests, newly exposed to *Yiddishkeit*, who will be insulted if told to make a *brachah*, and as a result may turn their backs completely on Torah and *mitzvos*? The Chazon Ish is stringent regarding this delicate issue and maintains that there is no *heter* to offer them food if they will not make a *brachah*. The *Minchas Shlomo* is lenient, saying that in this case we would be permitted to "assist" the guest in violating a lighter *issur* if it is likely to save him from more serious violations in the long run. (Practically speaking, when the suggestion is made with a modicum of tact, most non-Torah-observant guests are willing to go along with requests such as repeating a *brachah* after their hosts or washing their hands for bread.) (*Mishpetei Hashalom* 11:21, 24)

| 3 Teves | 3 Iyar | 3 Elul |

One Who Has Only Shimon met his neighbor, Zevulun, near the pub-
Himself to Blame lic trash bin, busily marking a number of bags and
boxes. After watching him for a few minutes, his
curiosity got the better of him. "What are you up to, Zevulun?" he asked.

"My wife went all out Pesach cleaning yesterday, and she sent me out
with old utensils, broken carriages … you name it. I think some of these
things are fixable, and someone might want to take them, so I'm writing 'hefker' — ownerless property — on those items. Otherwise, someone
might think they were not abandoned but were rather just left here for a
moment, and then if he takes them away he might be guilty of *gezel* —
stealing."

"Here, you missed this box," Shimon said, trying to be helpful.

"Oh, I'm not going to mark that one. Some company once sent us
this box with forty cans of shrimp — a promotion of some kind. Anyone
who takes home such obviously nonkosher food deserves to be guilty of
stealing, too. I don't have to go out of my way to help him," Zevulun explained.

ALTHOUGH IT IS prohibited to cause someone to sin, if he brings the
sin upon himself by his own misdeed, then we follow the principle of
"*Hal'iteihu larasha veyamos* — You dug your own grave."

Thus, for example, during the *shemittah* year, when everyone in
Eretz Yisrael has equal access to the fruits of private orchards, a person
who has trees in his orchard that are still *orlah* (in the first three years
of growth, when it is prohibited to consume the fruit) should mark them
clearly as such, so that no one will partake of them in error. If the trees
are in their fourth year of growth, and the fruit is *neta revai* — which can
be eaten only in Yerushalayim, or after being properly redeemed — then
during *shemittah*, the proper thing to do is to clearly identify them, or,
as an act of piety, to redeem them, so that the public will not inadvertently eat unredeemed *neta revai*. The same would apply to any *issurim*
where someone might be caused to transgress unknowingly.

However, during years that are not *shemittah*, anyone who comes
into the orchard and takes fruit is stealing. There would be no obligation
to mark the *orlah* trees in order to protect a thief from transgressing
this *issur*. Even though by eating the forbidden fruit he is transgressing

unintentionally, nevertheless, since he is stealing intentionally, we follow the principle cited above — "*Hal'iteihu lerasha veyamos.*" This rule applies anytime a *rasha* sins intentionally; even if we have the ability to minimize his sin or prevent it, or to prevent him from an additional, different sin, we should ignore these opportunities and let him suffer the consequences of his actions.

But the moment we see that the *rasha* has the slightest inclination to do *teshuvah*, even though we certainly cannot assist him in carrying out a transgression, we should do what we can to save him from sinning to whatever extent possible, because Hashem "does not desire the death of the *rasha*, but rather that he return from his ways and live." (*Mishpetei Hashalom* 11:26–27)

4 Teves	4 Iyar	4 Elul

Refraining From Giving Poor Advice; Giving Good Advice "How will I ever get rid of the last refrigerator from this stock?" Mr. Rosen, the appliance store proprietor, wondered to himself. "It was never a very successful model, and I've gotten plenty of complaints, but I must make room for the new ones."

Just then a young couple speaking in a foreign accent walked in. "We're looking for a good refrigerator, and we want your advice. These are the measurements ..."

"I have just the item for you — an excellent appliance at an excellent price," Mr. Rosen said, smiling in satisfaction at the instant solution that had just presented itself. *They'll swallow whatever I tell them — this is going to be an easy sale*, he thought smugly to himself.

ANOTHER ASPECT OF the *issur* of *lifnei iveir* is the prohibition to give someone bad advice. This prohibition applies to advising a Jew, although ethically we should try to give good advice to anyone who asks it of us. This does not apply, however, to a *rasha*. Whether we are giving bad advice for our own personal profit, as in the case of the storekeeper above, or for some other reason, and whether the issue is relevant to the adviser or not, offering advice that will be detrimental to another person is a violation of *lifnei iveir* and is subject to the curse stated at Har Gerizim (*Devarim* 27:18): "Cursed is the one who leads a blind man astray." Therefore, it is very important for a salesman to resist the temptation to persuade a customer to buy something that would not be for his benefit.

| "Oh, but I only meant it for his own good," one might insist.

That might be the case; no human being can know what another person's intentions really were. Therefore, the *passuk* that presents the *issur* of *lifnei iveir* concludes, "*veyareisa mei'Elokecha*" — fear Hashem; He knows exactly what is going on in your heart.

According to some opinions, the "positive side of the coin" is also a part of this *mitzvah*: not only should we refrain from giving bad advice, but we are obligated to give good advice to someone who seeks our counsel. Preferably, we should give serious thought before replying and should offer substantial, practical ideas, not just offhand suggestions. By offering good advice to another Jew on issues such as *shidduchim*, business practices and the like, we fulfill the *mitzvah* of *lifnei iveir* and also perform an important *chessed*. (*Mishpetei Hashalom* 11:28–29)

5 Teves	5 Iyar	5 Elul

Good for One;   SOMETIMES, THE DEFINITION of "good advice" is
Bad for Another   not so black-and-white. For example, if by giving the asker the advice that is best for him, you yourself would suffer a loss, then ideally, you should discuss this problem directly with the one consulting you. If that is not possible, then you may abstain and not give him any advice at all, following the principle in interpersonal matters that "Your life takes precedence."

If you sense that the asker has evil intentions, then not only should you not give him good advice; it would be a *mitzvah* to deliberately deceive him. For example, someone you suspect of dishonest leanings comes over and asks you: "I see your neighbor is away on vacation. I wanted to speak to him. Do you know when he'll be coming back?" If you have reason to suspect that he is plotting a break-in, then you might be concerned that giving him good advice and telling him when the neighbor will be back would also reveal to him when the house will be empty and vulnerable. Therefore, you can deceive him and say, "Oh, it could be that he's back already. They don't always answer the door or the phone."

Sometimes, giving Reuven good advice will harm Shimon. In such a case, you should not volunteer unsolicited advice, since you have no legitimate reason to prefer the good of one person over that of another. However, if one of the two is a close relative or friend whose loss or gain is felt by you as if it were your own, then you should offer him good advice even if it will be at someone else's expense. Also, if someone requests your advice specifically, even if he is a stranger, then you should give him advice that is for his benefit, even when someone else will lose out as a result.

Certain kinds of advice are always prohibited. We should never advise another Jew to transgress, even for a huge profit. Nor should we advise someone to engage in tricky or deceitful actions or any other disreputable behavior, even if no real *issur* is involved. *Chazal* call one who gives such advice a *"rasha arum"* — a cunning evildoer. (*Mishpetei Hashalom* 11:30–32)

In summary: The *mitzvah* of *lifnei iveir* prohibits us from causing another Jew to sin or assisting him in transgressing. This *mitzvah* also applies to causing an *akum* to violate one of the seven *mitzvos* in which he is obligated. According to some opinions, doing something that would assist an *akum* or a Jewish apostate in his sin would be permissible under certain circumstances. There are many practical applications of this *mitzvah*, such as, for example, regarding a woman who causes men to sin by her provocative public appearance, or selling or renting items to someone who will use them for *chillul Shabbos*. Also included in the purview of *lifnei iveir* is the prohibition to offer bad advice and the obligation to provide good advice.

⇾ 17 ⇽

לא תחמוד ולא תתאוה
Coveting the
Possessions of Others

The Grass
Is Greener
Strolling down the street, Moishe noticed his neighbor's sleek new car, parked right behind Moishe's old jalopy. *I wish that car was in my driveway*, he thought wistfully, pondering how he might persuade his neighbor to sell him the automobile at a good price.

A NATURAL REACTION, wouldn't you say? After all, doesn't everyone think the grass is greener on the other side? Nevertheless, as we have seen, the Torah expects more of us than "natural reactions"; Hashem gives us the power to control even our instinctive emotions — including the feeling of desiring attractive items that we see in other people's possession.

"*Lo sachmod* … — Do not covet your neighbor's wife, and do not desire your neighbor's house, nor his field, servant, maidservant, ox, donkey or anything that is his" (*Devarim* 5:18). This command is not a *middas chassidus* — an extra stringency; it is the tenth of the *Aseres Hadibros*. *Chazal* describe the chain of events that is set into motion by desire: "Desire leads to coveting; coveting leads to stealing, and it can

169

even lead to bloodshed, as occurred in the story of Achav and Navos." In addition, the habit of desiring what others have distracts us from our Torah and *mitzvah*-observance, and also indicates a weak link in our belief in Hashem's *hashgachah*. ("After all, if Hashem meant for that car to be mine, it would be in my driveway...") (*Mishpetei Hashalom* 12:1)

7 Teves	7 Iyar	7 Elul

Coveting Versus Desiring   AT WHAT POINT does an admiring glance turn into a prohibited, covetous look? The prohibition of *lo sachmod* consists of two parts, and according to many authorities, two distinct *mitzvos*.

The first step is *taavah* — desire. We see a nice item that belongs to someone else — an item the person has no intention of selling — and are attracted to it. If in our desire to acquire it we begin to think of strategies by which we might get it from the other fellow, then we have violated the *issur* of *lo tisaveh* — do not desire. Notice that no action has yet been taken and not a word has been said. The violation lies in the scheming thoughts running through our minds. On the other hand, the prohibition does not begin until we have started making plans to acquire the item. Simply admiring the item does not constitute an *issur*.

The second step is *chemdah* — coveting. Once the desire and the strategies one has come up with take the form of action, the act becomes a violation of *lo sachmod* — do not covet. We are not talking here about taking by force something that is not ours — that would be stealing. Rather, we refer to exerting unusual pressure to force someone to sell or give us something that he really does not want to part with. We might accomplish this by sending emissaries to persuade him to agree or by bombarding him with repeated pleas to his conscience. Asking once or twice is not considered exerting undue pressure, but pushing him against the wall repeatedly would fall into that category. If he finally gives in and sells us the item, even if we pay him the *full price* for it — the moment we take it, we are violating the *issur* of *lo sachmod* and are in fact violating two *issurim* at the same time.

In most cases a sale that is made under pressure is valid, and *halachah* does not require that the item be returned. Nevertheless, the buyer is

guilty of _lo tisaveh_ and _lo sachmod_, and he may even be disqualified from giving testimony in _beis din_ because of his covetous nature.

Needless to say, if we desire the item, pressure the owner and then finally take it _without_ the owner's permission, we violate the _issur_ of _gezel_, stealing, as well. (_Mishpetei Hashalom_ 12:4–7)

8 Teves	8 Iyar	8 Elul

What Items Fall into the Category of Lo Sachmod? THE OBJECTS THAT we may not desire or covet vary from the smallest to the most valuable. According to the _Minchas Chinuch_, the prohibition of _lo sachmod_ applies even to an item that is worth less than a _perutah_ (a coin of small monetary value — which might _not_ count toward other prohibitions).

The _passuk_ we cited from the _Aseres Hadibros_ mentions a field, servants, livestock, house and wife. Included in the first four items of this list are all kinds of real estate, household objects and personal items.

But what about the "wife"? Obviously, we would not step up to our neighbor and persuade him to sell his wife. Still, unfortunately, this prohibition may apply if a person covets his neighbor's wife and takes measures to influence him to initiate divorce proceedings. Even in a case where the neighbor has already begun a divorce process, urging him along in that direction for the purpose of later marrying his ex-wife would constitute a violation of this _issur_.

It is also prohibited to covet someone's job or his position of power, as we see in the case of Korach, who desired Moshe's leadership position. It is permissible, however, to persuade a professional to teach you his trade.

In terms of real estate, a common case of _lo tisaveh_ and _lo sachmod_ arises when a person wishes to buy from a neighbor land or a storeroom or garage that abuts his home or property, in order to expand his home. Even though there is much to be gained by the prospective buyer and little for the neighbor to lose in this transaction, and even if the buyer is willing to pay a high price for the purchase, he still cannot exert more-than-average pressure if the neighbor has no interest in the deal. (_Mishpetei Hashalom_ 12:5–6)

לא תחמוד אשר לאחרך ואת אשתו

For Sale or Moishe took another look at his neighbor's sleek car and
Not for Sale? was pleasantly surprised to notice a for-sale sign in the
back window. Moishe may not realize it, but those two
words change the whole picture, in terms of the transgressions of *lo ti-saveh* and *lo sachmod.*

THE *ISSURIM* WE have been discussing apply only to items that are not
on the market. Once something is for sale, we are allowed to desire it
and to take measures to acquire it. In addition, the *halachah* permits us
to use all our persuasive efforts to bargain down the price, since that is
considered normal negotiation.

In fact, whenever we are *uncertain* about whether someone is willing to sell the item we have our eye on, there is nothing wrong with
simply asking the owner once or twice if he would agree to sell; that
is not considered pressure. The exception would be when the relationship is such that even if we asked him only once, the owner would feel
obliged to agree. Common examples of this abound: a boss asking his
employee, a Rav asking his congregant, a parent asking his child. In all
of these cases, even if the owner had no intention of selling the object,
he will feel that he simply cannot refuse, due to his fear of or respect
for the asker. Therefore, even asking once could lead to a violation of *lo
sachmod.*

Consider the following all-too-common scenario:

Mindy arrived, huffing and puffing, at the door of the silver store, only to
find the owner locking up the shop. True, closing time was ten minutes
ago, but she just remembered that she must buy a gift for the wedding
she planned to attend that evening. Mindy implored the owner to reopen
just for a moment, and when he insisted that he was already late and had
to rush home, she practically got down on her knees to plead her case.
Grudgingly, he opened the door, and she made her purchase.

This too may constitute *lo sachmod.* At this moment the owner has
no interest in selling the item; he wants to go home. Certainly, we are
allowed to ask him politely to open his door to us. He might be more
than willing to get the unexpected business, despite the inconvenience.
But if we see that he is definitely not interested in making a sale at that

time, then according to some opinions, pressuring him is a violation of this *issur*. (*Mishpetei Hashalom* 12:8)

10 Teves	10 Iyar	10 Elul

Just One,   PLEADING WITH YOUR friend to give you something
Ple-e-ease …   as a gift when you know that he prefers not to do so
                     is also a violation of this *issur*. Scenarios of this kind
begin in earliest childhood — "Please, please give me a lick/a few potato
chips/a chance on your new bike …," and continue in various forms to
adulthood — "Just one cigarette — come on, you don't mind, do you?"
or, "Please, you must sign on this permit so I can build out on our building's shared courtyard — you just have to do it."

When an uninvited guest imposes himself on a host who does not
have sufficient means to provide for that guest, in some cases this can
fall under the same category.

A *chassan* who exerts pressure on his future father-in-law to provide
him with gifts beyond what was agreed on at the *tena'im* is similarly
guilty of coveting. (On the other hand, at the point of negotiations before the *tena'im* agreement is finalized, each side is entitled to pressure
and persuade, just as in any financial negotiation.)

In a case where *halachah* would *require* the owner to give or sell the
item (even if it is a Rabbinical requirement exhorting him to act *lifnim
mishuras hadin*, such as if someone is selling property and is expected to
give the first chance at buying it to the neighbor who owns an adjacent
unit, who might wish to expand his home), we are permitted to plead,
pressure or use any other reasonable means to force the owner to do
what is required of him. (*Mishpetei Hashalom* 12:9–10)

Who Is   THE MITZVOS OF *lo tisaveh* and *lo sachmod* apply in all
Obligated   places and at all times, to men and women. The prohibi-
                   tion is desiring something that belongs to men or women,
to someone who is physically or mentally challenged, and even to
children. However, no *issur* is violated when we desire something that
belongs to an *akum*.

We are required to train our children in these *mitzvos* from their

youth. It is not sufficient to tell them, "Keep your eyes out of your sister's plate," or, "You don't have to get a prize just because your brother did." Rather, a parent should give his child the tools to overcome the tendency to desire, such as by repeating often, "In our home, everyone gets just what he/she needs," or, "Hashem knows what is best for each one of us. If someone else has it, it wasn't meant for me." (*Mishpetei Hashalom* 12:2–3)

11 Teves	11 Iyar	11 Elul

The Green-Eyed Monster   THE UNDERLYING FLAW that leads a person to desire something that belongs to another and to take measures to acquire it is *kinah* — envy. According to the letter of the law, feeling envious of another's possessions does not constitute a violation of either of the two *mitzvos* we have been discussing, as long as we have not begun to map out strategies and have not taken action or spoken up in order to acquire the item. Nevertheless, the *middah* of envy is considered very crass and should be assiduously avoided.

Chazal tell us how destructive envy can be: "When a person has his eye on what is not his, then even what is his will be taken away from him." The Torah offers many examples of people who experienced this principle: Kayin, Korach, Bilam, Haman and others.

The envious person is truly unfortunate: "His entire life is pain, and he will never be happy" (*Sotah* 9). One extreme illustration is the classic parable of a royal minister who was extremely envious of his fellow minister. One day, the king generously offered to give him anything he asked for — but the king would give his companion twice as much. After much thought, the minister finally asked that the king gouge out one of his eyes…

Were it not for envy, a person would be able to manage with only the minimum requirements of food, clothing and living accommodations. People in our generation have become rather obsessed with "keeping up with the Joneses" — exerting themselves physically and emotionally to gain a lifestyle based on society's superficial and extravagant standards. Eliminating this nonconstructive trait would greatly enhance the true quality of our lives.

Therefore, even if envy is not an actual violation of either of these _mitzvos_, _middas chassidus_ would demand that we work on ourselves to avoid even _wanting_ someone else's possessions, even if that desire is not accompanied by any thought or action to acquire it. (_Mishpetei Hashalom_ 12:11)

In summary: The _mitzvos_ of _lo tisaveh_ and _lo sachmod_ forbid us to desire another Jew's possessions and to take measures to acquire them. The _issur_ applies whether we are pressuring another person to sell the items to us when he is not interested in selling, or whether we are pleading with him to give something to us as a gift. If the item is for sale, pressuring the seller to reduce the price is considered normal negotiation techniques and is permissible. The root of these violations is the _middah_ of envy, which is a very destructive trait that should be carefully avoided.

"_Envy, desire and [pursuit of] honor remove a person from this world_" (_Avos_ 4:21).

"_Who is wealthy? One who is satisfied with his lot_" (ibid. 4:1).

⇜ 18 ⇝

אחיך, רעך, בני עמך, עמיתך

Your Brother, Your Friend,
a Member of Your People,
Your Equal

12 Teves	12 Iyar	12 Elul

A Brother Remains Nat — once Nosson — was caught off guard when
a Brother his cousin Dovid tapped him on the shoulder at the
bus stop. Ever since Nat had left *yeshivah*, moved
out of his parents' house and thrown aside all traces of his *Yiddishkeit*, he
had not seen any of his cousins, but he was sure he knew exactly what
they thought of him.

"Nosson, I haven't seen you in months! What a nice surprise!" Dovid said
with a friendly smile.

"Cut the act, Dovid," Nat said with a bitter half-smile. "I'm not one of you
anymore and you know it. I don't look like you, I don't think like you, and
I'm free of the endless list of obligations that the rest of you have. So don't
pretend otherwise. Just forget I ever existed and leave me alone."

"Listen to me," Dovid said urgently, as he pulled his cousin over to a
quiet spot. "I don't sanction what you've done and where you've gone.
But remember one thing: Once a Jew, always a Jew. On the one hand,
that means that you aren't free of your obligations, you're just evading
them, and you'll have to answer for them. But it also means that the door

176

is always open for you to come back, because a brother remains a brother, no matter what. Remember that — we'll always be here waiting…"

SOMEONE WHO IS born a Jew remains a Jew for the duration of his life, no matter how he conducts that life. Even if he does not observe Torah and _mitzvos_, even if he constantly and deliberately commits serious transgressions, even if he turns his back on his nation and rebels against them by becoming an informer or a nonbeliever and drawing others into sin, even if he converts to a different religion — none of these affects his identity. He remains a Jew and is responsible for all the _mitzvos_ that obligate all his fellow Jews. (_Mishpetei Hashalom_ 18: Introduction)

13 Teves	13 Iyar	13 Elul

Privileges within While strolling through their new neighborhood,
a Deserving Max Smith and his wife Gloria noticed a small sign
Community outside a fenced-in estate: "Association of Volunteers — Golden Country Club." Listed below the name were a number of interesting activities and attractive privileges the association offered.

"Let's go in and see for ourselves what goes on there," Gloria suggested. "Maybe I'll sign up for one of those trips or enroll in some classes."

"Don't you see what it says at the bottom of the sign?" Max pointed to some small print that read, "For Members Only."

"That's not fair. Why should I be excluded? Why can't I benefit from all the special privileges too?" Gloria was indignant. "This is such discrimination!"

"Gloria, you can't call this discrimination. This is a club for dedicated community volunteers. If you want to be eligible for all those activities, you have to devote yourself to community work and prove yourself as a volunteer, and then you'll be able to become a member and can enjoy the privileges. Nobody's stopping you. Go ahead and earn your privileges!"

MANY OF THE _mitzvos_ that guide our interpersonal relationships are mentioned in the Torah as being relevant toward _achicha_ (your brother), _rei'acha_ (your friend), and _amecha_ or _amisecha_ (a member of your

nation). *Chazal* deduce from this choice of terms that these *mitzvos* are obligatory only toward Jews who are "your brother/your friend/with you — in observing Torah and *mitzvos*." These *mitzvos* represent an elevated level of conduct, beyond the norm, which is a privilege reserved for those who have, through their dedication to Torah observance, proven themselves eligible for membership in the "club." Toward others, we are expected to conduct ourselves only in a normally polite and civil manner, sometimes bestowing on them "club" privileges as necessary to avoid their feeling deprived and to avoid arousing enmity.

This apparently "preferential treatment" cannot be perceived as racism or discrimination, since membership in the "club" is actually open to all. This privileged society is composed of the many individuals who have chosen to live their lives according to the Torah's rules and to behave toward each other with high social standards. Any Jew may be part of this group and will be treated with the same standards, provided he or she acts like the members of the group and lives up to the same responsibilities.

On the other hand, someone who voluntarily abandons these practices relinquishes his privileges, of his own will, and automatically excludes himself from the "club." In that case, the remaining members no longer need to relate to him with these superior rules of social conduct.

Membership in this society is not based on a common genetic strain, either, since a gentile may at any time convert sincerely to Judaism through the accepted *halachic* procedures. Once he attaches himself to the "society" by adopting their Torah standards, a convert will be accepted as a full-fledged Jew and granted all the elite privileges inherent in the Torah network of personal relationships.

Another consideration in relating with those outside the "club" is the need to keep a safe distance from people with negative traits, so as to avoid being influenced by their actions or becoming a victim of their unprincipled practices. Obviously, there are many levels of people who have deserted Torah practice, and there are many *mitzvos* that have individual categories and specific details of their own. Therefore, we must be careful not to make generalizations based on the *halachah* in any specific case. (*Mishpetei Hashalom* 18: Introduction)

Our Relationship to Akum   THE WORD *"AKUM,"* used often in the course of this book, is actually an abbreviation of the Hebrew words *"ovdei cochavim umazalos"* — worshippers of stars and constellations. In its literal sense the term refers to idol-worshippers, whose bizarre conduct — often including the sacrifice of their own children to their gods — earned them our deep repulsion. As we have mentioned in connection with many *mitzvos* discussed in the book, *akum* are generally excluded from the interpersonal obligations Jews have toward other Jews; for instance, we don't have to give them free loans, and we may take interest that they've agreed to pay — although we certainly may not steal from them.

Nevertheless, in many cases we are still obligated to act toward *akum* in accordance with some of these *mitzvos* — such as visiting their sick, burying their dead, and so on — as a manifestation of good character traits, and also in order to preserve peace and to protect ourselves from their hostilities. Even if the *akum* is in a lowly position at present, it is not wise to antagonize him, since "there is no man who does not have his moment" (*Avos*, 4:3); he may later rise to power, and the anger we roused in him in the past will crouch within, awaiting an opportunity for revenge.

The Jewish people are a tiny nation among many enemies — "a sheep amid seventy wolves" — and it is always wise to avoid crossing the wolves' path, even if the sheep is awake now and the wolves are sleeping. Therefore, even if the *halachah* may permit us to act in certain ways against the *akum*, Rabbi Yehuda HaNasi advises us as a general rule always to choose the path "that is a credit for himself and will earn him people's esteem" (*Avos* 2:1).

Many Torah authors throughout the generations would write in the prefaces to their books that wherever terms such as *akum*, *goy* and *nochri* appear in their writings, they definitely do not refer to the gentiles of their country, who are so kind to their Jewish residents, but rather to wicked gentiles of earlier generations, such as Pharaoh, Haman and Antiochus, the Crusaders and the members of the Inquisition, who treated the Jews with terrible cruelty. (According to many opinions, however, these declarations were forced upon these authors by the censorship authorities of their generation. Nowadays, in our modern world that champions freedom of expression, there are those who feel that there is no need for sensitivity in our use of language, which they perceive to be a form of censorship. The author of this work feels otherwise, since much negative criticism may be triggered by being politically incorrect, undiplomatic, or simply tactless.)

In the course of this chapter we will try to clarify the rules and regulations of when the higher social standards of *mitzvos bein adam lechaveiro* need not be applied, as well as the rationale for this apparent "discrimination," mentioning many points we have cited earlier. In doing so, we will provide definitions for terms like *achicha*, *bnei amecha* and *amisecha*, and their negative counterparts — *min*, *apikorus*, *akum*, *meisis* and *mumar*. (*Mishpetei Hashalom* 18: Introduction)

15 Teves	15 Iyar	15 Elul

A Jew Forever, but ... AS WE MENTIONED at the opening of this chapter, a non-Jew can convert and become a Jew at any time, by acceptance of the *mitzvos*, immersion in a *mikveh* in the presence of a three-member *beis din* and, for a male, having a *bris milah*. However, a Jew can never become a non-Jew. "A Jew — even if he sinned — remains a Jew." This, as we said, is true even if he became a *mumar* or an *apikorus*, or even a *meisis* or an informer. As Yechezkel Hanavi prophesied, "What you are thinking — that you shall become like the nations ... worshipping wood and stones — shall not come to pass!" No Jew can shed his true identity. Thus, if someone who claims or acts in such a way as to show that he wishes to relinquish his identity as a Jew, performs an act of *kiddushin*, the woman is wed to him and would require a *get* — a *halachic* divorce — in order to remarry.

However, some *halachos* differ in their application to such a Jew: Meat *shechted* by him may not be considered kosher; his wine is considered *yayin nesech* (the wine of a non-Jew) and we may not drink it; he cannot be automatically included in a normal *eiruv chatzeiros*. We do not accept a *korban* from him, nor may he donate an object to a shul (although we may accept a donation of money from him). (*Mishpetei Hashalom* 18:1)

| 16 Teves | 16 Iyar | 16 Elul |

Definition of Terms WHAT IS A *mumar*? While generally translated as *convert to another religion*, the term *mumar* actually includes several subcategories:

▫ A ***mumar ledavar echad*** is someone who does not obey the Torah in respect to one particular *mitzvah*. He may do so *lehach'is* — for no other reason than to anger his Creator, or *letei'avon* — to satisfy his desires.

▫ A ***mumar letei'avon*** is someone who cannot control himself when he sees tasty food and eats it whether it is kosher or not, and similarly lacks control when encountering other physical or monetary temptations.

▫ A ***mumar lehach'is***, when given a choice between two equivalent foods, one kosher and one nonkosher, intentionally and knowingly chooses the nonkosher one. Some say that even if he has no conscious intention of defying Hashem but simply does not care what he chooses, he would still be considered a *mumar lehach'is*.

A step beyond the *mumar* are the categories of people who have not only defied Hashem but actually denied Him and His Torah, to varying degrees:

▫ An ***apikorus*** is defined in various ways, among them: A Jew who denies the Torah or prophecy (Rambam); one who denies Hashem's communication with humans, denies the prophecy of Moshe Rabbeinu or denies Hashem's knowledge of human activities (Rabbeinu Nissim); one who treats a *talmid chacham* — or someone else, in the presence of a *talmid chacham* — contemptuously (Beis Yosef).

▫ ***Kofrim*** are those who deny the origin of the Torah or the existence of Hashem. The term is often translated as *atheists* or *agnostics*.

- *Minim* are heretics, Jewish apostates who have adopted another religion, or clerics of other religions.
- *Malshinim* are informers, who betray Jews or the property of Jews to authorities who will deal with them in ways that are not in accordance with Jewish law.
- *Meisisim* are those who attempt to persuade Jews to leave their religion for another religion.
- *Meshumadim* are apostates, who live like adherents of another religion, abandoning the Torah entirely. (*Mishpetei Hashalom* 18:1, 4)

| 17 Teves | 17 Iyar | 17 Elul |

Privileges Denied THE *RASHA* WHO has not yet done *teshuvah* is treated differently from other Jews in regard to certain aspects of *gemilas chessed*, which are the "privileges of the club" — reserved for "your brother in Torah and *mitzvos*." Some examples would be in the application of our obligations: to save his life and return his lost property; to lend him money; to refrain from taking interest on loans to him; to provide him with *tzedakah* or medical assistance; to offer help in loading and unloading his donkey; and to ransom him from captors. The Torah demands that we exert ourselves to extend these privileges only to those who observe Torah and *mitzvos*, not to those who have chosen to reject the Torah and have excluded themselves from the common soul of the Jewish people. In any case, as we have mentioned, we are obliged to keep a safe distance from sinners so as not to be influenced by them.

For the same reasons, we are not obligated to apply many of the other *mitzvos bein adam lechaveiro* to those who violate Hashem's Will. However, the details vary from case to case, based on the way *Chazal* interpreted the related *pesukim* and the *halachos* derived from the understanding of these *pesukim*, and as we have cited in the relevant chapters of this book. For example: there is no obligation to judge a known *rasha* righteously (chapter 1); it is permissible, and in fact a *mitzvah*, to despise the *rasha* (chapter 2); there is no prohibition of *nekimah* or *netirah* against them (chapter 3); we may quarrel with them (chapter 5); some authorities permit striking them (chapter 7) and cursing them (chapter 8), as well as hurting them with words (chapter 9); there is no obligation to rescue them (chapter 11); in many cases we do not have to rebuke them (chapter 12); nor must we love them (Volume II, chapter 22); and in many cases, the laws forbidding *lashon hara* and *rechilus* are not applicable in regard to them (Volume II, chapter 28).

However, since there are so many fine distinctions between the *halachos* in each of these *mitzvos*, it is very important not to jump to conclusions and draw comparisons from one case to another. Each *mitzvah* must be learned separately, in all its details. For instance, in the case of judging righteously, the *halachah* states that when we see a person who is generally good doing what seems to be a sin, we must assume that his intentions are good, while in the case of a sinner, we assume he had malicious intentions in mind (see chapter 1). In this case, the latter *halachah* applies not only to an outright *rasha*, but even to someone for whom the majority of his actions are negative in the specific area in question.

In another example, when we say that the *mitzvah* of *lo sisna* — "Do not hate your brother" — does not apply toward a *rasha*, that would also include an otherwise righteous person whom we see committing one wrong act, but only after we have attempted without success to rebuke him; we would be permitted only revealed hatred in the heart but not hatred expressed in action. Similarly, according to some opinions, *ona'as devarim* is permitted not only toward outright *resha'im* but toward anyone who is not considered a *yerei Hashem*, even someone who commits just one transgression regularly. (*Mishpetei Hashalom* 18:2–3)

18 Teves	18 Iyar	18 Elul

Out of the Fold NO MATTER HOW deeply entrenched in *aveiros* a Jew is, he is always connected to the community of the Jewish people, even if only by a few threads, and the *halachos* that apply to him reflect that connection. However, once someone rejects Hashem and His Torah, he strains the last of these threads to the

breaking point. While he still remains a Jew, as we have stressed, the last vestiges of our human relationship with him dissipate, and none of the above *mitzvos* are applicable in regard to him.

The following are considered to have forfeited all rights to consideration as "brothers," "friends," "our people," and so on: the idol worshipper, or anyone who violates the *mitzvos lehach'is*; the denier of Torah and prophecy; the *min*, the *apikorus, malshinim, meisisim* and *meshumadim* (as defined earlier in this chapter).

In former times, when the *Sanhedrin* had sufficient power, these people were dealt with very severely, so much so, that it was permissible to act in ways that would bring about their deaths if an opportunity arose. When circumstances permitted, they were executed publicly, and when that was not possible, their deaths could be brought about through indirect means.

Nevertheless, throughout the generations, it was very rare for anyone to resort to implementing these powers. When Jews lost their judicial independence, these actions were stopped because of the danger it posed to Jewish lives and property.

Furthermore, the Chazon Ish writes that the practice of bringing about the death of these people was applicable only in earlier times, when Hashem's *hashgachah* was open and revealed, when miracles were common occurrences, and when we were worthy of being guided by a *Bas Kol*. At that time, everyone perceived clearly the breaches created by the *apikorsim* and recognized the fact that the devastating disasters and punishments in this world were consequences of such conduct.

However, today, when Hashem's providence is concealed and such a large segment of the Jewish population is weak in their *emunah*, taking action in this way would certainly not serve to heal the breach in community life. On the contrary, it would merely widen the rift, since most people would see such actions as nothing more than brutality and violence.

Therefore, since this approach is no longer effective or practical, it is our duty to draw these sinners back to Torah observance with "cords of love" and to enlighten them to the truth through whatever means possible. (*Mishpetei Hashalom* 18:4–5)

Various Categories of Sinners ONE CATEGORY OF sinners is comprised of those who are habitual transgressors of a specific sin, although they do not do so *lehach'is*. The classic example cited in the sources is that of the "*ro'ei beheimah dakah*" — keepers of sheep and goats in settled regions of Eretz Yisrael in the times of the Mishnah — who were known to graze their flocks on other people's fields and thus were constantly guilty of *gezel*. Such people were certainly not executed. At the same time, because of their constant sinning, they are excluded from the title of *amisecha* in regard to our obligations to help them out financially with loans or *tzedakah*, to provide them with medical assistance, and to return their lost property. However, if they are taken captive we are obligated to ransom them. The Chasam Sofer points out that this *halachah* is not referring to someone who commits the same sin two or three times over, but to individuals who base their *parnasah* on their transgression and therefore are unlikely to repent.

A separate category is the *mumar letei'avon*, who does not sin all the time but is sometimes overcome by his passions and succumbs to sin to satisfy his desires, such as for a nonkosher item of food, yet he believes in all the thirteen fundamental principles of faith. He is dealt with more leniently: We are obligated to save him from danger and come to his assistance, as well as to return his lost object. If he is taken captive, we may — and according to some opinions we *must* — redeem him. When lending him money, the prohibition to take interest is in full effect.

On the other hand, we relate to a *mumar lehach'is*, who intentionally chooses the prohibited option just to anger his Creator, in a much more severe manner: We are prohibited from returning his lost object (and the same is true for the *apikorus*, the idolator and one who is *mechallel Shabbos* publicly); nor are we permitted to ransom him if he is taken captive, or to support him with *tzedakah*. Some opinions maintain that we may lend him money with interest, as may be done to an *akum*. Others disagree, explaining that the Torah excused us from doing the *mitzvos* toward the *mumar lehach'is* himself but did not give us the liberty to do as we wish with his money, since there is always the possibility that he will have a son who will return to *Yiddishkeit*, and we do not want to deprive that heir of the money he could inherit. In any case, we are not permitted to borrow from him with interest, because he is still obliged to keep all the *mitzvos*.

In regard to the various sects that broke away from full Torah observance, the same *halachos* apply to *Kusim* (Samaritans of ancient times) as those that apply to the *mumar* who has converted to another religion. *Kara'im* (Karaites), however, are not treated as *mumarim*; both lending and borrowing from them with interest is prohibited.

The Rambam writes that anyone who believes that there is one G-d, but maintains that He has a body and form, is considered a *min*. The Ra'avad disagrees with this assertion, saying that "many greater and better than he have fallen into this error, having been misled by their interpretation of *pesukim* and *aggados* in their literal meaning, which confused their understanding."

An *avaryan* — a sinner who disregards a community resolution or who commits *aveiros* — even serious ones — *letei'avon*, may still be included as part of a *minyan* of ten for any *davar shebikdushah* (such as for reciting Kaddish), except for a *mezuman* for *bentching*, so as to avoid close association with him.

But a *mumar*, who has left his religion, or one who is publicly *mechallel Shabbos*, as well as one who denies Torah *shebe'al peh*, is treated like an *akum* and is not eligible to be counted toward a *minyan*. (*Mishpetei Hashalom* 18:6–12, 15)

20 Teves	20 Iyar	20 Elul

The "Lost Children" A PERSON WHO was taken captive by *akum* as a small child and grows up knowing nothing of Judaism, as well as someone who was born to a Jewish mother and a non-Jewish father and was not brought up as a Jewish child, falls into the category of *tinok shenishba* — the "captured" child — and is related to with much more lenience than the adult who left Torah of his own will. We may not charge interest or pay interest to a *tinok shenishba*.

Based on this premise, the Chazon Ish maintained that any Jew who was denied a Jewish education, and therefore does not appreciate the seriousness of an *aveirah* — as long as we have not made a sufficient effort to inform him of his heritage — should be treated as a Jew in every respect, including admitting him as a partner in an *eiruv* and permitting his *shechitah*. Although he is sinning, he is considered to be doing so as an *anoos*, one acting under duress, having never had the opportunity to learn otherwise.

However, the Chazon Ish concludes, once such a person has been exposed to the Torah and adequate efforts have been made to persuade him to observe it, to the degree deemed by *beis din* to be sufficient, and he still does not adopt a Torah way of life, he may be treated as a *meizid* — an intentional sinner. An example would be someone who was raised in an antireligious secular environment but was exposed to proper religious training in some form.

Since we do not find this distinction in the rulings of earlier authorities, some *poskim* differ with the conclusion of the Chazon Ish, even in respect to recent immigrants from Communist countries, who would certainly not have been held responsible for sinning in their ignorance of Torah under the antireligious rule of their former country. However, after such an immigrant has lived in Eretz Yisrael for some time, and was approached by religious elements there to persuade him to adopt a Torah way of life, his status may change. When such a case arises in practice, a qualified *posek* should be consulted.

Similarly, the *poskim* discuss whether Jews who are *mechallel Shabbos* in America should be considered *tinokos shenishbu*, since their grandparents came to a spiritual wasteland, and their violation of Shabbos never stemmed from an intentional rejection of the fundamentals of *emunah* but rather from a lack of knowledge. The *poskim* also differentiate between the members of Reform congregations, most of whom grew up with a distorted religious framework drilled into them from childhood, and would therefore be considered *tinokos shenishbu*, as opposed to the early leaders of the Reform movement, who knew what true *Yiddishkeit* was and intentionally abandoned it or twisted it out of its original form. Another question that has been raised relates to the Conservative movement, whose adherents are more aware of their Judaism and should know better, a circumstance that might render them more responsible for their violations. Regarding Jews whose status as *avaryanim* is unclear, a Rav should be consulted when questions arise regarding such matters as our conduct toward them and their qualification to give testimony.

Keep Your Distance CHAZAL ADVISED US: "Stay away from a bad neighbor, and do not associate with a *rasha*" (*Avos* 1:7). We should not associate closely with such people for the purpose of a business partnership, nor even with the intent of drawing him to Torah or for the purpose of working on a *mitzvah*-project together, because association brings with it the risk of learning from his ways.

Various aspects of our relationships to sinners have been addressed in chapter 15, on flattery, and in chapter 9, where we discussed reasons to try to bring them back to the Torah path. In Volume II, chapter 33, we will discuss the opposite side of the coin — the positive effects of associating with *talmidei chachamim*. (*Mishpetei Hashalom* 18:13–14, 16)

In summary: A Jew remains a Jew, no matter how distant his conduct is from Torah observance. However, once he leaves the Torah way, he is no longer eligible to receive all the privileges that are part of the special conduct of the *mitzvos bein adam lechaveiro*. Therefore, depending on the category into which his sins place him, we may not be obligated to refrain from revenge, hate and other prohibitions, and we may also be exempt from loving him, judging him favorably and other similar *mitzvos*. However, each *mitzvah* has its own details that must be studied carefully. The *minim*, *apikorsim* and others who deny Hashem and his Torah are excluded completely from our brotherly relationship in regard to these *mitzvos*, and they may not be counted toward a *minyan*. The *tinok shenishba*, who is considered an *anoos*, falls into a different category, and is treated as a Jew in every respect.

מדבר שקר תרחק
Avoiding Falsehood

Seal of
Hashem

"Late again, Dov Ber? Did you bring a note?" the rebbe demanded sternly. It was the third time that week, and the rebbe was fed up.

"Uh, my mother wasn't home. That's why I overslept. She, uh, was with my grandmother in the hospital all night," Dov Ber said softly.

"Hmmm… Sorry to hear that," the rebbe responded, looking a bit skeptical. "Well, we all wish your grandmother a *refuah sheleimah*. Now go to your seat quickly and find the place."

At the first recess, Dov Ber's friend, Shmaya, rushed over to him and asked, "When did your grandmother get sick? What's wrong with her? I just saw her at your house on Shabbos!"

Dov Ber looked around to make sure the rebbe was not in sight, then whispered, "Actually, my grandmother is fine. My mother told me yesterday that she refused to write me another late note, so I had to make up something."

"You mean you lied to the rebbe?" Shmaya was aghast.

"I didn't really lie. I just stretched the truth a little. Do you know what he would have done to me if I had told him what really happened? He'd have sent me straight to the principal's office to get a punishment. Then my mother would have had a fit, and if my grandmother had heard about

189

it, she might have fainted and ended up in the hospital, *chas veshalom*, and then my mother would really have had to spend the night there. So you see, it was a *mitzvah* to say what I said, and it wasn't so far from the truth."

"I don't know, Dov Ber, it sounds a lot like a lie to me..."

A POWERFUL KING carries with him a signet ring with the royal seal at all times. Once an edict is stamped with that seal, it is as good as done. Hashem, the King of all Kings, also has His personal stamp, so to speak. His seal is *emes* — Truth — and with that stamp He created the world. When we adhere to the *emes* and strive to become men of truth, we become partners in building Hashem's world.

When we begin the moral education of our young children, one of the first lessons we instill in them is the imperative that one must speak the truth and avoid falsehood. At the same time, we introduce them to a number of areas in the Torah that would, on the surface, appear to contradict that message: Avraham Avinu tells his wife, "Say you are my sister ... so that I shall live in your merit." Yehudah blatantly tells the "viceroy of the king" that Binyamin's brother died, when he had every reason to believe that Yosef was still alive.

Interestingly, we rarely find our innocent children asking, "How can it be that our *Avos* lied?" This is because their intrinsic purity of heart and clarity of spirit enables them to sense the simple truth — that in certain cases we are permitted to alter the facts in order to prevent others from hurting us or taking what is rightfully ours (as in the case of Yaakov's acquiring the birthright that was inherently his); this is not considered falsehood.

However, as children grow older they begin to apply these concepts to other situations independently. At times, they are *morah heter* — give themselves dispensation — in cases that do not justify bending the facts, often as a result of social influence. When they do so repeatedly, this occasional habit can become second nature to them. This results in great confusion, in both directions, with some people allowing themselves prohibited liberties and others prohibiting things that are permissible; either of these choices is contrary to Hashem's Will.

One of the major reasons for this perversion of the proper balance in this area is a dearth of knowledge on the subject, since the details of this topic are scattered throughout the Gemara and *poskim*. Therefore, in this and the next two chapters we hope to bring these *halachos* together into one organized body that will enable the reader to locate the relevant *din* easily, if only to know when to bring his question to a competent Rav.

22 Teves	22 Iyar	22 Elul

The Liar — Banished from Hashem's Presence CHAZAL TELL US (*Shabbos* 149) that someone whose words veer from the truth is not allowed to enter the environs of Hashem. They derive this from the incident involving the spirit of Navos, whom Achav had executed unjustly. Navos wished to go back to Earth and bring about Achav's downfall by bringing false inspiration to the self-proclaimed prophets of Baal, whom Achav consulted. Hashem tells him, "*Tzei!* — Get out of here!" *Chazal* learn from this particular response that since Navos was a speaker of falsehood, Hashem told him to "get out" — to leave His Presence.

The *Sefer Hachinuch* writes that there is nothing more disgusting than falsehood; it is the cause of many of the diseases and curses in this world. *Chazal* say that someone who speaks a distortion of truth is like an idol worshipper. *Chazal* also count liars among the four groups of people who cannot receive the *Shechinah* (*Sotah* 42).

The Chazon Ish, in his work *Emunah Ubitachon*, explains that a person who says an untruth *occasionally* retains his basic human form though it is tainted by sin. But someone who makes a habit of lying adopts the form of a *shakran* — a liar — and his human aspect is nullified.

The World to Come is known also as the World of Truth. It is understandable, therefore, that people whose essence is falsehood have no place there. The core of our reward in the World to Come is the opportunity to receive the *Shechinah* and enter Hashem's inner circle; the thought that we may be banished from this everlasting reward is terrifying!

When a person dies and is brought before the Heavenly Tribunal to be judged, one of the first questions he is asked is, "Did you conduct your business honestly?" (*Shabbos* 31). Whatever he may have gained by his falsehood — he loses many times over. Furthermore, David Hamelech warns us that "Men of bloodshed and deceit shall not live out half their days" (*Tehillim* 55:24). (*Emes Kenei*, Introduction)

23 Teves	23 Iyar	23 Elul

Virtues of the Speaker of Truth THE *ORCHOS TZADDIKIM* tells us that when someone accustoms himself not only to speak truth but even to think only thoughts of truth, then at night he will be shown visions of truth and will have glimpses of the future in the manner of the angels. The *Sefer Chassidim* goes even further and says that when a person always speaks the truth, without saying or even thinking a word of *sheker*, then whatever he says shall come about — he decrees below and Hashem carries it out from Above.

So why doesn't everyone adhere to the truth? The Me'iri explains metaphorically that "The truth is heavy; therefore, its bearers are few" (*Me'iri*, *Avos* 4:14). Moreover, in this world we see how the *resha'im* seem to succeed in life with their falsehood. We do not yet see the actualization of the *passuk* (*Mishlei* 12:19), "The lips of truth shall be established forever, but a lying tongue is just for a moment"; falsehood has no lasting existence at all.

When trying to acquire friends, some people make the mistake of using falsehood and prohibited *chanufah* — flattery. They don't realize that when a person speaks honestly and means what he says, he is loved much more than the smooth talker who is always trying to charm others with insincere accolades (Gra on *Mishlei* 28:23).

Rabbenu Bachyai points out that the Torah is referred to as *emes*, as we say, "*Emes kenei ve'al timkor* — Acquire truth and do not sell it away." David Hamelech said (*Tehillim* 119), "*Rosh devarecha emes* — Your very first utterance is truth." The Me'iri points out that one of the outstanding signs in the character of a *talmid chacham* is that he does not alter the truth. (*Emes Kenei*, Introduction)

A Delicate Topic ONE OF THE foundations of our *emunah* is the knowledge that our ancestors did not lie to us. This is in stark contrast to the leaders and fathers of other religions, who fed their followers mistruths and then suffered the inevitable consequence — that even when they said the truth, no one believed them.

Therefore, it is extremely important for us to examine carefully all the places mentioned in *Tanach* and in the Gemara where our ancestors spoke in ways that seemed to veer from the truth for one reason or another, and to understand how these principles apply to us. The problem, as we have mentioned, is that when discussing *sheker leto'eles* — constructive, justified distortions of the truth — the chances of misapplying the principles involved are great. On the other hand, if we don't study the topic at all, the ostensible stringencies that we adopt may turn into unwarranted leniencies.

Consequently, we chose to follow the directive of the Gemara (*Bava Basra* 89), citing the incident in which Rabbi Yochanan ben Zakai struggles with the dilemma, "I am in trouble if I speak and I am in trouble if I do not speak," and concludes that "Hashem's ways are straight; *tzaddikim* shall walk in them and sinners shall stumble in them."

We will present the principles as clearly as possible in the hope that the reader will "walk in them" — derive from them the proper *halachah* or learn when to ask a Rav for guidance, with a prayer that we will not, *chas veshalom*, be the cause of error. (*Emes Kenei*, Introduction)

24 Teves	24 Iyar	24 Elul

True or False "Mina, the van is outside and all your friends are getting on already," ten-year-old Benny said urgently to his sister, who was standing in front of the mirror for what was in his opinion a bit too much time.

"Oh, no, if I miss the van I'll never be able to get to the wedding," Mina said, panicking. She grabbed her brush and her bag and ran down the steps, nearly tripping on the way. When she got outside she saw one friend and no van. "What, they left already?"

> "Of course not. We're the first ones here," her friend Bella reassured her.
>
> "But Benny said ..."
>
> "I made it up. I said it so you would hurry," Benny piped up from behind her, rather proud of himself. "Otherwise you would have been standing by that mirror until after your friend finished her *sheva brachos*."
>
> "Oh, Benny, you're impossible. But seriously," Mina said with great feeling, taking her younger brother off to the side, "much as I want to get to this wedding, I would rather miss the van than have you say words that aren't true. Please, don't ever, ever do that again!"

FOR THE TORAH'S injunction not to speak *sheker* — falsehood — unique phrasing is used: "*Midevar sheker tirchak* — Stay far away from falsehood" (*Shemos* 23:7). Apparently, the Torah did not find it sufficient to use the more common wording of "*Tishamer* — Guard yourself." When it comes to *sheker*, we have to keep a great distance and flee from every trace of falsehood. *Sheker* is regarded as something repulsive, leading us to steer clear of anything related to it.

Therefore, when a person speaks words of *sheker* he violates this positive *mitzvah*, even if he merely includes some falsehood in a true report, and even if the words are literally true but their implication is false, as we shall see later in this chapter. Although some authorities stipulate that the Torah prohibition of *Midevar sheker tirchak* is limited to testimony in *beis din*, many authorities expand the Torah *issur* to include any *sheker* that causes harm to another person.

The prohibitions that relate to this *mitzvah* are applicable to men and women, in all places and at all times. Adults should accustom children from a young age to say only the truth. When the Vilna Gaon left his home, he instructed his wife to punish his children mainly if they veered from the truth. Naturally, at a young age children may find it difficult to draw the line between truth and imagination, and we might hear them report stories that have little to do with reality as if they had actually happened. This is to be expected and is generally a stage that they will outgrow. However, when the child show signs of intentionally misrepresenting the truth for his own benefit, it is crucial that his parents set him straight. (*Emes Kenei* 1:1–2, 11)

25 Teves   25 Iyar   25 Elul

What Is   NOT ONLY IS speaking *sheker* prohibited; we are also not
Included?   permitted to voluntarily and willingly lend an ear to words
we know to be false, or even to a report whose truth is
questionable.

Sheker includes saying things that can be construed in two different
ways, when our intention is to mislead others into believing the false
interpretation of our words. The only time this may be permissible is in
a case where we are allowed to bend the truth for the sake of peace, as
we shall discuss in chapter 20.

Similarly, if we say things that are true but deliberately omit crucial
details so that the report will be taken in a false manner, this too is
considered *sheker*, even though the words we uttered were absolutely
correct. The classic example of this tactic is the person who tells his
friend, "I read in the *Shulchan Aruch* that 'It is prohibited to learn or
daven'" — but leaves out the final words of the text, "... in a place where
there is a bad odor."

Even if we do not utter a word, but the falsehood emerges from our
actions or body language, this is a violation of the *issur*. Certainly, writing falsehood is no less reprehensible than saying it. We may not even
mislead others through our silence. Relating true facts, but mentioning
them out of context, is another common violation of this *issur*.

Nor may we cause others to lie. Rabbi Shimon ben Shetach alerted
us to this danger when he said regarding a *beis din*, "Interrogate the witnesses extensively, and be careful with your words, lest they learn to lie"
(*Avos* 1:9). If the interrogator does not invest a great deal of thought into
his every word, the direction of his questioning may give the witness
an idea for how to fabricate his testimony. Although Rabbi Shimon was
speaking about the possibility of giving false testimony, no doubt this
warning extends to distancing ourselves from causing any type of *sheker*.
For example, when we "interrogate" our children regarding an incident
in which they may have been at fault, it is vital to encourage them to tell
the truth without fear of extreme punishment, so that our questioning
should not lead them to lie in order to cover up their misdeed.

A number of authorities maintain that it is *middas chassidus* — a worthy level — to refrain from saying things that aren't true, even as a joke, if what we say might possibly mislead someone. However, when our purpose is purely to cheer people up and bring smiles to their faces, and no one is being misled by our words, there would seem to be no *issur* at all.

Some people who strive to achieve lofty levels of personal stature are careful to avoid *sheker* even in their thoughts. This is certainly a valuable effort, since, as is well known, one's deeds are drawn after one's heart, and if we do not even entertain thoughts of falsehood, we are not likely to slip into saying or doing things that are contrary to the truth. In addition, as we have mentioned, a person whose thoughts are *emes* achieves lofty levels of vision and endows his words with great power. (*Emes Kenei* 1:3–10)

26 Teves	26 Iyar	26 Elul

Other Related Prohibitions NOT ONLY DOES the Torah prohibit saying an outright lie, it also obligates us to avoid anything that may cause or strengthen falsehood. In many cases these violations will constitute a transgression of other related *issurim*, depending on the circumstances:

- When a person wrongly denies that he was entrusted with an item for safekeeping or as collateral, or denies that he owes a debt, or denies that he owes payment to a worker, he violates the *issur* of *Lo sechachashu velo seshakru ish ba'amiso* — "do not deny falsely and do not lie to one another" (*Vayikra* 19:11).

- A person who gives false testimony violates both the *issur* of *lo sa'aneh berei'acha eid shaker* — "do not bear false witness against your friend" (*Shemos* 20:13) and the *issur* of *lo sisa sheima shav* — "do not bear a false report" (*Shemos* 23:1).

- Dishonesty and deceit in business transactions and partnerships are a violation of *lo sonu ish es achiv* — "one man should not defraud his brother" (*Vayikra* 25:14). The relevant *halachos* on this subject are elaborated fully in *Shas* and *poskim*.

▫ Even when the falsehood in itself is not a direct cause of imme-diate damage and loss to someone else but may be an indirect cause of future damage — such as when Reuven falsely presents himself as a faithful friend to Shimon so that Shimon will not be wary of him and Reuven will be able to cause Shimon harm at a later point — this is considered to be in the category of "Lips of falsehood are an abomination to Hashem" (*Mishlei* 22:12) and "I despised the perverse mouth" (ibid. 8:13).

▫ When someone uses falsehood or deceitful words to prevent some good thing from reaching someone else, or to redirect to himself a gift or benefit of some kind, which was on its way to another person who in fact deserved it, *Chazal* say of him, "Someone who distorts his words is considered as if he worshipped idols." Included in this *issur* would be to claim falsely that one is interested in buying a house or business that another person has plans of purchasing, so that the other party will "buy him off" with a gift.

According to Rabbeinu Yonah, all of the above examples of false-hood are prohibited even for justifiable reasons, such as altering the truth for the sake of peace (see chapter 20). Other authorities distin-guish between those that are violations of explicit Torah prohibitions and those that are not. (*Emes Kenei* 2:1–4, 6–8)

27 Teves	27 Iyar	27 Elul

Honesty — the Only Policy IN THE EXAMPLES cited here, the falsehood is a cause of damage, either immediate or delayed. However, even when a person makes up stories or alters reports that he hears, for no particular personal benefit and without causing a loss to anyone else, he is still considered a liar. His punishment will be lighter, however, since he did not harm anyone. On the other hand, in one way his transgression is more profound, since he demonstrates an affinity for falsehood without the "excuse" of motives of self-interest. In any case, his love for falsehood may well lead him at some point to bear false testimony or to violate one of the other transgressions we have listed above.

Therefore, we should be careful to make sure every word that leaves our mouth, is absolutely, unequivocally true. We should not say "I will do …" or "I will not do such and such" without adding the phrase *bli neder* — "without the obligation of a vow." Otherwise, if, despite the best of intentions, we do not carry out what we said, we may be guilty of violating *midevar sheker tirchak*.

Similarly, if we owe someone money, we should not tell him, "Come back tomorrow, and then I'll pay you" if we know that we won't be able to pay him the next day either. However, if we know that by making the statement we will feel obligated to make a genuine effort to do what we said we would, or if we say, "I will try to have the money ready tomorrow," that would likely be permissible. (*Emes Kenei* 1:9, 11–16)

> ***No Matter to*** "Uncle Reuven, did you bring me a lollipop?" little Sara'le
> ***Whom*** asked in her sweet, appealing voice.
>
> "Oh, I'm sorry, sweetie. My pockets are empty today. I'll bring you one tomorrow, all right?" Reuven apologized.
>
> "Thank you, Uncle!" Sara'le answered graciously, skipping happily out to the porch.
>
> "Reuven, how could you tell her that? You know you're leaving to go to *Eretz Yisrael* tonight, and you can't bring her anything tomorrow," Mrs. Schwartz, Reuven's older sister, chided him.
>
> "Ah, come on, she's just a kid, practically a baby. She won't even remember what I said," Reuven said, brushing aside her concern.
>
> "I'm not one to teach you *halachah*, my *talmid-chacham* brother, but if I'm not mistaken, a lie is a lie, even when it's said to a four-year-old …"

THE *ISSUR* TO lie is no different whether the lie is told to a man or a woman, an adult or a child, a Jew or a non-Jew. As long as a misleading falsehood is expressed by the deeds or words emanating from a pure Jewish mouth, it is considered a violation of the *issur* in all cases. In fact, some say that we have to be even more careful not to lie to a child than to an adult, since, as *Chazal* warn us, a child who has been lied to will learn to lie to others.

Regarding a non-Jew, there is no basis for making an exception and permitting the speaking of a falsehood to him, since the *issur* is in having an untruth leave our lips — no matter to whom it is directed. Even those authorities who are lenient regarding our obligation to correct an inadvertent wrong done to an *akum* agree that intentional deceit is forbidden. In addition to the basic prohibition, there is also the risk of a *chillul Hashem* in the event that the falsehood is discovered. (*Emes Kenei*, 1:17)

28 Teves	28 Iyar	28 Elul

A Manner of Speaking THE MAIN ADVANTAGE man has over the animal world is his ability to communicate with others through the gift of speech with which Hashem endowed him. Through speech we form bonds with other people, since it enables us to reveal facts and intentions to others through the words we say, using the "local spoken language" — that which is understood by the people around us and is appropriate to the situation.

As we have mentioned, saying something true, but out of context, can lead to falsehood; at the same time, saying things that would appear inaccurate, but in the right context, may assume the character of *emes*. The benchmark is whether or not the goal and effect of our speech is to mislead other people.

When we say "local spoken language," we refer not only to languages such as English, Russian or Yiddish. The "spoken language" involves one's manner of speaking as well, as we will see. Some of these styles of speech may appear to veer from the truth, but since they are the accepted mode of communication, they are not considered *sheker*. (*Emes Kenei*, 6:1)

Exaggeration and Euphemism THE DEFINITION OF *guzma* — exaggeration — is saying something that is not accurate, but saying it without intending to lie; this mode of speech is common in the spoken language. Exaggeration is generally not used with the intention to mislead others and does not constitute a violation of the *issur* of *sheker*; it is simply a manner of expressing oneself. When a housewife tells her husband hysterically that "there are millions of ants in the pantry," she is certainly not intentionally and methodically distorting the truth; nor is the frustrated secretary who tells her boss

that she tried to place his call a thousand times and keeps getting an answering machine. We find *lashon guzma* used in the Torah, *Nevi'im*, Mishnah and Gemara, where it was deemed necessary; in most cases, no one is being misled by this and it is not included in the category of prohibited falsehood.

Similarly, we find in our primary sources that *lashon sagi nahor* — euphemistic language — is used in order to avoid saying something unpleasant; this is absolutely permitted for us as well. Another example of acceptable inaccuracy is the practice of being *toleh kilelaso ba'acheirim* — saying something negative in a way that implies that it will happen to someone else, not to ourselves.

It is both permitted and a *mitzvah* to use *lishna ma'alya* — elevated language, that is, to say things that are not so honorable in a more respectable manner. For example, whenever Iyov talks about cursing Hashem, *chas veshalom*, he uses the opposite term — *mevareich es Hashem* — "blessing Hashem."

When speaking with friends and students in a loving way, it is fully permissible to address them as "brothers" or "children." A common related term is when children call a friend of the family "Uncle" even though he is not a blood-relative at all. This is not *sheker*; it is but simply a manner of speaking. (*Emes Kenei*, 6:2–4)

29 Teves	29 Iyar	29 Elul

Business Language "Rabbi Levine, this is Moshe Rosenberg. I am looking into a *bachur* for a *shidduch*, and I understand that he is a *talmid* of yours."

"Glad to be of assistance, Reb Moshe," Rabbi Levine replied. "Which *bachur* are you referring to?"

"His name is Berel Lerner, and he should be about twenty-two years old," Mr. Rosenberg said.

"Ah, my dear *talmid* Berel!" Rabbi Levine proceeded with a five-minute soliloquy on the virtues of the Lerner boy, concluding with a definitive statement, "One of the best boys in the yeshivah."

After the phone call was concluded, Esther Levine couldn't help commenting to her husband, "I like Berel as much as you do, but I didn't think

you considered him among the top few boys in the yeshivah."

"Look, Esther, I've discussed *shidduchim* with Moshe Rosenberg in the past. I have to talk to this individual in the style that he'll understand — otherwise I'll be misunderstood. In his society, it's taken for granted that everyone greatly exaggerates when describing candidates for *shidduchim*. If I would state the facts as they are — that Berel is a good boy who sits and learns as he should and understands the *shiur* well, Moshe would interpret it to mean that the boy is mediocre, gets by with the minimum and barely follows what the *maggid shiur* says. In order to give him a proper picture, I have to exaggerate each of the *bachur*'s virtues and call him a 'top boy.' Then, when Reb Moshe takes everything down a notch, he'll have the right picture."

A MANNER OF speech commonly used by salesmen is to say that they will not budge from a certain price, or that they have other people who are willing to pay this price, in order to pressure the customer to close the deal. Salesmen who use these and other phrases in business dealings do not violate the *issur* of *sheker, as long as this is the prevalent mode of speech in their society* and everyone knows what they really mean. An example would be in the marketplaces in some cultures, where haggling is the rule, not the exception.

This principle can be applied to many everyday situations: If we are using a common manner of speaking and it is clear that we are not misleading anyone, since the listener understands our intent, there is no violation of *sheker*. For example, a certain Rosh Yeshivah once told an older *bachur* that if he gives his accurate age in *shidduchim* he is guilty of *sheker*, because the practice of taking off a few years is so well accepted in that particular yeshivah that the listener will surely "add back the difference," resulting in his mistakenly assuming the *bachur* to be older than he really is.

Another example would be when security authorities at the airport ask, "Do you have anything with you that you did not pack yourself, or that someone else gave you?" The authorities are rightfully concerned for terrorist activity or narcotics smuggling and do not want the passenger to accept packages from strangers. However, it is understood that they are clearly not referring to items given to the flyer by close relatives and friends whom he knows very well. Security personnel have no interest

in hearing small details about which you are totally confident — if they did, they would not be able to complete their work on time. Therefore, it would not be *sheker* to answer *no* to that question, even if one is carrying in his suitcase letters and packages given to him by such people. (*Emes Kenei*, 6:7)

1 Shvat	1 Sivan	1 Tishrei

Stories and Speeches
EVEN THOUGH THE *issur* of *sheker* includes written falsehoods, the writer of books, articles or pamphlets who wants to conceal his identity may use a pen name if that is common practice in his place and time. However, the author may not add a title to his name — such as "Doctor" or "Rosh Yeshivah" — in order to deceive his readers, and he certainly should not do so where the work contains medical or rabbinical content.

We are allowed to use a fictional story as a *mashal* — a parable — to enable us to illustrate a point — the *nimshal* — in a clear manner or to instill *yiras Shamayim* in the listeners, as we find in *Tanach* and in the words of *Chazal*. However, we should be careful to make it clear that the story is just a *mashal*, or we should say something like, "The story goes …" to emphasize that it is not a true story.

It is common practice for speakers to exaggerate in praising, for instance, their host, or a *chassan* and *kallah*, and also when eulogizing a *niftar*. Also, a speaker will often open his speech with words of assumed humility — "Who am I to stand and speak before such an honored assemblage?" At times the speaker will pretend to laugh or cry, as necessary, to accentuate his words. It would appear that there is no *issur* violated in any of these cases, as long as he does not go beyond the accepted standards for that place and time. (*Emes Kenei*, 5:10, 16)

A Man of Truth
AS WE HAVE said, *emes* is a concept that goes far beyond "reporting the facts." In business transactions the Torah requires us to follow certain guidelines absolutely, to avoid *geneivas da'as* (see chapter 21), *gezel* and other such *issurim*. In addition to these guidelines, however, the Torah expects us to strive for a higher

level of *emes* and imposes certain sanctions on those who follow the letter of the law yet ignore its spirit. The concepts of *mi shepara, hin tzedek* and *mechusar amana* are broad areas with many relevant *dinim*. Application of these *dinim* on a practical level are complex and remain the scope of an expert *dayan*. We will merely summarize the general idea behind each of these terms.

- *Mi shepara*: The major factor concluding a business transaction is the actual *kinyan*, acquisition, wherein the item is removed from the ownership of the seller and transferred to the ownership of the buyer. For movable property, according to Torah law, once the buyer gives money to the seller — even a portion of the full price — this is considered a transaction even though the article has not changed hands. *Chazal* stipulated that the buyer or seller can still back out until there has been a *kinyan hara'ui*, a suitable form of acquisition, and the item has actually changed hands, but they stress that this is not proper practice. Someone who backs out after putting down some money toward the transaction is cursed in *beis din* with the formula of "*Mi shepara* … — He Who punished the generation of the Flood … will punish the one who does not keep his word."

  Certain factors may permit backing out of the deal without being subject to "*Mi shepara*" — for example, if the item was damaged between the time of the transaction and the *kinyan*, or if a messenger carried out the transaction and was negligent in his duty, causing a loss to the one who sent him.

2 Shvat	2 Sivan	2 Tishrei

- *Hin Tzedek*: *Chazal* learn from the *passuk*, "*Hin tzedek yihyeh lachem*—You shall have correct measures" (*Vayikra* 19:36): "Your *hein* — 'yes' — should be a sincere 'yes' and your *lav*—'no' — should be a sincere 'no'." In other words, we should not say something without meaning it. When we "speak out" a transaction, even when there has been no *kinyan* nor even an exchange of money, we should have in mind to follow through on the words

that we have uttered. If a person has no such intention when he speaks, then even if he has second thoughts later and carries out his words, he will not have cleared himself of the violation of *hin tzedek* until he has specifically repented for his insincere or misleading speech.

◻ *Mechusar Amana*: Not only are we expected to mean what we say; as men of truth we are also expected to follow through on our words. When someone closes a transaction, even when there has been no *kinyan* and no exchange of money, and even if at the time, he intended to carry out the agreement, if he afterward regrets his words and withdraws from the transaction, he is called a *mechusar amana* — one who lacks integrity. The *Chachamim* strongly disapprove of such practice.

Keeping Our Word THE CONCEPT OF keeping our word even when there is no *kinyan* to obligate us has many applications. We will enumerate just a few:

◻ **Gift** — If we tell a friend we will give him a small gift, or even if we promise to give him a large gift or to do him a favor, or if we state publicly that we plan to do so, we should carry out our word, even though, according to the letter of the law, the gift has not yet become the recipient's property and ostensibly one ought to be able to back out of his commitment to give it.

◻ **Honor** — If the father of a baby tells a certain *mohel* that he wants him to perform the *bris* for his son, or if he tells a particular *kohen* that he intends to redeem his firstborn from him, then although it is not prohibited for him to back out, the *Chachamim* disapprove of such practice, and we may even call him a *rasha* for doing so.

In certain cases, backing out of a deal is a more serious violation. For example, when we tell a poor person that we will give him a donation, this is considered a *neder* — a vow to do a *mitzvah* — and if we backed out it would be considered a violation of "*Lo yachel devaro*" — nullifying a vow.

In summary: *Emes* is the seal of Hashem. People who speak *sheker* are considered very lowly, and speakers of truth reach lofty levels. The Torah tells us to keep a distance from all types of falsehood. This includes saying things that will mislead our listeners — saying things that are false, omitting relevant details, implying falsehood by our body language, and reporting true facts out of context. The *issur* applies to men and women, and toward Jews and non-Jews, adults and children. Certain modes of speech that sound untruthful are actually permitted as the accepted spoken language — such as exaggeration and euphemisms. The Torah expects us to be honest and reliable in our transactions, beyond the letter of the law, as seen by the concepts of *mi shepara*, *hin tzedek* and *mechusar amana*.

"Therefore love the truth and peace" (Zechariah 8:19).

אמת ואת לבבות

20

שקר לתועלת
Sheker Leto'eles

3 Shvat	*3 Sivan*	*3 Tishrei*

For a Constructive Purpose

"Am I glad that's over with!" Tzivia collapsed into the undersized chair with a sigh of relief. "Now I can start sleeping again. I've been so nervous about this model lesson, I haven't slept well in days!"

"You were great, Tzivia," Mimi assured her. "Those second-graders were hanging on to your every word."

"Were they really?" Tzivia smiled. "I was too nervous to even notice. What did you think of the lesson, Yehudis?"

"You repeated yourself a lot, and looked at your paper too much. The girls in front listened, but the ones in back were fooling around. You should have walked around while you spoke. And you forgot all about having an exciting introduction and a summary at the end." Yehudis rattled off her answer without even pausing to take a breath.

"Oh. Thanks for your opinion." Tzivia's smile disappeared, and she quickly retreated from the classroom.

"Yehudis, how could you say that?" Mimi was appalled.

"She asked my opinion, so I told her the truth," Yehudis replied, unmoved by Mimi's reaction. "I always tell the truth. I can't stand anything that smacks of *sheker.* Admit it — wasn't everything I said true?"

AS WE NOTED earlier, it is forbidden to say words that are true in a manner that will strengthen *sheker* — such as by making a statement that is true but that omits an important detail. By the same token, there are times when we are permitted and even obligated to say words that appear false, and we are prohibited from saying the truth, when the purpose is to restore the ultimate *emes* to its rightful place. As we shall see, this principle does not in any way contradict what we have said thus far about the importance of uttering only the truth; It does, however, require us to gain a deeper understanding of what constitutes *emes*.

Many people have a very simplistic view of truth; they think that *emes* means always stating the facts as they occurred, and *sheker* means veering in our report from what really took place. At times, however, saying things as they are will not have positive repercussions but will, rather, have a destructive effect. If the outcome is bad, one's words are considered falsehood. On the other hand, there are times when what appears ostensibly to be *sheker* will lead to an outcome of good and of fulfillment of Hashem's Will — and that is considered *emes*. The cases in which we are told to bend the truth are those situations where saying the unembellished truth is in fact a lowly act.

The concept of permitting *issurim bein adam lechaveiro* — prohibitions in interpersonal matters — for a constructive purpose is not new to us. We have devoted an entire chapter to the area of *lashon hara leto'eles*, which is justified when a number of conditions have been met. When circumstances permit speaking up, within the constraints of *halachah*, that speaking is not considered *lashon hara*. The same applies in the area of *emes* and *sheker*. When *halachah* permits — or obligates — us to speak words that appear false, they are no longer considered *sheker* at all.

Rav Yaakov Kaminetzky gives a telling example to prove this point: Reuven is running away from Shimon, who wishes to harm him, and he finds refuge in Levi's house. When Shimon comes banging at Levi's door, and Levi, in his "pious honesty," tells him the truth — that Reuven is in the attic — enabling Shimon to carry out his evil intent, Levi's words are not *emes*. Though the words are true in the simple sense, the outcome demonstrates the *sheker* of uttering those words.

Certainly, there are times when there is no choice but to follow the principle of "*im ikesh tispatal* — with the crooked, act deceptively" — as Yaakov Avinu did with Esav to obtain the *brachos* that were rightfully

his, and as Yaakov's sons did when dealing with Shechem. These deeds in no way detract from our forefathers' righteousness or from their inner quality of *emes*.

Two benchmarks for determining whether something is *emes* or *sheker* are the outcome and the intention. If the outcome of our words is evil, then the means by which we achieved that end is considered *sheker*, and vice versa. As the Maharal writes, if it is the proper thing to do, it is inherently *emes*.

Our intentions also determine the status of our words and deeds. Rav Shlomo Wolbe writes that even *lashon hara* that includes only true facts is considered "*sheima shav*," a false report, since our evil intention in reporting it renders it *sheker*.

Needless to say, this is not meant to give anyone carte blanche to lie when it is convenient, with the excuse that "our intentions are good." Specific guidelines, which we shall present here, determine when veering from the apparent truth is permitted or even required. Beyond that, we are fully obligated by the requirement to allow no word of *sheker* to leave our lips. It should be stressed that where a *beis din* is concerned, no *sheker* whatsoever is justified. The *beis din* is in partnership with Hashem in creating and upholding the world. The seal of *emes* must be an inherent characteristic of the *beis din*, as it is of the Creator. (*Emes Kenei* 4:1)

4 Shvat	4 Sivan	4 Tishrei

For the Sake of Peace A PRIMARY EXAMPLE of our broader understanding of *emes* and *sheker* lies in the principle that "we alter the facts for the sake of peace." The first application we see of this principle is when Hashem Himself reported to Avraham Avinu that his wife, Sarah, said, "I am old," when what she actually said was, "My master [Avraham] is old," in order to prevent any traces of antagonism that Avraham's hearing her actual statement might have aroused.

We know that the stamp of Hashem is *emes*, and upon that foundation He created the world. How then could He have spoken *sheker*? According to the definition we cited above, we understand that though Hashem did not report Sarah's words as she said them, He did not veer from the *emes*, because the essence of *emes* is to uphold the purpose of

the world — and one aspect of this purpose is peace. When doing so requires an altering of facts, that change is not a violation of *midvar sheker tirchak*; the changed facts themselves become the *emes*.

Peace is a supreme value in Torah. We are permitted and even obligated to deviate from the facts or to embellish them for the sake of preserving peace. Doing so is permitted not only to restore peace when *machlokes* exists, but even to maintain peace when matters are still stable, if our intent is to prevent a possible outbreak of antagonism.

This principle applies not only to the person who is directly involved in the *machlokes*, but also to anyone who may have some influence in defusing it. Aharon Hakohen, for example, would go to each of the parties involved in a *machlokes* and report to him — with little or no basis — that the other side was overcome with shame for having initiated the disagreement and was interested in pursuing peace. His efforts would result in bringing the two parties back together. (*Emes Kenei* 4:2)

Praising the Kallah AT A WEDDING, when the *kallah* is not at all pretty or when she has some defect — for example, if she is lame or blind, *Chazal* instruct us to sing her praises to the *chassan*, declaring how beautiful and charming she is, even attributing to her virtues that she does not possess at all. Note, however, that this is the *halachah* once the two are married, in order to endear the *kallah* to her husband and to promote peace. When we are asked for information about someone for the purpose of a *shidduch*, we need to answer in accordance with the intricate details of the *halachos* outlined in Volume II, chapters 30–31, sometimes remaining silent regarding shortcomings, sometimes volunteering information even if not asked, and sometimes reporting a flaw only if specifically asked about it.

Regarding a widow, or, according to some authorities, anyone who is having a difficult time finding a *shidduch*, we are allowed to imply that we are interested in a *shidduch* with her or to say that she is our relative, in order to get other people interested in her as a *shidduch*-prospect. Here, too, however, we need to know when it is necessary to reveal a flaw, based on our obligation of *lo saamod al dam rei'echa*, and when we are required to remain silent. In many cases, especially when dealing with someone who is having a difficult time finding a *shidduch*, the

advice of a Rav should be sought to rule on these complex issues. (*Emes Kenei* 4:3, 9)

| 5 Shvat | 5 Sivan | 5 Tishrei |

Other Cases Justifying Alteration of the Facts

"Faigie, Shuly — what do you think of this outfit I just picked up at the clearance sale? You wouldn't believe what a bargain it was!" Mindy seemed quite pleased with her purchase as she pulled the outfit out of the bag to show her friends.

"Why in the world did—" Shuly's response was cut short by Faigie's elbow jabbing her unceremoniously in the rib.

"Mindy, you are some shopper! How do you always manage to find such special bargains? What a pretty color, and such a unique pattern! Wear it well," Faigie wished her heartily before continuing on her way, pulling Shuly away with her.

"Faigie, how could you bring yourself to speak so nicely about such an ugly, outdated *shmatteh*?" Shuly said when they were at a safe distance. "I'm surprised at you! You're always so careful to be honest and open."

"Shuly, you know these clearance sales have a no-return policy. Whatever you buy, you keep. So what would be the point of telling her what's wrong with it? She won't be able to bring it back, and she'll just kick herself for making a bad choice. Besides, I didn't really lie; I just focused on the nicer aspects of the suit, that's all."

"I guess you have a point there. I never thought of it that way," Shuly admitted.

WHEN SOMEONE MAKES a bad purchase, and there is no option of returning it, we should praise it even before the buyer asks us our opinion, in order to make him feel good about his purchase. Naturally, if someone has been deceived in a manner that would entitle him to reimbursement, and he is able to exercise that right and reclaim his money, there is no justification for altering the facts; we should be open with him and help him retrieve his money.

Chazal say that as a general rule, we should always try to get along well with people and speak positively of them and their possessions, even when the virtues we speak of do not exist. However, some authorities specify that we should use vague language that can be construed in two ways, as opposed to saying something that is not anchored in reality at all.

Thus, for example, if someone has a homely child, we can tell him in clear conscience, "What a beautiful baby," since every child is beautiful to his parents, and by saying so we bring the mother and father immeasurable pleasure.

We are also allowed to lie in order to raise the spirits of someone who is depressed and feeling downtrodden. For example, if a friend failed a test, we may say, "I know how you feel; I once got an even lower grade after studying for weeks," even if the facts are not quite accurate, since "a sorrow shared is a sorrow halved." Or, when comforting someone who has suffered a financial disaster, we might tell him, "I once went bankrupt too, and I was in even worse straits," even if our experience was not really that bad.

When we are given the unpleasant task of giving someone bad news, such as reporting to him that a loved one has passed away, we may alter the facts to cushion the blow, as Rabbi Meir's wife Bruriah did when revealing to her husband news of the tragic deaths of their two sons. When they passed away on Shabbos, Bruriah made excuses for their absence and did not tell her husband the truth until after Shabbos.

6 Shvat	6 Sivan	6 Tishrei

Another situation where we would be permitted to lie would be to save another person from shame. For example, we may admit to something we did not do in order to take the blame in place of someone else, or at least imply that we too were involved in the misdeed, so as to minimize the embarrassment of those who are actually guilty. This tactic is commonly applied in giving *tochachah*, when the speaker will often choose to include himself in the reprehensible behavior he is decrying, since the listeners are more apt to accept words of rebuke when the speaker presents it as if he too is guilty of the same fault.

At times, distinguished individuals who suffer from poverty are ashamed to accept *tzedakah*, although they are in desperate need of help. Under certain conditions we would be permitted to say things that are not true in order to provide such a person with a respectable

livelihood. For example, we might write a letter in which we inform the individual that he has been awarded a special grant for his Torah achievements from a nonexistent organization that we have conjured up, since he will be more likely to accept financial assistance in the guise of such a scholarship. (*Emes Kenei* 4:4–8)

When a Talmid Chacham Bends the Truth CHAZAL TELL US that *talmidei chachamim* who would never lie under ordinary circumstances are still expected to "bend the truth" in three areas, and these are considered legitimate distortions: in learning, in private matters, and in matters relating to hosts and their guests. The *poskim* imply that ignorant people are also allowed to lie in these three areas.

In Matters of Learning IN MATTERS OF learning there are several interpretations, all of which have their own practical differences, as follows:

◻ **Humility:** When asked if he knows a particular *masechta*, where there is no particular necessity involved, he may alter the truth and say, "I don't know," or "I haven't learned that," although he really knows it. This is considered a sign of humility. Similarly, a person who is fasting a voluntary fast and does not want to flaunt his piety may conceal that fact when asked if he has eaten. Humility, though often exhibited through masking the facts, is a quality well-rooted in the World of Truth.

◻ **Shame:** When asked if we are involved in a particular *masechta*, we are allowed to say that we are learning a different one, in order to avoid being asked questions in learning that might put us on the spot and cause us embarrassment. Certainly we would be permitted to alter the truth in order to save someone else from such embarrassment.

7 Shvat	7 Sivan	7 Tishrei

Even though we learn in *Pirkei Avos* (5:7) that there is a distinct virtue in a Rav's admitting when he has made a mistake and not

hesitating to retract a statement he has made previously, this refers to a case where a practical *halachah* is involved. However, when there is no relevant *halachah* at stake, some authorities hold that he would be permitted to conceal his error to save himself from shame.

Included in this area would be allowing a *baal teshuvah* to bend the truth regarding his past in order to spare himself embarrassment, though according to some authorities, this prerogative is limited to sins that he did not do publicly.

❑ **To avoid an unnecessary interruption:** When we do not have time to respond to someone's questions, or when we are concerned that the interruptions will distract us from our concentration, and we are afraid that telling the truth will offend the other person, we are allowed to tell an untruth in order to avoid the disturbance.

Some authorities rule that this *heter* applies in all cases where we are not obligated to do something for another person, and they maintain that we would be allowed to alter the facts in order to gracefully evade the issue without hurting anyone. For example, if we are rushing to catch a bus and someone stops us to ask if we have a pen, according to this opinion we would be allowed to say "No" even if we do have a pen, if we know that telling the person openly and abruptly, "I can't, I'm in a hurry," is likely to insult him, and stopping to explain politely, "My bus is about to leave…" is likely to result in our missing it.

The same would apply, according to this opinion, if someone comes to the house and we do not want to deal with him at that time, for whatever reason. In such a case, the person answering the door would be allowed to say, "He's not here," or, better yet — "He'll be here later," since we are not obligated to deal with the person, nor are we obligated to tell him what we are doing that prevents us from inviting him in. Admitting that we are home and making excuses for our unavailability might be perceived as an insult — "What? Whatever he is doing is more important than my needs?!" Therefore, altering the facts in this case is actually for the sake of peace and is not considered lying. Of course, if someone owes another person money or a service, or if for some

other reason he is obligated to speak to the person, this *heter* does not apply and he may not use it to avoid fulfilling his obligation.

We should be careful not to use this *heter* in front of a child, since he will not understand the nuances involved, and, not being able to differentiate between one situation and another, he may jump to the wrong conclusions and learn to lie. (The same care should be taken in speaking *lashon hara* for a permitted, constructive purpose when there are children within earshot, for the same reason.)

In a similar case, when someone suggests a *shidduch* that does not appeal to us, we are allowed to say that we are busy with another *shidduch*, even if that is not the case, when saying outright that the suggestion does not interest us may cause hard feelings.

▫ **To avoid misunderstandings:** If we are afraid that when we answer the question posed to us, the asker will not fully understand our response, we are permitted to evade the question and say, "I don't know," even when we know the answer very well. (*Emes Kenei* 4:10–11, 13–15, 33)

8 Shvat	8 Sivan	8 Tishrei

In Matters of Privacy WHEN ASKED ABOUT private matters that are not meant to become public information, it is commendable to alter the facts and is an application of the quality of *tznius*, modesty. Thus, for example, if one is asked if his wife is expecting, he need not respond truthfully. Similarly, if a *bachur* is going to meet someone for a *shidduch* and does not wish to speak about it publicly, he may say that he is going elsewhere, for the sake of *tznius*.

If a woman had a miscarriage and afterward gave birth to a baby boy, when asked about the *pidyon haben* (which will not take place because the child is not considered a firstborn), she may alter the truth and claim to be the daughter of a *kohen* or a *levi*, in which case her child would not need a *pidyon haben*, in order to protect her privacy regarding the miscarriage.

Disclosing personal conversations between spouses to outsiders is a breach of *tznius* and a lack of *derech eretz*. Needless to say, matters that are private and intimate between a couple should not be anyone else's business. Certainly when pressed for such information, we should alter the truth to avoid answering. (*Emes Kenei* 4:21)

In Matters of Hospitality ◻ If we enjoy the hospitality of a generous and gracious host, we should certainly feel grateful and sing his praises, but only in a private milieu, or among people whom we know to be decent. If unscrupulous characters ask about our host, we should answer their queries by misrepresenting the facts and downplaying the host's goodwill, so that they will not take advantage of his good nature, though we should not go so far as to speak derogatorily about him. The same rule would apply regarding someone who gave us a loan or a large amount of *tzedakah*.

◻ Likewise, if we are guests in Reuven's home and someone asks us where we are staying, then if we know that the inquirer will also want to enjoy Reuven's hospitality, we can alter the facts and say, "I'm staying with Shimon," or with someone else, so as not to overburden Reuven.

◻ If someone presses us to find out how our host conducts himself in the relaxed privacy of his home, we should certainly not divulge any secrets or private matters, nor should we discuss his casual ways of relaxing, which he may prefer not to publicize, even if we need to lie to get out of doing so, since no one wants others to know his personal matters.

◻ If our host troubles himself in caring for our needs, we are permitted to bend the truth and say, "That isn't necessary, I've had enough to eat..." even if we have not had our fill, in order to spare him the trouble. Similarly, if someone wants to give us a ride, and we don't want to inconvenience him, we may alter the truth and say that we have to get to a place that is nearby, rather than troubling him to go out of his way to take us all the way to our true destination. By the same token, the driver who senses a passenger's discomfort may pretend that he needs to get to precisely the area his passenger needs and that he is not going out of his way at all.

◻ The host himself is also allowed to bend the truth for a good purpose. For example, if a guest has overstayed his welcome and the host's wife or children have had enough of him, the host might tell them that he owes this guest a great debt of gratitude, even if there is no basis for such a claim, or that the guest is a hidden *tzaddik* and it is a great honor to host him, even if that is a gross exaggeration. When a host notices that his guest senses there is not really enough food to spare for company, the host may say that there is plenty of food left in the kitchen, even if that is not the case, so that the guest will feel at ease eating his fill. (*Emes Kenei* 4:22–25)

| 9 Shvat | 9 Sivan | 9 Tishrei |

Bending the Truth to Prevent Loss AT TIMES, WE are permitted to lie in order to prevent others from causing us an unjustified monetary loss or other damage — for example, if others might create a situation in which our freedom of movement is limited. Therefore, we are allowed to alter the facts in order to obtain an exemption from taxes or other levies in a case where we are really eligible for the exemption and the authorities want to impose payment illegitimately.

Similarly, we may mark boxes of merchandise belonging to us with stickers reading "Danger" or "Glass" or "Government Property," in order to prevent others from mishandling them. For example, the *poskim* ruled that one may send a box of matzos by mail and mark it "Glass," so that the workers will treat it with care and the matzos won't break, if one is concerned that writing "Fragile" will not be sufficient.

It is permissible to deceive a swindler in order to save ourselves from his deception. Therefore, for example, if Reuven owes a hundred dollars to Shimon and is lax about repaying the debt, Shimon may offer to sell him an item at the price of a hundred dollars, and once Reuven gives him the payment, Shimon can say, "I accept the hundred dollars as payment of the loan, and I will keep the item."

In certain cases, when necessary, we can bait a swindler in order to catch him in the act of deception and hand him over to *beis din* for punishment, although a Rav should be consulted before carrying out such a plan, since the issue of *lifnei iveir* — causing others to sin — must be addressed.

If someone is compelled to sell land or merchandise against his will, he can make a *modaah*, a pronouncement in front of witnesses who understand his situation, stating that he is making the sale unwillingly. Then he may go ahead with the bogus sale in a normal fashion, and then, when he has the opportunity, he can retrieve his property through *beis din*. This is not considered *sheker*. However, since the details involved in such a case are complex, one should not utilize this tactic without first consulting a Rav.

Another case in which we may go back on our word without being guilty of *sheker* is when workers who have obligated themselves to complete a job at a set price wish to back out in the middle, causing us a loss. In such a case, the employer may pursuade them to finish the job by saying, "I'll pay you double," and then, when they have completed the work, he may pay them the original set price. Here, too, the *halachos* are complex and one should never go ahead with this tactic without discussing it with a Rav first. (*Emes Kenei* 4:27–32)

10 Shvat	10 Sivan	10 Tishrei

Lying to Prevent a Transgression
"Miriam, you must tell me what they were saying about me at your table," Tzipora said, cornering Miriam at the side of the dance floor. "It was about my upcoming divorce, wasn't it? I could see all those glances in my direction. Come on, if you're really my friend, you'll tell me every word they said!"

Miriam was at a loss. The moment she heard the direction the conversation at her table was taking, she had found an excuse to get up and move somewhere a safe distance away. Before she had a chance to leave, though, she had heard who the subject of the conversation was and who was leading the conversation, but she certainly wasn't going to reveal either of those facts to Tzipora and be guilty of first-class *rechilus*.

Suddenly, she had a brainstorm. She shrugged her shoulders apologetically and motioned wildly at her throat, putting on an excellent show of someone suffering from laryngitis.

"Oh, your throat again. What timing. I was counting on you to fill me in.

Too bad. I guess I'll find someone else to ask. At least I know you weren't talking about me...." Tzipora bought the act! What a relief!

WHEN PEOPLE WANT to prevent us from carrying out a *mitzvah* in the Torah, we are allowed to alter the truth if that will enable us to do the *mitzvah*. This applies not only to positive *mitzvos* but to Torah prohibitions as well. Therefore, if, for example, someone is trying to elicit from us *lashon hara* or *rechilus*, we may lie in order to prevent ourselves from transgressing the *issur*, even where there is no issue of preserving peace involved. The same is true regarding any *aveirah*, even a Rabbinically ordained *issur*. However, when it is possible to sidestep the problem by saying something ambiguous that can be construed in two ways, as opposed to saying an outright lie, that is always preferable.

For example, if someone offers us wine that we suspect is *stam yeinam*, forbidden wine, we may lie and say that we are fasting. When a certain *Gadol baTorah* used to be present at meals where the kashrus of the food was questionable, he would say, "My doctor doesn't allow me to eat these foods," having in mind the Rambam, who was a renowned physician besides being a great *halachic* authority.

If we know that others will make fun of us when they know we are keeping a certain *mitzvah*, we may conceal from them the *mitzvah* we are doing or even lie about it in order to enable ourselves to do the *mitzvah* without subjecting ourselves to their scorn.

We are allowed to alter the facts in order to guard someone else's secret, since revealing it would be a violation of an *issur*. Therefore, for instance, if we are privy to the fact that a friend is getting engaged, and he wants us to keep the news a secret, then if someone asks us about it, we should say, "I don't know" or "What are you talking about?" But if an elusive answer would be understood as a concession that the rumor is true, we may even say an outright lie in order to guard the secret.

When a Jew is obligated to perform a particular *mitzvah*, such as saving a life, performing *chalitzah* or giving a *get*, and he does not want to do it, we are permitted to lie to him and, for example, promise him a huge sum of money so that he will perform his obligation, and then afterward pay him no more than his expenses and the cost of his time.

Needless to say, when we want to save a Jew from transgressing an

issur, we are allowed to lie. Therefore, if a woman is chronically late in getting ready for Shabbos, her husband may tell her that Shabbos begins at an earlier time than it actually does. Similarly, we may set the clocks in the house for an earlier time, so that the men in the house will get up in time for *davening*. (*Emes Kenei* 4:35–39)

11 Shvat	11 Sivan	11 Tishrei

Lying to Prevent Damage or to Avoid Physical Danger IN A CASE of potential danger, we are permitted to alter the facts in order to protect ourselves. For example, if a person of suspicious character asks where we are going, we are allowed to respond with an incorrect destination, so as to avoid meeting up with him and suffering physical harm or robbery at his hands. Yaakov Avinu used such a tactic when he told Esav to go ahead of him and wait until he would get to Esav's land of Sei'ir (where he did not plan to arrive until the days of Moshiach). Even if the deception will be found out, there is no risk of *chillul Hashem* involved. On the contrary — such quick thinking demonstrates the cleverness of *talmidei chachamim*.

Similarly, if such a person asks us where we are staying, and we suspect that he harbors malicious motives, we can lie and say that we are staying elsewhere in order to save ourselves from danger or from possible damage. Certainly, if we suspect foul play, we may lie, even using Hashem's Name, if our life is endangered.

At times, a sick person — for example, one who has been overcome by hysteria — may need to be shaken up to cure him. If that is the case, we are allowed to invent some frightening report, such as saying that a snake is about to bite him, or that his enemy is nearby, in order to help him.

If we were told the simple formula of a particular medication, even if it was revealed to us on condition that we do not let the secret out, we are permitted to reveal it to the public, since in this case, keeping our word is actually *sheker*, while revealing it for the benefit of mankind is the essence of *emes*. (At the same time, in the case of a complex secret formula, we must make a serious effort not to cause undue loss to the inventor or patent holder, who may have invested enormous amounts of time, money and effort into his project, with the expectation of future

profits to compensate him for his investments.)

Although generally, we are expected to lie in a case where it would enable us to avoid danger to life, a Jew is not permitted to lie by stating explicitly that he is a gentile, even if this would enable him to save himself, since that would be equivalent to denying Hashem, and we are required to submit to death rather than to deny Hashem; in that way we exhibit our love for and belief in Hashem to the extent that we are willing to sacrifice our lives for it. If a Jew says that he is a gentile, it is considered *avazraihu de'avodah zarah* — something that closely resembles idolatry. Even though we have not actually shed our Jewish belief, since the understanding is that we would be killed if we did not accept their religion, merely identifying oneself as a non-Jew is tantamount to denying Hashem. However, some authorities challenge this stance and allow a Jew who is in danger to make such a statement without believing it, if that is the only way to escape death.

In any case, it is only the explicit declaration that is forbidden. In times of danger we are allowed to don gentile-style clothing, as long as we do not say, "I am a gentile." Also, we are permitted to make an ambiguous statement that would lead others to understand that we are gentile, when our true intent is an alternate interpretation of our words. Certainly we are allowed to mislead others so that they will reach this incorrect conclusion on their own. (*Emes Kenei* 4:42–43, 45–48)

| 12 Shvat | 12 Sivan | 12 Tishrei |

Lying in a Case
of Spiritual
Danger

IF A *RASHA* says words of wisdom that are true, and we are concerned that the masses will be misled and will flock to him, we are allowed to say that he is a liar and that his words are nothing but falsehood, in order to prevent people from falling into his clutches. It is also permitted to lie in order to make fun of a heretical philosopher, for the sake of ridiculing his arguments and degrading him, to reveal his infamy before his audience.

Lying is permitted in order to counter the words of a *rasha* or a *meisis* — an instigator of sin — or in order to prevent a *chillul Hashem*. If we are allowed to alter the facts to protect our own honor (as in the

case of private matters, or for the sake of peace), we certainly should do so for the sake of Hashem's honor.

One area in which bending the truth is not justified even for a spiritual purpose is in dealing with *kiruv rechokim* — drawing back to the fold those who are far from *Yiddishkeit*. Even when our intentions are lofty, such as to ease their way in accepting upon themselves full *mitzvah* observance, we may not lie and tell them that something prohibited is actually permitted. This is considered a display of the utmost insolence toward the Torah. Rather, we should give our warm support to these newcomers to Torah and encourage them to add to their *mitzvah*-observance gradually, little by little, according to their ability, until they are able to keep the entire Torah properly. (*Emes Kenei* 4:51, 54, 58)

Lying to Conceal IF SOMEONE'S LOVED one has passed away — even
Bad News a parent — and he is not aware of his loss, we do not have to tell him. It is even permissible to invite him to participate in a joyous occasion during the time when he has not been informed of his loss and would otherwise be in mourning. In fact, if someone takes the liberty of informing him unnecessarily, that person is considered a fool.

Nevertheless, if someone asks us directly about the well-being of his relatives, we are not allowed to lie and say they are alive, since that would be a violation of *midvar sheker tirchak*. But we can answer in an ambiguous manner, such as by saying, "I haven't seen them in a long time," or, "We need to *daven*."

However, in the case of a sick or elderly person whose health might be endangered if he hears the bad news, we are permitted and even required to actually lie and say that the relatives are fine, in order to shield him from a shock that could endanger his life. (*Emes Kenei* 5:8)

| 13 Shvat | 13 Sivan | 13 Tishrei |

Not a "Free AS WE MENTIONED earlier, the areas in which we are
for All" permitted or obligated to alter the facts are rather clearly defined in *halachah*. In all other cases we are required to adhere to the truth in the most basic sense — to state the facts as they

appear. Even when we are permitted to bend the truth, we are limited by certain constraints.

First of all, as we have mentioned, in any matters related to procedures in *beis din*, our obligation to adhere to the actual facts is much stricter, and no *heteirim* are applicable. Thus, even if our goal is to recover something that is rightfully ours from someone who took it from us without any justification, we are not allowed to do so by altering the facts in *beis din*, since this would constitute a distortion of the judicial process and a falsification of testimony in a monetary matter.

Secondly, according to some authorities, the *heter* of altering the facts even for the sake of preserving peace is indicated only for occasional use; we are not meant to make a habit of it; doing so could have a dire effect on our whole character. If that is the case when it comes to preserving peace, which is the primary *heter*, it certainly applies to the other situations we have mentioned.

Third, even when there is justification for lying, such as for the sake of peace, if we can achieve the same purpose in a different manner, we are required to attempt that before resorting to the *heter* of lying, even if that approach demands more effort on our part.

Fourth, some authorities maintain that an outright lie was never permitted, even for a constructive purpose; they rule that we are allowed only to use ambiguous language that can be construed in two ways. In practice, the *poskim* rule leniently and allow us to utilize an outright lie if necessary. Nevertheless, we are obligated to limit the falsehood as much as possible, avoiding explicit untruth whenever possible and opting for ambiguous language when that will do the trick.

It seems logical to assume that most of the *heteirim* we enumerated above do not apply to children, since they would not understand the fine points of distinction and would simply become accustomed to speaking *sheker*. (*Emes Kenei* 5:1, 3, 6–7, 9)

| 14 Shvat | 14 Sivan | 14 Tishrei |

Middas Chassidus — A Commendable Level

IN CONCLUSION, IT is highly commendable to make every effort not to lie at all, even in situations where doing so is permitted. In

this way we can strive for the elevated status of an *"ish emes"* — a man of truth. Also, if we find ourselves in a place where people are generally careful not to alter the facts at all, even where technically it would be permissible to do so, we should try to follow the custom of the town.

In any case, before going ahead with saying an untruth in any form, we should consider the matter carefully, several times over, before uttering a word, especially when our purpose is to save ourselves from damage or loss, or if we stand to gain personally from the untruth, since in such cases we are prone to err in our judgment.

When it comes to preserving peace, there is an *obligation* to veer from the facts, no matter where we are; *middas chassidus* does not apply when peace is at stake. When the fire of *machlokes* is raging, we should not seek ways to keep quiet or sidestep the matter, nor should we excuse ourselves with other occupations. We should not even maneuver our language to find an ambiguous term that can be interpreted in alternate ways. When a fire is raging, the only priority is to put it out as quickly as possible. Likewise, when a *machlokes* is heating up, we cannot take any chances by delaying the matter or tiptoeing warily around it, as this may allow the argument to mushroom to monstrous proportions. (*Emes Kenei* 5:10–12)

> **In summary:** While truth is a basic value, we see from *Tanach* that at times, facts were altered to protect someone from harm, or for other reasons, and this was not considered falsehood. In certain cases we too may be advised to "bend the truth" for a constructive purpose. In these cases, the altered report becomes the *emes*. A delicate balance is necessary in order to know when to apply such principles. Examples of cases when it would be permissible to tell an untruth include when it is necessary for the sake of peace, in matters of privacy, and regarding a host or guest. At times we may also bend the truth in order to prevent a loss, a transgression, physical or spiritual danger, and other negative outcomes. These *heteirim* do not indicate a "free for all"; they are greatly limited by various constraints and are absolutely taboo in the realm of *beis din*.

⚛ 21 ⚛

איסור גניבת דעת
Misrepresentation

| 15 Shvat | 15 Sivan | 15 Tishrei |

Say What You Mean, Mean What You Say

"Oh, Rina, I'm so thrilled to see you!" Shira interrupted her conversation with Penina to welcome her sister-in-law to Berel's bar mitzvah. "I've been waiting anxiously for you to get here. What an important guest — you've made my evening! Here, let me seat you with our cousins in this corner." Shira oozed smiles and compliments as she walked Rina over to the cousins' table. Then she returned to Penina to resume their discussion.

"The last I heard, you and Rina weren't exactly on speaking terms. I'm happy to see that you've made up," Penina said.

"Made up? Ha! I'm as upset with her as ever, if not more so. I know I shouldn't be speaking *lashon hara*, but you should know, I can't stand her!" Shira hissed.

"But ... but ... the way you were talking ... I was sure ..." Penina stuttered.

"So ... I was talking. I don't want to make a scene at the bar mitzvah, and besides, you know how rich they are; I want to make sure they write out a fat check for Berel. What I was saying has nothing to do with what I'm feeling. I'm a good actress, no?"

Yes, a good actress — if you were on stage, Penina thought to herself in

224

disgust. *But in real life, that kind of performance is not going to win you an award — just a reputation for* geneivas da'as....

ONE OF THE three categories of people whom Hashem despises is the one who is *echad bapeh ve'echad balev* — someone who says things that he does not feel in his heart. We are not allowed to speak in an insincere manner or in a smooth, manipulative way. Rather, what we show on the outside should reflect how we feel on the inside; our words should be a mirror of our heart.

If we mislead our friend, giving him the impression that we've done him a favor or spoken highly of him when we did not really do so, we are guilty of *geneivas da'as*. The *Peleh Yo'eitz* says that even showing excessive affection for our friend (beyond the polite minimum) when we do not feel such affection would be considered *geneivas da'as*. Yosef's brothers were praised for the fact that they did not make any pretense of loving Yosef by speaking to him in an affectionate manner. Since they disliked him, they chose not to say anything at all rather than to speak insincerely. We are not permitted to deceive anyone, Jew or non-Jew, when the *halachah* considers it *geneivas da'as*.

The *poskim* differ regarding the source of this *issur*, defining it as an offshoot of either *geneivah* — theft, *ona'ah* — cheating or hurting verbally, or *sheker* — falsehood. There is also some debate on the question of whether this *issur* is Torah-based or *mideRabbanan*, a Rabbinical injunction.

The *issur* of *geneivas da'as* may be violated without saying a single word; even if we mislead our fellow man through our deeds, or by remaining silent when we should have spoken up, we are guilty of transgressing this prohibition.

The *issur* of *geneivas da'as* applies to monetary matters as well, such as deceiving someone in a business exchange by concealing a defect in the item being sold — even in a case where the final price is not more than the accepted price for a defective item. The other area of *geneivas da'as* is verbal misrepresentation, such as giving a friend the impression that we are doing him a favor or that we are speaking up on his behalf when in fact we have not done so, so as to cause him to feel beholden to us without reason. (*Emes Kenei* 8:1–3, 21)

אסור גניבת דעת

Monetary Fraud MONETARY FRAUD INCLUDES the following situations:

- Selling — even to a non-Jew — nonkosher meat with the implication that it is kosher. This is prohibited even when the meat is a gift and there is no monetary exchange involved (details of this *halachah* will be explained later in this chapter), and according to some opinions, the prohibition of deceiving someone about the kashrus of a gift applies even when giving the gift to a non-Jew. However, we are allowed to advertise "low-cost meat" and sell it to a non-Jew as "bargain merchandise" without referring to its state of kashrus; if the buyer assumes that it is kosher, he has deluded himself. (Naturally, we must be careful that the non-Jew will not later sell the meat to a Jew, mistakenly telling him that it is kosher meat.)

- Concealing a defect in an item, even if we sell it at a lower-than-standard price that is in keeping with the value of the defective merchandise (as mentioned above). When we sell defective merchandise, including a house or car, we have to inform the potential buyer of the flaws even if we are planning to ask for a fair price that is reasonable for an item with that defect.

- Discount tickets: Certain bus companies offer a round-trip ticket at a rate that is much lower than the cost of two one-way tickets; or they may offer discounted multi-trip tickets, specifying that the tickets are nontransferable. If another person uses the ticket, then even though there may be a way of understanding it as not being actual *gezel*, since the trip *was* paid for, nevertheless, as long as the company does not specifically agree to the practice, it would certainly be considered *geneivas da'as*. The same would apply when a store features a sale in which the second item can be purchased at half price. If two people, each of whom wishes to buy one item, get together and have one person pay for the two items so as to obtain the discount, this may be considered *geneivas da'as* if the proprietor does not agree to the arrangement.

In certain similar cases, there may be an actual violation of *gezel* — for example, when Reuven buys a ticket for unlimited use of the local swimming pool for the month, and Shimon uses it; or when a service or privilege of some kind is granted to employees of a particular company, and a worker gives his identity card to a friend to use in his stead.

Certain privileges in the area of interpersonal relationships are reserved for the "club" of Torah Jews. Therefore, although we may not intentionally mislead even an *akum*, nevertheless, in a case where an unintentional omission is involved and the *akum* is not aware of it, in some cases we are not obligated to correct the error. For example, if we pay for an item and the owner, who is an *akum*, gives us too much change, and there is no chance that he will notice the mistake, then according to the letter of the law there is no obligation to inform him of the error and return the difference. However, if we do return it with the intention of making a *kiddush Hashem* — sanctifying Hashem's Name — (but not for reasons of personal benefit or out of pity for him), then it is a very commendable deed. The same would apply, for example, if we find a lost item belonging to an *akum* and decide to return it. (*Emes Kenei* 8:4–5, 7, 15)

17 Shvat	17 Sivan	17 Tishrei

Misleading Words   THE SECOND CATEGORY of *geneivas da'as* has nothing to do with financial matters, but rather involves intentionally misleading someone in regard to our deeds or intentions toward him. The *issur* of this type of *geneivas da'as* would include the following:

❒ Offering something insistently when we know the other person will refuse. For example, we should not beg a friend to join us for a meal or to accept a gift when we are certain that he will not do so. Similarly, we should not offer him wine or some other drink from an empty container when we know that he will decline our offer anyway. In all of these cases, we put the other person in a position of feeling grateful to us when there is no reason for him to feel that way.

▫ In all of the above cases, what is prohibited is requesting in a manner that is *excessive*. A polite request expressed once or twice, as a matter of protocol or as a gesture of respect, is permitted and is the common practice. In fact, if we fail to do so it may be perceived as an insult to the other person's honor. Still, in the case of offering someone wine, we should offer it only if there is some wine in the decanter, even if we know that the other person is likely to refuse; if the decanter is empty, then even a polite offer would be considered *geneivas da'as*.

▫ If we are sincere in our requests, for example, if we are serving a meal and we genuinely would like our friend to join us, then we are permitted to plead with him to accept our offer, since we honestly wish to do something for him. Even if he declines and is left feeling indebted to us, his gratitude is well-founded, as it was not gained by deceitful means.

Sometimes a person who is well-off feels obligated to invite guests whom he does not really wish to host. If they accept, however, he will welcome them in and serve them; he certainly does not lack the necessary food. In such a case he is permitted to invite them, insincere as his invitation may be, and this is not considered *geneivas da'as*. (*Emes Kenei* 11–13)

Putting on a Show of Generosity   GENEIVAS DA'AS MAY be accomplished through deeds, without a word being said. For example, we should not come to the house of a mourner bearing an empty food container, since this misleads the *aveil* into thinking that we were kind enough to bring him a meal. Coming into a wedding with a conspicuous gift-wrapped item not meant for the *chassan* and *kallah* can be equally misleading, as can be an elaborate, showy *mishlo'ach manos* package that is virtually empty of content other than space-filling confetti and such.

If, however, our purpose is to enhance someone's honor — for example, to demonstrate to the many people gathered at the mourner's home how prominent the *aveil* is, by showing them how we honor him with what appears to be generous gifts of food, then it is permissible.

The same would apply in the case of the wedding gift, as well as if we publicly appeal to someone to honor us with his presence at a meal, showing all those present how dear he is to us. Since our purpose is not to force a feeling of unearned gratitude on the person, but rather to build up his image, these acts would be permissible.

Care must be taken, however, not to inadvertently cause the recipient shame. For example, we should not send our friend a large bakery box with a few cookies on top, if there is a chance he may count on that supply and offer it to a large group of guests, not realizing that the rest of the box is full of Styrofoam packing material. The Gemara relates a story of someone who received a barrel of wine with a layer of oil floating at the top as a gift from a friend. The recipient invited guests with the assumption that the barrel was full of oil (which was commonly used in large amounts during meals in the times of the Gemara), and that it was more than enough for his needs. When he saw that beneath the thin layer of oil was wine, and he had nothing to serve his guests, he strangled himself from the shame of it. (_Emes Kenei_ 8:14, 16–17)

| 18 Shvat | 18 Sivan | 18 Tishrei |

"Especially for You"   "Sholom, I'm opening up that big bottle of expensive champagne we got last Purim. We've been saving it for so long, and it will be just the thing for tonight's _'lechaim,'_ don't you think?" Ora was almost as bubbly as the champagne as she contemplated the celebration of her oldest daughter Basya's engagement, which would take place in just a few hours.

"A wonderful idea, Ora," Sholom agreed.

Ding-dong! The doorbell? Who could it be? The _mechutanim_ weren't expected for at least another four hours.

"Oh, Auntie Matilda and Uncle Menachem," Ora said with a flourish as she opened the front door, trying to conceal her surprise. How could she have forgotten? Two weeks ago, her great-aunt Matilda had called to say that she and Uncle Menachem would be traveling to their city on this very date and would stop in for a visit. With all the excitement of Basya's _shidduch_, she had forgotten all about it. Well, they certainly had enough cake on hand to serve these unexpected guests …

> "What an honor!" Sholom came to the foyer and took up his role as host. "What do you say, Ora, don't you think that for such important guests, we should open a bottle of champagne?" He winked at Ora and reached for the bottle on the table.
>
> Only the next day, when Sholom finished accepting *mazal tov*s and told his Rav the amusing story of the unexpected guests did he hear that his gallant gesture may have actually been a violation of *geneivas da'as* ...

WE MAY NOT mislead a guest into thinking that, especially for him, we are opening a barrel or large bottle of wine or any other package of perishable food that is likely to spoil if not used up shortly, when we know that we can actually sell the remainder without suffering a loss, or that we were planning to open it anyway and use it up for a *simchah*. If we give the impression that we are doing so only in this guest's honor, the guest will feel indebted to us for no reason; therefore, we have to inform him that it was not done exclusively for his sake.

However, if the guest is so dear to us that even if we had nothing to do with the remainder, we would still have opened it for him, we do not have to inform him that in this particular case we do have a use for the rest of it.

Also, if we did not give any indication that we made the effort especially for him, and he should have understood on his own that we have additional uses for it, yet he deluded himself into thinking that we went out of our way on his behalf and in his honor, then we are not obligated to set him straight. For example, if we meet up with a friend on the outskirts of town, and he thinks that we came out especially to greet him, we are not obligated to inform him of his error.

We may find a common application of this principle if we go to a distant hospital to visit one patient, and while we are there come across someone else we know who is hospitalized in the same facility. On the one hand, we are not permitted to say, or even to hint, that we came especially to see the second person. On the other hand, if the patient jumps to this conclusion on his own and thanks us for our trouble, we are not required to reveal the truth, since it is he who has deluded himself.

Similarly, if we have to be in a distant city on business and stop in

at a wedding that is taking place there, we may not imply that we came so far just to attend our friend's *simchah*. However, if he assumes that we did so, we do not need to refute his assumption and announce that we never would have come just on his account and that we stopped in merely because we were in town anyway. In fact, "honesty" in such cases may not be a virtue at all, since by being so open we may insult the other person deeply. (*Emes Kenei* 8:18–20, 38)

Business Ethics   MARKETING TACTICS NOWADAYS are geared toward touting the virtues of a product and downplaying any disadvantages, in a manner that may at times border closely on deceiving the buyer. Long before consumerism was a household word, *halachah* gave us guidelines on avoiding misleading advertising and sales. We are not permitted to dress up merchandise so as to give the wrong impression of its quality or condition. In the times of the Gemara, that meant not brushing up the cattle's hair to make it appear fatter, and not painting old vessels so as to make them appear new. As we have mentioned, we are not allowed to conceal any defect that most people would care about.

A storekeeper may give out treats to children to encourage them to frequent his store; this is not in violation of *geneivas da'as*. He may also lower his prices to attract customers. However, he may not advertise that his prices are lower than other stores when they are not. Nor may he claim that items are on sale when in fact he raised the ticket prices and then "reduced" them to the original cost. As to claiming that "for *you*, I will give such and such a price," when he actually offers the same or a lower price to any customer — this is a questionable practice; the *halachah* may depend on whether all the salesmen in the vicinity use such ploys, and how seriously consumers take them.

While we may not attempt to pawn off old items as new, we are allowed to paint new items and enhance the appearance of old ones, even though this will raise their value, because it is accepted practice to pay extra for beauty. In these cases there is no concealing of a defect

and no deceitful act. For this reason we are allowed to paint a car or a house that is for sale.

A greengrocer may not mix lower-quality with higher-quality produce in order to sell them all as top quality. If it is known that the storekeeper gets his produce from a number of sources, some better and some worse, and it is up to the customer to pick out the better ones, then the proprietor can mix them together, as long as he does not misrepresent the mix as all coming from the better source. Some produce comes naturally with a certain amount of waste material, such as clods of earth stuck to potatoes, and the storekeeper does not have to separate that out; however, if he did so he may not be allowed to mix the waste material back in. In these matters, the common practice in that area is an important factor in determining whether or not *geneivas da'as* is involved.

If there is a mix of fruits, the greengrocer can sort them all out to remove the spoiled produce, so as to attract customers; however, he is not permitted to sort out the fruits in the top layer alone, as this can be deceptive.

All of these points relate not only to fresh produce; the same rules can be applied to any other merchandise.

Needless to say, it is strictly prohibited to place fruit or other food items, or any other merchandise, into boxes and/or wrappers that are marked with the logo of a well-known company. Doing this may involve violations of several serious *issurim*. It is certainly a violation of *geneivas da'as* and may be outright *gezel* as well, because it would lead to a *mekach ta'us* — a transaction based on error. It would also be a violation of *hasagas gevul* — in the category of theft of copyright or usurping business from that company. In any case, it is forbidden for an advertiser to exaggerate the quality of a product and to overprice it.

A butcher may not soak meat in water so as to give it a light, robust appearance. Nor may a wine merchant mix water into wine beyond the amount that all the vendors in the area do; the buyer must know exactly what he is getting. If bottled wine is marked "all natural" or "100% pure," the product has to meet that standard. Otherwise, in addition to being a deceitful practice, this may be considered *mekach ta'us* as well as causing people to say incorrect *brachos* and disqualifying their

Kiddush, since the buyer may himself add more water to the wine, on the assumption that none has been added by the producer.

In short, a person who engages in business should make sure that his words can be relied on and that he does not misrepresent his merchandise in even the smallest degree. This is, unfortunately, a far cry from today's business practices, where an advertising agency's success is measured by the degree to which it can stretch the truth and deceive consumers within the limits of the law. (*Emes Kenei* 8:25–31)

20 Shvat	20 Sivan	20 Tishrei

Personal HYPOCRISY IS A despicable quality. Even outright
Misrepresentation *resha'im* fear and despise those who falsely present themselves as fine, religious, G-d-fearing people, whose "deeds are [evil] as the deed of Zimri, yet they expect reward like that of Pinchas." The Heavenly *beis din* punishes those who wrap themselves piously in a *tallis* and put on a show of religiosity while they conceal their evil deeds from others (*Sotah* 22b).

It is a *mitzvah* to publicize the wicked ways of such people, so as to prevent the *chillul Hashem* that would ensue if people were to learn from their example, assuming that they are really *tzaddikim*. Another important reason to uncover the deception of such people is so that when they are duly punished, others shouldn't wonder at why such a "*tzaddik*" should need to suffer in that way.

Even when we are not intentionally misrepresenting ourselves, we still have to be careful not to inadvertently give a wrong impression of what we are. Therefore, we may not accept praise for qualities that are actually lacking in us. For example, if a *talmid chacham* comes to town and is received with the honor due to someone who knows two *masechtos*, while in reality he knows only one *masechta*, he is obligated to tell the townspeople his true level. Needless to say, he may not intentionally mislead them into thinking that he knows more than he actually does. In practice, the *minhag* is to exaggerate a bit in titles awarded to a *talmid chacham*, whether in writing or in a public introduction; in that case it is permissible to follow the local practice. (*Emes Kenei* 8:32–33)

Geneivas Da'as —
Additional
Examples
THERE IS NO justification for copying or using any other deceptive tactic when taking a test for school. If someone forges a professional diploma and receives a higher pay based on that document, he is also guilty of stealing.

The Rambam wrote in his time that magicians who use sleight of hand to do things that are not as they appear — such as putting a rope up his sleeve and pulling out a snake, or throwing a ring in the air and subsequently retrieving it from the mouth of someone in the audience, are guilty of *geneivas da'as.*

Today, some *poskim* are lenient in this matter, especially when the magician explains in advance that his act is based on optical illusions and sleight of hand. However, many authorities retain a stringent approach, and therefore it is best not to follow the lenient view. (*Emes Kenei* 8:22, 38)

Permitted
Deception
ALTHOUGH SPEAKING OR acting hypocritically is generally an abhorrent practice, there are times when it may be commendable, when our intentions are well-placed. For example, it is a great *mitzvah* to flatter our students and colleagues, and in fact any other person, in order to attract them to us so they will be willing to lean Torah and *mitzvos* from us and accept our rebuke. Similarly, we can praise a student for qualities that he does not (yet) have, or bend the truth in order to encourage and motivate him so that he will have greater success in the future.

It is especially important for parents and teachers to provide children with powerful words of praise and encouragement, even if it means exaggerating the truth, so as to motivate them to reach their full potential. For example, if a child who is quiet and introverted gathers up the courage to ask his rebbe a question, the rebbe can grasp the opportunity to magnify the significance of the question and build up the child's self-esteem. Sometimes a small incident like this can change the course of the child's development. (*Emes Kenei* 8:35)

In summary: *Geneivas da'as* includes both monetary fraud and deceptive speech that misrepresents our deeds, our intentions or ourselves. Monetary fraud includes unauthorized use of a bus ticket, concealing a defect in merchandise, and many other such deceptive practices. Verbal deception includes pleading with someone to accept, for example, a meal or a favor when we know that he will not accept it in the end, thereby leaving him feeling indebted to us. Business ethics require that we be open and honest in pricing and advertising, and in describing the quality of the merchandise. Cheating on tests, and also magic shows, can be violations of *geneivas da'as*. Hypocritically misrepresenting oneself as an upstanding person while concealing evil deeds is a lowly form of *geneivas da'as*. One case where deception is permitted is when we exaggerate the positive qualities or actions of a student in order to encourage his emotional and/or spiritual growth.

אמת ואמונה

VOLUME II

⟿ **22** ⟾

ואהבת לרעך כמוך \ והלכת בדרכיו
Love Your Fellow as Yourself /
Walk in Hashem's Ways

21 Shvat	21 Sivan	21 Tishrei

"Kamocha" —
As Yourself
Arriving early at school, Chavie dropped her schoolbag in a pile with the others and ran to join a quick game of jump rope until the bell would ring to signal the start of the school day. Her good friend Faigie drew up into the line right behind her, and they both waited for a turn to jump in.

"Oy, look — somebody's schoolbag popped open and her notebooks are scattering on the floor," Faigie said. "Maybe we should go pick them up and stuff them back in before they get stepped on."

"Not now, Faigie. I don't want to lose my turn." Chavie shrugged her shoulders. "Let somebody else worry about it."

"Hey, Chavie, isn't that your schoolbag, and aren't those your notebooks?" Faigie asked suddenly.

"What?!" Chavie ran out of line, forgetting all about her turn, and rushed to gather the items that had tumbled out of her bag. As she did so, she heard her teacher's voice echoing in her mind: "Loving someone as yourself means caring about them as you care about yourself, and caring about their property as if it were your own." Chavie blushed. Her early-morning experience had taught her that lesson more clearly than any lecture could have done.

239

THE OBLIGATION TO care for one's fellow man is expressed in the Torah in the form of two separate but closely related *mitzvos*: "*Ve'ahavta lerei'acha kamocha* — Love your fellow man as yourself," and "*Vehalachta bidrachav* — Walk in the ways of Hashem." The scope of each of these *mitzvos* is defined differently by the various *poskim*.

According to one opinion, the *mitzvah* of *ve'ahavta* requires that we feel love in our hearts, which we express by refraining from doing anything to hurt our fellow man, and by making efforts to protect him from monetary loss, anguish and any affront to his dignity. On the other hand, the *mitzvah* of *vehalachta bidrachav* is the obligation to emulate Hashem by performing positive acts of kindness, just as Hashem acts with kindness toward His creations.

A second opinion makes a different distinction between the two *mitzvos*. According to this view, in addition to the obligation to feel love in one's heart, the *mitzvah* of *ve'ahavta* also includes doing acts of *chessed*, while the *mitzvah* of *vehalachta* refers to the obligation to cleave to Hashem through refining our *middos* (which is commonly achieved by doing acts of *chessed* repeatedly). According to this opinion, even if you felt a powerful love in your heart for the other person, you will not have fulfilled the *mitzvah* of *ve'ahavta* until you did an actual act of *chessed* for him. At the same time, if you did a tremendous act of kindness for the person but did it in a cold, apathetic way, without being moved to increase your love for him, you may not have fulfilled the *mitzvah* of *vehalachta*. (*Mishpetei Hashalom* 13:1)

22 Shvat	22 Sivan	22 Tishrei

Love Your Fellow Man — Who Is Obligated? "LOVE YOUR FELLOW man as yourself; I am Hashem" (*Vayikra* 19:18). The obligation to love one's fellow man applies to men and women, rich and poor, in all places and at all times. Children should be trained in this *mitzvah* from a young age and should be encouraged both within the family circle and without to seek ways to make others feel good and to "*fargin*" — to take joy in the success of others.

The centrality of this *mitzvah* is stressed time and again in our sources. Rabbi Akiva called it "a great principle in the Torah." Hillel Hazaken went so far as to say that the rule, "Do not do to your friend anything that would be loathsome to you [were you in his position]," is the crux of Torah; "the rest is just explanation." Indeed, we find that many of the *mitzvos* in the Torah derive from this principle: the *issurim* of stealing, adultery, swindling, hurting with words, hatred, revenge, bearing a grudge and many others.

In order to carry out the *mitzvah* properly, it is not enough to consider how you — with your weaknesses and strengths — would feel under the circumstances. For example, you may be particularly thick-skinned and truly do not mind when others kid you about your faults. That does not give you license to joke at another person's expense, rationalizing that "I wouldn't care if he treated me that way." Rather, you have to put yourself into the other person's shoes and imagine how you would feel if you were *he*, and act toward him accordingly. (*Mishpetei Hashalom* 13:2–3)

What Does the Mitzvah of Ve'ahavta Entail? THE RAMBAM EXPLAINS the *mitzvah* of *ve'ahavta* as an obligation to love every Jew as you love yourself. In practice, this means that we should be concerned for his personal welfare and for the safety of his possessions as we are concerned for our own welfare and our own possessions. Just as we wish people would think and speak highly of us and would look out for our interests, so should we speak positively of our friend, look out for his honor and his possessions, and do what we can to protect him from any kind of loss.

If we truly feel love for another person, then we will be free of the nasty pangs of jealousy when he surpasses us in financial success, reputation, intellectual achievements and so on. In fact, we will feel personal joy in his success, just as we would feel at our own. King Shaul's son Yonasan achieved this level in his boundless love for David, which was untainted by envy, even when the position of king was taken from Yonasan and given to David. If we could all adopt this attitude, we would have a sure formula for peace and harmony. (*Mishpetei Hashalom* 13:4–5)

Vehalachta Bidrachav — How? IN THREE DIFFERENT places the Torah commands us the *mitzvah* to "Walk in His [Hashem's] ways" (*Devarim* 28:9; see also ibid. 11:22 and ibid. 13:5). *Chazal* ask the obvious question: "How can a mortal man walk in the way of the *Shechinah*? Isn't the *Shechinah* a 'consuming fire'?" How can we be expected to model ourselves in the image of such an inaccessibly lofty Reality? *Chazal* answer by explaining that the *mitzvah* is to try and cleave to Hashem by emulating His acts of kindness — performing acts of *chessed*, clothing the needy, visiting the sick, consoling mourners and burying the dead, as we see in the Torah that Hashem did (e.g., Hashem visited Avraham when he was sick, consoled Yitzchak after Avraham's death, buried Moshe Rabbeinu, etc.).

This *mitzvah* too applies to men and women, in all places and at all times. If a person does not make a conscious effort to improve his behavior, overcome his *yetzer hara* and refine his thoughts and deeds to love Hashem and follow in His ways, then he will have violated this positive *mitzvah*.

In certain cases, a dignified and honorable person may be exempt from engaging in acts toward his fellow man that flow from the *mitzvah* of "*ve'ahavta*," when it would be beneath his dignity to do so. On the other hand, acts that derive from the *mitzvah* of "*vehalachta bidrachav*" (such as visiting the sick, showing hospitality to guests, participating in burial of the dead, and gladdening a *chassan* and *kallah*) apply even in the case of a great Torah scholar attending to the needs of an ordinary person (as will be explained).

Educating Children in Doing Chessed CHILDREN SHOULD BE trained in this *mitzvah* as well, and should be reminded from time to time that when we are kind to others, we are imitating the ways of Hashem, Who is so kind to us.

In the same context, it seems fitting to point out here how important it is to involve children — both boys and girls — in helping at home. Besides the obvious fulfillment of the *mitzvah* of *kibbud av va'em*, the child who learns to pull his weight in the realm of household responsibilities, especially in helping out his younger siblings, is getting "on-the-job training" in *vehalachta bidrachav*. In addition, participating in the family effort teaches him how to be *nosei be'ol* — to share the burden, instead of expecting to have others serve him, and it also fosters several other valuable *middos*, such as *zerizus* (alacrity) and *chessed*.

These goals are so important that we would be well advised to give children jobs in the house even if it might be easier to get the work done without their "assistance." Also, we should keep in mind that our main goal is to educate the child and cultivate willing effort on his part, not necessarily to benefit from his work; therefore, we should not be sticklers for perfect results. (*Mishpetei Hashalom* 13:1, 7–8)

24 Shvat	24 Sivan	24 Tishrei

Unconditional Love   "Give me a piece of your new stationery, and I'll be your best friend…"

"I applied for a job in the office where you work. Could you recommend me to your boss?"

"Sure, on condition that you speak to your brother-in-law to help get my son into his yeshivah…"

SOME PEOPLE ARE always willing to do a favor — as long as they are getting something in return. Their so-called "love" is actually an expression of their unspoken motto: "You take care of me, and I'll take care of you." This can be compared to the person who claims that he "loves fish." "If so," he is told, "why do you kill them and eat them? Why don't you throw them back into the water? It is clear that the one you love is yourself!"

Genuine *ahavas Yisrael* and *gemilus chessed* does not work that way. When we love our fellow Jews and help them out, our act should in no way be tied to expectations of gaining anything in return from the other person. Just as Hashem is merciful, gracious and giving to His creations without expecting anything in return, so are we expected to conduct ourselves in the same way with every other Jew, whether he is a relative, a friend or a total stranger. This is one of the hallmarks of the Jewish people, and is a theme that runs through the entire Torah, which begins with *chessed* — Hashem's clothing Adam and Chava — and concludes with *chessed* — Hashem's burying Moshe Rabbeinu.

True love is the ability to give purely for the sake of benefiting the other person. The act of giving must not be geared toward bringing pleasure to ourselves; on the contrary, we are willing to relinquish our own comfort and pleasure so that the object of our love will benefit. In our genuine love for every other Jew, we are concerned for his physical, emotional and financial well-being as well as for his personal honor. It was with this selfless love that Hashem created the world, and by emulating this genuine love when we relate to others, we fulfill the *mitzvah* of following in His ways. (*Mishpetei Hashalom* 13:9)

25 Shvat	25 Sivan	25 Tishrei

Your Life Comes First ALTHOUGH THE TWO *mitzvos* of *ve'ahavta lerei'acha kamocha* and *vehalachta bidrachav* require us to be genuinely concerned for another person's needs, there is a different *passuk* that limits this concern to a certain extent: "*Vechei achicha imach* — And your brother shall live with you" (*Vayikra* 25:36). *Chazal* deduce from these words that your life takes precedence over your friend's life. Consider the example of two people who are traveling through the desert, and only one of them has a flask of water. If they both drink from it, they will both die of thirst; but if only one drinks from it, he will reach a settlement and survive. The *halachah* in this case states that the owner of the water should drink all the water in order to save himself in the long run, rather than give half of it to his friend, which will save them both but only for a short time. This ruling is based on the principle of "your life comes first."

In earlier times, before there were modern, sophisticated water systems, people were dependent on the water source near their town. If two cities shared one water source, the *halachah* allowed residents of the city that was situated higher up to obstruct the water from flowing downward until they had drawn enough water for their own drinking needs, because of the principle of "your life comes first."

After the people of the lower city had gotten their necessary share of drinking water, those of the higher-up city could again obstruct the water flow so that their animals could drink, because, according to the same principle, their animals take precedence over the animals of others. So too, their need to do laundry using that water precedes others' need to launder.

In fact, some are of the opinion that in a case where inability to do laundry will cause the higher-up community great discomfort, then water for the laundry needs of that city would take precedence even over the life-sustaining drinking water of the lower city. (This principle probably applies only in a case where the people of the lower city are able to acquire water from another source, albeit for pay. Otherwise, it would be forbidden for members of the upper city to do laundry at the expense of the lives of residents in the lower city, based on the *mitzvah* of *lo saamod al dam rei'acha*.) (*Mishpetei Hashalom* 13:10–11)

26 Shvat	26 Sivan	26 Tishrei

Your Needs Come First FOLLOWING THE SAME principle, your personal livelihood takes precedence over someone else's livelihood.

Therefore, we are not obligated to give *tzedakah* to support others unless we have enough money for our own basic needs.

The same applies to other acts of *chessed*; while we are obligated to help others, we are not required to do so if it will lead to damage to ourselves. For example, if someone asks for our help in doing some work, we do not have to take time off from our own work and suffer a monetary loss in order to help him in his work. Nor are we expected to invest time and effort to do work for another instead of taking care of the same matter for ourselves.

Certainly, in a case where we would not have done that act for ourselves at all, we would not be obligated to do that same act for others. For example, if a revered *Rosh Yeshivah* would not ordinarily carry bags of groceries through the street for his own family, as it is beneath his dignity, then he would not be required to do so to help another person. (However, there are certain matters, such as *simchas chassan vekallah* and burying the dead, for which the *mitzvah* of *vehalachta bidrachav* would still oblige us to act, as we will discuss in later chapters.)

An important exception to this rule is in matters that affect one's wife. *Chazal* tell us that a husband should love his wife exactly as he loves himself and honor her even more than he honors himself.

Therefore, for the sake of his wife a man would be obligated to exert himself even in acts that he would not perform for the sake of his own needs. (*Mishpetei Hashalom* 13:12–13)

| ***Your Spiritual Needs Take Precedence*** | "Binyamin, what are you doing up at one o'clock in the morning?" Mr. Rosenberg asked his twelve-year-old son in surprise. |

"I'm almost finished reviewing the Gemara for tomorrow's test, Abba. I'll go to sleep soon," Binyamin explained.

"But, Binyamin, why are you studying so late? How will you be able to concentrate tomorrow morning?" Mr. Rosenberg's eyes radiated genuine concern.

"Well, I got home at six, but then Shmuel called and asked me to explain one difficult point to him, and then when I finished with that, Reuven knocked at the door and asked if I could learn with him the part he missed when he was sick, and then Shauli called, and before I turned around, it was eleven, and I hadn't started doing my own reviewing," Binyamin responded with a gaping yawn.

"Binyamin, I'm proud of you for being so helpful to all your friends, and I don't want to discourage you from doing that, but your learning has to come first. And that's not just my opinion — it's the *halachah*," Mr. Rosenberg said definitively.

THE PRINCIPLE OF "your life comes first" prevails in the spiritual realm as well. A person may not give time to another when he needs that time to fulfill his own *halachic* requirements. Similarly, he cannot put the Torah learning of others before his own Torah learning.

Nevertheless, the *poskim* do indicate that *some* time should be dedicated to helping others in their Torah study — perhaps a tenth of one's time, or, according to some sources, even a fifth. (*Mishpetei Hashalom* 13:13)

| 27 Shvat | 27 Sivan | 27 Tishrei |

| ***Your Lost Object Takes Precedence*** | When David and Shlomo got off the bus that brought them home from yeshivah, they were appalled to find that their suitcases were not in the baggage compart- |

ment. Shlomo was in a rush to get home, so he gave up on searching for

the suitcase and decided that he would call the bus company later. David, however, was determined to trace his missing item immediately.

He walked back toward the previous bus stops and, sure enough, after a half-hour trek, he found the two suitcases on the sidewalk. Apparently, someone had taken them out of the baggage compartment to get at his own bag and had forgotten to put them back in.

Now what? He couldn't possibly carry both of the heavy suitcases, and he didn't have money to hail a taxi. There was no one around to help him, and he did not know anyone in the area. On the other hand, if he left one of the suitcases there, it might get stolen. What should he do?

IF YOU LOSE an object and then come across both your own lost object and that of your friend, then if you can return both, you must do so. But if that is not possible, your own object takes precedence over that of others (even those that belong to your Rav or father). *Chazal* derive this *halachah* from the *passuk*, "There shall be no poor man among you" (*Devarim* 15:4) — we are required to protect ourselves from poverty and financial loss. The same rule would apply in any case where performing a *mitzvah bein adam lechaveiro* would cause us monetary loss or would cause us to neglect our job.

However, even though *halachah* provides us with this "out," the proper conduct is to go beyond the letter of the law and not be overly particular about giving our own property priority when the loss is not a certainty but is only a possibility. If a person is so meticulous about protecting his interests that he constantly wheedles his way out of helping others, it is considered as if he has thrown off the yoke of *chessed*. In the end, his punishment will be that he himself will be forced to rely on the help of others. (*Mishpetei Hashalom* 13:14–15)

Miscellaneous Applications CHAZAL TELL US that in a case where one person benefits from another without causing loss to him, there is no need for the beneficiary to pay. For example, if Reuven illegally squats on Shimon's empty dwelling but does not cause loss to Shimon by living there, then in some cases, even though Reuven used the property without permission, he is not required to pay Shimon. However, if the owners protest from the outset, then the user would have to either pay or vacate the premises.

These rules apply only to real estate, not to moveable property. In the case of moveable property, using an item without explicit permission would be considered theft. The *Shulchan Aruch* explains the numerous detailed rules that govern this area.

At times we find that *Chazal* allow us to force a person to cooperate with another when he is displaying senseless selfishness (known as "*middas Sedom*"). *Chazal* also advise us that a person should not wastefully empty his well when others need the water. This principle applies to a variety of circumstances. In places where the *beis din* was authorized to do so, *beis din* could apply pressure and even use lashes or excommunication to prevent a person from acting in these ways. (*Mishpetei Hashalom* 13:16–17)

28 Shvat	28 Sivan	28 Tishrei

Interrupting Torah Learning WHEN THERE IS a *mitzvah* that cannot be delegated to another or is incumbent on the person himself to fulfill, he must interrupt his Torah learning in order to do it. If others could theoretically carry out the *mitzvah* but are lazy about doing so, it is considered as if they aren't there, and in that case as well, he must stop his learning to do the *mitzvah*. However, after the *mitzvah* is completed he should return to his learning as soon as possible.

Talmud Torah derabbim — public learning — is in a different category from individual learning, and opinions differ on the question of when such learning may be interrupted, for example, to attend a funeral or a wedding. Some say that even public Torah learning or a *shiur* may be interrupted for the performance of such a *mitzvah*. Others maintain that *talmud Torah derabbim* may be interrupted only to recite the obligatory first *passuk* of *Krias Shema*.

Yet others maintain that only when the speaker is a great *talmid chacham*, who stimulates his listeners to do *teshuvah* through his inspiring words, should there be no interruption. Otherwise, even a public *shiur* should be interrupted for the performance of a *mitzvah* such as attending a funeral or wedding.

We mentioned above that when a person can delegate the performance of a *chessed* to someone else, he should not stop learning to do the *chessed*. However, where he is presented with an opportunity to do a specific *mitzvah*, such as giving *tzedakah*, returning lost objects, or even a Rabbinically ordained *mitzvah*, the sources seem to imply that, although he is not obliged to, he is allowed to fulfill the *mitzvah* even though his Torah learning will be interrupted. If in doubt, he should consult a rabbinic authority. However, one should not go looking for other *mitzvos* at times when one should be learning.

Women and girls, though not obligated in Torah learning for its own sake, can miss vital lessons in practical *halachah* or in *yiras Shamayim* if they are absent from school unnecessarily. They should certainly think twice before missing such a class, the price of which may be lifelong ignorance of a particular topic in *halachah* or *hashkafah* (Jewish thought). In addition, neither students nor their teachers, who must adhere to the structured requirements of their school, should leave class to attend any *levayah* that passes by. In a sense, they are considered *anoos* — forced to refrain from doing the *mitzvah* — since anyone associated with a specific institution has no choice but to follow its governing rules.

When it comes to *hachnasas kallah*, *halvayas hameis* and other, similar *mitzvos*, even though these *mitzvos* could be fulfilled by others, a person should interrupt his learning as much as is necessary to ensure that they are carried out properly, with the requisite honor, as will be explained in upcoming chapters.

Regarding Shabbos preparations, the Rema says specifically that a person should take some time from his Torah learning in order to take part, at least in some small way, in preparing for Shabbos, even if he has servants who could do the work in his stead. It is also well known that, over the generations, *Gedolei Torah* would interrupt their Torah learning in order to personally take part in other *mitzvos*, such as baking matzos, building the *sukkah* and the like. (*Mishpetei Hashalom* 13:18–20)

29 Shvat	29 Sivan	29 Tishrei

Relatives Take Precedence "I'm looking for a babysitter to take my children out for a few hours today. I'm recovering from surgery, and I must get some rest," Mrs. Danziger explained to the secretary of the community *chessed* committee."

> "Danziger ... Danziger ... that name sounds familiar," the secretary muttered. "Say, isn't your daughter the one in charge of all the volunteer work in the local high school?"
>
> "Yes, that's her," Mrs. Danziger sighed. Her daughter was a real doer — out helping everyone in the world ... except her own family.

JUST AS RELATIVES take precedence in the *mitzvah* of *tzedakah*, so should they be first priority in all *mitzvos* of *chessed*. Therefore, we are obligated to care for our parents' needs before tending to the needs of our children (assuming that it does not impinge too much on the smooth running of the household, depending on the situation), our children's needs before those of our siblings, and so on. Similarly, the needs of our community take precedence over those of another city, and the needs of a *talmid chacham* take precedence over those of a layman (as explained in *Yoreh Dei'ah* 251).

A common illustration of this principle is the housewife who will be unable to attend to the needs of her own home properly if she goes to do *chessed* for another family. It is important to keep in mind that just as a person cannot give *tzedakah* from funds he should be using to pay his belated debts, so a woman cannot extend herself for the sake of others before she carries out her obligations to her own family. Her household takes precedence. For example, when time and energy is limited, a mother should give higher priority to baking a cake for her own children for Shabbos than to doing so for the local bar-mitzvah *chessed* society.

An exception would be a case where in doing a *chessed* for others, her intention is to teach her children important lessons. For example, by sending food to a neighbor who is an *almanah*, she hopes to show her children how we must cater to the special needs of others; or by preparing elaborately for guests, she teaches her children that *orchim* are to be served better and more plentiful food. (*Mishpetei Hashalom* 13:21)

30 Shvat	30 Sivan	30 Tishrei

To Whom, and How, Do These Mitzvos Apply ? WE ARE OBLIGATED to love and do *chessed* for all Jews — poor and rich, men and women, children, people of unsound mind and even people who are no longer alive. Acts of kindness to the deceased (such

as burying and eulogizing them) are of particular value, because we perform them without any expectation of reward. Included in the *mitzvah* of *chessed* is offering *gemachim* (free lending arrangements) of utensils, books, money and any other items or services that are needed. Another valuable form of *chessed* is giving good counsel and advice to others.

There is no *mitzvah* to love *akum* (although in some cases, for the sake of peace and to avoid hostility, we are compelled to conduct ourselves in a manner of *ahavah*, such as by visiting their sick or burying their dead). Likewise, there is no obligation to love those in the various categories of extreme sinners — *apikorsim, minim, meisisim, mumarim lehach'is* and informers. According to some opinions, in the case of any *rasha* whom we are permitted to hate, we are not required to relate to him with the *mitzvah* of *ve'ahavta*. (See Volume I, chapter 2.)

On the other hand, the Torah demands that we be caring even toward someone who is to be executed by the Sanhedrin, in which case the *mitzvah* of *ve'ahavta* applies. Although we are required to execute him, we are obligated to spare him any unnecessary pain, disgrace or disfigurement.

We have to be especially careful regarding *geirim*, converts, since besides the *mitzvos* of *ve'ahavta* and *vehalachta bidrachav*, there is an additional obligation to "love the *ger*" (*Devarim* 10:19) and to "love him as [you love] yourself, because you yourselves were *geirim* in Mitzrayim" (*Vayikra* 19:34). Similarly, one must show special sensitivity toward widows and orphans.

Therefore, we have to be particularly careful to treat *geirim*, widows and orphans lovingly and to refrain from hating them or doing anything that may be distressing to them or cause them pain. On the contrary, we should be concerned for their honor and their financial security as if it were our own and do for them all that we would want others to do for us. The same applies in all the other *mitzvos* of kindness. (For more details on *geirim, almanos* and *yesomim*, see Volume I, chapter 9.)

Although this *halachic* requirement refers specifically to a *ger tzedek*, we can deduce from here the importance of being supportive to anyone who is a stranger to his surroundings, such as an immigrant in a foreign country, a new member of a particular group or society, a *baal teshuvah* or even a new boy in yeshivah. Such people are more vulnerable, more easily taken advantage of and less capable of helping themselves. (*Mishpetei Hashalom* 13:6, 22–25)

The Common Denominator THE *MITZVAH* OF *ve'ahavta lerei'acha kamocha* is closely connected to almost every *mitzvah bein adam lechaveiro*. Therefore, if we violate any one of these *mitzvos*, in most cases we also violate the *mitzvah* of *ve'ahavta*. Examples of this would be the prohibitions against stealing, causing damage, adultery, *ona'as devarim*, *nekimah*, *netirah*, not judging favorably, striking, cursing and speaking *lashon hara*.

On the other side of the coin, when we fulfill any one of these *mitzvos*, and when we perform any acts of *tzedakah* or *chessed*—such as unloading or loading someone else's animal, saving a life, returning lost property, honoring parents, visiting the sick, hosting guests, comforting mourners, attending to the burial of the dead, and so on—we also fulfill the *mitzvah* of *ve'ahavta*.

The Rambam wrote, "It is a positive Rabbinic *mitzvah* to: visit the sick, console the bereaved, escort the deceased, bring a *kallah* to the *chuppah*, accompany guests, and occupy oneself with all the needs of a burial—carrying the *aron* of the *meis* on one's shoulder, walking in front of him, eulogizing him, digging the grave and burying him—and also bringing *simchah* to the *chassan* and *kallah* and providing them with all their needs. These are acts of *chessed* that one personally exerts oneself to perform and that have no set maximum measure.

"Even though all these *mitzvos* are Rabbinically ordained, they are all included under the general *mitzvah* of *ve'ahavta lerei'acha kamocha*; anything that you would want other people to do for you, so should you do for every Jew who lives according to the laws of Torah and *mitzvos*." (*Mishpetei Hashalom* 13:6, 26–28)

The Four Special Categories of Chessed THE *HALACHAH* PROVIDES us with certain guidelines and rules of precedence to use when two different acts of *chessed* conflict with each other. For example, if a funeral procession and a bridal

entourage meet on a road, the funeral procession should stop and make way for the *kallah*. Moreover, if there are not enough people in the city to both bury the *meis* and accompany the *kallah*, precedence should be given to accompanying the *kallah*; the *meis* should be buried afterward.

However, once the *kallah* has been brought to the *chuppah*, and you have the option of consoling the *aveilim* or dancing for the *chassan*, consoling the *aveilim* takes precedence. Similarly, providing the *seudas havra'ah* — the first meal for the *aveilim* — takes precedence over taking part in the *seudah* for the *chassan* and *kallah*.

However, this principle applies only when you have sufficient resources to perform both *mitzvos*. If not, preference is given to providing a *seudah* for the *chassan* and *kallah*. The same rule applies regarding other relevant honors — for instance, precedence is given to a *chassan* and his entourage, before the *aveil* and his consolers, in leaving the shul.

When you have to choose between attending a burial and attending a *bris*, precedence is given to a *bris*. However, if the deceased is a *meis mitzvah*, where there is no one but you to take care of burying him, the burial takes precedence, as a *meis mitzvah* takes precedence over all other *mitzvos* of the Torah. (These rules are explained in *Shulchan Aruch, Yoreh Dei'ah* 374.)

According to the Rambam, *nichum aveilim* takes precedence over vi'*chessed* both for the living and for the dead. However, some are of the opinion that this applies only when you won't be able to perform both *mitzvos*. However, when you will be able to do both, visiting the sick comes first, because it gives you the opportunity to fulfill his needs and pray for him.

The Rambam enumerates specific *chessed* requirements in relation to five categories of people: (a) the sick, (b) the deceased, (c) mourners, (d) the *chassan* and *kallah*, and (e) guests. The details of the laws pertaining to each of these five categories are explained in the following chapters. (Other *halachos* of *tzedakah* are explained in *Yoreh Dei'ah*, Vol. 3, and in *sefer Ahavas Chessed*.) (*Mishpetei Hashalom* 13:6, 28–33)

In summary: The *mitzvos* of *ve'ahavta lerei'acha kamocha* and *ve-halachta bidrachav* require us to love our fellow Jews and emulate Hashem's *middos* by doing *chessed* for others. We should care for the well-being and the possessions of others as we care for our own. However, when helping others may cause harm to us, we act in accordance with the principle of "your life comes first." This applies in cases involving financial loss, Torah study, retrieving a lost object, and in other matters. Particular attention should be given to loving *geirim*, widows and orphans. Specific laws govern priorities regarding *chessed* done with the sick, the deceased and mourners, the *chassan* and *kallah*, and guests.

⇒ 23 ⇐

ביקור חולים
Visiting the Sick

2 Adar	2 Tammuz	2 Cheshvan

An Invaluable Visit   Rina had to practically drag her friend Aviva through the hospital entrance.

"I told you I'm terrified of hospitals. Even the smell of the disinfectant makes me dizzy," Aviva protested. "And besides, I'm sure that the moment I see Rochel I'll just burst into tears."

"No, you won't," Rina insisted. Rochel was their newly married friend. "I agree that it's painful to see Rochel languishing in the oncology ward. But our job now is to smile, make light conversation and cheer her up, as hard as that may be."

The visit was easier than Aviva had imagined it would be. Rochel, though pale and weak, was thrilled to see her friends. Before long they were actually joking together as they reminisced about their not-so-long-ago high-school days. When the medical staff came to do some routine checks, Rina and Aviva stepped discreetly out to the hallway, where Rochel's husband and mother were sitting quietly.

A few minutes later one of the doctors called Rochel's husband into the room. Concerned, he rushed in. A moment later he emerged, all smiles, and reported to his mother-in-law, "The doctor just told me that Rochel's vital signs are better than they've been in weeks. He asked me if we've tried some dramatic new treatment he hadn't heard about. I told him the treatment was nothing more than her dedicated friends' *bikur cholim* visit,"

255

ביקור חולים

he said, casting an appreciative glance in Rina and Aviva's direction. "They were literally *'mechayeh nefashos'* — they revived her spirit!"

ONE OF THE ways we emulate Hashem is by visiting the sick — as Hashem Himself visited Avraham Avinu. When we visit the sick, attend to their needs and *daven* for their recovery, we fulfill both of the positive *mitzvos* discussed in the previous chapter — *Ve'ahavta lerei'acha kamocha* and *Vehalachta bidrachav*. In a case where the visit is crucial and life-saving, we also fulfill the *mitzvos* of "*Vechai achicha imach*" — saving a life; "*Vehasheivosa*" — returning a lost object, which, according to *Chazal*, includes saving someone's life; and "*Lo saamod al dam rei'echa*" — not standing by while someone's blood is being shed (as we discussed in Volume I, chapter 11).

A person who visits the sick is promised great reward. He will be saved from the judgment of *Gehinnom*, protected from the *yetzer hara* and treated with respect by all. In contrast, laziness in visiting the sick is considered tantamount to murder. (*Mishpetei Hashalom* 14: 1)

Who Should Visit and When? EVERYONE IS OBLIGATED to visit the sick. Even dignified and revered personages should visit simple people. One should not hesitate to visit someone who is *ben gilo* — born in the same *mazal* as him, even though in such a case, according to *Chazal*, the visitor takes away with him a sixtieth of the *choleh's* (sick person's) illness. Although there is no *mitzvah* of *ve'ahavta lerei'acha kamocha* in respect to *akum*, we are obliged to visit the sick among them, for the sake of peaceful relations.

If necessary we should visit the patient even several times a day — the more the better — as long as we are careful not to burden the patient. Keep in mind, however, that when a person becomes ill, it is usually not beneficial for him to have all types of visitors come and go indiscriminately. Relatives and close friends who spend time with the patient regularly should visit him immediately; he relies on their help and benefits from their company even when he is weak. Less familiar acquaintances would do better to wait until three days have passed before visiting the patient. However, if he takes a sudden turn for the worse, then even more distant friends should visit him without delay.

We are permitted to visit the *choleh* on Shabbos. Ideally, however, we should not put off visiting the sick until Shabbos just because it is a convenient, free day. Rather, we should make an effort to do our main visiting during the week.

The issue of men visiting women and vice versa will be discussed later in this chapter. (*Mishpetei Hashalom* 14:2–3, 10, 18)

| 3 Adar | 3 Tammuz | 3 Cheshvan |

What Does the Mitzvah Entail?   "Did you hear that Cohen had a heart attack Monday night? He's in Har Sinai Hospital. Maybe we should go visit him; he does *daven* with us every day," Yissochor suggested.

"Cohen, that multi-millionaire?" Naftali guffawed. "I'm sure he has three nurses on call all the time, a private room, and the head of the department as his personal physician. He doesn't need our visit, believe me."

Is Naftali right?

THE *MITZVAH* OF *bikur cholim* is not limited to matters relating to physical and/or medical assistance. There are actually four main components to the *mitzvah* of *bikur cholim*:

1. Taking care of the patient's physical needs
2. Giving him emotional support by showing that you share his pain
3. Praying for him in his presence
4. Divesting him of a sixtieth of his illness

Therefore, we should fulfill this *mitzvah* not only when the patient is poor and may lack doctors, medicines, or adequate food and heating, but even when the patient is wealthy and we can assume he is getting the best medical care and attention. Similarly, when a patient is obviously being well-tended by family or hospital staff, and there is nothing for us to do to support him physically, we would still be obliged to visit him; he still is in need of our prayers and emotional support.

Picture a sick person lying in bed, lonely and depressed, feeling that no one takes the least bit of interest in his misery. There might be no one coming by to attend to his various needs, to boost his spirits and raise his morale, or simply to serve as a listening ear for his worries and emotional distress. We can easily understand how this overall feeling of abandonment can weaken him and actually aggravate his illness. Therefore, by coming to visit the patient and and helping to relieve his distress, the visitor may actually be saving his life.

It is a *mitzvah* to sit with the patient and keep him company. If he is lying on the floor or on a low bed, we should be careful not to sit on a seat higher than his head, because *Chazal* tell us that the *Shechinah* hovers over the head of the sick person. If we cannot sit beside him, such as in a case where a patient is in the intensive care unit of the hospital, we should come to the hallway outside his room to inquire after his welfare. If even that is not possible, for example, if a patient is quarantined with a highly contagious illness, then we should still inquire after his health from his family and close friends.

If we are not able to visit the sick person, we should still try to send a message or a letter, or even to phone him. Even though this may not be a complete fulfillment of the *mitzvah*, it accomplishes the purpose of the *mitzvah* in part and is certainly a form of *chessed*.

Every community should establish a *bikur cholim* organization that will see to it that the physical and emotional needs of the sick are tended to properly. (*Mishpetei Hashalom* 14:6–8)

| 4 Adar | 4 Tammuz | 4 Cheshvan |

Tefillah for the Choleh   AS WE HAVE mentioned, one of the main components of the *mitzvah* of *bikur cholim* is *tefillah* — to daven to Hashem on behalf of the *choleh*. Whoever visits the sick and does not pray for Hashem to have mercy on the patient has not fulfilled the *mitzvah* properly.

For this reason we are advised not to visit the *choleh* during the first three hours of the day, when he usually looks and feels better, because, seeing how well he appears, we might not pray as intensely for him. Nor should we visit him during the last few hours of the day, when he is feeling at his worst, since upon seeing his worrisome condition we might give up and not pray for him at all.

These time constraints are not ironclad. In fact, some authorities say that these guidelines are suggested purely for practical reasons, since visiting the patient at these times is likely to interfere with the daily care of the patient, which is usually carried out at these hours. Therefore, if a visitor has a limiting time schedule, or has to deal with a hospital's strict visiting hours, making it difficult for him to visit during the appropriate times, he is certainly better off visiting at other hours as opposed to not performing the *mitzvah* at all.

Praying for the patient in his presence is of special value for two reasons. Firstly, when you see his suffering you are likely to daven with greater *kavanah*. Secondly, as we mentioned, the *Shechinah* rests near the bed of the *choleh*; therefore prayers uttered there are more effective. (*Mishpetei Hashalom* 14:8, 11)

5 Adar	5 Tammuz	5 Cheshvan

Formulating the Tefillah WHEN IN THE presence of the patient, we may *daven* in whatever language we choose. When we are not in his presence, the *tefillos* should, ideally, be in *lashon hakodesh*.

Some authorities maintain that when praying for a *choleh* we do not have to mention his name. Others say that this is true only when praying in his presence; in his absence the name must be mentioned. The *minhag* is to mention the patient's given name and his mother's name (*Ploni ben Plonis*) — not his father's name, unless his mother's name is unknown, and not his family name, nor any honorary titles, such as *Rabbeinu*. Whenever we pray for a *choleh* we should include the words "... *besoch she'ar cholei Yisrael* — among all the other sick people of *Am Yisrael*." Counting him as one of the *klal* makes the *tefillah* more effective.

It is questionable whether merely saying the words "*refuah sheleimah*" is considered a *tefillah*. Certainly, it is preferable to say an actual prayer on behalf of the *choleh* and not stop with expressing this brief wish.

When someone in our family is sick, we should go to a revered local Torah personality for a *brachah* and to ask him to pray for the *choleh*.

It is also customary to pray for the *choleh* publicly in shul. Nowadays this is usually done during *krias haTorah*, in the form of a "*Mi shebei-rach* — He who blessed our Forefathers … should bless…*"

On Shabbos we are not permitted to pray for the *choleh* directly. Therefore, on Shabbos, instead of conveying our prayer for his recovery with the regular expression of "*Refuah sheleimah*," we should say, "*Shabbos hi milizok, urefuah kerovah lavo* — On Shabbos we do not cry out, but a recovery should soon be on the way." Some add, "*Verachamav merubim veshivsu beshalom* — His mercy is great; have a tranquil respite." (*Mishpetei Hashalom* 14:10–15)

Giving Precedence WHEN SOMEONE HAS to choose between the *mitzvah* of visiting the sick, which is considered a *chessed* for the living, and the *mitzvah* of *nichum aveilim*, which is a *chessed* for both the living and the deceased, he should console the *aveilim*, as this *mitzvah* takes precedence.

However, if he will be able to do both *mitzvos*, then he should go to visit the sick first, because when we pray for the *choleh* and take care of his needs it is considered as if we are sustaining him.

When meting out funds for *tzedakah*, the *halachic* order of priorities states that giving money for the building of a shul takes precedence over most charitable causes; however, according to some opinions, *tzedakah* to pay for the medical and other needs of the poor who are sick takes precedence even over building a shul. (*Mishpetei Hashalom* 14:16, 37)

6 Adar	6 Tammuz	6 Cheshvan

Exemptions from the Obligation WHEN THE *CHOLEH* suffers from a contagious illness that poses a definite danger to visitors, only those who are absolutely needed at his side should visit him. Even where there is only a possible danger, it is not wise to take the risk and visit, since, according to the rule we learned in the previous chapter, our own life takes precedence. Therefore, even the possible personal risk involved in exposing ourselves to the illness outweighs the definite danger in which the *choleh* finds himself.

However, in the case of a slightly contagious, mild illness, we should not rush to excuse ourselves from visiting the *choleh*. Nor should we shed our responsibilities to the sick by exaggerating every imaginary distant possibility of catching his illness. Each case should be considered rationally, on an individual basis, depending on the factors involved in the illness and the physical vulnerability of the visitor.

Some *poskim* say that you should not visit a person with whom you are at odds, so as not to give him the impression that you are happy to see him suffer. However, this depends on the individuals involved and the nature of their hostilities. Sometimes the opposite is true; if handled properly, a well-intentioned visit could be an excellent opportunity to settle differences. If in doubt, we can first send a messenger to the sick person to say that we would like to visit him and "make peace," and then make the visit only upon receiving the *choleh*'s agreement.

Since the whole purpose of visiting is to help the *choleh,* we should be sensitive to the patient's needs and not visit someone who may find it a burden to have visitors. This would include *cholim* with embarrassing stomach disorders, patients who find it difficult to converse, or those who suffer from severe headaches, eye strains or any other uncomfortable symptoms. For such *cholim*, carrying on a friendly interchange may be more straining than invigorating.

However, it is still important to show our concern. Therefore, we can remain outside his room, inquire warmly about how he is feeling and whether all his needs are being taken care of, hear the patient's suffering, and pray for him from there. (*Mishpetei Hashalom* 14:4–5, 17)

| 7 Adar | 7 Tammuz | 7 Cheshvan |

Men and Women WHEN A *CHOLEH* is in need of assistance, men and women may attend to each other's needs, with some limitations, and may even make physical contact if necessary, since no amorous intentions are involved. Doctors and nurses may assist patients in standard ways, since this is their profession and they are therefore less likely to become aroused. However, physical and visual contact

should be kept to the minimum that is necessary. The *halachos* of these matters are complex, and one is advised to seek the counsel of a Rav in any question of this kind.

When a *choleh* suffers from a digestive disorder and requires assistance in matters related to elimination, the rule is that women may assist male patients, but men may not assist women. The same applies with any illness that may involve private parts of the body. In these and other illnesses, care should be taken to avoid *yichud* (the *issur* of a man and woman being alone together). Also, one should minimize as much as possible physical contact with the *choleh* and gazing at her, and should keep one's intentions focused purely on the *mitzvah*. *Chazal* praised highly those male professionals who made great efforts wherever possible to minimize or avoid physical or visual contact with female patients. Of course, this was only when it could be accomplished without delaying or interfering with necessary treatment.

During the time when a woman is a *niddah*, if she or her husband is sick, they must try to adhere to all the laws that guide their behavior at this time (as outlined in *Shulchan Aruch Yoreh Dei'ah* 195). When this is impossible, and there is no one else available to help, a Rabbinical authority must be consulted regarding how to proceed.

If those involved are enjoying the contact and find it arousing, then even if there is no one else available to take care of the patient and his life will be at risk, the contact is forbidden. This prohibited conduct is in the category of *gilui arayos* and therefore is subject to the rule of *yeihareig ve'al yaavor*, a sin for which we must be prepared to sacrifice our lives rather than transgress.

Generally, a man is not permitted to be overly friendly when greeting a woman — beyond the minimal polite exchange of words that are acceptable in their community — even when doing so through a third party or through her husband. However, we are permitted to inquire about her welfare through her husband, especially if she has been sick. Some are of the opinion that a man should not enter the sickroom of a female patient to visit when she is not dressed in her usual modest and respectable attire; rather, he should stand outside, inquire about her welfare, ask if she has everything she needs and pray for her recovery. (*Mishpetei Hashalom* 14:19–23)

Deterioration of the Patient's Condition WHEN A PATIENT'S condition becomes critical or life-threatening, it is sometimes necessary to add a name in order to annul the Heavenly decree.

A seriously ill person should not be informed of the death of a close relative or friend, because in his weakened condition such news could lead to emotional collapse. If he does hear about a death, others should not tear _kri'ah_, cry or give a _hesped_ in his presence, even if the person who passed away is not a close relative of the _choleh_. Because of his delicate condition, we are concerned that witnessing any of these actions may cause him to become brokenhearted by his fear of his own death.

Therefore, all visitors should be warned not to offer their consolation, and if necessary one should even cover up the truth to prevent the patient from finding out about the death. However, when it is clear that the _choleh_ will understand on his own what happened — if, for example, he and the _meis_ were in a car accident together — it would be pointless to lie to him. Each case should be dealt with according to the factors involved.

From the third day of his illness, or in the case of sudden deterioration, the _choleh_ should be advised to settle his financial affairs — for example, to check if he has to receive or repay loans, and retrieve belongings that he deposited with others for safekeeping or return those that others deposited in his keeping. Before bringing up the subject we should reassure him that it is customary for people who are even mildly ill to settle their financial affairs, and that it does not at all imply that we fear something very bad will happen to him; we certainly do not want to frighten him or cause sudden changes in his emotional condition, which could have serious consequences.

There are specific _halachos_ that relate to people who are seriously ill, which apply to dealings in areas such as the laws of _kinyanim_ (acquisitions) as they relate to the execution of a written or verbal will; to a hurried _get_ (divorce contract) that should be written in order to save his widow from problems relating to _chalitzah_; and the laws of _amirah le'akum_ (telling an _akum_ to do a forbidden _melachah_ on Shabbos). (_Mishpetei Hashalom_ 14:24–26)

Preparing for Death WHEN ATTENTING TO a *choleh* who appears to be close to death, we must walk a fine line between the tremendous *chessed* of helping him approach his death spiritually prepared, and the risk of frightening him in a way that might accelerate his passing, *chas veshalom.*

If a person appears to be nearing death, or if we have reason to be concerned that he may pass away suddenly, we should advise him to say *viduy.* This should be told to him in a gentle, tactful way. For example, he can be told that "in certain communities, all *cholim* are told to say *viduy.*" According to some opinions, we should assure him that "many have said *viduy* and did not die, while many others did not say *viduy* — and died...." We can remind him that anyone who does *teshuvah* and recites *viduy* sincerely is guaranteed a place in the World to Come.

The *choleh* should not be told to say *viduy* when there are women or children nearby, or in the presence of simple people with little emotional control or little tact, since they might break down in tears upon hearing the suggestion, and this could demoralize him. Therefore, these people should first be asked to leave the room.

If the *choleh* is not capable of reciting the *viduy* aloud, he may say it to himself in his heart. The accepted *nusach* is: מוֹדֶה אֲנִי לְפָנֶיךָ ה' אֱלוֹקַי וֵאלוֹקֵי אֲבוֹתַי שֶׁרְפוּאָתִי וּמִיתָתִי בְּיָדְךָ שֶׁתִּרְפָּאֵנִי רְפוּאָה שְׁלֵמָה, וְאִם אָמוּת תִּהְיֶה מִיתָתִי כַּפָּרָה עַל כָּל חֲטָאִים וַעֲווֹנוֹת וּפְשָׁעִים שֶׁחָטָאתִי וְשֶׁעָוִיתִי וְשֶׁפָּשַׁעְתִּי לְפָנֶיךָ וְתֵן חֶלְקִי בְּגַן עֵדֶן, וְזַכֵּנִי לְעוֹלָם הַבָּא הַצָּפוּן לַצַּדִיקִים — "I acknowledge before You, Hashem ... in Whose Hands lie my healing and my death, may you allow me to have a complete recovery. If I die, let my death be an atonement for all my sins, transgressions and rebellious behavior that I have committed before You. Please grant me my portion in *Gan Eden* and provide me with the merit to take part in the World to Come, which is reserved for the righteous."

If the *choleh* wishes to recite the full *viduy* of Yom Kippur, he may do so.

At this point the *choleh* should also be told to ask forgiveness from anyone he may have sinned against, whether these are personal sins or

sins involving money. Death does not atone for sins of this kind unless the person was first forgiven by the injured party, and if _mechilah_ is not obtained, the _neshamah_ will need to return to this world in the form of a _gilgul_ (reincarnation) in order to return anything he owes to others. Helping someone correct his sins and repent before death is a great _mitzvah_ and a _chessed_, since it will save him from harsh Heavenly judgment and strict punishment.

The _choleh_ should also be advised to give _tzedakah_ generously, since _tzedakah_ saves a person from death. Even if he does pass away, the _tzedakah_ will come to his aid, since, as _Chazal_ teach us, whoever sets aside a portion of his wealth for _tzedakah_ will be saved from _Gehinnom_, and the _zechus_ will accompany him on his last journey. "_Ki lo bemoso yikach hakol, lo yeired acharav kevodo_ — For he shall not take everything with him when he dies; his honor shall not descend with him [to the grave]" (_Tehillim_ 49:18). (_Mishpetei Hashalom_ 14:27–30)

| 10 Adar | 10 Tammuz | 10 Cheshvan |

The Threshold of Death PART OF THE _mitzvah_ of _chessed_ toward the _choleh_ is to ease his departure from this world. When a patient is deemed a _gosses_, on the verge of death, he should not be left alone, since he can become very frightened at the moment the _neshamah_ leaves his body. The _gosses_ may not be moved, since any movement may hasten his death. Chairs should be placed around the patient's bed so that a hand or foot should not jut out beyond the bed; if a limb does extend out, we may not move it back onto the bed. The _minhag_ is to light candles near the _gosses_ to fend off _mazikin_ (evil spirits).

At the moment of _yetzias haneshamah_ — when the _neshamah_ departs from the body — those around the _meis_ say the _passuk_ of "_Shema Yisrael …_" one time, "_Baruch Shem kevod Malchuso le'olam va'ed_" three times, "_Hashem Hu ha'Elokim_" seven times, and "_Hashem melech …_" one time. These _pesukim_ should be said as close as possible to the actual moment of death; however, they should not be said loudly, in case the _choleh_ is still in a condition of _gosses_. Also, loud sounds prevent the _neshamah_ from leaving the body.

Once the *choleh* has died, the *minhag* is to have people guarding his body continuously until the burial. The *halachos* of *taharas hamess* that are usually performed by the *chevra kadisha* — including washing the *meis*, cutting his nails, shutting his eyes, tying his jaw, blocking up his openings, and other tasks performed for a *meis* — are outlined in the *Shulchan Aruch*. (*Mishpetei Hashalom* 14:22, and footnote 34)

Seeking Medical Assistance   Menachem went over to the *mashgiach* to explain why he had to leave the learning *seder* early that day. "I have an appointment with Dr. Lewis, the top specialist who deals with the problem I've been having. Now I can finally take care of this business once and for all. After all, he's the best in his field."

The *mashgiach* nodded and asked quizzically, "Top specialist, you say? Best in his field? Then I'm afraid you are headed in the wrong direction."

"I don't understand," Menachem said in confusion. "Does the *mashgiach* know of a better specialist?"

"The best Doctor in every field is the One you can reach anytime, without an appointment, whenever you open up a *siddur* or *Tehillim*, or when you just open your heart. He is the One Who will bring your *refuah*," the *mashgiach* said gently. "I understand that today you have an appointment with his *shaliach* — his emissary."

Menachem got the message, and he echoed the *mashgiach*'s words with an understanding smile. "Yes, of course. Just an emissary."

A TRUE RECOVERY from illness depends on *tefillah* to Hashem. He is the One Who strikes a person with illness, and He is the One Who cures. However, few people are on the level of awaiting and meriting a direct, miraculous cure from Heaven. Therefore, the Torah allows doctors to practice medicine. Nowadays we are obligated to seek proven medical care, since our lives depend on it. Very few individuals in our generation are at a level of *bitachon* that would entitle them to shun medical assistance and rely exclusively on Hashem's direct help. In fact, if a person arbitrarily refuses to see a doctor when he is ill, in most cases we have to force him to seek medical care against his will, both because of his obligation to take the best possible care of the body he was entrusted with and because of our own obligation not to "stand aside while your brother's blood is spilled."

However, the Torah granted doctors only the right to try and cure a _choleh_, not to despair of his recovery, even from a terminal illness. Rather, he must continue to provide medical assistance and keep trying in every way possible to help the patient. _Chazal_ teach that even when an executioner's sharp sword is already positioned on a person's neck, he should keep praying to be saved. (_Mishpetei Hashalom_ 14:31)

11 Adar   11 Tammuz   11 Cheshvan

The Doctor's   DOCTORS MUST BE extremely diligent and cautious
Obligations   when practicing medicine, as their actions may prove
to be either lifesaving or life-endangering. A doctor who is qualified to help may not stand by casually when others are suffering or are in life-threatening situations; he is required to do everything in his power to help the patient. We are obliged even to desecrate the Shabbos in order to save a person's life, in addition to other leniencies in _halachah_ that we must use for the purpose of curing the sick.

A doctor who assists a _choleh_ medically fulfills several positive _mitzvos_ (as we cited regarding _bikur cholim_ in the beginning of this chapter), especially in cases where the care is lifesaving. In contrast, if a doctor refrains from helping a _choleh_, it may be considered as if he is spilling blood. This is true even if there are other doctors available, because they may not be as qualified in that particular area, or he may have the _mazal_ to correctly diagnose this symptom and its cure, or he may be the one who was designated by Heaven to be the emissary to bring about that _choleh_'s cure.

An inexperienced doctor should not treat a complex case when there are more qualified doctors available. In earlier times it was customary to receive permission from _beis din_ in order to practice medicine; nowadays a physician must obtain all the necessary legal certification before he may practice. If someone practices medicine without having completed all the requisite training and qualifications, he must take responsibility and rectify or compensate for any damages he may have caused erroneously.

The doctor is permitted to cause pain or discomfort to a patient in order to heal him, including carrying out procedures such as drawing

blood, bursting blisters, pricking the patient with a needle to remove a splinter, or even amputating limbs if necessary. The Torah teaches us to love others in ways that we would want to be loved and to refrain from harming others in ways we would not want to be harmed. A doctor would certainly be willing and happy to receive the pain he is administering in order to be properly treated, rather than to be spared the pain and not receive any treatment. Therefore, he may cause pain when he treats others.

When a doctor treats his own parents, he should avoid treatments that may result in bruising or bleeding, even if the wound is minor or accidental. The reason he has to be so careful is that when such action is carried out deliberately, not for the sake of necessary treatment, it is an extremely serious sin that would have made him liable for a death sentence in the times when the Sanhedrin was functional. The same situation may arise even for a child who is not a doctor, when his parent must receive regular injections or intravenous treatment administered at home, or when he is washing a parent's open wound or changing the bandages on a burn, any of which may cause slight bleeding. If someone other than the child can administer the treatment — such as a son-in-law or daughter-in-law, a grandchild or neighbor — then that is preferable. However, if no one else is available or capable of helping, and the parent is suffering or in danger, a child may administer any treatment necessary, after receiving rabbinical advice.

The *halachah* does not permit a doctor to ask for payment after curing a patient, since *mitzvos* must be done without receiving compensation. However, he may take payment for his time and effort, and for any losses he may have incurred. If the patient promised a high fee, this must be paid, as the doctor sold him his knowledge and expertise, and that is something that has no set monetary value. In any case, when it comes to any of the positive *mitzvos* that are actually the responsibility of all of *Klal Yisrael* to perform, we cannot force any one individual to do the *mitzvah* for free.

It is prohibited to raise the cost of medicines above their true market value. Even if the patient, out of desperation, said he would pay the inflated price for the medication, without intending to pay the price, this agreement is not halachically binding, and he has to pay only the market value. However, if when he agreed to the price he sincerely intended to pay it, and certainly if he already paid, the deal is halachically binding.

The laws of saving other Jews from danger are discussed in Volume I, chapter 11. (*Mishpetei Hashalom* 14:31–36)

In summary: The obligation of *bikur cholim* is one of the expressions of *ve'ahavta lerei'acha kamocha* and *vehalachta bidrachav*. Everyone is obligated to visit the sick; even an important person is obligated to visit a simple person. The *mitzvah* is not just to provide for the *choleh*'s physical needs, but to offer him emotional support as well as our *tefillos* on his behalf. Specific guidelines govern the care that a man may offer a woman and vice versa when he/she is ill. When a *choleh*'s situation deteriorates, we are obligated to help him prepare spiritually for his death, without frightening him. While true recovery can come only from Hashem, doctors were given permission to engage in medical assistance. The doctor himself has specific obligations regarding the *choleh*.

ביקור חולים

⇥ 24 ⇤

חסד של אמת
Attending to the Deceased

Chessed for Aharon and Levi waited impatiently for the light to turn
the Deceased green so they could get to their friend Efraim's house.
Efraim was making a *siyum* and had invited them to join
his family for the *seudah*. They knew that Efraim's uncle, the renowned
Rosh Yeshivah, would be there for a short time, and they didn't want to
miss seeing him and maybe even receiving a *brachah* from him.

Just then they noticed a crowd pouring down the street. "Ah, that must
be the *levayah* of Mr. Schwartzman, the *gabbai* from the Kehillas Emes
shul," Aharon said. "My father mentioned that it would be leaving about
this time."

"Well, let's zoom across the street and avoid them, before we get stuck
waiting for the whole crowd to go by and get to Efraim after it's all over,"
Levi suggested.

"That doesn't seem right. If the *levayah* of a fine Jew is passing right
before us, I think we have to follow along with the rest of the crowd, at
least for a short distance," Aharon insisted. "That's the least we can do out
of respect for Mr. Schwartzman."

"You're right," Levi agreed grudgingly. "I guess I got so carried away with
Efraim's *siyum* that I got my priorities a little mixed up. There — I can see
the people carrying the *aron*. Let's walk after them for a little while."

270

AMONG THE *MITZVOS* that are included in the categories of *ve'ahavta lerei'acha kamocha* and *vehalachta bidrachav* is the *mitzvah* of *hotzaas hameis* — attending the funeral and seeing to all the needs of the deceased, including carrying the *aron*, coffin, on one's shoulder, walking before the *meis*, eulogizing him, digging the grave and burying him. The *mitzvah* of *hotzaas hameis* is considered a *chessed shel emes* — a true *chessed*, since there is no expectation of reward from the recipient of the kindness. (*Mishpetei Hashalom* 15:1)

Burying the Meis BESIDES THE TWO general *mitzvos* mentioned above, burying the deceased is also a fulfillment of the *mitzvah* of "*kavor tikberenu bayom hahu* — you shall bury him on that day*" (*Devarim* 21:23). Even an honored personage must occupy himself with the burial (such as by helping with the digging and other tasks related to the burial), even though it may appear to be beneath his dignity. The *minhag* is for each of the men present at the graveside to take a shovelful of soil and deposit it over the grave, and then put the shovel down for the next person to use. Even the senior *Gedolim* of the generation are not exempt from the *mitzvah* of *levayah* — accompanying the deceased on his last journey.

If the deceased has no family or friends to tend to his burial, he is called a *meis mitzvah*, and all Jews share the responsibility of seeing to it that he is buried with proper respect. (*Mishpetei Hashalom* 15:2)

| 13 Adar | 13 Tammuz | 13 Cheshvan |

Before Sundown IN ADDITION TO the *mitzvah* of burying the *meis* on the day of his death, there is also a prohibition of "*lo salin nivlaso* — his body shall not remain through the night*" (*Devarim* 21:23). Delaying the burial unnecessarily is a violation of this prohibition and also causes great anguish to the *niftar*.

The only exceptions to this rule are when the delay is for the purpose of honoring the *meis* — for example, to arrange an appropriate *aron* and *tachrichim*, to announce the *levayah* in outlying areas, to await the arrival of close relatives or to obtain the necessary burial permit from the authorities. In Yerushalayim the *meis* is not left overnight, even for the

sake of honoring him. In any case, we should try very hard to complete the burial before sunset. For *halachic* purposes, burial is defined as the time when the *meis* has been placed in the ground and covered with soil. Merely placing the *niftar* in the *aron* or in a mortuary cooler is not considered burial.

If the burial is delayed until after sunset without a justified reason, this constitutes a violation of the *mitzvah* of *kavor tikberenu bayom hahu*, and if it is delayed until the following morning, then the *issur* of *lo salin* is also transgressed. (*Mishpetei Hashalom* 15:3)

"Hotzaas Hameis" — Escorting the Deceased

GIVING THE DECEASED proper honor by attending his *levayah* is so important that we even interrupt Torah learning in order to do so. However, this is warranted only in a case where there are not at least ten people to attend to the needs of the *meis*. Otherwise, only people who are not involved in Torah study should interrupt their affairs to tend to the deceased. According to most opinions, public Torah learning (such as a group *shiur*) should not be interrupted under any circumstances.

In the case of the death of a *talmid chacham*, however, one should interrupt Torah learning to join the *levayah* even if many people are already attending, since their numbers will not have reached the minimum necessary to honor a *talmid chacham*, that minimum being 600,000 people. A teacher of Torah — and some say one who devoted himself to serving a *talmid chacham* as well — deserves an extra measure of respect, and there are no limits to the number of people who must be there to honor him; therefore, everyone's Torah learning is to be interrupted for such a *levayah*.

| 14 Adar | 14 Tammuz | 14 Cheshvan |

Generally, young children are not taken away from their Torah studies to accompany the *meis*; we do not interrupt their learning even for the building of the *Beis Hamikdash*. In practice, some schools will take their boys out to attend the *levayah* of a great Torah leader, or even of a staunch financial supporter of the institution, as this would be considered an inspiring educational experience, no less so than any other school outing. A Rav should be consulted when deciding what to do in such cases. Similarly, as we discussed in chapter 22, girls' studies should not be interrupted to attend funerals if because of this they may remain ignorant of some information that is vital to them (such as a particular _melachah_ of Shabbos or a theme of _yiras Shamayim_), which will not be adequately reviewed afterward. Usually, teachers and pupils in educational institutions are not permitted to come and go as they please. This renders them _anoos_ — forced — to abide by the school rules, and thus prevents them from being free to perform this _mitzvah_ during school hours.

According to some opinions, nowadays everyone's Torah learning may be interrupted for any _niftar_, since everyone in the Jewish community is involved in Torah learning on some level — whether he is learning _Chumash_, Mishnah or any other Torah subject — and anyone might fall into the category of _talmid chacham_. The _poskim_ differ regarding the status of the _levayah_ of a woman and whether that too should be treated as a _levayah_ of a _talmid chacham_. In practice, the _minhag_ is to interrupt _talmud Torah_ for the _levayah_ of a woman as well as for that of a child.

When someone passes away, it is forbidden for any Jew in that city to carry on his work until the _meis_ is properly buried. However, if there are others attending to the burial, such as a _chevra kadisha_, which most communities have nowadays, then the rest of the Jews in the city are permitted to conduct their business until the _levayah_ actually begins. At that point, the people should all stop their work out of respect for the _meis_.

In big cities, where there may be several _levayos_ each day, the _minhag_ is not to interrupt Torah learning if we are unacquainted with the _niftar_ or the _aveilim_, especially if we are merely aware that a _levayah_ is to take place but are not clearly informed about when and where it will. However, if we actually see the funeral procession passing by, we must interrupt our learning and join the procession.

Similarly, a person who is learning Torah does not have to go out and check to see whether the _meis_ is in fact getting all the attention he needs, as long as he knows that someone — such as the _chevra kadisha_ — is taking responsibility. In this case, his Torah learning takes

precedence. However, some opinions say that this is true regarding an ordinary person, for whom we can assume that there will be the requisite ten men attending to the *meis*. But in the case of a *talmid chacham*, there will certainly not be the required 600,000 people attending, and even more so in the case of a teacher of Torah, in which case there is no limit to the number of people required to attend the funeral. Therefore, for the *levayos* of such people we should interrupt Torah learning in any case in order to attend.

| 15 Adar | 15 Tammuz | 15 Cheshvan |

Someone who sees the *meis* being carried out and does not bother to accompany the funeral procession is guilty of being "*lo'eig larash*" — mocking the less fortunate, incapable person and thus disgracing him — and is subject to *nidui*. Even if there are enough people attending the *levayah*, we should accompany the *meis* for at least four *amos*.

Often the eulogies at a funeral take a very long time, and we are compelled to leave even before we have had a chance to see the *meis* taken out and accompany him on his final way. The prevalent *minhag* in such a case is to consider one's obligation fulfilled by having listened to the *hespeidim*. Ideally, however, if we suspect that we may not be able to stay until the end, we should try to accompany the *aron* at the beginning of the *levayah* as it is brought the short distance from the *chevra kadisha* van to the place where the *hespeidim* will be delivered, and in this way we will definitely have fulfilled our minimum obligation. (*Mishpetei Hashalom* 15:4–8)

A Respectable Burial   GENERALLY, NOT EVERYONE who attends a funeral accompanies the *meis* to the cemetery, due to the difficulty or inconvenience involved. However, all those present should make sure that there will be at least ten men continuing on to the cemetery, even when this involves great effort, such as when the cemetery is located some distance away, or in cold winter weather. The *minyan* is necessary both so that the *aveilim* will be able to say Kaddish and the *birkas aveilim*, and also for the honor of the *meis*, so

that he will not depart on his final journey with only a few people seeing him off.

Those who cannot continue on to the burial should not turn around to leave the _levayah_ until the funeral entourage is out of sight.

Even though women should follow the _aron_ of the _meis_, they should be discouraged from continuing on to the cemetery. In some communities, as in Yerushalayim, the _minhag_ is that, after initially accompanying a male _niftar_ a short way, none of his children follow him to the cemetery. (_Mishpetei Hashalom_ 15:9–10)

| 16 Adar | 16 Tammuz | 16 Cheshvan |

Exemption from Other Mitzvos   THERE IS A Torah principle that someone who is occupied with one _mitzvah_ is exempt from performing another _mitzvah_ that becomes incumbent upon him while he is involved in the first _mitzvah_. For this reason, those carrying the _aron_, as well as their substitutes, who must be available at any moment to take over doing the _mitzvah_, whether they are walking in front of the _aron_ or behind it, are all exempt from _Krias Shema_ and _tefillah_. The same applies to anyone who is directly involved in carrying the _meis_, guarding him until the _levayah_, digging the grave and other related tasks — all are exempt from _Krias Shema_, _tefillah_ and all other _mitzvos_. The other people attending the _levayah_, who are not needed for these purposes, should slip away to recite _Shema_ and _tefillah_, and should then come back to resume their involvement with the _niftar_.

In order to avoid the need to fall back on this principle, ideally the funeral should not be set for an hour that is close to the required time for _Krias Shema_ or even for after that time, until such time as they can assume that most of the attendees will have had a chance to daven. Nevertheless, once the _levayah_ has begun, anyone who is required to assist with the _aron_ should not stop to say _Krias Shema_. Similarly, on Purim and _erev Pesach_ a funeral should not be set for a time that will interfere with the reading of the Megillah or with the burning of _chametz_.

After the burial, it is important to accompany the _aveilim_ from the

graveside to the place where those present will line up to give their condolences and to where the mourners will begin their observance of *shivah*. At that point, if those who have not yet had a chance to say *Krias Shema* will be able to start and finish even the first *passuk* before the *aveilim* arrive at the designated location, they should do so. If they see that they will not have time to finish, they should not begin.

However, if they see that by waiting to give *tanchumim* to the *aveilim* they will miss the final time for *Krias Shema*, they should first say *Krias Shema* and should afterward comfort the *aveilim*. In this case, the rule of "someone involved in a *mitzvah* is exempt from another *mitzvah*" does not apply, because at the point when they realized that they must say *Krias Shema* immediately, they had already completed the *mitzvah* of *hotzaas hameis* and had not yet begun the *mitzvah* of *tanchumim*. (*Mishpetei Hashalom* 15:11–13)

17 Adar   17 Tammuz   17 Cheshvan

**Hespeidim —
Eulogizing the
Niftar**

Although Mr. Weinstein died at the ripe old age of 90, his son, Avraham Weinstein, was broken by the loss of his dear, special father. Everyone understood that Avraham would step up at the *levayah* to speak some words of *hesped*. Avraham was flustered. He hadn't spoken publicly since his bar mitzvah; he was a quiet fellow, easily moved to emotion, and as much as he loved his father, he wasn't sure he could express how much he appreciated his father's character in words.

Hesitantly, he stepped to the lectern and began to speak. After every few words he would break down in tears, and the crowd sobbed along with him. After several attempts to continue his *hesped*, he gave up and stepped down. Later on, during the *shivah*, he confided to his friend Baruch, "I feel that I failed in my task. There was so much I could have said, and I couldn't get the words out."

Baruch opened a *sefer* on *aveilus* and showed him that one of the main purposes of the *hesped* is to rouse the listeners to shed tears for the *niftar*, and that is precisely what Avraham had done. Avraham was consoled.

EULOGIZING THE *NIFTAR* in a fitting manner is a great *mitzvah*. The proper way to fulfill the *mitzvah* is to raise one's voice and say heartrending words that will move the listeners to tears. The Gemara (*Shabbos* 105b) states that "When a person sheds tears over the passing of a good man, Hashem counts out the tears, places them in His treasury and forgives all the sins of the one who wept. In contrast, one who is slack in weeping over the *niftar* does not merit long life and deserves to be buried alive."

The *hesped* should include praise of the *niftar*. We are allowed to exaggerate slightly in our praise, but not to overdo it; nor may we praise him for attributes that he did not possess at all.

Women too should be properly eulogized, just as men are, even in front of a crowd of *talmidei chachamim*. A *talmid chacham* who passes away, and the wife of a *talmid chacham*, may be eulogized in a shul or *beis medrash*, although laymen may not be eulogized there.

A child, too, is eulogized from the time he has reached a certain age. If he has elderly or impoverished parents, then we say a *hesped* for him from age five. If he is from a wealthy family (and if his parents are not elderly), then we eulogize him only from age six. However, *tzidduk ha-din* and Kaddish are said even for a baby who lived for just thirty days, or, according to other opinions, for a child who lived twelve months.

If the child was old enough to have had his own dealings in life, we praise him for his own merits when we eulogize him. If not, we can praise him for the deeds of his parents or relatives.

Generally, we are careful not to speak words of Torah in front of the *meis*; rather, we should have only basic conversations and discuss things that pertain to the *meis* himself, such as matters regarding the burial. This is because the *neshamah* of the *meis* is aware of what is going on around him. Therefore, learning Torah in his presence is considered to be *lo'eig larash*, causing him pain, and mundane chatter about things that do not pertain to his needs would be disturbing to him. However, it is permissible to cite *pesukim* and give Torah *derashos* as part of the *hesped*, which is for the honor of the *meis*, even within the immediate area where the *meis* lies, or at the cemetery.

Once the burial has been completed, we interrupt further *hespeidim* to say *Krias Shema* or to *daven*. However, when the *meis* still lies before us, the people should slip away one at a time to say *Krias Shema* and *daven*. (*Mishpetei Hashalom* 15:14–19)

Days When AS WE HAVE mentioned, one of the purposes of the
Hespeidim Are *hespeidim* is to rouse the listeners to sorrowful tears.
Not Said Therefore, on certain joyous occasions through the
year *hespeidim* are limited, so as not to dampen the
simchah of the day. On some days all *hespeidim* are prohibited; on other
days, we deliver a *hesped* only for a *talmid chacham*; on yet other days
we may eulogize a *talmid chacham* only in his presence.

All *hespeidim* — except for a *talmid chacham* in his presence — are
prohibited during the month of Nisan, and on Pesach Sheni, Lag
Ba'omer, Chanukah, Purim and Purim Katan, Shushan Purim and
Shushan Purim Katan, Tu BiShvat, Tu B'Av, *isru chag*, the four days
between Yom Kippur and Sukkos, and Rosh Chodesh.

Likewise, *hespeidim* should not be given — except for a *talmid chacham* — on *erev Shabbos* and *erev Yom Tov* after midday, and on *erev Yom
Kippur* from the morning. Even a *talmid chacham* is not eulogized, even
in his presence, on Shabbos or Yom Tov or on *chol hamo'ed*. *Hespeidim*
may be said on Tishah B'Av, even though that day is called a *mo'ed*, since
the day is set aside for crying and mourning. No eulogy may be said for
any *meis* after twelve months have passed from the time of his departure
from this world.

The Torah also limits the mourners' expressions of grief. We may
not pluck out even one of our hairs in our grief over the *meis*, nor may
we scratch our flesh, even when not in the presence of the *meis*. Striking
one's hands in grief until blood flows is permissible. However, some
opinions qualify this *heter* and permit it only when the *meis* was a great
man and our grief flows from anguish over the loss of his Torah; in regard to an ordinary person who died, such action would be prohibited.
(*Mishpetei Hashalom* 15:20–21)

Burial WHILE IN MANY societies burial of the dead is an ex-
Expenses travagant ceremony, the Torah way is not to use expensive
shrouds; the *meis* is buried in simple white linen *tachrichim*, which may be made from *shaatnez* (the generally forbidden
combination of wool and linen). The *poskim* differ as to whether the

meis may be buried in a _tallis_ with _kosher tzitzis_ on it. (All the details concerning preparation of the body of the _meis_ for burial are explained in the _Shulchan Aruch_.) _Tachrichim_ should not be prepared for a dying person as long as he is still alive. However, a healthy person may prepare _tachrichim_ for himself in advance.

When an impoverished person dies, funds should be collected discreetly to pay for his burial needs; the purpose of the collection should not be revealed to anyone who does not need to know. Anyone who has settled in the community as a permanent resident, or who has been living there for at least nine months, may be compelled to contribute toward a burial fund for the needy of the community. In some communities today, participation in such a collection is required from the time one has been a resident for just thirty days.

| 19 Adar | 19 Tammuz | 19 Cheshvan |

When funds have been collected specifically to pay for a particular person's burial needs, any money that is left over may be given to his heirs. However, if the money was not collected specifically for him, then the remaining funds should be set aside to be used to help cover the costs of future burials.

If before his death someone requested that burial costs should not be taken from his own assets (but inevitably will come from the public coffers), his request is ignored; he has no right to leave a larger sum for his heirs at the expense of the community.

Instead, money should be taken from the assets his heirs inherited in order to cover the costs of burial, along with any other costs that families living on his standard would normally spend on a relative's passing, such as for the erection of a suitable tombstone over the grave.

If, on the other hand, a poor person requested before his death that he not be given a respectful burial, so that public monies will not have to be used, we ignore his request as well, since although he may forgo his own honor, doing so would also disgrace the living.

If the heirs who inherited the assets of the _meis_ refuse to pay for someone to eulogize the _niftar_, they are to be forced to come up with the funds. A _hesped_ is an honor for the _meis_, and the heirs have no right

to dispense with it. On the other hand, if the *meis* himself requested before his death that he not be eulogized, his request should be honored, for he is entitled to give up his own honor. However, if he asks that the mourners not sit *shivah* or that they not observe the laws of *shloshim*, we are not to heed his request.

Even though many respected people request, out of humility, that they not be eulogized, the leaders of the community often opt to overlook that request and deliver *hespeidim* anyway in order to arouse the assembled to repent and learn from the actions and character of the *niftar*. (*Mishpetei Hashalom* 15:22–25)

20 Adar	20 Tammuz	20 Cheshvan

Conduct in the Cemetery   AS WE MENTIONED, the *neshamah* of the *meis* is aware of what is going on around him. Since he can no longer perform *mitzvos* himself, seeing others flaunting their *mitzvos* would cause him pain. For this reason, we may not enter a cemetery, nor walk within four *amos* (about 6 feet or 2 meters) of the *meis*, when we are wearing *tefillin* or *tzitzis* that are showing. Doing so is considered being *lo'eig larash*.

Similarly, we may not carry a *sefer Torah* in our arms, even without reading from it, nor may we daven or *lein* (read from the Torah), even by heart, within four *amos* of the *meis*, unless it is for his own honor. However, if someone stands farther away than four *amos*, he may read from the Torah or *daven*, even if he is still in sight of the grave or the cemetery. If there is a *mechitzah*, a *halachic* partition, then he may do so even within four *amos* of the *meis*.

A cemetery should be treated with respect; therefore, we do not eat or drink, tend to mundane matters or relieve ourselves in the cemetery. A cemetery should not be used as a shortcut from one point to another. (*Mishpetei Hashalom* 15:26–27)

In summary: The obligation of *hotzaas hameis* is one of the expressions of *ve'ahavta lerei'acha kamocha* and *vehalachta bidrachav*. In addition, burying the *meis* is also a fulfillment of the *mitzvos* of *lo salin* and *kavor tikberenu*. A burial may not be delayed unless it is for the honor of the *meis*. Torah study is interrupted in order to accompany the *meis*, with certain qualifications. A person who is involved in the needs of the *meis* is exempt from other *mitzvos* until after the burial. It is a great *mitzvah* to properly eulogize the *meis*. The heirs of the deceased can be forced to pay for the costs of burial. The community should discreetly provide for the burial costs of the needy. Certain rules guide our behavior in the immediate area where the *meis* is resting, as well as in the cemetery.

חסד של אמת

⋙ 25 ⋘

ניחום אבלים
Consoling the Mourners

| 21 Adar | 21 Tammuz | 21 Cheshvan |

Comfort for the Mourner, Honor for the Deceased Aviva dragged her feet as she approached the *shivah* house with her friend Rina. "It looks like you've been chosen to break me in to all the *mitzvos* I've always been hesitant to do, Rina. First you got me to visit Rochel in the hospital, and now you've persuaded me to do the *mitzvah* of *nichum aveilim* with you for Miriam Werner, since her mother passed away."

"I'm sure you would have gone even without my convincing," Rina protested. "Miriam is our good friend."

"I know," Aviva agreed. "But I don't know what to say and what not to say. I'm afraid I'll put my foot in my mouth and make her feel even worse."

"Don't worry. The main thing is to show her we care," Rina asserted as she opened the door that was slightly ajar.

Aviva and Rina sat quietly until Miriam began to talk about her mother. Before long the friends were sharing their memories of Mrs. Werner's warmth and *chessed*. Twenty minutes passed quickly, and the girls realized it was time to leave. They said the traditional words of *tanchumim* that were posted on the wall, addressing their words to Miriam's sisters and aunts as well.

"I appreciate your coming," Miriam said softly. "I know it wasn't easy for you, but it's so comforting to know that you're there for me, and it is a real *kavod* for my mother, *a"h*, too."

282

ONE OF THE ways of fulfilling the *mitzvah* of *vehalachta bidrachav* and emulating Hashem is by exerting ourselves to do the *chessed* of *nichum aveilim* — consoling mourners after the loss of a close relative — as Hashem comforted Yitzchak Avinu after the passing of his father Avraham Avinu (*Bereishis* 25:11).

If we were in the position of the *aveil* we would certainly want others to comfort us; therefore, by consoling the *aveil* we also fulfill the *mitzvah* of *ve'ahavta lerei'acha kamocha* — acting toward others as we would want them to act toward us.

Even though *akum* are not included in the *mitzvah* of *ve'ahavta lerei'acha kamocha*, we still bury their dead and console their mourners, in order to promote peace. (*Mishpetei Hashalom* 15:31, 48)

| 22 Adar | 22 Tammuz | 22 Cheshvan |

Seudas Havraah   THE FIRST MEAL the *aveil* eats after returning from the funeral is known as the *seudas havraah*. The *aveil* should not eat of his own food for this meal; it is the neighbors' responsibility to provide him with all that is necessary, from their own resources. The second meal may be his own food, even if he eats it on the first day of *shivah*.

Needless to say, if the *aveil* is alone in a strange city, or if for whatever reason his neighbors do not bring him the meal, he does not have to afflict himself and go hungry; he can eat from his own food. (The laws of *Birkas Hamazon* in the mourner's house are explained in *Shulchan Aruch Yoreh Dei'ah* 379.)

The *seudas havraah* for a woman *aveilah* should be provided by women, not by men. If she is married, her husband may not provide this meal for her. (*Mishpetei Hashalom* 15:29–30)

Nichum Aveilim — Dual Purpose   THE *MITZVAH* OF *nichum aveilim* is a *chessed* both for the living — the mourning relatives of the *niftar* — and for the deceased — the *meis* himself.

Regarding the *aveilim*, the crux of the *mitzvah* is to comfort them in their pain, to offer them emotional support, and to say comforting words that will relieve their worries and ease their pain. This is an even greater *mitzvah* when the *aveil* is a poor person, since a poor person's anguish is greater than that of a wealthy person; moreover, the poor person usually has fewer friends coming to console him.

The *minhag* is that not only women but also men console women mourners; however, care should be taken to avoid *yichud* (the prohibition of a man being alone with a woman). Usually, even when only female mourners are present, *tefillos* will take place in the *shivah* house, and it is customary for men to offer their consolation after the *tefillos*.

By consoling the mourners we do a *chessed* for the *meis* as well. Therefore, even if the *niftar* did not leave any living relatives who could sit *shivah*, some opinions say that ten people should come and sit *shivah* in the home of the *niftar* and that people should gather there to honor the *niftar*. In practice this is not usually done; however, when possible, a minyan should gather to daven in the home of the *niftar* during the seven days of *shivah*.

If someone is unable to come personally to the *beis aveil*, the house of mourning, due to illness or other difficulty, he can perform the *mitzvah* of *tanchumim* by speaking to the *aveil* on the phone. However, this is not a complete fulfillment of the *mitzvah*, because it is lacking the aspect of *chessed* for the *niftar*, which can be accomplished only by actually visiting the *shivah* house. (*Mishpetei Hashalom* 15:31–32)

| 23 Adar | 23 Tammuz | 23 Cheshvan |

Conduct in the Beis Aveil

Aharon Weinstein glanced at the clock. It was a quarter to eleven. Exhausted by the long day of *aveilus* that started at seven o'clock, when the *minyan* began, he hoped that they would soon be able to call it a day. Just then the door opened and Chaim Rudman walked in. Aharon tried to stifle his groan.

"Hope it's not too late," Chaim said cheerfully, and he began a long monologue that had little to do with either the pain of the *aveilim* or memories of the *niftar*. The *aveilim*'s repeated yawns and glances at the clock did not seem to register with him at all, as he kept talking and asking inappropriate questions. Nor did he seem to notice that all the other visitors had left. Finally, at 11:30 p.m., he rose, said the requisite words of *nichumim*, and apologized — not for coming late, but for being unable to stay longer.

IF A MAJOR purpose of *nichum aveilim* is to alleviate the pain of the *aveilim*, it stands to reason that the *mitzvah* should be performed in a way that does not aggravate their discomfort. This relates to when we come, how long we stay and what we say on our visit of consolation.

Some opinions say that we should not visit the *aveilim* during the first three days after their relative's death, since these days are meant for crying, and the mourner is not yet ready to be comforted. However, others allow *nichum aveilim* even during the first three days.

Nichum aveilim may be done day or night. However, the needs of the *aveilim* should be taken into consideration, and visitors should not come too late at night, nor should they come during afternoon hours if the mourners might want to take a break to rest or eat at that time.

A person should not visit his enemy who is sitting *shivah* if it is likely to appear as if he is gloating over the *aveil*'s misfortune. Each situation should be weighed according to its particular factors. (*Mishpetei Hashalom* 15:33)

The Aveil Sets the Tone THE *AVEIL* SHOULD sit at the head of the table. Generally, visitors should not speak until the *aveil* opens the conversation. However, if they see that it is difficult for him to begin, then the visitors should take the initiative and start speaking as necessary.

The *aveil* does not have to stand up even in honor of the Torah leader of the generation who enters the room. If the *aveil* does rise to honor his friend, he should not be told, "*Sheiv* — Sit down," since that sounds as if the visitor is telling the *aveil* to sit — that is, to remain — in his mourning.

Since the *aveil* cannot say "*shalom*," as we will discuss, the consoler should be sensitive to the *aveil*'s signals in his direction. It is especially important to do so when the hour is late, or when mealtime approaches. When the *aveil* hints that he is ready for us to go, we may not remain there any longer.

When parting from the *aveil*, the *minhag* is to comfort him with the words "*HaMakom yenachem eschem* [plural]/*oscha* [singular] *besoch she'ar aveilei Tzion ViYerushalayim* — May Hashem console you among the other mourners of Tzion and Yerushalayim."

On Shabbos, we can console the *aveil* with the words "*Shabbos hi milenachem unechamah kerovah lavo* — On Shabbos we do not console, but a consolation should soon be on the way." Some opinions are more lenient and even allow one to say, "*HaMakom yenachemcha* — May Hashem console you" on Shabbos. (*Mishpetei Hashalom* 15:34–37, 41)

24 Adar	24 Tammuz	24 Cheshvan

She'eilas "Shalom" — Inquiring of Another's Welfare Using Hashem's Name "Shalom" AS WE DISCUSSED in Volume I, chapter 6, one should generally greet other Jews with a *she'eilas shalom* — an inquiry after his welfare. *Shalom* also has an implication of completeness, both in the physical and in the emotional sense. With the loss of a loved one, a mourner experiences a sense of incompleteness, and the sorrow he feels at the loss is a form of honor for the *niftar*. Exchanging greetings of *shalom* would imply that the *aveil* is lacking that feeling of bereavement. For this reason, the *aveil* is forbidden to give or receive a *she'eilas shalom*, in keeping with the following guidelines:

- During the first three days, he may not greet anyone. If others greet him, out of ignorance or not realizing that he is an *aveil*, he should not return the greeting but rather should inform them of his status.

- From the third to the seventh day he may not greet others, but if they greet him unknowingly he may respond.

- From the seventh to the thirtieth day, he may greet others, but others should not greet him. However, if they do, he may respond.

- On Shabbos, the *aveil* himself can greet others with a *gut Shabbos*, since refraining from doing so would be considered conspicuous mourning on Shabbos, which is prohibited. Whether or not others can greet the _aveil_ on Shabbos depends on local _minhag_; in some communities the custom is to greet the _aveil_, and in others, the custom is not to do so.

- After the _shloshim_, the _aveil_ returns to his regular status, unless he is mourning for a parent. In the case of the passing of a parent, the consensus of _poskim_ is that we should not greet the _aveil_ using the term "_shalom_" for a full twelve months, nor should we send him _mishlo'ach manos_ on Purim.

Even though the _aveil_ is generally prohibited from _she'eilas shalom_, if a large group of consolers gets up to leave, he is allowed to say to them, "_Lechu leveischem leshalom_ — Go home in peace," since the prohibition is mitigated for the sake of showing honor to the public.

If the _aveil_ is not allowed even to give a short greeting, we can understand that he should also not talk more than is necessary. During the week of _shivah_ he should not leave the house at all, and during the second and third weeks, he can leave the house but should not talk unnecessarily. However, some opinions allow the _aveil_ to bless others with long life, _refuah sheleimah_, _mazal tov_ and similar blessings, and he is also allowed to shake hands with a person while blessing him. (_Mishpetei Hashalom_ 15:38–40)

| 25 Adar | 25 Tammuz | 25 Cheshvan |

Nichum Aveilim
after the Shivah

WHEN WE MEET a person whom we know is a mourner, if it is still within the _shloshim_ — thirty days from the time of his loss — we can still console him, and we should not greet him. After the _shloshim_, we greet him in the normal fashion and do not console him directly, but rather "_min hatzad_" — in an indirect manner, that is, without mentioning the name of the _niftar_ and by saying to him in a more general way, the word "_Tisnachem_ — Be comforted."

When someone is mourning the loss of a parent, we may console him for a full twelve months. After that time we should console him only indirectly. When a person has lost his wife, we may console him until

Shalosh Regalim (the three festivals of Sukkos, Pesach and Shavuos) have passed. However, if he remarries in the interim, we should console him only if we meet him outside but not in his home. (*Mishpetei Hashalom* 15:42–44)

Accepting the Decree EVEN THOUGH LOSING a loved one can be a devastating experience, the *aveil* is expected to adhere to certain *halachic* limitations of mourning. Someone who mourns excessively may bring upon himself another loss, *chas veshalom*.

The Torah allots three days for crying, seven days for *hesped*, and thirty days for refraining from haircuts and wearing laundered, pressed clothing. However, when a *talmid chacham* passes away, the extent of mourning depends on his stature and thus the magnitude of the loss. In any case, we do not cry for someone for more than thirty days and do not eulogize him for more than twelve months.

The *aveil* should never say, "I have not been paid according to my deeds," implying that he deserves even harsher punishment, since we should not "tempt the *satan*."

When the life of a loved one is in danger, we do whatever we can to prevent his death — taking practical steps and engaging in *tefillah* and fasting. Nevertheless, after the person dies, it is natural for us to feel guilty and think, "Perhaps we did not do enough." However, once there is nothing more that can be done, we have to realize that this was Hashem's Will and accept the decree with equanimity.

Therefore, one should never say to an *aveil*, "What can you do — we cannot change the *din*," since this kind of talk has a blasphemous tone, implying that if we could change Hashem's decrees we would, and if it were up to us we would run the world differently. Rather, we should accept Hashem's decree with love, as difficult as it may be, secure in the knowledge that Hashem loves us and that everything He does is only for our benefit.

The remaining laws of *aninus* (the period before the burial), *aveilus*, *tziduk hadin* and related *halachos* are beyond the scope of this work; these laws are explained fully in *Shulchan Aruch Yoreh Dei'ah*. (*Mishpetei Hashalom* 15:45–47)

In summary: The *mitzvah* of *nichum aveilim* is another expression of *ve'ahavta lerei'acha kamocha* and *vehalachta bidrachav*. The *mitzvah* has a dual purpose — comforting the *aveil* and honoring the *niftar*. The *seudas havraah* for the aveil should be provided by neighbors. While sitting *shivah* the *aveil* should open the conversation, and we should act in accordance with his hints as to when the *nichum aveilim* visit should be concluded. It is forbidden for the *aveil* to give or receive *she'eilas shalom*, according to halachic guidelines. He should not overreact in his grief, but should accept the decree of Hashem lovingly and adhere to the limitations applicable to the first three days of mourning, the *shivah* and the *shloshim*.

ניחום אבלים

26

חתן וכלה
Chassan Vekallah

26 Adar	26 Tammuz	26 Cheshvan

Bringing Joy   "How are you getting to the wedding tonight?" Rabbi Dovid Abrams asked his friend and fellow rebbe, Rabbi Aronowitz, as they gathered up their *sefarim* and prepared to head home.

"You mean Yaakov Rubin's wedding? Actually, I was planning to sit that one out. There are so many *simchah*s these days — relatives, neighbors, friends — I can't get to the wedding of every former talmid, too."

"I know what you mean. But didn't you mention that he made a special visit last week to invite you personally? You were pretty close with him when he was in *yeshivah*, weren't you? Don't you think your absence might cast a shadow on his simchah?"

"You have a point there, Reb Dovid," Rabbi Aronowitz conceded, rubbing his beard thoughtfully. "If my being there is important for his *simchah*, then I just may be halachically obligated to attend, even if it is a bit difficult for me. I guess I'll pick another wedding to skip. I'll just check with my wife, and assuming there's no problem, I can pick you up at seven."

AMONG THE RABBINICAL *mitzvos* derived from the *mitzvah* of *ve-halachta bidrachav* are our obligations toward a *chassan* and *kallah*, which include escorting the *kallah* to the *chuppah*, gladdening the *chas-*

290

san and *kallah*, and providing them with their needs. These are acts of *chessed* that we should personally exert ourselves to do, and they are not limited by any prescribed measure. By carrying out our obligations in this regard, in addition to *vehalachta bidrachav*, we also fulfill the *mitzvah* of *ve'ahavta lerei'acha kamocha*. (*Mishpetei Hashalom* 16:1)

Hachnasas Kallah — Escorting the Kallah ESCORTING A *KALLAH* to the *chuppah* is so important that it supersedes the *mitzvah* of Torah learning. Therefore, if we see such a procession in progress we are obligated to honor the occasion with our participation, even if we must interrupt our Torah study to do so. Some opinions say that even if we do not actually see the *chuppah* but are merely aware that it is to take place at this time in the town, we are obligated to interrupt our Torah learning in order to participate. In large cities, however, where weddings are common, and especially when we are not familiar with either of the two sides, the *halachah* is lenient and we need not interrupt our learning.

We mentioned in chapter 24 that according to most opinions there is no limit to the number of people who should interrupt their Torah learning in order to participate in a funeral. Regarding the numbers required to escort a *kallah*, there are differing opinions. Some maintain that since *hachnasas kallah* is an honor only for the living — that is, to endear the *kallah* to the *chassan* — it is sufficient for her to be accompanied by a number of people appropriate for the *kallah*'s personal stature. Others disagree and say that escorting the *kallah* is greater than escorting the *meis* and has no prescribed limit. Therefore, everyone should interrupt his Torah learning for *hachnasas kallah*, since the more people there are present, the greater the honor of the *chassan* and *kallah*, and the more we add to their joy and mutual endearment. (The rules regarding what takes precedence when one must attend both a wedding and a funeral are outlined at the end of chapter 22.)

When we are invited to a wedding, the Gemara states that we should make every effort to attend and to sit down at the *seudas mitzvah*. However, this obligation is not considered as strong as is an invitation to the *seudah* of a *bris*. In addition, according to many opinions, the printed invitations of our day are not considered personal invitations regarding this obligation, and the same is often true even of an invitation delivered verbally, which may be offered simply as a polite gesture. However, if someone has reason to believe that the family would be hurt by his absence, then he may be obligated to attend in order to fulfill his obligation to provide the *chassan* with "that which he is lacking." (*Mishpetei Hashalom* 16:2, 4)

| 27 Adar | 27 Tammuz | 27 Cheshvan |

Escorting the Kallah — How and Who? HACHNASAS KALLAH IS defined in the Gemara as escorting the *kallah* from her father's home to the place of the *chuppah*. In our times, this stage of the *mitzvah* is done by women, while the men fulfill their obligation by walking along with the *chassan* on his way to the *badeken* (the covering of the *kallah*'s face). Others say that the *mitzvah* is fulfilled by the men walking toward the *kallah* and then, when they draw near, turning back and returning toward the *chuppah*.

When it comes to the *mitzvah* of *hachnasas kallah*, no one should be inhibited by a concern that it is not fitting for him to accompany a simpler person to the *chuppah*. After all, the Gemara points out to us that Hashem Himself tended to the needs of the first couple, Adam and Chava, and even braided Chava's hair to bring her to her *chassan*, as we learn from the words "*Vayiven ... es hatzela* — He built up the side." Therefore, even respected people should not consider such efforts as being beneath them, and they should make an effort to arrange *shidduchim*, to see to the needs of the wedding feast and to bring joy to the *chassan* and *kallah*. (*Mishpetei Hashalom* 16:3, 5)

Beautifying the Mitzvah IN EARLIER TIMES, the greatest *Amora'im* would involve themselves personally with decorating the *chuppah*, and the *Tanna'im* would adorn the *chassan* with crowns and ring chime bells before him.

Once the *Beis Hamikdash* was destroyed and the painful exile commenced, some of these *minhagim* were prohibited. The *chassan* is no longer adorned with a crown, nor is the *kallah* given a tiara of gold,

silver or precious stones, from the night before the *chuppah* and for the duration of the seven days of *sheva berachos*. However, she is permitted to don a crown of multicolored embroidered material, although opinions differ as to whether this crown may include threads or pieces of gold and silver. (*Mishpetei Hashalom* 16: 6)

28 Adar	28 Tammuz	28 Cheshvan

Simchas Chassan Vekallah

"Naftali, did you see Asher anywhere?" Shraga asked his friend. "Since we came to the wedding together, I've hardly seen him — not at the table, not schmoozing in the hallway with the rest of the fellows ..."

"Have I seen him? I've been watching him the whole time," Naftali responded. "He's a nonstop model of *simchas chassan*. When we first came he gave a full five-minute *brachah* to the *chassan*. Then he started to rave to him about the *kallah*; his sister was in school with her, and she must have given him a booklet full of compliments to say. And now ... well, just look."

The two of them watched as Asher magically appeared at the side of the red-faced *chassan* with a cool drink of soda. He reappeared shortly afterward with a chair for the *chassan*, and moments later he was back with two more for the *chassan*'s father and father-in-law. Then, when there was a slight lull in the dancing, he suddenly began a one-man juggling and dancing performance that brought a huge smile to the *chassan*'s face.

"He's working hard," Shraga said, astounded at Asher's untiring efforts. "When is he going to enjoy himself?"

"Take a look at him," Naftali said, pointing out Asher's beaming face, beaded with sweat. "Do you really have any doubt that he's enjoying himself? He's just doing it with an emphasis on the *mitzvah* and not on himself having a good time, like some of us tend to do..."

IT IS A *MITZVAH* to be *mesamei'ach* — to gladden — the *chassan* and *kallah*, both by dancing for them and by saying things that will make them happy. A primary way of being *mesamei'ach* the *chassan* is by singing the praises of his *kallah* and saying how beautiful and charming she is — even if the compliments are a bit of an exaggeration — to reassure him that his choice was a good one. Naturally, we should not say an

outright lie, but we can use ambiguous language, such as saying that the *kallah* is beautiful, even if her outward appearance is not particularly attractive, since it can also be taken to mean that she is beautiful in her *middos*, and her beauty clearly found favor in the *chassan*'s eyes if he decided to marry her.

When being *mesamei'ach* the *chassan*, we should do so in accordance with his level. To a *ben Torah* we offer intellectually stimulating *divrei Torah*, since that is the main source of *simchah*. A simpler person will derive pleasure from hearing *divrei aggadah*, and for a yet simpler *chassan*, light conversation and amusing words are appropriate. However, we should be careful to avoid frivolous talk, and even the *milei debedichusa* — the humorous words — should carry a moral message for the couple.

Other ways that the *mitzvah* of *simchas chassan vekallah* can be fulfilled include being *mesader kiddushin*, saying one of the *brachos* under the *chuppah* or after *bentching*, giving the *chassan* something to eat or drink, getting the *chassan* to laugh with a good joke, and so on. An important person may fulfill the *mitzvah* simply by his presence at the wedding. The same can be said of someone who comes from afar and makes an unusual effort to attend the *simchah*.

Musical instruments are an important element in bringing joy to the *chassan* and *kallah*, and in areas where music is traditionally played at weddings, it is considered as much of a requirement as is the *seudah*. In Yerushalayim, the *minhag* among *Ashkenazim* is to limit musical accompaniment to one instrument, due to the proximity to the site of the *churban*, the site of the destroyed *Beis Hamikdash*. (*Mishpetei Hashalom* 16:7–8, 10)

29 Adar   29 Tammuz   29 Cheshvan

Simchas Chassan Vekallah — Who Is Obligated? ALTHOUGH ORDINARILY A *chacham* may not forgo his *kavod*, since his honor is the honor of Torah, nevertheless, when it comes to exerting himself for a *davar shebikdushah* — a holy purpose — he may do so. Therefore, we find that David Hamelech danced publicly before the *Aron Kodesh*, and that *chachamim* involved themselves in ostensibly menial tasks of preparing for Shabbos, digging a grave, building a sukkah and drawing water for matzah-baking.

Similarly, the greatest *chachamim* of the Mishnah and Gemara are known to have set their honor aside to be *mesamei'ach chassan vekallah*: Rabbi Yehudah bar Ilai would take a *hadas*, a stalk of a myrtle tree, and dance with it before the *kallah*, singing, "The *kallah* is beautiful and charming," and Rabbi Shmuel bar Rav Yitzchak would dance while juggling three items at a time.

Chazal say that anyone who partakes of the feast of a *chassan* and is not *mesamei'ach* him degrades the five *kolos* — the five "sounds" with which Hashem blessed *Am Yisrael* ("*Kol sasson vekol simchah ...* — The sound of joy and the sound of gladness ..."). On the other hand, someone who is *mesamei'ach* the *chassan* merits the Torah, which was given with five *kolos*, and it is considered as if he offered a *korban todah* and rebuilt one of the ruins of Yerushalayim.

According to some opinions, anyone who is present at a wedding, even if he does not partake of the *seudah*, is obligated to be *mesamei'ach* the *chassan*. However, if he fails to do so in such a case, he is not guilty of degrading the five *kolos*.

When attending a wedding we are permitted to derive personal enjoyment from the occasion; in fact, seeing the guests enjoying themselves definitely adds to the pleasure of the *baal hasimchah*. However, the focus should not be on our personal enjoyment but rather on bringing joy to the *chassan* and *kallah* and their families. The rule is to place oneself in the shoes of the *chassan* and *kallah* and do for them whatever we would like them to do for us if we were in their position. (*Mishpetei Hashalom* 16:10–11)

1 Nisan	1 Av	1 Kislev

Retaining an Aura of Tznius — Modesty WHILE ALL AGREE that there is a *mitzvah* to dance before the *kallah*, there are different *minhagim* regarding a male relative or Rabbi dancing ("*mitzvah tantz*") *with* the *kallah* — with the separation of a handkerchief, of course — in order to endear her to the *chassan*. According to some opinions it is prohibited to do so, and a *talmid chacham* should be stringent

and refrain. In communities where this is the norm and the intentions of those participating are *lesheim Shamayim*, one should not protest the *minhag*, but where it is not the accepted *minhag*, such dancing is forbidden. In any case, the *poskim* prohibit men gazing at the *kallah*.

At wedding celebrations we should be careful to ensure complete separation between men and women, especially during the dancing. If, *chas veshalom*, there is any mixing between boys and girls at the time of dancing, many *issurim* are violated, including: "*Lo sikrevu …* — Do not approach …" (*Vayikra* 18); "*Lo sasuru …* — Do not turn after your eyes" (*Bamidbar* 15); and "*Venishmarta …* — Keep away from all evil thoughts" (*Devarim* 23). In fact, if men and women sit together during the wedding meal, the meal loses its designation as a *seudas mitzvah*, and we do not add the *brachah* of *Shehasimchah bime'ono* with the *bentching*, since Torah obligations are likely to be violated at such a gathering. Whoever is in a position to influence the *baalei simchah* should do whatever is in his power to prevent this practice.

When a *sheva brachos* takes place in a private home, with the participation of only close family, in some places the custom is for men and women to sit separately in the same room, without a *mechitzah* separating them, and still say the *brachah* of *Shehasimchah bime'ono*. However, if there are young men or women from outside the family present, such as friends of the *chassan* and *kallah*, then there should certainly be a *mechitzah*. (*Mishpetei Hashalom* 16:12–13)

2 Nisan	2 Av	2 Kislev

Providing the Couple with Their Needs   A FATHER IS obligated to make every effort to provide whatever is necessary to marry off his sons and daughters when they come of age, even if this requires him to greatly extend himself financially. For example, *Chazal* tell us that a person should "sell everything he owns so as to marry off his daughter to a *talmid chacham*." If he has a large family and will not be able to marry his children off from his own resources, he is required to accept *tzedakah* for this purpose. If he refuses to accept financial assistance because he is too proud to do so, he is considered a *choteh* — a sinner.

In addition to the special obligation a father has toward his children, every member of *Klal Yisrael* is required to provide the needy with "*dei machsoro asher yechsar lo* — the needs that he is lacking" (*Devarim* 15). *Chazal* explain that *lo* — to him — refers to a wife, as we see from the *passuk*, "*E'eseh lo eizer kenegdo* — I will make for him a helpmate" (*Bereishis* 2:18).

We see, therefore, that one aspect of the obligation of *tzedakah* is to try and find suitable *shidduchim* for single people and help marry them off. Even if our *shidduch*-efforts are unsuccessful, we do a *chessed* with our efforts by assuring the singles that we have them in mind (as long as the suggestion is a fairly suitable one and not insulting), and we also keep their names in people's awareness, increasing their chances of receiving another *shidduch*-suggestion.

According to *Chazal*, the words "*Hatzneia leches im Hashem Elokecha* — Walk modestly with Hashem your G-d" (*Michah* 6) — refers to *hachnasas kallah*. The basic explanation for this *passuk* is that even though the wedding celebration is a public affair, there too we should eat and rejoice in a refined manner and not act frivolously. Another interpretation, however, is that when providing for a poor *kallah* we should be discreet in our efforts and not reveal our actions to anyone who does not need to know.

A poor person who is provided for through *tzedakah* funds must be given "*dei machsoro asher yechsar lo*," as mentioned above. This includes food, dress, living quarters and household items. If he is single and is now getting married, we rent living accommodations for him, provide necessary household utensils and help him make the wedding. If an impoverished woman is to be married and the community *tzedakah* funds suffice, her needs should be provided to suit her dignity.

A *gabbai tzedakah*, who is responsible for the dispensing of community *tzedakah* funds, should use any surplus funds to marry off needy girls, since there is no greater *tzedakah* than this. When the community does not have the necessary funds, the *gabbaim* should sell the shul or other *devarim shebikdushah*, even a *sefer Torah*, in order to raise the money necessary to marry off orphans. (*Mishpetei Hashalom* 16:14–18)

In summary: The *mitzvos* of *hachnasas kallah* and *simchas chassan vekallah* provide an additional opportunity to fulfill the *mitzvah* of *ve'ahavta lerei'acha kamocha* and *vehalachta bidrachav*. Torah learning is interrupted in order to escort a *kallah* to the *chuppah*. The *mitzvah* of *hachnasas kallah* is unlimited; therefore there is no specific number of people who are required to attend. Great and distinguished people should occupy themselves with the wedding needs of simple ones. We are obligated to be *mesamei'ach* the *chassan* by speaking highly of his *kallah*, dancing for him and engaging in other activities that will gladden him. The protective barriers of *tznius* should be carefully retained at a wedding, including full separation between men and women at the meal and dancing. A father must exert himself personally and financially to marry off his children. For a poor *chassan* or *kallah*, the community is obligated to provide whatever is necessary to marry them off, and for an orphan they must do so even if this requires selling *devarim shebikdushah* to raise the money.

⇌ 27 ⇌

הכנסת אורחים

Hospitality to Guests

3 Nisan	3 Av	3 Kislev

True Hospitality   Yerachmiel checked again to see that his wife Yehudis was comfortably ensconced in her hospital bed, then he began to think about his own accommodations. When Yehudis had suddenly gone into labor just after *bentching Shabbos licht*, they were taken quite by surprise. More than a month before her due date, they were unprepared, both emotionally and practically, for this moment. Somehow they managed to summon an ambulance and get to the hospital just in time, and *Baruch Hashem*, mother and baby boy were doing well. But Yerachmiel had not had time before they left to think of grabbing a bottle of grape juice for *Kiddush* or a roll for *Hamotzi*, and now he was stuck in this remote hospital without any basic Shabbos necessities.

Just then, like a *malach* appearing from *Shamayim*, a bearded face peered into the room. "My name is Nochum Kleiner. Would you do us the honor of joining us for a Shabbos *seudah*?" the man pleaded with Yerachmiel. "We live right down the block, and you'd do us a great favor if you would agree to come and enhance our Shabbos table."

Yerachmiel accepted the timely invitation gratefully. Accustomed to hosting guests himself, he was not used to being on the receiving end, but Rabbi Kleiner made it sound as if Yerachmiel would be giving, not receiving, by joining him. "He must have a quiet Shabbos table, where every

299

guest is appreciated," he figured. To his surprise, however, when he arrived at the Kleiner home he found a huge table, where the large Kleiner family and at least five other guests sat.

Before long the guests felt like family, as they were served generously and made to feel at home in every way. The Kleiners even put together an impromptu *Shalom Zachor* for all the fathers of newborn boys among the guests. A few hours later Yerachmiel left, physically and spiritually sated, but not before he had assured his host that he had a suitable bed to sleep in at the hospital, and not before he had promised to return for the *seudah* the next day. After his experience of being a guest, he knew that his own *hachnasas orchim* would take on a new dimension from that point on.

WELCOMING GUESTS AND seeing that their needs are met is one more expression of *vehalachta bidrachav*, as well as being a fulfillment of *ve'ahavta lerei'acha kamocha*. Therefore, whenever we meet up with someone who is traveling or who needs sleeping and eating accommodations for other reasons, we are obligated to do for him whatever we would wish that others would do for us were we in the same position. Some opinions maintain that we fulfill the *mitzvah* even when we invite friends to our home who are not necessarily in need, as long as we are doing it for their honor.

The *mitzvah* includes welcoming the guest into our home, providing him with food and drink, arranging sleeping accommodations for him and accompanying him when he departs, along with meeting any other particular needs he has.

Since this is such an elementary requirement, the people in a city can compel each other to bring in guests and to contribute to the local *hachnasas orchim* fund.

This *mitzvah* applies to men and women, in all places and at all times. Even a poor or sickly person should perform this *mitzvah* to the extent that he is able to do so, as long as he follows the rules of "*chayecha kodmin*" — your own life takes precedence, as well as the principle of "*mibesarcha*" — relatives take precedence. Therefore, he must first see to it that the needs of his family members are adequately met.

Even though the general rule is that it is preferable to do a *mitzvah* personally than to delegate it to an agent, in the case of *hachnasas or-*

chim, we should allot some part of the *mitzvah* to our children, since it is important to train them in welcoming guests. We learn this from Avraham Avinu, the *machnis orchim* par excellence, who involved his son Yishmael in serving the three angels, even though the boy was also still aching from his recent *bris*. As we shall see, we derive many basic principles of *hachnasas orchim* from Avraham Avinu's encounter with the angels. (*Mishpetei Hashalom* 17:1–3, 9)

Hachnasas Orchim — A Top Priority THE IMPORTANCE THAT the Torah accords *hachnasas orchim* can be seen from the priority *Chazal* place upon this *mitzvah* relative to other obligations. "*Hachnasas orchim* is greater than receiving the *Shechinah*"—as we learn from Avraham Avinu, who "kept *Hakadosh Baruch Hu* waiting" (with His approval, of course), while he ran to tend to his guests. "*Hachnasas orchim* is greater than rising early to go to [the] *beis medrash*"—that is, in a case where the guest specifically needs the host, and not anyone else, to serve him, the host may miss *tefillah betzibbur* or interrupt his Torah learning in order to care for his guest.

Similarly, due to the importance of this *mitzvah*, we are lenient in certain specific *halachos* in order to facilitate the proper performance of *hachnasas orchim*. For example, if it is raining on the first night of Sukkos, ordinarily we are required to wait for a while, in the hope that the rain will let up, before giving up and making Kiddush in the house. However, when there are guests, we might be obliged not to wait but rather to make *Kiddush* immediately and commence the meal indoors, so as not to keep them waiting. (*Mishpetei Hashalom* 17:3)

4 Nisan	4 Av	4 Kislev

Making the Guest Feel at Home "Hi, Mom! I'm back from the hike," Yoni called out as he piled into the door with his backpack. His friend trailed hesitantly behind him. "Moishie's parents aren't home and his door is locked, so I brought him home to have dinner with us. I hope you don't mind!"

"I suppose not," Mrs. Rosen said with a sour face.

Moishie sat down at the edge of his chair. Dusty and sweating from his

trip, he really would have liked to wash up a bit, but no one gave him a towel to use or told him where the washroom was, and he was embarrassed to ask. He was also thirsty, having finished his water supply hours earlier, but since it didn't occur to Yoni to offer him a drink just a little while before dinner, he had to wait.

Famished from their long hike, Moishie was relieved when the family finally washed and sat down to eat. He eagerly took a portion from the central plate, but his appetite waned when he sensed Mr. Rosen watching him eat. Had he taken too much? Was he not eating politely enough? Moishie took a few more nibbles and excused himself, asking if he could use the phone. He tried calling home and was thrilled to hear his mother's voice answering. After *bentching* and saying a quick thank you, he ran with great relief to his own house, where he felt "at home."

THE CHOFETZ CHAIM derives many nuances of the *halachos* of proper hospitality from the incident that the Torah relates, at uncharacteristic length, of the hospitality Avraham showed the angels. Even though Avraham was ill, he sat out in the hot sun, hoping to find guests. When he saw what appeared to be simple, dusty wayfarers, he bowed before them and respected them as though they were distinguished gentlemen, begging them to enter. He immediately offered them the opportunity to wash up from their journey and arranged a shady place for them to rest up. Realizing that they might be anxious to continue on their way, he assured them that he would just bring a bit of bread and water, which he indeed brought before them right away. Meanwhile, however, he prepared a full, substantial meal with unusual alacrity, and then insisted on serving them himself, after which he personally escorted them on their way.

Following Avraham Avinu's lead, we should provide for the needs of our guests — food, drink, a place to wash and rest, etc. — enthusiastically and quickly. The host should always serve with a smile, as if he is wealthy and has plenty to spare, and should apologize that he does not have more to offer them. If they need a place to sleep, he should offer them the most comfortable beds, even if that means displacing his own family members to lesser accommodations.

Whenever possible, the host should dine together with his guest. When separate rolls or small loaves of bread are not being served to

each person at the meal, it is preferable that the host (taking precedence over even a _kohen_ or a _talmid chacham_) be the one to make the _brachah_ of _Hamotzi_ and slice the loaf of bread, since he will be sure to cut generous slices. The host should not invite more people to his meal than he has room to seat and food to serve.

We should never look at a person — especially a guest — while he is eating, nor should we look at the portion on his plate, so as not to embarrass him. The host should also be extremely careful to maintain a positive demeanor at the table, not to lose his temper or act in a fussy or irritable manner, since that would make all present feel uncomfortable and might discourage his family members from inviting guests in the future. Nor should he display sadness or relate his misfortunes, since the guest might surmise that _he_ is actually the cause of his host's unhappiness.

(The _halachos_ regarding serving a guest who might not wash or make a _brachah_ are discussed in Volume I, chapter 16.) (_Mishpetei Hashalom_ 17:4–6)

5 Nisan	5 Av	5 Kislev

Rich and Poor THE _MITZVAH_ OF _hachnasas orchim_ should be performed even for a wealthy guest who can afford to pay for his accommodations — such as a rich businessman who is stuck in a strange town for Shabbos. And we are certainly required to provide for the needs of a poor guest, where the _mitzvah_ of _tzedakah_ is also fulfilled. A host should not be distressed if his guest curses him or offends him, since the _zechus_ of the _mitzvah_ far outweighs any harm or pain he may sustain.

Even though keeping an open house is very praiseworthy, we should still be careful not to invite wicked people into our homes, since they could have a negative effect on the household.

The purpose of _hachnasas orchim_ is not to "grab the _mitzvah_ for ourselves" but rather to provide for the guest in the way that is best for him. Therefore, if there are others with greater resources, who are willing to host the guest and are more capable of properly honoring him, we should relinquish the _mitzvah_ and allow them to take the opportunity.

If, however, there is no one else available, then it is certainly preferable to offer the guest our simpler accommodations than to leave him out in the cold. If a guest is in a hurry, or insists that he does not want to trouble the host, we should not delay him in our homes.

Ideally, anyone who has the financial means should set aside a room in his home, or build a special guest room, for the purpose of properly fulfilling this *mitzvah*. Every community has the responsibility to make sure that accommodations are available for guests. At one time, towns would set up a special lodging house for guests, or the *gabbai* would see to it that every stranger in shul was paired up with a suitable host. Today, a widespread network of *hachnasas orchim* organizations exists to carry out this function, and anyone who takes part in their activities has a great *zechus*.

It is especially important to host poor guests at our table on Yom Tov (or to send them the necessary food, when that is a preferable arrangement). The Rambam writes that someone who locks his door and sits down to eat and drink with his wife and children without including the poor and unfortunate at his table is not fulfilling the requirement of *simchas mitzvah* — joy in the *mitzvah* of Yom Tov; he is merely indulging in the pleasures of filling his stomach, to his disgrace! (*Mishpetei Hashalom* 17:7–8, 10–11)

6 Nisan	6 Av	6 Kislev

Women's Hospitality A WOMAN IS obligated in the *mitzvah* of *hachnasas orchim* even toward male guests. However, she should not indulge in light conversation more than is absolutely necessary to make the guest feel welcome, and she should be careful in regard to all the accepted rules of separation between men and women. Naturally, she should make sure to dress and conduct herself with strict modesty and should also be careful not to be secluded with the guest in violation of the laws of *yichud*, especially if she is unmarried or a widow, or if her husband is out of town.

Women are known to be personally involved in this *mitzvah* more than men and to excel in providing for the needs of their guests, as we see from the case of the Shunamis woman (*Melachim II*, ch. 4) who offered hospitality to Elisha and was rewarded commensurately, as well as in the case of the wife of Mar Ukba (_Kesubos_ 67b), who merited a miracle because of the unique efforts she made in fulfilling this _mitzvah_. Nevertheless, since there are potential moral dangers involved in a woman hosting a man, especially when other family members are not present, she should ask a _sheʾeilas Rav_ in each particular situation. Furthermore, a woman should not go out to offer food and drink to wayfarers, as this violates the rules of modesty, but should fulfill the _mitzvah_ only for guests who come into her home. (_Mishpetei Hashalom_ 17:11)

Hachnasas Orchim — Assorted Points WHEN WE INVITE a guest into our home, we should not say to him, "Come eat with me that which you have fed me," implying that we are repaying a debt; for then, if he ends up eating more than you ate at his home, it might appear as if you are paying him interest. However, we may say, "Come eat with me, and another time, I will eat at your home," in order to persuade him to join us without the uncomfortable feeling that he is getting a free meal. In that case, there is no problem if we eat a larger portion of food at a later time at the guest's house.

If we know that someone will definitely not take us up on our invitation, we should not implore him repeatedly to be a guest at our table just to flatter him or cause him to feel indebted to us, since this is considered _geneivas daʾas_ — deceit. However, we may invite him once or twice, without imploring him, as a gesture of respect.

When the _Beis Hamikdash_ stood, _Chazal_ tell us, the _korbanos_ would atone for our sins. Nowadays, a person's table — that is, his hospitality to guests at his table — provides atonement. If the guest is a _talmid chacham_, then the _hachnasas orchim_ is tantamount to offering a _korban tamid_. Hosting needy _yeshivah bachurim_ is especially meritorious, since in addition to the basic _mitzvah_ of _hachnasas orchim_, we fulfill the _mitzvah_ of _tzedakah_ and also enhance our table with _divrei Torah_.

In describing the power of _hachnasas orchim_, _Chazal_ say, "The sip [that we offer guests] is so great that it distances those who are close [Amon and Moav], draws close those who are distant [Yisro], causes Hashem to look away from sin [Michah], causes the _Shechinah_ to rest

on *nevi'ei haBaal* [a false prophet who tricked the *navi* Ido], and, when inadvertently violated, is treated with the severity of intentional neglect [David and Yonasan]." (*Mishpetei Hashalom* 17:12–15)

7 Nisan	7 Av	7 Kislev

***Levayah —
Accompanying
Departing Guests***

"Thank you so much for your hospitality," Miriam said as she got up to leave. "Everything was delicious. I'd better get going; I have to be back at the dorm for a meeting with my teacher soon. I just hope I'll find my way to the bus stop. These Yerushalayim neighborhoods with their winding streets are so confusing to me…" Knowing that her sense of direction was virtually nonexistent, as was her Hebrew, Miriam really hoped that her host, Mindy, would offer to walk her at least part of the way, though she didn't want to ask her directly.

"You'll be just fine," Mindy said, oblivious to the heavy hint. "Go left to the end of the street, cross over and bear right, take the first steps you see, and then, if you walk about 50 feet down the road, you'll see the bus stop. Got that?"

"Uh, I think so…" Miriam mumbled as she walked out the door.

Miriam missed her meeting that evening, and she might have continued wandering around the neighborhood looking for the bus stop until the next morning had she not had the good fortune to meet a classmate and join her on her way back to the dorm.

THE *MITZVAH* OF *levayah* — accompanying a guest when he departs — is even greater than that of inviting him in. If a person is lax about escorting his guests, it is considered as if he has shed blood, as we learn from the *parashah* of the *eglah arufah*, which directs the elders of the city to exonerate themselves from the guilt of a traveler's death by declaring that they did not send him off without accompaniment. On the other hand, when someone escorts his guest even for the minimum four *amos* within the city limits, we are assured that the guest will not be harmed that entire day.

Just as the members of a community can be compelled to give the designated amount of *tzedakah*, so can they be compelled to accompany their guests as required. In fact, at one time the commnity leaders used to appoint agents to escort travelers from town to town.

The main purpose of the accompaniment is to make sure that the guest understands clearly how to proceed toward his destination. Therefore, the host should either walk along with his guest until the guest is confident of the route or should give him clear directions that he can remember and follow, so that he will not run into trouble finding his way.

The Gemara cites the vast reward given to the man who merely pointed out with his finger the entrance to Beis El so that the people of Shevet Yosef could capture it — he was _zocheh_ to build the city of Luz, where the _malach hamaves_ has no power. How much greater will be the reward of someone who takes the trouble to walk along personally with his guest.

We can derive from this incident that anyone who offers directions to someone — not just a host for his guest — fulfills the _mitzvah_ of _levayah_. Another offshoot of the _mitzvah_ that we can deduce is the obligation to post clear street signs, and addresses on buildings, to make it easier for people to find their way.

According to Rashi on the _parashah_ of the _eglah arufah_, the elders also declared that they did not send the guest off without food for the journey. From this we learn an additional responsibility of the host seeing off his guest — to provide the guest with provisions for the continuation of his journey. Yonasan was severely punished because he did not offer David Hamelech provisions when David was fleeing from Shaul, even though it was an inadvertent omission. (_Mishpetei Hashalom_ 17:16–17)

How Far to Accompany? THE REQUIRED DISTANCE one must accompany a guest in order to fulfill the _mitzvah_ of _levayah_ is contingent on certain factors relating to the host and his guest. In the times of the Gemara, the rules were as follows: A Rav should accompany his visiting _talmid_ until the edge of the city. A person should accompany his friend as far as _techum Shabbos_ — 2,000 _amos_ outside the city. A _talmid_ should walk his Rav for the distance of a _parsah_ (approximately 4 kilometers), and he should accompany his Rav _muvhak_ (primary teacher from whom he received most of his Torah knowledge in any given subject) for three _parsa'os_.

Many opinions maintain that these rules are no longer relevant, since in our times the roads are well posted, wild animals and highwaymen do not endanger the travel routes, and teachers of Torah generally forgo the respect that is due them. While a guest cannot excuse his host altogether from the *mitzvah*, the *minhag* nowadays is for the host to walk his guest until the gate, or for at least four *amos*. (*Mishpetei Hashalom* 17:18)

8 Nisan	8 Av	8 Kislev

The Guest's Responsibilities A GUEST SHOULD be alert to the situation of his hosts and should make sure not to eat a meal with people who do not have food to spare, since, according to the Rambam, doing so is tantamount to *gezel*, stealing, as the guest is, in a sense, "stealing" the food that the host needs for himself. If the guest does not give thought to the matter, he might not even realize his error, since he may innocently assume that he has permission to eat anything. However, even if the invitation was initiated by the host, he might have invited the guest just to be polite, while in fact he does not have the wherewithal to provide for a guest. The stress experienced by a host who is ashamed that he does not have a respectable amount of food to offer his guest can at times be so intense as to be life-endangering.

For the same reason, a guest should not show up at the end of a meal, since the host may be greatly ashamed if he does not have any food left to offer. Even though *Chazal* advise that someone who does not leave over a bit of bread on the table at the end of a meal, in case a poor person should come, will never see blessing, the guest should not rely on the fact that his host follows this principle of *Chazal*.

Generally, a woman whose husband is not present at the table should not drink any wine or other intoxicating beverage. However, if she is accustomed to drinking such beverages when her husband is there, she may drink a bit at her own table even when he is absent. But when she is a guest at someone else's table she should not partake of such drinks at all, even if her husband is with her.

It is not proper for one guest to invite another guest into his host's home. A person should never walk suddenly into his friend's home — or even into his own home, for that matter — without first knocking to inform those inside of his arrival, to avoid causing embarrassment to anyone who might be engaged in private matters.

Generally, a guest should not take food that was put in front of him and offer it to children of his host without asking permission, since he may inadvertently cause the host embarrassment if there is subsequently not enough food to go around. However, if he can see that there is an abundance of food, or when the meal has already concluded and food remains on the table, then he is permitted to offer it to the children.

When a son is eating at his father's table, or a worker at his employer's table, he can give a small portion, such as a slice of bread, to a poor person or a friend without being concerned that he is violating the prohibition of _gezel_, since this is a generally accepted practice, and he can assume that the _baal habayis_ agrees.

It is not befitting the honor of a _talmid chacham_ to sit at a meal with _amei ha'aretz_, ignorant people. Therefore, the _neki'ei da'as_, pious people, of Yerushalayim in years gone by would not sit down at a meal unless they knew in whose company they would be sitting. However, in a case where the _talmid chacham_'s presence would enhance _kevod Shamayim_, such as to aid a worthy cause or to have a positive influence on those present, it would be permitted and even meritorious for the _talmid chacham_ to attend. Also, if he is personally surrounded by other _talmidei chachamim_, then even if there are many _amei ha'aretz_ present, such as at a large wedding, he need not be concerned about being there.

Even though _Chazal_ spoke strongly against someone who is invited to a _seudas mitzvah_, such as a _bris_ or a wedding meal, and does not come, there is no obligation to participate in the meal if there are people there who are of questionable reputation. (_Mishpetei Hashalom_ 17:19–25)

9 Nisan	9 Av	9 Kislev

The Host/Guest Relationship ONCE A PERSON has become a guest in someone's home, a relationship of indebtedness is created between him and his host, which is manifest in a

number of aspects. If he stayed at one person's home when he came to a certain town, he should remain loyal to his hosts and return there each time he visits the town — except in extreme, justified circumstances, such as if he suspects the hosts of *gezel* or if they have acted abusively toward him — so that people should not surmise that the hosts and/or guest are difficult people and could not get along with one another.

When in the host's home, the guest must do whatever his host tells him to do. Even if the guest is normally humble and self-effacing, if the *baal habayis* asks him to act in an arrogant, lordly manner, he should do so. On the other hand, if the host tells him to go out and do menial work in the marketplace, which would be demeaning for him, he is not obligated to agree.

If the guest generally conducts himself in a manner of *prishus* — such as by abstaining from certain permitted pleasures — he should conceal his deeds from his hosts. However, if the host instructs him to do something which borders on the prohibited — such as if he requires his guest to rely on a lenient opinion or skeptical testimony — then he is not obligated to comply. Nor does he have to partake of food or drink that could be harmful to him, even if the host insists.

The *poskim* differ as to whether the guest has *halachic* ownership of the portion he receives from his host. This issue can have a variety of ramifications, such as whether he may be *mekadesh* a woman for marriage with that portion, or if he may make a condition before Shabbos that would enable him to separate *terumos* and *maasros* on Shabbos.

There are also various rules concerning guests in regard to making an *eruv chatzeros* to permit carrying from one property to another, kindling Shabbos and Chanukah lights, and making the *brachah* of *hatov vehameitiv* on wine, as well as regarding the meal's ending with "*hav lan unvareich,*" said by him or by the host. We will not elaborate on the details of these *halachos* here.

| 10 Nisan | 10 Av | 10 Kislev |

A person who is suspected of eating prohibited foods cannot be relied on to attest to the *kashrus* of the foods he serves. Therefore, in the home of such a host, the guest should not partake of the host's food.

If the host is a Jew whom the guest has no reason to suspect of such violations, even if the guest is not personally familiar with him as being reliable, then he may rely on him as a host and eat at his table anything about which he does not have a particular concern. However, when the guest is paying for the meal, we cannot rely on the owner unless we are certain that his kashrus is trustworthy, either because we were told this by people who know him personally or because he has a reliable _hechsher._ In any case, if we have a reasonable concern that the _baal habayis_ might unintentionally serve something prohibited, we should certainly check out the matter carefully before eating at his table.

"What does the good guest say? 'Look how much trouble the _baal habayis_ went to for me! See how much meat and wine and fine food he served for me. And all this work — all for my sake!' [And the bad guest says the opposite]." The good guest appreciates every detail of his host's work. However, he should sing his host's praises aloud only privately, or among fine, decent people. In public, or when there are unscrupulous people around, there is a danger that these people might take advantage of his host's good nature, at great cost to the host. Therefore, he should not praise his host at all in such circumstances. In fact, if such people ask him about his host, he can even misrepresent the facts in order to protect the host. He certainly should not divulge any secrets or private matters that he saw in his host's home, even if asked about them.

A guest should express his thanks to his host and should inquire after his well-being regularly. If speaking at a gathering at his host's home, a guest should preface his words with praise of his host. If he has any opportunity to help his host, he should do so. In fact, a guest's gratitude should be so tangible that if the guest is a _dayan_, he should avoid judging a case involving his host, so that he should not be an indirect cause of damage to the host in case the host loses the case, nor should he sway the case in the host's favor due to his being subconsciously "bribed" by the host's gratitude.

The guest can express his appreciation by leaving small gifts for the members of the household at the end of his stay. Also, _Chazal_ formulated a special _brachah_ for the guest to say for the _baal habayis_ in the _nusach_ of _bentching._ (_Mishpetei Hashalom_ 17:26–31)

In summary: The final application in our discussion of the *mitzvos* of *ve'ahavta lerei'acha kamocha* and *vehalachta bidrachav* is the *mitzvah* of *hachnasas orchim*, which is incumbent on everyone, toward rich or poor — whoever is in need of hospitality. Many details of *hachnasas orchim* are derived from the Torah's narrative of Avraham's experience of welcoming the angels. The *mitzvah* includes welcoming the guest, giving him food and drink and sleeping accommodations, as well as washing facilities when necessary, and accompanying him when he departs. The host should do everything possible to make the guest feel comfortable. Women are obligated in this *mitzvah*, even toward male guests, within the bounds of *tznius*. The *mitzvah* of accompanying the guest is even greater than inviting him in, and failing to do so is a serious omission. The guest, for his part, has a number of responsibilities in his relationship toward his host, including a debt of appreciation.

28

לשון הרע ורכילות
Lashon Hara and Rechilus

11 Nisan	11 Av	11 Kislev

One Word — An Avalanche of Spiritual Destruction　When Shaindy returned from the supermarket she deposited her bags of groceries on the table, balancing the eggs precariously on top, while she sat down to catch her breath. With a pang of guilt she mentally reviewed the conversation she'd had with her friend Rivky as they waited in the endless line at the checkout. "It was just one little sentence," she told herself in an effort to pacify her conscience.

"But it was a sentence about your common friend, Raizy, and it was not very complimentary!" her conscience retorted.

"I know, but what harm could one little sentence of *lashon hara* cause?" Rivky persisted.

At that moment, one-year-old Avi saw his bottle peeking out from under the pile of grocery bags. With determined effort he pulled and pulled until he managed to yank out the bottle.

Instantly, the delicately balanced pile of groceries was shaken, the bags came tumbling down, and the eggs smashed into a gooey mess all over the floor, mingling with the shattered bottle of grape juice and the punctured bags of flour and sugar.

313

> Avi looked with amazement at the scene and held up his bottle in won-
> derment, as if to say, "It was just one little bottle …"

SOMETIMES, JUST ONE word can create absolute havoc, leading to the
violation of numerous *mitzvos*, incurring irreparable damage to the
people involved, and penetrating the highest spiritual spheres. That is
the power of *lashon hara*…

The laws governing what we may say about others and what we may
not say are complex and are the focus of a multitude of *sefarim*. We have
attempted to capture the main principles of the subject as clearly and as
concisely as possible.

Nevertheless, there is much to be said even in a brief presentation
of the subject.

12 Nisan	12 Av	12 Kislev

What Is Lashon Hara and Rechilus? WHILE IN THE secular world it is often said that "words
can never harm me," the Torah asserts that the real-
ity is quite the opposite, and teaches us that words of
lashon hara and *rechilus* are far more potent than we
may ever have imagined.

The *mitzvah* of "*Lo seileich rachil be'amecha* — Do not be a gossipmonger among your people," includes several prohibitions: (1) *lashon
hara* — speaking derogatorily about someone, even if what you are saying is true; (2) *motzi sheim ra* — giving a person a bad name by saying
derogatory things about him that are not true; (3) *rechilus* — peddling
gossip — going from one person to another and saying, "Reuven told me
this," or "I heard such and such about Shimon." Even if the information is true, and even if it does not include anything derogatory, if it is
something that may cause animosity between the listener and a third
party, it is considered *rechilus*.

Let us define some of these terms in more detail: *lashon hara* is
violated when Reuven either speaks derogatorily about Shimon or says
something that is likely to cause him physical harm or financial damage, or — if it gets back to Shimon — to disgrace, aggravate or frighten
him.

Lashon Hara includes any statement that would bring disgrace to the subject, such as speaking about the reprehensible conduct of his family or ancestors, his own past misdeeds, or *aveiros* he committed *bein adam laMakom* — toward Hashem — and *bein adam lechaveiro* — toward other people.

Also prohibited would be to speak of his bad attributes, to imply that he is lacking in intelligence, talent, strength or wealth, or to point out his unwillingness to do favors for others. Even speaking negatively of the other person's possessions is prohibited, such as saying that a storekeeper's merchandise is overpriced or of low quality, unless there is a halachically valid reason to do so, such as to save another person from being cheated.

Even if the speaker intends no harm, and even if he is speaking the absolute truth and the subject of the *lashon hara* himself would not deny the truth of his words, the *lashon hara* still may not be said, because Hashem does not want His children to disparage one another.

Rechilus is violated when Reuven goes to Shimon and reports to him what Levi said about him or did against him, with the potential result of bad feelings being incurred between Shimon and Levi. This is true even if the report is true, and even if Shimon and Levi were already at odds and the *rechilus* merely intensifies their antagonism. Even if the report contains nothing derogatory, and Levi himself would not deny it — perhaps Levi even thinks he did something positive — still, if reporting it will cause enmity between Shimon and Levi, this constitutes *rechilus*.

A classic example of this is the incident in *sefer Shmuel* in which Achimelech supplied David with food and arms — the special dagger of Goliath. Not knowing that David was on the run from King Shaul, Achimelech himself thought he was doing a fine act, helping out the king's son-in-law on an important mission.

Nevertheless, when Do'eg reported to Shaul that Achimelech was feeding and arming David, the result of his *rechilus* was that Achimelech was executed and Shaul's animosity against David was intensified.

Subsequently, as a further consequence of this *rechilus*, Shaul and his son were killed in battle, and Do'eg lost his portion in the World to Come. (*Mishpetei Hashalom* 19:16–17, 20)

14 Nisan	14 Av	14 Kislev

Mitzvos Likely to Be Violated EVERY *MITZVAH* IS precious, and every prohibition must be assiduously avoided. However, special care must be exercised to avoid speaking or hearing *lashon hara* and *rechilus*, because with each transgression, we may potentially violate not just one *mitzvah* but many *mitzvos* simultaneously. The following is a long list of *mitzvos* that are likely to be violated by the ***mesaper*** — the speaker, by the ***shomei'a*** — the one who intentionally listens to the report, and/or by the ***mekabel*** — the one who accepts and believes the report:

- "לא תלך רכיל בעמיך": When Reuven tells Shimon *lashon hara* or *rechilus* about Levi, even if his words are absolutely true, Reuven violates the *mitzvah* of "**do not be a gossipmonger among your people**" (*Vayikra* 19:16).

- "מדבר שקר תרחק": If his words are not true, or even if there is some untruth mixed in, he also violates the *mitzvah* to "**keep far away from falsehood**" (*Shemos* 23:7) and is considered a "*motzi sheim ra*." If the matter was confidential, then he also violates the *divrei kabbalah* that prohibit us from being in the category of "a gossipmonger reveals secrets" (*Mishlei* 11).

- "לא תשא שמע שוא": Both the *mesaper* and the *mekabel* violate the Torah prohibition of "**do not accept a false report**" (*Shemos* 23:1) — the listener, for believing the report, and the *mesaper*, for leading him to believe it.

- "השמר בנגע הצרעת": All those involved violate the *mitzvah* to "**guard yourself from the punishment of *tzaraas* ...**" (*Devarim* 24:8), since *lashon hara* is the primary transgression for which *tzaraas* is the punishment.

- "זכור את אשר עשה ד' אלוקיך למרים": For the same reason, they also violate the positive *mitzvah* to "**remember what Hashem did to Miriam**" (ibid. 9) — who was punished with *tzaraas* for her minor violation of *lashon hara*.

15 Nisan	15 Av	15 Kislev

□ "ארור מכה רעהו בסתר": If Reuven related his report secretly, taking precautions to ensure that it should not get back to the one about whom he spoke, he is also subject to the *arur*, "**cursed is the one who strikes his friend secretly**" (*Devarim* 27:24).

□ "לפני עור לא תתן מכשל": Generally, both the *mesaper* and the *shomei'a* — even if he does not believe the report — transgress the prohibition of "**do not put a stumbling block before the blind**" (*Vayikra* 19:14) and are subject to the *arur* of "**cursed is he who misleads the blind on his way**" (*Devarim* 27:18), since each causes the other to sin (see Volume I, chapter 16). The more people there are listening to the report, the greater is the sin that has been committed, since for every individual listener there is an additional sin.

□ "הוכח תוכיח את עמיתך": Both the *mesaper* and the *shomei'a* are guilty of refraining from doing the *mitzvah* to "**reprove your fellow**" (*Vayikra* 19:17), since each one actually has the responsibility to interrupt the prohibited exchange and give *tochachah* — reprove the other — to stop him from sinning (see Volume I, chapter 12). This *mitzvah de'Oraisa* applies only in a case where the rebuke would be accepted. If rebuke would merely fuel the fire and increase the transgression, we should remain silent and not reprove the other person.

If, however, the rebuke will not make him stop, but also will not make matters worse, then we are obligated to speak up. Even if we know that direct rebuke will not be of any benefit, we should at least try to change the subject in order to prevent those involved from further sin, and if there is no one listening but ourselves, we should get up and leave the scene, effectively putting an end to the *lashon hara*.

◌ "ואהבת לרעך כמוך": The *mesaper* and the *mekabel* are inevitably guilty of transgressing the *mitzvah* to "**love your fellow man as yourself**" (*Vayikra* 19:18), about which Rabbi Akiva said, "This is a great principle of the Torah." As Hillel Hazaken paraphrased it: "'Do not do to others that which is loathsome to you' — this is the entire Torah; the rest is just explanation" (*Shabbos* 31a). We know our own faults better than anyone else knows them, yet we continue loving ourselves and go to great lengths to conceal our shortcomings. If by chance word gets out of some defect, we hope desperately that no one will believe it is true. Therefore, we should be equally eager to conceal the faults of others and disbelieve negative reports about them. By the same token, every Jew is expected to love every other Jew as he loves himself and, consequently, to speak highly of him and seek to maintain or restore his money and his honor, just as he would do for himself (see chapter 22).

◌ "והלכת בדרכיו": Speaking or listening to *lashon hara* is incompatible with the *mitzvah* to "**walk in His ways**" (*Devarim* 28:9), which demands of us that we be merciful, kind, and so on, emulating Hashem's attributes (*Shabbos* 133b) (see chapter 22).

◌ "לא תונו איש את עמיתו": When Reuven speaks about Shimon in Shimon's presence, he causes pain to Shimon, transgressing the *mitzvah* of "**do not aggrieve one another**" (*Vayikra* 25:17) (see Volume I, chapter 9).

◌ "לא תשא עליו חטא": If he said the *lashon hara* in the presence of the subject, frightening or embarrassing him, he has also violated the *mitzvah* of "**do not bear a sin on his account**" (*Vayikra* 19:17); and if he embarrassed the subject publicly, he loses his share in the World to Come! (See Volume I, chapter 10.)

◌ "בצדק תשפט עמיתך": If Reuven speaks derogatorily about Shimon in a situation in which he should have judged him favorably, then he has also violated the *mitzvah* of "**judge your fellow man righteously**" (*Vayikra* 19:15). In the case of a *tzaddik*, even if there is no evident explanation for his conduct, we are not permitted even to harbor suspicions in our mind, and if we do so, this falls under the category of *choshed biksheirim* — suspecting the person who is worthy, which incurs corporal punishment from *Shamayim*. If we speak about the *tzaddik*, even *leto'eles* — for a constructive purpose, having met all the conditions — if we have decided unnecessarily that he is certainly wrong, we transgress the *mitzvah* of judging favorably. On the other hand, if we speak about the average person, even in a case where there is no obligation to judge him favorably, if there is no *to'eles* involved, we are guilty of speaking *lashon hara* (see Volume I, chapter 1).

□ "לא תשנא את אחיך בלבבך": If we harbor hatred in our hearts when speaking or listening, we have violated the *mitzvah* of "**do not hate your brother in your heart**" (*Vayikra* 19:17) (see Volume I, chapter 2).

□ "לא תקם ולא תטר": When the *lashon hara* is an expression of a grudge or an act of revenge, we violate the *mitzvos* of "**do not take revenge and do not bear a grudge**" (*Vayikra* 19:18) (see Volume I, chapter 3).

| 18 Nisan | 18 Av | 18 Kislev |

□ "ולא יהיה כקרח וכעדתו": Where the *lashon hara* incites a fight or strengthens an existing fight, we violate the *issur* of "**do not be like Korach and his congregation**" (*Bamidbar* 17:5) (see Volume I, chapter 5).

□ "לא תהיה אחרי רבים לרעת"; "ובו תדבק": Joining a group of people speaking *lashon hara* is a violation of the *issur* of "**do not follow the multitude to do evil**" (*Shemos* 23:2) and also of the positive *mitzvah* of "cleave unto Him" (*Devarim* 10:20), which commands us to attach ourselves to *talmidei chachamim* (and not to *resha'im*) whenever possible. (*Mishpetei Hashalom* 19:2–12)

Mitzvos Violated Under Certain Circumstances

IN ADDITION TO the *mitzvos* we have already mentioned, which are very frequently violated when speaking *lashon hara*, there are additional *mitzvos* that we may transgress, depending on the circumstances, such as the nature of the person about whom we are speaking and even the place where the *lashon hara* is said:

ס "והדרת פני זקן"; "וקדשתו"; "כיבוד אב ואם"; "ומקדשי תיראו": If the *lashon hara* spoken or accepted concerns a *talmid chacham* or an elderly person, we violate the *mitzvah* to "**honor the presence of a sage**" (*Vayikra* 19:32) (see chapter 33). If we speak about a *kohen*, we have transgressed the *mitzvah* of "**you shall sanctify him**" (*Vayikra* 21:8) (see chapter 34), and if the *lashon hara* is about our parents, then in addition to violating the *mitzvah* of **honoring and revering parents**, we also become subject to the *arur*, "Cursed is one who dishonors his father and mother [including his older brother]" (*Devarim* 27:16) (see chapter 32). If the conversation of *lashon hara* is conducted in a shul or a *beis medrash*, we also violate the *mitzvah* of "**revere My sanctuary**" (*Vayikra* 26:2).

| 19 Nisan | 19 Av | 19 Kislev |

ס "כל אלמנה ויתום לא תענון"; "וגר לא תונה": If the subject of our *lashon hara* happens to be a widow, an orphan or a *ger* (convert to Judaism), then we aggravate the violation by transgressing the *mitzvos* that are repeated several times in the Torah, "do not afflict the widow and orphan" (*Shemos*, 22:21) and "do not hurt or oppress a *ger*" (*Shemos* 22:20).

At times, the tone of our *lashon hara*, our motives for speaking it, or the results can add to the list of *mitzvos* violated:

ס "לא תקלל חרש"; "לא תחניפו את הארץ"; "השמר לך פן תשכח את ד'"; "וחי עמך": Sometimes, in our anger, we may curse the subject of our *lashon hara*, thereby adding a violation of "**do not curse**" (*Vayikra* 19:14) (see Volume I, chapter 8). If the motive of our *lashon hara* is to flatter or praise the unworthy person to whom we are speaking or listening, then we also transgress the *mitzvah* of "**do not sully the land**" (*Bamidbar* 35:33) (see Volume I, chapter 15). When we speak out of arrogance, then we are also guilty of violating the *issur* of ga'avah, "**be careful not to forget Hashem**" (*Devarim* 6:12). If the *lashon hara* causes another Jew to lose his *parnassah*, a not-uncommon phenomenon, then those involved have also violated the obligation of "**that [your brother] may live with you**" (*Vayikra* 25:35).

Potentially, a seemingly "harmless" exchange of *lashon hara* can be a violation of some of the most severe prohibitions in the Torah:

- ס "לא תחללו את שם קדשי"; "את ה' אלוקיך תירא"; "ביטול תורה" Any time a person does an *aveirah* that he was not swept into by desire or pleasure — as is often the case with regard to *lashon hara* — the violation reflects a certain degree of throwing off the yoke of Hashem, and constitutes a violation of the serious *issur* of *chillul Hashem*, "**do not profane My Holy Name**" (*Vayikra* 22:32). The violation is greatly intensified if the transgressor is an important person whose deeds have an impact on those who observe him, and certainly even more so if the *lashon hara* was publicized. In any case, every sin transgressed shows a nick in the transgressor's *yiras Shamayim* and is a violation of the *mitzvah* to "**fear Hashem Your G-d**" (*Devarim* 6:13).

  Moreover, it causes him to neglect his obligation to learn Torah at every free moment, leading him to be subject to the *arur*, "Cursed is he who does not uphold all the words of this Torah" (*Devarim* 27:26).

20 Nisan	20 Av	20 Kislev

A brief glance at the above list emphasizes just how many severe *aveiros* are involved in speaking *lashon hara*. The *gemara* in *maseches Arachin* (15b) states that someone who speaks *lashon hara* "builds a tower of *aveiros* up to the Heavens," citing the *passuk* in *Tehillim* (73:9), "*Shatu baShamayim pihem* ... — They thrust their speech up to the Heavens." Each sentence of *lashon hara*, multiplied by the many

mitzvos violated, may add scores of *aveiros* to one's account. (*Mishpetei Hashalom* 19:13–15)

Who Is Obligated?   Efraim Brown was distraught. How long had he been unemployed before he found this excellent programming job?

It was at least five long, trying months. When this position fell in his lap, he could hardly believe it — the pay was good, the work was challenging, his coworkers were friendly. For the first week, everything was fine. Then the boss called him into his office and dropped the bombshell:

"Well, Brown, I'm pleased with your work. You'll go far in our business here. But I have an important additional assignment for you. I need to know exactly what is going on in the outer office. I want you to report to me at the end of each day and tell me exactly what every worker had to say about me, about job conditions and so on. Got it?"

"B-b-but I can't," Efraim stuttered. "I mean, I-I-I-"

"Listen, Brown, I'm not asking you, I'm telling you. You do your part, and you're on the way up. If not, well then, if I'm not mistaken you know where the unemployment office is. I'll be waiting for your answer tomorrow morning."

What should he do? That evening, Efraim headed straight for his Rav's house before setting foot in his own home and presented his dilemma to the Rav: How could he violate the *mitzvah* of *lashon hara* daily? On the other hand, how could he give up the job he had waited so long to get?

"And if he told you to come in to work on Shabbos, what would you have said?" the Rav asked gently.

"Of course I wouldn't," Efraim answered without hesitation. "That's an *issur de'Oraisa*!" As the words came out, he realized that he had answered his own question. He knew exactly what he would tell his new boss.

The next day Efraim knocked on the door of the boss's office, walked in and said with confidence, "I'm sorry, but the task you want to give me is against my religious principles. I can't do it." The boss glared at him for a long moment, then broke into a smile.

"You passed the test, Brown. I'm glad you refused. In my business, I want principled, loyal workers who won't sell their souls for a buck. You've proved your mettle, and you're in!"

THE *ISSUR* OF speaking and believing *lashon hara, hotzaas sheim ra* and *rechilus* applies to men and women, at all times and in all places. A parent who hears his young children speaking *lashon hara* should scold them and stop them from doing so.

Some opinions maintain that once a child has reached the age of *chinuch*, it is a *mitzvah* for any adult to stop him from transgressing. And it is certainly forbidden for us to instruct a child to violate the *mitzvah* and tell us *lashon hara*.

21 Nisan	21 Av	21 Kislev

Although every parent has a responsibility to train his child in all *mitzvos*, this is especially vital in the area of prohibited speech. The speech habits we acquire in our childhood are especially difficult to change later in life, while the child who is accustomed to speaking according to the principles of *shemiras halashon* will find it much easier to avoid transgressing in the future.

As is the case with all *aveiros*, even if a parent or teacher asks us to violate the *mitzvah* and tell them *lashon hara*, we are not permitted to submit to their request, unless they explain to us that the *lashon hara* is for a constructive purpose and is permitted according to all the necessary conditions (see chapter 29). Nor should we agree to violate the prohibition if someone pleads with us and tries repeatedly to persuade us.

Even if refusing to participate in a conversation of *lashon hara* will cause us to be disparaged by those present, and even if we will lose our job because of our refusal, it is still prohibited to speak or listen to *lashon hara* or *rechilus*. Though the challenge may at times be daunting, *Chazal* assure us that "it is better to be called a fool by others for one's entire life rather than transgress before Hashem for even one moment."

Contrary to the common misconception, the fact that someone spoke negatively about us does not give us license to speak derogatorily about him. The only exception would be if there was constructive benefit in doing so, as in preventing future damage, and even then, speaking against him would be permitted only if all the necessary conditions have been met. (*Mishpetei Hashalom* 19:18)

About Whom Are We Forbidden to Speak

IT IS PROHIBITED to speak *lashon hara* or *rechilus* about any Jew — man or woman, elderly or young, friend or enemy, relative or stranger. The *issur* applies whether we are speaking about a prominent person or a lowly one, a *talmid chacham* or an ignoramus, whether in his presence or out of his hearing.

Regarding children, we may not speak about them if harm could result from our words, or if they are old enough to be hurt or embarrassed by what is being said. As to speaking about relatives, the prohibition includes talking about one's spouse and children, even though in close family circles people tend to be forgiving about light remarks that were made without any malicious intent. Also, special care should be taken when speaking with siblings or brothers-/sisters-in-law about parents and in-laws, since the conversation can easily slide into prohibited remarks. While parents may choose to forgo their honor in some ways, they may not allow their children to speak of them disparagingly.

A *cherem* from earlier generations prohibits us from slandering the deceased, even a simple person, and certainly a *talmid chacham* and his Torah. A person who speaks about the deceased has to atone for his transgression by fasting, doing *teshuvah* and paying a monetary fine set by the *beis din*, as well as going to the graveside of the *niftar* or sending a representative on his behalf to ask the *niftar*'s forgiveness.

From the incident of the *meraglim* we learn that there is a special prohibition against speaking *lashon hara* about Eretz Yisrael — its fruits, its inhabitants, its weather or anything else connected to it. In speaking negatively about the land, the *meraglim* brought about the decree that forced our ancestors to wander in the *midbar* for forty years and established the day of Tishah B'Av as a day of weeping for all future generations. (*Mishpetei Hashalom* 19:19, 23–24)

Exceptions to the Rule

LASHON HARA AND *rechilus* may be spoken and believed about *akum*, as long as there is no risk of *chil-*

lul Hashem involved. However, we should not make a habit of sitting around and speaking about *akum*, both because such idle chatter is considered a *moshav leitzim* — sitting in a gathering of scorners — and because the conversation is likely to slip into negative talk about Jews as well and to create a habit that is hard to control even when speaking about Jews.

It is permitted to talk about Jews who have by their deeds excluded themselves from the Jewish people, such as an *apikorus* or well-known *rasha* — that is, someone who willfully violates Torah prohibitions and has not yet repented. Such people may even be publicly shamed and scorned, in keeping with the words of *Chazal* advising us to "publicize the pretenders."

Needless to say, this rule applies only to willful sinners; we have no license to speak negatively about Jews who fall into the category of *tinokos shenishbu* — for example, those who were never given a Jewish education and don't know any better — unless there is a constructive purpose in doing so, such as to prevent them from being a negative influence on our children or students.

In a case where the *beis din* ordered a person to do something and he brashly refused to obey, without justification, we may speak derogatorily about him and even record his misdeed in the community records for future generations. If a messenger of *beis din* was scorned, the messenger is permitted to report this to the *beis din*, and this would not constitute prohibited *lashon hara*.

Although ordinarily, testimony of a single witness before the *beis din* would be prohibited as *lashon hara*, there are certain cases where such testimony is permitted: to prevent a sin from taking place, such as when the person witnessed a married woman committing adultery, which renders her forbidden to her husband; or when someone knows that a litigant who is due to take an oath is planning to swear falsely; one may also testify in a monetary claim, since another witness may come later and complete the necessary testimony.

In certain cases, there would be no prohibition to speak *lashon hara* about a person of unsound mind, if the report will not cause that person damage and will not insult them. However, as in the case of a child, if they are aware enough to suffer embarrassment or anguish, or if the

attitude of those caring for them will be affected, leading to damage to the individual, then the *lashon hara* is prohibited. Just as we find that anyone who willfully shames such a child is held fully responsible. (*Mishpetei Hashalom* 19:25, 27–28)

24 Nisan	24 Av	24 Kislev

Lashon Hara About Oneself — The substitute rebbe walked in to the bustling fifth-grade class and stood at the desk, waiting for quiet. Yanky, whose mouth, unfortunately, worked much faster than his conscience, turned brazenly to the rebbe and said, "Forget it, rebbe. You'll never get a word in edgewise over here. You know what we did to the last substitute? Dovie and I took a specimen from Shmerel's frog collection…"

"Stop!" the rebbe said loudly, putting his hands over his ears. The unusual reaction captured everyone's attention. "You are about to speak *lashon hara*, and I don't want to hear it!"

"But I admitted that I did it too," Yanky said in his own defense, "so it's allowed, right?"

"No, it's not," the rebbe repeated, "not if you're talking about others as well. And even about yourself, it's not so simple. I suggest that after we **daven**, we start the day with a few *halachos* of *shemiras halashon*." By then the boys were in their seats, all ears — even Yanky.

IN PRINCIPLE, WE are allowed to speak *lashon hara* about ourselves — as long as we do not include others in the derogatory comment, as Yanky did in the example above. However, this *heter* should be employed only when speaking negatively about one's weaknesses or shortcomings. When it comes to actual *aveiros* we may have transgressed, *Chazal* say that revealing such deeds openly is an act of chutzpah, since it indicates that we are not ashamed of our transgressions and aren't bothered much by the fact that we've done them.

When a constructive purpose is served, then openly admitting the *aveirah* would be permitted. If, for example, the *aveirah* was committed publicly, it would be appropriate to shamefully admit one's error so as to undo the *chillul Hashem* that was caused. Similarly, if we sinned against another person, it might be in place to reveal our *aveirah* in order to conciliate the victim. Needless to say, if someone else may be

wrongly accused of a transgression we committed, we should imme-diately take the blame and admit our sin in order to remove suspicion from him.

In general, the Torah approach is to conceal one's wrongdoings *bein adam laMakom* — toward Hashem, so as to prevent the negative effects of publicizing them. Only when we need guidance in correcting the damage done and in finding the proper path to atonement do we turn to a respected Rav, reveal our sin and accept his directives. (*Mishpetei Hashalom* 19:26)

25 Nisan	25 Av	25 Kislev

Listening to and Believing Lashon Hara

"Come, Rivkie, let's find a table with a couple of empty seats and move over to there," Shira whispered desper-ately to her cousin.

"Why?" Rivkie didn't understand what was so urgent. "What's wrong with this table? The band is too loud for you? Anyway, they're right in the middle of an interesting story. Shhh!"

Shira would not give up. Firmly pulling Rivkie up and to the side, she said, "That's just the point. This table is teeming with *lashon hara*. They won't listen to us if we tell them to stop, or even if we try to change the topic. Let's just get away."

"Oh, don't go overboard, Shira. We're not saying a word — just sitting and listening," Rivkie persisted.

"Rivkie, don't tell me you forgot that listening is just as bad as talk-ing — or worse. I'm going. Stay here and collect *aveiros* if you want...." Shira walked away, and after a brief moment of hesitation, Rivkie followed humbly at her heels.

THE TORAH PROHIBITION of *lashon hara* and *rechilus* applies not only to speaking but also to listening to what someone else is saying and believing it to be true. An even greater offense is to express agreement with the prohibited statement. The *issur* to believe *lashon hara* applies no matter who the speaker is — old or young, Jew or non-Jew. The Chofetz Chaim maintains that deliberately listening to *lashon hara* that is being spoken is also a violation of a Torah prohibition, even if the listener does not believe what he hears. However, in a case where there is a specific

constructive benefit to listening to what is being said — such as to prevent future damage — we may listen and take precautions, as long as we do not accept what was said as the truth.

If we hear a negative report about someone, and are able to interpret what took place in a positive way, then we do not have to disbelieve the facts. On the other hand, if we were aware of the facts beforehand, and the speaker now shed a negative light on what took place, we are not permitted to believe his negative interpretation, as that would constitute accepting *lashon hara.*

Even in a case where it appears obvious that the report is true, such as when the *lashon hara* is said in the presence of the subject and he remains silent, not making any attempt to defend himself, we are still not permitted to believe the *lashon hara.* In fact, even if the subject is not a quiet person by nature, but rather usually speaks up, we still cannot take his silence as proof of the truth of the report.

If one witness testifies in *beis din,* we may not accept his report as true; only the testimony of two witnesses is acceptable. On the other hand, if we hear a report from two people, as long as it is not delivered properly in *beis din,* the report is not considered reliable testimony but rather the words of nasty plotters, and it may not be accepted as truth.

26 Nisan	26 Av	26 Kislev

Even when we hear *lashon hara* or *rechilus* from someone who is *meisi'ach lefi tumo* — who innocently mentions it in passing, without meaning to disgrace the subject or arouse contention — we are not allowed to believe what he said.

If a report is already common knowledge, we still may not believe it to be true, but we may take precautions based on what we heard and may even mention it to others as a vague, unproven concern until the matter is clarified, as long as our intention is not to deliberately spread the rumor and make it even more widespread.

A general principle is that whatever we are not allowed to say, we are also not allowed to listen to. (*Mishpetei Hashalom* 19:21–22, 30, 70)

Avoiding the Company of Speakers of Lashon Hara

IF WE KNOW that the people in a certain group are speaking *lashon hara* or are the type of individuals who are likely to do so, we may not sit down together with them, even if we make up our minds in advance not to believe a word they say. Moreover, if we did not realize their nature in advance, and they started speaking only after we sat down with them, we should get up and leave if at all possible.

At times it may not be practical to leave — for instance, if we are sitting with them on a long taxi ride on the highway. In such a situation, we should try to stop them or change the subject. If that does not help, then ideally, we should put a finger in each of our ears to demonstrate dramatically our objection and to protect ourselves from hearing what they are saying.

If we cannot summon the gumption to utilize this last option, yet we have no way to escape their company, we are required to make it absolutely clear that we are not a willing part of their conversation. Therefore, if possible, we should display a sour face to indicate our disapproval, be sure not to indicate in any way that we agree to or enjoy their words, and make every effort not to listen to, and certainly not to believe, what they are saying.

These rules apply even in a case where a major loss will be incurred as a result, such as having to give up one's job in a workplace where *lashon hara* is commonly spoken. (*Mishpetei Hashalom* 19:21–22, 30)

27 Nisan	27 Av	27 Kislev

Rechilus — Peddling Wares of Gossip

"Hello, Mrs. Steiner!" Mrs. Weinman said with a warm smile. "What an amazing coincidence. For months I haven't bumped into you or your family, and now, in the same week, I see both you and your daughter-in-law."

"Oh, Rochel? How nice. Where did you see her? Were you in Monsey for a *simchah*?" Mrs. Steiner inquired.

"Monsey? Is that where she lives? Oh, no, I saw her right here in Boro Park just yesterday," Mrs. Weinman explained.

"In Boro Park?!" Mrs. Steiner seemed shocked. "I don't understand. How

can it be that she came to Boro Park and didn't stop by to visit me? A daughter would never do that. Rochel was always a bit of a cold fish…"

Mrs. Weinman wished she could swallow her words. She just wanted to be friendly, but she should have remembered that this was a sore topic. Why couldn't she have stopped at "Hello, how nice to see you…"?

AS A GENERAL rule, any speech prohibited under the category of *lashon hara* is also prohibited under the category of *rechilus*. However, some forms of speech may not be *lashon hara* — since they are not intrinsically derogatory — yet still fall under the category of *rechilus*, since they cause the listener resentment against a third party. Therefore, this type of report may not be said to the person involved or to his close friends and family, who might also feel resentment on his behalf, nor should it be revealed to anyone who is likely to pass it on to the subject. But there is no *issur* in relating something of this sort that contains no derogatory information to someone who will certainly not have cause to tell it to any of the people (mentioned here), to whom it should not be revealed.

If Reuven hears a derogatory report about Shimon and tells it to others, this constitutes both *lashon hara* and *rechilus*. However, if he tells it only to Shimon, then his report is considered *rechilus*, since it arouses bad feelings, but is not *lashon hara*, since it does not disgrace the subject.

In any case, spreading gossip from one person to another is a violation of *rechilus*, even when we do not report it to the subject of the *rechilus*, and the violation is even greater if it is said in a manner that renders it likely to get back to the subject.

Some people have the unfortunate habit of always wanting to know what others say and think of them. If someone asks us, "What did so-and-so say about me?" or "What did he do to me?" we should try to evade the question or answer him in an ambiguous manner that the asker can also take in a positive sense.

If we see that our evasive tactics are not effective, we can actually lie in order to preserve the peace — and it is even a *mitzvah* to do so, but we may not take a false oath for this purpose. (*Mishpetei Hashalom* 19:31–33)

28 Nisan | 28 Av | 28 Kislev

Rechilus — IN PRACTICE, WE should not relate the _rechilus_ even to
Even If ... people who are not directly involved in the report, even
if we warn them not to disclose it to the subject, because
generally, word eventually does get back to him. Certainly, we should
never tell a person what others said about his wife, his children or other
close relatives, because that is equally likely to cause him pain and is
therefore considered _rechilus_.

Even if the speaker does not reveal any new information to his
listener but just stirs up old bad feelings or casts new light on what
he already knows, and certainly if the matter was originally in doubt
and the speaker effectively reinforces the listener's resentment — it is
considered _rechilus_.

Even if the speaker had no intention of rousing hatred in the heart of
the listener, if his words result in antagonism, this constitutes _rechilus_.

Even if the speaker sees nothing wrong in what the person did, if
mentioning that deed may arouse hostility, he may not say it. For this
reason, when speaking to someone we should not praise his wife or
partner for having helped us out with a donation or a loan. While we
may be genuinely grateful and sincere in our praise, it is rather common
for such talk to stir up resentment if the spouse/partner thinks that his
counterpart is being overly generous on his account.

If we are not careful, one bit of _rechilus_ can easily lead to another.
Therefore, we should be careful never to tell someone, "I heard that you
said such and such about me," since in the likely case that the listener
will figure out who delivered the report to us, we will have been the
cause of enmity between them, and therefore such words are _rechilus_.
(_Mishpetei Hashalom_ 19:34–38)

Revealing IF SOMEONE TELLS us a secret, or calls us into his house or
a Secret into some private corner to tell us something — implying
thereby that he wants the matter kept quiet — _Chazal_ say
that we are not permitted to reveal that information to others, unless
and until we hear from the speaker that he doesn't mind if it is passed
on.

If the speaker tells his "secret" in the presence of a crowd, or at least a minimum of three people, this indicates that he doesn't really mind if the word gets out, and in that case, there would be no *issur* in revealing the information to others. However, if the "secret" includes derogatory information, or might cause pain or loss, or could arouse contention, then it would be forbidden for us to relate it under any circumstances. (*Mishpetei Hashalom* 19:73)

29 Nisan	29 Av	29 Kislev

Making Matters Worse   CERTAIN CIRCUMSTANCES CAN give the transgressions of *lashon hara* and *rechilus* an even more severe character. Added factors, such as the status of the person spoken about, the manner in which the report was delivered and the effect of the report, can bring into play many additional prohibitions, as we have pointed out earlier.

When the person we are speaking about is a parent, a *talmid chacham*, an elderly person, a *kohen*, a widow, an orphan or a *ger*, we add the corresponding violations to the general prohibition of *lashon hara*. The same applies when the words are spoken out of hatred, a feeling of vengeance or a grudge, in a hurtful or embarrassing manner, or in a situation where we should have judged the subject favorably; each factor adds its own violation to the "collection." If the words spoken are even partially false, or even just exaggerated, another transgression is tacked on to the basic *aveirah*.

The same derogatory piece of information becomes much worse when it is said to more people. Therefore, it is far more severe when reported in a public forum or spread in the mass media, such as when it is printed in a newspaper or on a sign in the street. The violation is also multiplied when we speak about a large number of people, as is the case, for example, when we make statements about entire communities of Jews.

The transgression is also more serious when two or more people spread the damaging report, because people will more readily accept as true words that are "verified" by a second person, as opposed to a statement made by one person alone.

The degree of damage caused by the _lashon hara_ will also intensify the _aveirah_. For example, causing someone to lose his source of
income — whether it is a Rav deposed from his position, a hired worker
fired from his place of work, a store owner forced to close down his
shop, or a _chassan_ whose father-in-law reneges on dowry obligations as a
result of _lashon hara_ that was heard — all aggravate the basic transgression of _lashon hara_. And the damage is not always measurable in dollars
and cents. If the _lashon hara_ sabotages relationships and causes hatred
and _machlokes_, that is also considered a loss.

Certainly, when the _lashon hara_ is told to a non-Jew (as in reporting
a neighbor's actions to the police in a case where _halachah_ does not
sanction this for reasons of safety or other justified reasons), this will
often lead to damage and suffering, and may add to the prohibition of
the _lashon hara_ such violations as _halshanah_ — informing on a fellow
Jew, or _arka'os_ — bringing a case to a secular court without authorization of _beis din_, which _Chazal_ considered tantamount to "raising one's
hand against the Torah of Moshe." (_Mishpetei Hashalom_ 19:39–41)

30 Nisan	30 Av	30 Kislev

Watch What
You Say

"I can't believe it," Mr. Kaufman told his wife in shock.
"Yesterday I saw the Berman boy behind the shul, smoking — on Shabbos!"

"Shmuel, I don't think you ought to be talking about it. It sounds a lot
like _lashon hara_ to me," Mrs. Kaufman chided him.

"But I saw it myself! And this isn't the first time, either!" Mr. Kaufman
insisted.

"Are you sure that gives you license to speak about him? I think we
should get back to learning the _halachos_ every day at the table, so we can
brush up on the subject," Mrs. Kaufman concluded.

NOT ONLY IS it prohibited to talk about a person's transgressions from
years back, or to talk about the transgressions of his ancestors, but even
if we ourselves witness him doing an _aveirah_ several times — whether he
has violated a _mitzvah de'Oraisa_ or a _mitzvah deRabbanan_, and whether
it is against Hashem or against his fellow man — we are obligated to
judge him favorably. Perhaps he misunderstood the _halachah_, or he

committed the act in error, or regretted his action a moment later and did *teshuvah*. Nor should we hate him or disparage him because of what we have seen.

The same applies to negative character traits that we perceive in someone, such as arrogance, bad temper or even imperfection in positive attributes. Speaking about such faults could damage the subject and cause him anguish. For example, reporting that someone is physically weak could prevent him from being hired for a job. Letting out word that a businessman is not wealthy may keep others from wanting him as a business partner. Saying that someone is not a *lamdan* could affect his chance at finding a *shidduch* or retaining a position of Rav or *darshan*.

1 Iyar	1 Elul	1 Teves

Even if the speaker would consider the statement to be praise if it were said about him, that does not justify his saying it about another person if, in that context, the statement is derogatory. For example, a businessman may not say of someone in *kollel* that he learns a few hours a day; that would be a disparaging statement said about someone who is expected to put in a long day of learning, even though the businessman would be highly praised were the same thing said about him.

Speaking disparagingly of someone's property or possessions is also prohibited, if doing so might cause the person a loss or anguish, such as if one would speak negatively about a shopkeeper's merchandise. In short, we must think carefully before we speak, because not everything we see and know firsthand may be said, if saying it may cause pain or damage. (*Mishpetei Hashalom* 19:41–42)

Other Forms of Lashon Hara LASHON HARA IS not limited to words spoken and heard. Writing and reading prohibited statements would certainly also be considered *lashon hara*. Physical gestures too can convey *lashon hara* — for example, disparaging someone through a wink or a grimace — and are equally forbidden.

Telling a story without revealing the identity of the subject would not be prohibited if the subject will remain anonymous, but if the listeners are likely to eventually figure out who was spoken about, this would still constitute *lashon hara.*

Contrary to a common misconception, *lashon hara* that is said in the context of a joke or a Purim *shpiel* is also prohibited, even if it was not said maliciously but simply "in good fun." This kind of talk is compared to someone shooting poisonous arrows all about him, and then, after the damage is done, defending himself by saying, "I was just playing around…" The Rambam categorizes this as *avak lashon hara* (a subtle form of *lashon hara*, which is discussed below); however, all the other *poskim* designate it as absolute *lashon hara.*

2 Iyar	2 Elul	2 Teves

A person who relates potentially damaging information in a tricky, subtle manner, even if the information is not actually derogatory, transgresses the *issur* of *lashon hara*; likewise, one who inserts the comment shrewdly, as if it is an innocent part of the conversation, also transgresses this *issur.* This form of *lashon hara* is known as *lashon hara betzinah*, since the hurtful remarks are cleverly concealed.

For example, in an incident cited in the *Gemara Yerushalmi* (Pei'ah 1:5), the king drafted the people for shifts of forced labor. One person, named Bar Chovetz, managed to evade the summons and stayed home. A few of the workers envied Bar Chovetz for escaping the assignment and decided to get him into trouble. At the lunch break, one of them "innocently" asked the other, "What are we eating today?" and the other one replied, "*Chuvtza*" (a type of food). The taskmaster picked up on the hint and noticed that Bar Chovetz wasn't there, and a soldier was sent to fetch him. (*Mishpetei Hashalom* 19:45–46, 48)

Under Accusation IF AN IMPROPER act was done, and someone asks, "Who did it?" — we are not allowed to reveal the true culprit, even if the asker suspects that it is we who are at fault. However, one is allowed to say, "I didn't do it," even if the asker will understand from this response who really did it.

This *halachah* applies when the act was clearly an objective wrongdoing — an act that anyone would have seen as a misdeed. If it was a

wrong only in the eyes of the asker, then it is not clear that we are allowed to deny our guilt if that will cause the identity of the real culprit to be revealed.

Parents in a family setting, and teachers in a classroom, should be careful to avoid asking their children or students, "Who did it?" because such a question can only lead to *lashon hara*. It would be preferable to ask in a general way that the culprit himself later approach the parent/teacher privately.

In any case, a *baal nefesh* — a person with spiritual aspirations — should try to avoid answering "I didn't do it" when doing so would point a finger at the culprit, because we should always try to save others from shame. The Gemara cites examples of great people who actually stepped forward and accepted the blame themselves for things they had never done, in order to spare others from embarrassment. (*Mishpetei Hashalom* 19:50)

3 Iyar	3 Elul	3 Teves

Avak Lashon Hara "Hello, is this Sara Stern? I wanted to ask you about your classmate Dina Dorman, for a *shidduch*," the unidentified voice on the phone requested.

"I'm sorry, I can't help you on that. I don't want to get into *lashon hara*..." Sara answered self-righteously.

"Oh, I see," replied the caller, who deduced what was not said. "That answers my question. Thank you very much."

Sara was pleased with herself for avoiding saying all the negative things that she could have reported about Dina. But while her words were avak *lashon hara*, not openly derogatory words, the damage was just as deadly.

EVEN WHEN WE do not explicitly say something derogatory, if by our words, hints, motions or actions we imply a derogatory statement or one that will stir up resentment, then we have violated the *issur* of *avak lashon hara* or *avak rechilus* (more subtle forms of the *issurim*).

For example, saying, "Who would have thought that so-and-so would turn out as he is today?" would be *avak lashon hara*. Even though nothing explicitly derogatory was said, and even if it sounds like praise, still, there is a negative implication about the person's earlier conduct. Another common phrase that should not be used is, "I don't want to say what happened to so-and-so," which implies that there is something negative that could be said, although the speaker is not actually saying it.

A statement that can be interpreted in two ways — positive or negative — is considered *avak lashon hara* even when it does not lean toward the derogatory interpretation, since factors such as tone of voice and body language can easily imply the negative side of the coin. Such statements are especially taboo when there are already hostile feelings between the listener and the subject, or when the listener has a tendency to judge others in a condemning manner. (*Mishpetei Hashalom* 19:44, 46, 49)

4 Iyar	4 Elul	4 Teves

Even Praise Can Lead to Lashon Hara "I just heard that we're going to have Rav Sheinowitz as our *mechanech* this year. You don't know how lucky we are. My brother had him, and he's the most fantastic, brilliant, nice, thoughtful, creative rebbe in the whole world. There's nobody like him anywhere!"

"Oh, come on. Nobody's perfect. I know he once punished a boy for something he never did, and he wouldn't back down and apologize. And another time, he..."

SINGING SOMEONE'S PRAISES in the presence of his enemy, or in a crowd that knows him and might include his enemies, is considered *avak lashon hara*. The same is true of someone who praises his friend to the extreme, even if no enemies are around. In both cases, the statement is very likely to result in someone qualifying the praise or negating it with a derogatory counterstatement.

If the person under discussion is renowned as an upstanding *tzaddik*, then there is not a concern that anyone would attempt to undermine the speaker's laudatory words, and in such a case it would be permissible to praise him publicly. Also permissible would be to publicly extol the virtues of someone who is unknown to the listeners, or to speak highly of him at a gathering in his honor or at a private festivity, such as a bar-mitzvah or *sheva brachos*.

Praise can also constitute *lashon hara*, at times, if it can potentially cause the subject damage. For example, if a grateful guest praises his

host aloud in a public place, or if a person publicizes the fact that someone gave him a generous donation or loan, creating an opening for unscrupulous people to take advantage of the giver, the well-meant praise
may lead to damage to his benefactor, and is therefore prohibited as
lashon hara. There are differences of opinion regarding whether we can
disclose the identity of a philanthropist if people would then approach
him for assistance, but all agree that we should not reveal his name to
dishonest people or to collectors for unworthy causes.

It is important to keep in mind that praise is a very relative thing;
what is perceived as a compliment to one person of a certain status
or in a particular circle may be highly insulting to another. (*Mishpetei
Hashalom* 19:47)

5 Iyar	5 Elul	5 Teves

**Who Wants
Life?**
THE EARLY COMMENTARIES wrote that when a person
who speaks *lashon hara* and *rechilus* about his fellow man
will come to the *Beis Din shel Maalah* — the Heavenly
Tribunal after his death, he will see that some of his merits are missing
and that some *aveiros* he never committed are credited to him. When
he complains of the injustice, he will be told that Hashem transferred
some of his merits to the people about whom he spoke *lashon hara* and
transferred some of their *aveiros* to his account.

Even though the person who violates the *issur* of *rechilus* is not liable
for *malkos*, *rechilus* is a great sin and causes many Jewish lives to be lost,
as we see in the story of Do'eg, who was the cause of the deaths of the
kohanim of Nov and also of Shaul and his offspring, and who himself
lost his place in *Olam Haba*.

Those who constantly engage in *lashon hara* do not merit to have
the *Shechinah* revealed to them. We are warned not to reside in their
vicinity, and certainly not to sit around with them and listen to their
discussions.

Chazal say that the *aveirah* of *lashon hara* is the cause of drought
and the resultant loss of *parnassah*, and it brings *nega'im* (spiritual
afflictions) upon the person. The speaker of *lashon hara* ought to be
stoned, and the one who accepts *lashon hara* is fit to be thrown to the

dogs. It is the epitome of foolishness to violate this sin that brings no benefit or real pleasure.

Chazal say further that someone who speaks *lashon hara* habitually is equivalent to the violator of the three most severe sins — *avodah zarah* — idolatry, *gilui arayos* — immorality, and *shefichus damim* — murder. He is punished in this world and has no portion in the next world. He is considered a heretic. The sole reason for the decree that our forefathers had to wander for forty years in the wilderness was *lashon hara*.

"Which man desires life, who loves days of seeing good? Guard your tongue from evil, and your lips from speaking deceitfully" (*Tehillim* 34). The formula for a good life in this world and the next is to choose our words with care and to avoid saying or listening to anything that might lead to *lashon hara* or *rechilus*.

6 Iyar	6 Elul	6 Teves

Teshuvah —
Correcting
the Wrong

ONCE *LASHON HARA* or *rechilus* has been said, even if the listener did not believe the report and no damage or pain was incurred, the speaker has violated the *issur* of *lashon hara* and needs to atone for his sin against his Creator. In such a case, he would not have to ask forgiveness from his subject and may even be prohibited from doing so, since the apology itself can stir up bad feelings.

In the event that the listeners accepted and believed his report as true, the speaker must first try to remove the impression of his derogatory words from their hearts and then, according to the Chofetz Chaim, must also go to the person he spoke about, reveal his sin, conciliate him and ask his forgiveness. If revealing the details of the *lashon hara* will cause the subject even more pain or embarrassment, then the speaker should ask for general forgiveness, without divulging any details.

The people who were on the listening end and accepted the *lashon hara* must also do *teshuvah*. As a first step, they must wipe out the report from their hearts, which they can do by assuming the report was mistaken, exaggerated, misunderstood, etc. Then they should go through the steps of *teshuvah* — admitting their sin to Hashem, regretting it, and resolving not to repeat it. (*Mishpetei Hashalom* 19:43)

In summary: *Lashon hara* — speaking derogatorily or in a way that will cause someone damage — and *rechilus* — relating what someone did or said to another so as to cause strife between two people — are violations of *lo seileich rachil be'amecha*, but are also likely to entail violations of many other positive and negative *mitzvos*, depending on the circumstances. The *mitzvah* applies to men and women, at all times and places, and prohibits us from speaking about any Jews, old or young, learned or ignorant. The exceptions to the rule include *akum* and nonbelievers, as well as certain sinners. We may not violate the *mitzvah* even if it will lead to our being ridiculed or losing our livelihood. The *issur* applies not only to speaking but also to listening and believing, even in cases where it might seem obvious that the report is true. Also included in the *issur* is writing *lashon hara*, derogatory talk said in jest, and more. Certain forms of speech are not outright *lashon hara* but are forbidden as *avak lashon hara*, such as implied derogatory information and exaggerated praise that leads to *lashon hara*. The severity of the violations of *lashon hara* and *rechilus* is clear from the words of *Chazal* and from the punishments that they incur. Anyone who really yearns for the good life, in this world and the next, will avoid these *aveiros* at all costs. When doing *teshuvah* for *lashon hara*, we must not only go through the standard stages of *teshuvah* but must also ask forgiveness of the subject when necessary, and attempt to remove the negative impression from the hearts of the listeners. (Considering the breadth of the topic, this summary is far from comprehensive.)

⇁⇨ 29 ⇦⇀

לשון הרע לתועלת
Lashon Hara and Rechilus Leto'eles
and Other Special Situations

7 Iyar	7 Elul	7 Teves

Speaking Up When Necessary "Raizy, *mazal tov!*" Masha exclaimed enthusiastically when she met her friend on the street. "I haven't seen you since your daughter's wedding. How long ago was it—two months? How is the young couple?"

Raizy's sullen expression indicated that all was not well. "I guess you didn't hear. Shortly after the wedding, the *chassan* displayed some very irregular behavior, and then we found out that he had a serious psychiatric disorder that is not well-controlled. I don't know how he kept it hidden all the times they met before and after the engagement. After a few weeks, the marriage was over."

"Oh, Raizy, I'm so sorry. That's terrible," Masha empathized.

"Yes, it's very sad," Raizy solemnly agreed. "But you know what hurts the most? We spoke to so many people to ask for information about him before they met, especially since the *chassan* was from abroad and we didn't know him or his family from before. They all knew about the problem, and nobody said a word. I guess they thought they were being very pious and not saying *lashon hara*. But they didn't stop to think about the damage they could cause by not saying what the *halachah* required them to say, and to at least consult a Rav about the matter."

341

THE UNDERLYING FACTOR in the *issur* of *lashon hara* is the lowly, corrupt nature that characterizes the person who chooses to find fault with others, to seek out his weak points, to degrade him in the eyes of his peers and to take perverse pleasure in his downfall. The Torah wants us to be elevated people, not backbiters and lowly peddlers of gossip.

However, this would be true only if we were to say the *lashon hara* with the destructive purpose of denigrating the subject or instigating conflict. If we are speaking up for a constructive goal — such as to decry evil, to help someone who was wronged or to do a service for society — then under certain circumstances this would not be a violation of the prohibitions of *lashon hara* or *rechilus* but would rather fall into the category of *lashon hara leto'eles*, which is permissible — and sometimes even required — provided the following seven conditions are met:

1. **Truth:** We must be certain that the negative information is true, either because we saw it ourselves or because we have investigated the matter and confirmed that it is true.

2. **Wrong:** We must think the matter through carefully to make sure that the act was really a wrongdoing according to the Torah.

   If we are not sure on this point, we are obligated to judge the person favorably. We also have no right to denigrate a person's *middos* or to disparage the conduct of his ancestors or his own past misdeeds. If, however, there is a concern about potential damage to someone, then the *mitzvah* of *lo saamod* — "Do not stand aside while your fellow's blood is shed" — applies. In that case, we would have to relate the information to the person who is in need of protection even if we still have doubts on this point.

3. **Rebuke:** When possible, we must first try to gently reprove the sinner. Perhaps in this way we will achieve the constructive goal without having to relate the derogatory information to anyone else.

4. **Accuracy:** The information must be relayed accurately, without exaggerating the wrongdoing and without omitting any details that would mitigate its severity.

5. **Beneficial intentions:** Our intentions must be *leto'eles* — for the sake of helping or benefiting one or more of the parties involved — not in order to take pleasure in finding fault, and not stemming

from motives of personal hatred toward the sinner.

6. **Alternatives:** When it may be possible to bring about the constructive purpose through means other than relating the *lashon hara*, we are required to try the alternative method first.

7. **No more than the *din*:** We should not cause the subject more damage than would have been assigned to him had the case been brought to *beis din*. (For example, if we know that our information will cause the listener to unilaterally dismantle a partnership that was already finalized contrary to the *din*, or will lead to some other loss, we may not be permitted to speak.) (*Mishpetei Hashalom* 19:51–52)

8 Iyar	8 Elul	8 Teves

For Whose Benefit   LASHON HARA LETO'ELES is sometimes said for the benefit of the person spoken about.

One example of this kind of *to'eles* would be reporting someone's conduct to a mentor whom he respects, so that the listener will help the sinner do *teshuvah*. Another scenario would be when Reuven hears that Shimon is guilty of a wrongdoing, and Reuven is concerned that others may come and report the information in a manner that is extremely demeaning to Shimon. To prevent this from happening, he pre-empts them by reporting the wrongdoing first, playing it down and cushioning it with many justifications, so that later, when the vilifying report is made, the listeners will not be inclined to accept it. Here again, the *lashon hara* actually benefits the subject.

At other times, the *to'eles* is for others, such as to save them from a suspected theft or other anguish that the subject is plotting, or to help the victim retrieve a stolen item. In such a case, it is important that the listener *not* report back to the subject what he heard, as this would constitute *rechilus*, provided the information has not yet been revealed publicly. However, if there is a specific constructive purpose to be achieved by tipping off the subject of the *lashon hara*, letting him know that he was spoken about, such as so that he can take measures to prevent people from believing the report about him, then reporting back would be permissible.

If we need to reveal the information to others in order to prevent harm from coming to them, and we were unable to reprove the sinner first, then the *lashon hara* must be said in front of at least three people, so that the listeners will not suspect us of spreading *lashon hara* without justification, and we need to confirm that the listeners will only take precautions based on what we said but will not accept our words as absolute truth. If the sinner is a violent type and the speaker is afraid to antagonize him, or if the speaker is known as a person of impeccable integrity who would never flatter a wrongdoer and would speak the same way even in the presence of the sinner, then there is no need for this minimum of three listeners.

The *lashon hara* might benefit the listeners by serving as a warning to them to keep their distance from someone who could be a negative influence; in such a case, it is a *mitzvah* to speak up, especially when doing so will prevent the listeners from transgressing actual prohibitions.

9 Iyar	9 Elul	9 Teves

When a *machlokes* is going on, we are permitted to speak *lashon hara* about those engaged in the quarrel, in order to end the conflict. However, we have to be very careful that our words do not have the opposite effect and fan the fires of the dispute.

Sometimes the *lashon hara* will bring benefit to both sides. For example, when people are considering someone as a possible *shidduch* or business partner, each side is permitted to check out the other by inquiring about them, in order to learn whether the two parties are suitable for each other. They may ask as many people as necessary until they feel confident that they have a clear picture of the person's character and circumstances, even though the *lashon hara* is for their own *to'eles* — to avoid damage or potential conflict.

When inquiring, we must inform those being asked that our inquiry is for a permissible, constructive purpose; otherwise, we violate the *issur* of *lifnei iveir* — causing someone else to sin. The asker must be sure not to believe what he hears, but only to take precautions based on the information. The person who is asked should make sure he has beneficial intentions, that he does not exaggerate the candidate's shortcomings, and that he does not reveal negative points that he wasn't asked about specifically, unless they are in the category of "_chesronos atzumim_" — serious deficiencies — which he must volunteer even if not asked, because of his obligation in the _mitzvah_ of _lo saamod_.

Another possible example of _lashon hara_ that is for the benefit of the speaker is when a person speaks not for the purpose of denigrating the subject, but simply to "get it off his chest" — to alleviate the difficult feelings that are weighing on his heart. This is considered speaking for a future benefit; for the speaker, it is permissible to say, and for the listener, there is a _mitzvah_ to hear the person out, as long as he is careful not to believe what he hears. Certainly if the listener's intention is to help calm down the speaker, defuse his anger and dissolve his need to repeat the story to anyone else, we can be sure that there is no _issur_ involved here, but only the fulfillment of a _mitzvah_. (_Mishpetei Hashalom_ 19:53–58)

10 Iyar	10 Elul	10 Teves

The Right Way to Speak or Listen Leto'eles
AS WE MENTIONED earlier, the general rule is that anything we are not permitted to say, we are also not permitted to listen to. However, when there is a specific constructive purpose in listening, we are allowed to listen and even to inquire extensively from several people as much as is necessary in order to attain a clear understanding of the matter. Nevertheless, we may not believe what we hear as if it were the truth; we may only take it as a basis for concern. Certainly we should not cause the subject any damage or shame based on the report; he remains _bechezkas kashrus_ — presumed to be upstanding — in regard to returning his lost object, giving him _tzedakah_, and helping him in any other _mitzvos_ of the Torah. We also are not allowed to tell other people what we heard until we have clarified the absolute truth.

In any situation where we are relating _lashon hara leto'eles_, we are required to explain why we are saying it, so that the listener should not wrongly infer that _lashon hara_ of this kind is permissible even without a constructive purpose, and so that he will not be confused by the speaker's behavior.

When we see a *talmid chacham* or even an average person committing a well-known *aveirah*, such as eating *treife* food or engaging in
immoral conduct, then we should assume that he did *teshuvah* immediately afterward. If we witnessed the act together with another kosher
witness, as long as there is any chance that the sinner would accept our
rebuke, we should first gently and pleasantly reprove him before revealing the matter to *beis din*.

If we are sure that he would not heed our rebuke, or if we tried to
rebuke him and saw that he did not listen to our words, then we may
tell the *beis din*, and they can punish him discreetly. Likewise, we can
tell his Rav, relative or anyone he is close with and whose words are
valued by him, as long as that person is knowledgeable in the *halachos*
of *shemiras halashon* and can be relied on to deal with the sinner with
positive intentions — not for the purpose of degrading him and not
out of hatred, not by shaming him publicly and not causing him to sin
further.

11 Iyar	11 Elul	11 Teves

In the case of a persistent sinner, we may report the matter to his
rebbe even if the rebbe may publicize the information, as long as he does
so for a constructive purpose.

If we were the only ones to witness the sin and there is no second
witness, then we may not reveal the matter to *beis din* at all; anyone who
does so is considered a *motzi sheim ra*.

When the *to'eles* of the *lashon hara* is to decry evil actions and prevent others from being influenced, then, as *Chazal* learn from several
pesukim, we may speak up only after all the seven conditions have been
met. But when the *to'eles* is to save someone from a definite loss (in a
case where the *heter* is derived from the *din* of one witness requiring
an accused to take an oath in *beis din* and from the obligation of *lo
saamod*), we do not need to fulfill some of the conditions.

When our purpose in speaking *lashon hara* is to help someone who
was wronged by another person — through robbery, deceit, damage,
pain, embarrassment or insult — an individual may report the *lashon
hara* publicly, as long as he has first attempted to rebuke the sinner. In

this case we do not have to be concerned that the transgressor already did *teshuvah* if he has not yet compensated the victim for the loss and appeased him. This *halachah* applies when trying to retrieve someone else's loss. Regarding one's own loss, this would be permissible only if the victim can be sure that his main intention is to save himself from damage and not merely to disparage the offender.

When the purpose is not to correct past damage but to prevent a loss that has not yet taken place — such as to prevent a *shidduch* or a partnership that would be detrimental, or to save someone from a theft or damage that may occur — then the *halachah* is even more lenient, since we are bound by the obligation of *lo saamod* — "Do not stand aside while your fellow Jew's blood is being shed." In such cases, we do not need to fulfill the condition of reproving the subject before speaking up.

Also, when we have good reason to suspect a serious deficiency in one party, then even if we have not verified that the information is definitely true, we are still obligated to speak up, but we should make sure to indicate that we cannot vouch for the truth of the information and should only say that "we heard…" (*Mishpetei Hashalom* 19:59–64)

12 Iyar	12 Elul	12 Teves

Where To'eles Does Not Apply

When Gitty and Moishe Meirson came to her brother Shmuel's newly renovated house, they were given the "grand tour." After the requisite "ooh's" and "ah's," Moishe pointed to the kitchen sinks.

"Shmuel, didn't you say you ordered the same sinks that we have?"

"Yes," Shmuel replied, "I did, and I paid good money for them."

"But these are the regular-quality sinks, not the ones with the special scratch-proof enamel," Moishe insisted. "I'm sure of it."

"What?! I can't believe it!"

"That contractor cheated you. You are entitled to get the sinks replaced, or at least to get your money refunded," Moishe said definitively.

The discovery cast a slight pall on the visit, and the Meirsons were soon on their way home.

"Moishe, why did you have to speak up about the sinks and bad-mouth the contractor?" Gitty asked with annoyance in her voice.

"What do you mean? He's entitled to compensation. My words were one hundred percent *leto'eles!*"

"Come on, Moishe. You know my meek brother Shmuel. He wouldn't even return a carton of sour milk to the grocery store. He's certainly not going to call and argue with the contractor. He's just going to eat himself up for having been taken advantage of. So where is your *to'eles?* You talked about the contractor for nothing, and you only caused Shmuel aggravation."

SOMETIMES, EVEN THOUGH there would appear to be a constructive purpose in speaking *lashon hara*, we are still not permitted to say it, either because the listener will not accept our words, or because it is too late for him to use the information to correct the damage. In either case, such *lashon hara* would not be considered *leto'eles* at all.

If the one witnessing a wrongdoing is guilty of the same transgression himself, then he is not permitted to publicize it, since he clearly does not have any constructive purpose in mind; he only intends to demean the sinner and take pleasure in his downfall. However, if there is a concrete purpose that will be achieved by his speaking the *lashon hara* — such as retrieving a stolen item or contributing necessary information to an inquiry for a *shidduch* or partnership — then he certainly should speak up, despite his personal faults.

We may not relate *lashon hara leto'eles* to *resha'im*, since in that case the listeners are guilty of the same transgressions that we are decrying and may not even consider them to be wrong. Therefore, there will obviously be no benefit in telling them the *lashon hara*; on the contrary, it will only cause greater damage, since they are likely to convey the report back to the subject, violating the *issur* of *rechilus*, and leading to serious *machlokes* and perhaps even to the subject informing on the speaker to the authorities, contrary to *halachah*. (*Mishpetei Hashalom* 19:65–67)

13 Iyar	13 Elul	13 Teves

Stop! Check the Conditions! WHEN WE ARE approached by an unhappy relative or a close friend who complains to us of having been wronged in some way and asks for our assistance, the natural reaction is to sympathize with the loved one and to take his side.

Under the influence of our worked-up emotions, we begin making plans to help and protect the victim.

It is precisely at that moment that we must stop and make sure that all the conditions to permit *lashon hara leto'eles* have been met. This means that we have to verify the facts, check that the report is the absolute truth, and clarify the possible reasons and motivations of the person who committed the wrong. Can his actions be justified in any way?

Next, we need to check whether the report has been exaggerated or important details have been omitted. Might the report have been related out of context? Has it been related solely for a constructive purpose or is it motivated by feelings of hate or revenge?

It is important to consider whether it might be possible to reprove the sinner before taking more drastic action. Is there a way to rectify the situation without causing damage to either party? By acting on the information, will we cause the subject a greater loss than *halachah* sanctions? Are we permitted to believe the report?

We should remember to take the speaker's emotions into account. Listening to him empathetically will allow him to unburden his heavy heart in a controlled fashion, thereby alleviating his pain and anguish. The emotional support we provide may prevent him from complicating the situation, as long as we identify with his difficult feelings, while taking care not to show that we agree with his derogatory statements or to provoke him to take drastic or inappropriate action. (*Mishpetei Hashalom* 19:67)

| 14 Iyar | 14 Elul | 14 Teves |

As Reliable as IN THE TIMES of the Gemara, there was a concept of
Two Witnesses *kim lei begavei* — a person whom we are absolutely confident would never lie or exaggerate in any matter. When a statement of *lashon hara* was heard from such a person, who was *meheiman lei kevei trei* — whose word was as airtight as the testimony of two witnesses in *beis din* — then the statement could be believed.

For example, at that time, if a *talmid* who was absolutely reliable in this way told his Rav that a fellow student had deliberately committed a sin and that there was no possible justification, the Rav would be al-

lowed to believe his words and to cool his relationship with the errant student until the student did *teshuvah*. However, the Rav would not be allowed to relate the information to anyone else and would certainly not be allowed to strike the student or cause him any financial loss based on this information.

The Chofetz Chaim writes that the consensus of the *poskim* is that in our times, the concept of *kim lei begavei* no longer exists, since nowadays no one can be relied on to be so meticulously careful with his speech as to never exaggerate in any matter. Therefore, the Chofetz Chaim rules that when hearing *lashon hara* or *rechilus* that may have some constructive use for the future, such as to save oneself from damage, even if we hear it from someone we would consider a highly reliable source, we are allowed only to be concerned and take precautions, but not to believe the report.

Clearly, then, we are not allowed to believe a statement of *lashon hara* told to us by a parent or spouse, even though we might ordinarily rely on that person blindly. Nor may we discuss the derogatory report with others, including a spouse or children, unless the information affects them as well (or where we need to "get the matter off our chest" and gain emotional support, as we have discussed in this chapter under the subheading "For Whose Benefit"). In any case, a husband would be wise not to relate to his wife every little incident in which he felt he was mistreated or shown a lack of respect or where he argued with someone. Doing so would not only be a violation of *shemiras halashon* but would also result in his degrading himself and causing his wife to lose respect for him. (*Mishpetei Hashalom* 19:68–69)

15 Iyar	15 Elul	15 Teves

Circumstantial Evidence AN EXCEPTIONAL SITUATION where one might be permitted to believe *lashon hara* or *rechilus* is the case of *devarim hanikarim* — clear circumstantial evidence. To explain: Reuven heard *lashon hara* or *rechilus* about Shimon, in a situation where the seven conditions for permitting relating the information were fulfilled, and where there was *to'eles* in Reuven's hearing it (e.g., to protect himself from possible damage). If Reuven himself sees clear circumstantial evidence that seems to corroborate the report he heard, then he may believe the report, provided the following conditions are met:

- ◻ There is absolutely no room to judge the incident favorably.
- ◻ The evidence observed is very close in detail to what was heard, not just remotely related.
- ◻ The listener himself observed the *devarim hanikarim*. Hearing it from someone else is not sufficient.

Even when the conditions have been met, and we can believe the report, we still may not relate it to others, nor may we strike the person about whom the *lashon hara* was spoken or cause him financial loss based on what we heard. In certain cases, the *beis din* or the city's halachically ordained committee may be permitted to strike the subject of the *lashon hara* until he admits his wrongdoing (such as admitting that he stole), on the basis of strong circumstantial evidence pointing to his guilt.

When a person has seen *devarim hanikarim* that indicate someone's negative conduct, he is permitted to inquire from others about that person's conduct, but only if he has a constructive reason for doing so, such as for the purpose of protecting himself, and only if he fulfills all the conditions of *to'eles* cited at the beginning of this chapter.

If a person hears that someone informed on him to non-Jewish authorities, and he suspects that a particular enemy or competitor of his is the culprit, then even if he sees clear circumstantial evidence that this is the case, he is still permitted only to take precautions to protect himself from that person, but he may not strike the person or cause him a loss, and he certainly may not inform on him in response. (*Mishpetei Hashalom* 19:71–72)

16 Iyar	16 Elul	16 Teves

Public Knowledge   IF INFORMATION HAS been publicized and is known to everyone in a particular place, it is not *rechilus* or *lashon hara* to repeat it, as long as our intention is not to degrade the subject or to publicize the matter further, and only if relating the report will not cause anyone loss or pain or arouse further contention.

However, talking about the misdeeds of someone's ancestors or about the person's own past wrongdoings for which he has already done *teshuvah* is absolutely prohibited, even if these matters are common knowledge. Also prohibited would be to spice up the well-publicized story with a different emphasis or a small addition.

In any case, we may not *believe* the story even if it is common knowledge. The fact that it was publicized in the newspapers or radio does not prove its authenticity; on the contrary, the mass media is replete with exaggerations, inaccuracies, things taken out of context and outright lies. Nor may we relate the story to anyone who by nature believes everything he hears, or to someone who is likely to repeat it to others in a manner that is not permissible, since doing so would be a violation of *lifnei iveir* — causing someone to sin.

The *dayanim* in *beis din* may not reveal who wanted to exonerate the defendant and who was in favor of conviction, and how they arrived at their final decision. Similarly, when a meeting of the *tuvei ha'ir* — the assembled town committee — takes place, the members may not disclose each one's opinion, since there will always be some individuals who are dissatisfied with their decisions.

When a public appointment takes place that someone does not approve of, such as a *darshan* whose style is not to his liking, or a Rav who does not meet his approval, it is a serious violation of *lashon hara* and *rechilus* for him to disclose to others his feelings on the matter. (*Mishpetei Hashalom* 19:74–76)

17 Iyar	17 Elul	17 Teves

In the Subject's Presence

"Shimmy is the clumsiest player I ever saw. If he would get a chance at bat, he would bat himself out of the park and leave the ball here at home base — ha ha ha!"

Donny collapsed into hysterical laughter, while a few feet away, Shimmy turned as pale as the ball in Donny's hand.

"Donny, how could you talk like that? How could you say such outright *lashon hara* about Shimmy?" Nachman whispered furiously to his friend.

"But he's right here, so it's not *lashon hara*," Donny replied.

"No, you're wrong," Nachman disagreed. "He's right here, so it's worse!"

CHAZAL WERE LENIENT about speaking in the presence of the subject — *apei marei* — only when the report is *avak lashon hara* that can be interpreted in two ways, positive and negative, depending on the speaker's tone of voice and body language. Generally, when making such a statement in the presence of the subject, the speaker will be careful to avoid any gesture or tone that would indicate an insulting interpretation. Therefore, he is permitted to make such a statement in front of the subject.

In a case of actual *lashon hara* or even *avak lashon hara*, if the speaker makes it clear that his intention is to denigrate the subject, then not only is it forbidden, but it is actually much worse than *lashon hara* spoken elsewhere, because the speaker is also guilty of violating the *issurim* of *ona'as devarim* — hurting the subject's feelings — and *lo sisa alav cheit* — embarrassing him. (*Mishpetei Hashalom* 19:77)

18 Iyar	18 Elul	18 Teves

In the Presence of Three   THE GEMARA STATES: "Anything said in the presence of three — *apei telasa* — is no longer considered *lashon hara.*" There is much controversy among the *poskim* as to what this statement means to tell us.

Tosafos understood that this refers to a report that can be interpreted in two ways, depending on the way it is presented. Similar to the *halachah* above, in the case of *apei marei* (in the presence of the subject), here too, we assume that when in the presence of at least three people the speaker will certainly not intend the statement in its negative sense, since it is almost certain to get back to the subject. Nevertheless, if it is clear from the speaker's tone and body language that he *does* mean to denigrate the subject, the report is considered *avak lashon hara* and is prohibited.

The Rashbam, Smag and Rambam understand the statement of the Gemara differently. They maintain that the person who speaks *lashon hara* in the presence of three people is certainly guilty of violating the *issurim* of *lashon hara* and *rechilus*. However, we learn from this statement that if one of the three later relates the report innocently to someone else in the area, he will not have transgressed the *issur* of *lashon hara*, as long as he did not spread the information intentionally or present it in a manner that shows it as even more derogatory than the version he originally heard. The reasoning behind this is that once three people know the report, it is already considered common knowledge, since each one of the three is likely to tell it to several people, and before long everyone in town will have heard. This *heter* applies only to the three people who originally heard the *lashon hara*, not to the people to whom they tell it, and they may repeat the report only in the same town or community; they may not tell people elsewhere. Also, *apei telasa* (in the presence of three) is relevant only when there were three listeners present; if two people related the information to two other people, the *heter* is not applicable. Nor may the listeners believe the information they heard.

The Chofetz Chaim qualifies this explanation by pointing out that if one of the three is a *yerei Shamayim* — a G-d-fearing person — or a close friend or relative of the subject, who would not relay such information about his loved one, or if the speaker specifically warned the listeners not to pass on the report, then the *heter* of *apei telasa* does not apply, since the matter will not automatically become public knowledge. In that case, if one of the three relates the report, he *is* guilty of violating the *issur* of *lashon hara*.

Some opinions restrict the *heter* of *apei telasa* to *lashon hara*; in the case of *rechilus*, it would be forbidden for any of the three to repeat the report, since by spreading the information, one makes it all the more likely that the subject will hear about it and resentment will be caused.

The Chofetz Chaim closes the discussion by saying that it is very rare for all of the conditions of *apei telasa* to be met, and even if they are, many *poskim* maintain that this leniency is not well-based in any case. In short, the Chofetz Chaim concludes, we would be well-advised not to rely on the lenient opinions. (*Mishpetei Hashalom* 19:78–80)

19 Iyar	19 Elul	19 Teves

Apei Telasa —
Other Angles

RASHI TAKES AN entirely different approach to the abovementioned statement in the Gemara. He says that the statement refers to a person who speaks *lashon hara* about himself or reveals his own secrets — such as his busi-

ness affairs or details of his own illness — in the presence of three or
more people. Even though we are generally prohibited from revealing
other people's secrets, in a case like this, where he made it evident that
he doesn't mind if the information gets out, the listeners are allowed to
disclose it to others, as long as the speaker did not explicitly tell them
that he does not want the matter discussed.

Rabbeinu Yonah derives a different *halachah* from these words. He
says that when there is a *heter* to say something derogatory because of
the *to'eles* involved, the speaker should be sure to relate the information
publicly, or at least in front of three people, so that the listeners will
not suspect him of violating the *issur* of *lashon hara*. The details of this
halachah were discussed earlier in this chapter, under the subheading
"For Whose Benefit." (*Mishpetei Hashalom* 19:81–82)

In summary: When *lashon hara* or *rechilus* are spoken *leto'eles* — for
a constructive purpose — it is not prohibited, provided the seven
conditions are met, among them: checking that the statement is accurate and is indeed a wrongdoing, giving the subject rebuke before
speaking, and trying alternate methods to accomplish the constructive purpose. The *to'eles* may be for the subject, for the listeners, or
for the speaker himself. Under certain circumstances *to'eles* would
not apply, such as when the speaker is guilty of the same transgression as that which he is speaking about, or when the listener will not
take action in any case. The Chofetz Chaim also discusses special
situations — such as when the speaker says the *lashon hara* in front
of the subject or in front of three listeners, when the listener has circumstantial evidence confirming what he heard, or when the *lashon
hara* is already common knowledge.

30

לשון הרע בשידוכים: הוראות כלליות
Shemiras Halashon for Shidduchim:
General Guidelines

Hilchos Shemiras Halashon in Practice

"Reb Shmaya, this is Refael Friedner. I wanted to ask you about a particular *bachur* you teach in your *shiur*—for a *shidduch*, of course…." Refael cleared his voice a few times, as if hesitant to continue.

"Reb Refael, I can't believe it," Shmaya intercepted him. "Your daughter Chaneleh is already of marriageable age? When we were neighbors in Lakewood she was just a toddler. How time flies! I should have realized—after all, my Yankie and Motty are both married, and I even have a couple of adorable grandchildren. So how are you adjusting to the 'shidduch scene'?"

"It isn't easy. There's the emotional side of getting ready to send my daughter off to her own home, and of course there's the financial pressure. But what I really find hard to handle are the inquiries," Refael sighed. "After years of learning *hilchos shemiras halashon* and avoiding any talk about individuals, suddenly I have to call people and interrogate them about every little nuance relating to each candidate. I'm having a hard time putting my Chofetz Chaim aside and adjusting myself to this new role."

"*Chas veshalom*! Don't put your Chofetz Chaim aside! This is your opportunity to put everything you always learned into action! The Chofetz Chaim prepared you for exactly what you can ask and how to ask it, just as he prepared me for how I should answer and when. Now, what was the name of that *bachur* you wanted to know about?"

356

WHEN IT COMES to inquiries about *shidduchim*, marriage-candidates, the laws of *shemiras halashon* are no different from any other situation. Nevertheless, we felt the need to devote two chapters to the practical application of *hilchos shemiras halashon* in this area, in order to make the reader aware of and sensitive to the complexity of this topic, since it is one that the public encounters regularly and is familiar with on a very personal level. Of course, in certain matters relating to business, such as hiring employees and choosing business partners, these principles are equally applicable. We trust that the reader will use the knowledge he has gained from these chapters and apply it on practical levels in all walks of life.

After examining all the angles, we will find that in *shidduch* inquiries there are some matters that are clearly forbidden, others that are clearly permitted, and a large gray area in between. It is very difficult for a layman to navigate his way through this gray expanse and reach the correct conclusions unless he consults a *talmid chacham* and also learns to apply his common sense to know how the *halachah* changes with each situation. (*Mishpetei Hashalom* 20: Introduction)

21 Iyar	21 Elul	21 Teves

Basis for the Need to Check   IN PRESENTING THESE *halachos*, for the sake of illustration we've often used examples based on average yeshivah students or Bais Yaakov graduates, with their particular concerns and goals. Although the examples we've cited are not necessarily universal, the principles and the *halachos* derived from them are relevant to every situation, and readers can apply these to their own circumstances.

Chazal encourage every individual to seek an appropriate spouse, even if it means "stepping down" from the level of respect he feels is his due and marrying someone on a lower level than himself (*Yevamos* 63a). This does not mean, however, that a suggested spouse should be taken "sight unseen." On the contrary, the need to make inquiries about a *shidduch*-candidate is well-anchored in the words of the Sages: "When you are considering marrying a woman, first check out her brothers, as most children resemble their mothers' brothers" (*Bava Basra* 110a).

Although the influence of uncles may have been more significant years ago, when members of extended families lived in close proximity to one another, this rule still applies for a number of reasons. First of all, even though the children may see their uncles only at an occasional Yom Tov meal or family *simchah*, these brief encounters can often leave a strong impression on a child's aspirations. Second, the mother is likely to raise her children as she saw her own brothers raised. Third, while a person can always work on himself to acquire good *middos*, there are certain positive characteristics that are inborn, giving him a spiritual "head start." Often, these hereditary *middos* can be perceived by checking out the grown brothers of the *shidduch*-candidate.

22 Iyar	22 Elul	22 Teves

Chazal stress that "a person should sell all that he has in order to marry the daughter of a *talmid chacham*" (*Pesachim* 49). At one time, the sole *chinuch* a girl received was from within her family circle. Today, while the family still plays a strong role, religious girls learn in an equalizing Bais Yaakov-type framework, where they are instilled with Torah ideals. Consequently, the *Gedolim* have stated that in our times every Bais Yaakov graduate who is meticulous in her observance of Torah and *mitzvos*, and respects the Roshei Yeshivos and the Rabbanim, is considered a *bas talmid chacham* for *shidduch* purposes. Needless to say, there are still unique virtues to a girl who actually grew up in the home of a *talmid chacham*, suffused with Torah values and aspirations for achieving high levels in Torah learning and observance.

In discussing the incident of Eliezer, the servant of Avraham, *Chazal* say that Eliezer did not "ask properly" when he declared that the girl who would offer drinks to him and his camels would be the wife for Yitzchak, since he had not made any of the requisite inquiries; the girl who offered her generous assistance might have turned out to be lame or blind or of questionable lineage. After all, before we purchase a valuable item we check out its quality extensively; how much more thoroughly should we make inquiries about a spouse, who will be our life partner in both the spiritual world and the physical, in this world and the next. "If he has merit, she will assist him, and if not, she will oppose him"

(*Yevamos* 63a). Woe to the man who falls into a bad marriage, for "A wicked woman is more bitter than death" (ibid. 63b).

In fact, *Chazal* tell us, "Someone who marries a woman who is not appropriate for him violates the *issurim* of *lo sikom* and *lo sitor*, because it is inevitable that he will dislike her, and he is bound to end up building up hard feelings and taking revenge on her" (*Avos DeRabbi Nosson* 26). *Chazal* tell us, "A man is not permitted to marry a woman without seeing her first. Otherwise, after marrying her he might notice something repulsive and be disgusted by her, in violation of Hashem's command of *ve'ahavta* — to love your fellowman" (*Kiddushin* 41a).

When the marriage is peaceful, the *Shechinah* resides with the couple. But "when the couple is not worthy, fire devours them" (*Sotah* 17a). To avoid such a situation, *Chazal* advise young, inexperienced *talmidei chachamim* who seek to meet a marriage partner to take someone along who understands women better, so they will not fall into a marriage that is not for their benefit (*Bava Basra* 168a). (*Mishpetei Hashalom* 20:1)

For a Constructive Purpose AS WE DISCUSSED in the preceding chapter, derogatory words that are spoken for a constructive purpose do not constitute a violation of *lashon hara* or *rechilus*, as long as the requisite conditions have been met. In the case of inquiries for *shidduchim*, there is a definite *to'eles* — a constructive purpose — for the future: to ensure the success of the potential match; therefore, the person responding to inquiries may give derogatory information where necessary. Since his words are not for the purpose of degrading or harming the subject, there is no transgression being committed; on the contrary — he is doing a *mitzvah* by answering, provided the conditions of *to'eles* are met, as in any other case. (See chapter 29 for details.)

Unfortunately, a not-uncommon error committed by people providing information for a *shidduch* is that they say either too much or too little, and in doing so they cause terrible, irreparable damage. Sometimes all it takes is one unnecessary word to sabotage a *shidduch*.

When a person maliciously says something derogatory about the prospective *shidduch*, he is considered a *rasha*, and we can only hope and pray that he does *teshuvah*. Our goal in this presentation is to correct the unintentional bunglers who mean well but who may cause damage just because they did not learn the details of the *halachos* and do not realize how careful we have to be before letting a word cross our lips. (*Mishpetei Hashalom* 20:2)

24 Iyar	24 Elul	24 Teves

Matchmaking — A Mitzvah ...

As Penina and Shayna walked out of shul, Penina sighed. "Every time I see Dina Steinman," she said, "my heart aches. Such a wonderful girl, I can't imagine why she hasn't found a *shidduch* yet."

"Such a shame," Shayna agreed. "And she's over thirty already, even though she looks younger."

"I think I'll mention to her my neighbor's brother-in-law — remember, the one I told you about," Penina decided.

"But Penina," Shayna objected, "you told me yourself when I asked you for information about him for my niece that he's terribly hot-tempered, didn't you? And for Dina, of all people — she's such a sweet, soft-spoken person."

"Yes, that's true. But it's better than not suggesting anything, isn't it? I won't mention to her about his temper. Maybe it won't bother her."

"I don't know. I think you should ask advice. To suggest a fellow you know isn't good for her, just to assuage your conscience that you came up with something? It doesn't sound right to me."

THE BURGEONING NUMBER of single young men and women who have not yet found their *shiduchim* makes the heart of every sensitive person ache in sympathy. We watch their eyes turn heavenward as they wonder despairingly, "From where will my help come?" How we wish we could help each of these lonely fellow Jews find his or her complementary "other half" and fulfill the *mitzvah* of having children and bringing up a new generation in the ways of Torah and *mitzvos*.

Beyond our feelings of personal empathy, we've also been taught to pursue the *mitzvah* of "*vehalachta bidrachav*" — emulating the kind ways of Hashem, Who is the ultimate Matchmaker, as we read in *Tehillim*,

"He settles individuals into family units" (*Tehillim* 68).

Many people of stature have been known to go to great lengths to promote *shidduchim*. When a widow would have difficulty remarrying, Iyov would claim to be her relative, so as to make her a more desirable candidate. Similarly, in more recent times, the Chofetz Chaim agreed that an orphan be presented as his relative (since, after all, all Jews are at least distant relatives…), so that she would be able to find a *shidduch*.

The Gemara tells us about a certain individual who made a vow not to derive benefit from his niece. Rabbi Yishmael arranged for the girl to be brought to his own home and beautified, and then, once she had a new appearance, the vow could be annulled and the individual was allowed to marry her (*Nedarim* 66). A father is obligated to provide for his daughter generously so that she will be an attractive proposition for potential marriage partners (*Kiddushin* 30b). Hashem Himself personally arranged the *shidduch* and made the wedding preparations for Adam Harishon (*Brachos* 61a). (*Mishpetei Hashalom* 20:3)

25 Iyar	25 Elul	25 Teves

… But With a Word of Caution   HOWEVER, MUCH AS we would like to help these lonely individuals find *shidduchim*, we cannot do so at any cost. Some people are under the mistaken impression that if we are allowed to bend the truth about a *kallah* at her wedding, calling a bride who is lame and blind "beautiful and graceful" (*Kesubos* 17a), the same rule must apply when describing a candidate for *shidduchim*. But this could not be further from the truth. Hiding real faults in a *shidduch* proposal — and certainly altering the facts — can have disastrous results and even end up in divorce — a tragedy that causes the *Mizbei'ach* to shed tears.

Even when the married couple remains together, the agony can be so intense that *Chazal* say that one who suffers from a bad spouse in this world does not have to go to *Gehinnom* (*Eiruvin* 41b), for he has already experienced it in this world. Similarly, "A person cannot live together with a snake …" (*Kesubos* 72a). While there is great satisfaction in making a *shidduch*, we must keep in mind that the goal is not just to get two people engaged but to see them joined together in a happy marriage.

Interestingly, we often find people who are generally rather careless when it comes to *issurim* of *lashon hara*, but as soon as they are asked to report on the shortcomings of their friends for *shidduch*-purposes, they suddenly become exceedingly meticulous not to reveal the slightest hint of a negative trait, even in a case where they would be obliged to speak up. Before opening our mouths to speak, we need to picture a set of scales before us. On one side of the scale lies our obligation to help the match go through. On the other side lie all the *mitzvos* of not standing aside when someone is in danger or about to suffer a loss, not giving unsound advice, returning a lost item (which includes saving someone from potential damage), and, if a relative or close friend is involved, there is also the obligation of *mibsarecha lo tisalem* — not disregarding our own flesh and blood (*Yeshayahu* 58:7).

When we are asked information for a *shidduch*, we have to keep in mind that every word, even a subtle emphasis or an ever-so-slight gesture, can tip the scale toward one side or the other and can result in destroying or building the future of these two Jews and changing the whole course of their lives and the lives of their future generations, in this world and the next. The burden of responsibility for what we say and for the consequences of our words falls on our shoulders — whether we say too much or too little. Even if we are in a rush or under pressure for some other reason, we should always stop and think carefully before answering questions on this delicate topic. (*Mishpetei Hashalom* 20:3)

26 Iyar	26 Elul	26 Teves

What to Look for   EVEN THOUGH EVERY person is unique, there are some general requirements that everyone should see as paramount when seeking a *shidduch*. According to the Torah, the main things a Torah-true girl should seek in a boy are *yiras Shamayim*, good *middos* and *hasmadah* — diligence in learning and strict adherence to his yeshivah framework — and a good amount of common sense. She needs someone with whom she can set up a home and bring up children in the way of Torah and *mitzvos*.

In seeking a marriage partner, a boy should look for a girl with good *middos*, *tznius* and *yiras Shamayim* and should verify that she shows proper respect to her parents. Also, it is vital that the two share similar ambitions and aspirations.

Naturally, in addition to this general "list," every individual has his own opinions and needs. Generally, he will have some requirements that are a "must" for him, and others that he might want ideally but would be prepared to dispense with if necessary. Every *shidduch* suggestion will have different combinations of the items on his list, and everyone is entitled to endeavor to find the match that is as close as possible to his ideal.

27 Iyar	27 Elul	27 Teves

Consequently, it is permissible to research and investigate each candidate as much as a person feels is necessary to assure him of that candidate's compatibility, as long as the inquiry has some constructive purpose. (It is wise, however, not to be overly picky.) We are required to stand at the ready to assist someone who is seeking a *shidduch* by offering our sound advice wherever possible. By doing so we refrain from transgressing the *issur* of *lo saamod* — not standing by while our brother's blood is being spilled — and we also fulfill the *mitzvah* of *ve'ahavta lerei'acha kamocha* — loving our fellow man, paraphrased by Hillel Hazaken as "Do not do to others what you would not want them to do to you." Certainly, if we were in the position of seeking a *shidduch* we would want others to help us along the way.

The Torah tells us to provide the needy with *dei machsoro asher yechsar lo*, "that which is lacking *to him*." The Gemara learns from the term "to him" that we should help find him a spouse, deducing it from similar language in the *passuk*, *E'eseh lo eizer kenegdo*, "I shall make *for him* a suitable helpmate." If we are obliged to help those who are in need even when the effort requires an outlay of money, we should certainly do so when the *chessed* demands only an investment of time.

From the same term, "to him," we can also derive that we should help the person seek a spouse that is right for *him*, according to his particular wishes and requirements, while at the same time trying to see past his imaginary, unrealistic hopes and to discern what his *real* needs are. Some people are excessively influenced and perhaps even intimidated

by the need for social approval and therefore turn down excellent *shidduchim* because of their concern for "what people will say." Others are blind to their own faults while criticizing *shidduch*-candidates for those selfsame shortcomings. Yet others simply make unreasonable demands that are not at all appropriate to meet their real needs or levels.

In any case, our task is to put ourselves in the shoes of the person seeking a *shidduch* and to ask ourselves, "If I were in his exact position, what would I want others to do for me?" This is a true fulfillment of the *mitzvah* of *ve'ahavta*. (*Mishpetei Hashalom* 20:4–5)

28 Iyar	28 Elul	28 Teves

The Good of the Couple Is Foremost

"What's going to be with our Mireleh? There are no *shidduchim* coming in at all," moaned Mirele's father, Mendel Moseson.

Malka Moseson was puzzled. "But Mendel, just yesterday you showed me your notebook bulging at the seams with names of potential *chassanim*. I don't understand how you can say that there is nothing available!"

"Oh, sure, there are names, lots of names. But not one of them is good enough for my Mireleh," Mendel asserted.

"Look, Mendel, I love Mireleh as much as you do, but face it, she's not perfect. She's a wonderful girl with a heart of gold, but she was far from the top of her class, she's a little heavy, and no matter how we try we can't get rid of that acne. And besides, we're simple people. We don't have any big *yichus* in our family tree, and we can't pay a mint for a dowry or provide a five-star wedding in a fancy hall. Maybe you aren't being realistic …?"

"Nonsense, Malka. These things aren't important — a few pimples, a few pounds. Mirele is a treasure, and I won't settle for anything less than the top boy in a top yeshivah, from the family of a Rav or a Rosh Yeshivah. Let me call back that *shadchan* and give him a nudge …"

WHEN SUGGESTING A *shidduch*, the goal should be the genuine good of the couple — not pleasing their parents or friends. Sometimes people have an exaggerated image — either of themselves or of their children. They fail to see their own faults but are quite good at finding faults in those suggested to them. Nor are they willing to step down, as *Chazal* advise (*Yevamos* 62), and accept a *shidduch* that they perceive to be below

their level in some aspect. Unfortunately, some people who take this attitude end up remaining single — or keeping their children single — for years, because of trivial, tangential issues.

In such a situation, the *shadchan* or the person providing information sometimes has to take the initiative and conceal faults or exaggerate virtues of the other side in order to overcome the hurdle of the asker's overblown self-image. In this case it would be a *mitzvah* of *ve'ahavta lerei'acha kamocha* to do so, in order to neutralize the unreasonable demands that run counter to the real needs of the couple.

Of course, a person should not rush into using such tactics, since when all is said and done, parents generally do want what is best for the child. Even if it seems to us that they are being overly particular about certain points, to their child's detriment, we must keep in mind that even the most independent child tends to rely on his parents' opinions and financial backing, in the knowledge that the parent is more experienced and is acting in his best interests. Therefore, before we take the responsibility of analyzing the parents' motives and misrepresenting the other side in order to counteract the parents' unreasonable expectations in our hope to save the child from remaining single indefinitely, we would do well to consult with a *talmid chacham* who can give us objective direction. (*Mishpetei Hashalom* 20:6)

29 Iyar	29 Elul	29 Teves

General Guidelines   MOST SITUATIONS WE encounter in *shidduchim* are not "black and white." Therefore, even when we are well-versed in all the *halachos* of *lashon hara* and *rechilus*, and even if we also know all the details about both sides in a suggested *shidduch*, we still need to exercise common sense and good judgment — what is known as the "fifth *Shulchan Aruch*" — in order to respond to *shidduch*-inquiries in a properly balanced way.

When we possess derogatory information that would cause the asker to drop the *shidduch*, we should try whenever possible to discourage the *shidduch* without revealing the derogatory point, such as by saying, "It's not for you," or some other such statement. If we see that this vague response is not enough to dissuade the asker from continuing

the *shidduch*, then we are obligated to reveal the information, but we should be careful to reveal as little of the negative report as is necessary in order to achieve our constructive purpose. For example, if we saw the *bachur* in question hanging out in a pizza shop day after day during his yeshivah's learning hours, we might say, "He's not careful about keeping to the yeshivah schedule." Only if that does not accomplish the purpose should we give the full story.

When we are not certain how to answer a question posed to us, we should say "I don't know," rather than risk giving inaccurate information. However, if we sense that the asker will read into that answer and assume we are hiding something negative, we should find another way to evade the question.

If we possess confidential information regarding a *shidduch*-candidate — such as information regarding a medical or psychological condition — and we are the only ones who possess that information, we may be obligated to speak up and disclose the information. On the other hand, it may be prohibited for us to reveal it. In such a case a Rav should be consulted.

Whenever the intentions of the asker are vague, we should answer in a more general way and not reveal any derogatory detail that was not asked about specifically. For example, if people ask in a general way, "How does he get along socially?" we can respond in an equally general manner, "He gets along fine with people and is well-liked." But if they ask specifically, "Is he quiet or lively? Is he very shy in new situations? Does he keep the same roommates in the dormitory where he stays, or does he run into trouble with them and change rooms often?" — then we would have to answer more precisely.

We should not ask a person's enemy — or even his competitor — for information about him. If we are asked information about our own enemy or competitor, we should avoid answering, as long as there is someone else the person could inquire from instead. Inquiring about a divorcee is an extremely delicate situation. At times, in such a case there is no choice but to inquire of the ex-spouse, but this must be done very cautiously and tactfully by perceptive people who are also meticulous in the *halachos* of *shemiras halashon*; otherwise, it is almost impossible to avoid violating the *issur* of *lashon hara*. (*Mishpetei Hashalom* 20:7)

Keeping the Exchange "Kosher"   As Mrs. Sitner got on the bus, her thoughts distracted her. The *shadchan* had called a few days earlier to suggest a girl for her Baruch, someone by the name of Sara Abelson, but she was having difficulty finding out information about the girl. Advancing toward the back of the bus, she noticed an empty seat and was relieved to sit down.

"Hello, Mrs. Sitner," her seatmate said cheerfully.

"Oh, Bayla, I didn't notice it was you. I see you're back from seminary," Mrs. Sitner said. Bayla was the daughter of her friend Esther, from the other side of town.

"Yes, I'm back, and today we had a get-together from my old high school class. What a blast!"

Suddenly the gears started moving in Mrs. Sitner's mind. Didn't Bayla go to the same high school as that Abelson girl? "Oh, so you saw all your old friends. Tell me," she asked as nonchalantly as she could, "how is that Abelson girl doing?"

"Oh, don't ask. She was always a '*neb*,' and the year in seminary didn't help a bit…" Bayla, obviously unaware of the gravity of the *issur* of *lashon hara*, went on for the next five minutes pouring out everything Mrs. Sitner could possibly have wanted to know about the girl. Mrs. Sitner was quite pleased with what she perceived as *hashgachah pratis* — Divine providence. Too bad she hadn't realized that the omission of six little words — "I'm asking *leto'eles*, for a *shidduch*" — transformed the whole conversation into an *aveirah* for both her and Bayla.

WHEN WE MAKE inquiries for a *shidduch*, we must reveal the reason for our investigation, or — if for some reason we don't want the word out that it is for *shidduch* purposes — at least point out that it is for a legitimate *to'eles*. If we fail to do so, we may be guilty of *lifnei iveir* — causing the other person to sin. However, when it is clear that we are asking for a constructive purpose, such as if we have already asked about this same individual repeatedly, or if the other party knows that we have a son or daughter in *shidduchim* and the reason for our inquiry is obvious, then we may not have to spell out the fact that we are asking *leto'eles* each time, especially among people who are always careful about these *halachos*.

When we are asked for information by someone whom we suspect

is not proficient or exacting in the laws of *shemiras halashon*, we should preface our response with something like, "Please don't believe what I'm telling you as absolute truth; just use it as a basis for taking precautions or making further inquiries." If we are really not sure what to answer, we should hint to the asker in some way that he should look into the matter further.

As we have mentioned regarding suggesting a *shidduch*, the goal in responding to a *shidduch* inquiry should be for the benefit of the couple — not necessarily for that of their parents, *shadchanim* or friends. A word of caution: In situations such as these, where we are permitted to speak about others to some extent, the *yetzer* lurks in the background, eager to trick us into crossing over the bounds of the permissible. Talking too much is almost guaranteed to lead us to an *aveirah*, since a mere hairsbreadth marks the boundary between what we may say and what we may not. Since every extraneous word may constitute a violation of several *issurim*, we should keep our words as brief as possible, while retaining a polite and respectful approach, as the situation demands. (*Mishpetei Hashalom* 20:8)

2 Sivan	2 Tishrei	2 Shvat

As Much as Necessary WHEN MAKING A *shidduch* inquiry we are permitted to ask as many people as many questions as we feel are necessary in order to get a clear picture and ensure the success of the *shidduch*. No question is too picayune, as long as we feel it will be of benefit for the clarification of the *shidduch*. The Chofetz Chaim proves this from the Gemara in *Shavuos* 39b, where we learn that the person who does not make adequate inquiries before taking a business partner and consequently has to demand that he take an oath with Hashem's Name is called a *rasha*, since he could have prevented the need for that oath had he clarified the matter properly before entrusting this person with his money.

Messengers can also be employed to do the investigating, when we cannot do it ourselves. Some people find that when inquiring about a *shidduch* it is helpful to have a reliable, capable third party to act as a mediator between the asker and the one being asked for information. In this way, the person giving the information will not need to figure out who the other party is and to tailor his answers accordingly. In addition, the mediator will be able to sift through the information and pass on only what is necessary.

Others maintain that there is an advantage to asking for information directly, because then the asker can perceive the spontaneous response of the person giving the information and can read his body language and/or tone of voice. The response does not lose any of its enthusiasm — or lack of enthusiasm — as it would if it went through a third party. Moreover, when the responder knows who wants the information, he also has a better idea of what that person's concepts and expectations are — for example, in a *bachur*'s level of learning or in a girl's level of *tznius* — and is better equipped to answer his questions.

When we can find out the information without anyone else acting as a go-between, that is usually preferable, since fewer people will have to hear the derogatory report. If, however, we are the ones who are providing the information, we must be careful not to raise doubts and suspicions on the part of the listener when we do so — as might happen if a stranger calls the candidate's parents directly to divulge some derogatory point. In some cases, this approach to giving information directly may fall into the category of blowing the derogatory information out of proportion or of causing more damage than is appropriate. Sometimes a better option is to have the go-between ask the parents to call him, but this is not always practical; each situation should be considered on an individual basis.

3 Sivan	3 Tishrei	3 Shvat

In any case, if it is possible for us to verify the information we need without asking anyone at all, it would appear that we have the obligation to utilize that option first. (*Mishpetei Hashalom* 20:7, 9)

Clear Communication IN *SHIDDUCH* INQUIRIES it is vital that the asker and the one he is asking be "speaking the same language" and that they understand each other properly. Otherwise, misunderstandings are likely to ensue. For example,

when we say that a girl is a "*baalas chessed*," the term can have a wide range of meanings. It might refer to someone who is willing to lend you her blow-dryer for an hour, or it might be a girl who organizes all the babysitting help and meals for the young mothers in her neighborhood, helps her mother with the housework and with caring for the children and then spends her evenings studying with the weak students in her class. Therefore, it is important in such a case to give specific examples that will provide a picture of the nature, quality and quantity of the kind acts in which she engages.

The same is true of such vague, subjective descriptions like *masmid*, bright, modern, *machmir*, organized, *tzaddik*, *talmid chacham*, normal, yeshivish, nice, cold, sociable and punctual, to name just a few.

Even more potential for confusion arises when using terms that are perceived differently in different cultures. For example, when an Englishman uses the word "smart" he means "put together"; when an American uses the same word he means "intelligent." Outside of Eretz Yisrael the term "*iluy*" is a positive one, referring to an intellectual genius, while in Eretz Yisrael, it may connote someone who is "in the clouds" and a bit out of touch with reality.

4 Sivan	4 Tishrei	4 Shvat

In addition, the same quality may be presented as positive or negative, depending on the label we tack on to it. For example, a girl who is actively concerned about other people's problems, seems to know what they need and seeks to help them however she can might be called either a *baalas chessed* or a *yenta* who has her nose in everyone else's business.

Providing a number of examples can help give a clearer picture of the candidate's character. On the other hand, it is important not to jump to sweeping, positive conclusions about someone's character based on scattered individual incidents.

The same is true of generalizing a negative picture based on an isolated detail or two. Everyone has a "skeleton in his closet" — an embarrassing episode or shady aspect of his past; we must be careful not to take these isolated details out of context or inflate them out of proportion.

From each of these cases, we can see how important it is in a _shidduch_ inquiry to know a bit about the person with whom we are speaking — not only his cultural background, but also where his priorities lie, his manner of thinking and his style of speech. For example, some people have a tendency to speak bombastically, as if they are giving a _hesped_ or a _sheva-brachos_ speech. Their generous attitude leads them to praise others to the sky, even when the accolades are not justified. In order to get a more accurate picture of the _shidduch_ candidate, we might have to take their description and cut it down by half. Other people are extremely stingy with their praise, and if we are aware of that we will know to magnify their words to get a clear picture.

Many areas that are brought up in a _shidduch_-inquiry are very delicate and can be easily taken out of context and misunderstood. Therefore, we should avoid answering when the asker insists on hiding or misrepresenting his identity. If we cannot evade responding, we should try to make small talk for a few minutes to give ourselves an opportunity to tune in to the other person's wavelength before getting down to the nitty-gritty of the inquiry. (_Mishpetei Hashalom_ 20:10)

5 Sivan	5 Tishrei	5 Shvat

Timing Is Crucial NOT ONLY DO we have to be careful about _what_ we say; we also have to be cautious about _when_ we say it. Certain flaws in a _shidduch_-candidate will be enough to sabotage the _shidduch_ if they are revealed before the couple ever meets, but those same flaws will not loom so threateningly if heard about at a later point, after the candidate has already made a positive impression.

Therefore, the _Gedolim_ have ruled that it is permissible and even advisable to delay revealing certain flaws or derogatory information until after the two have met, and even then, perhaps to do so through an intermediary. In certain circumstances it is best not to disclose the information until close to the engagement or after the engagement, and in rare cases, when the information will not affect the couple's life together in any way, it should not be divulged until after the wedding, or perhaps not at all. Of course, such a decision should be made with rabbinical guidance.

In all of the above cases, even though we are dealing with information that we would be permitted to disclose eventually, if we reveal the derogatory information before the time designated according to *din Torah*, we would be guilty of violating the *mitzvos* of *lo seileich rachil* (do not be a gossipmonger), *zachor eis asher asa Hashem leMiriam* (remember how Hashem punished Miriam for her *lashon hara*), and *hishamer benega hatzaraas* (guard yourself from the punishment of *tzaraas*). (Some opinions disagree and maintain that as long as disclosure of the information is permitted, these *issurim* are not violated when we speak ahead of the prescribed time.) (*Mishpetei Hashalom* 20:11)

In summary: We are permitted and encouraged to check out a candidate for a *shidduch*, since our inquiry is for a clearly beneficial purpose. It is a *mitzvah* to suggest *shidduchim* and to offer our help by providing information. In doing so, the good of the couple should be uppermost in our minds; we should act, to the best of our ability, precisely as we would want others to act toward us were we to find ourselves in an identical situation. In asking information we must point out that our inquiry is *leto'eles*. In responding, we should keep our comments general unless we are responding to specific questions. Keep in mind that withholding necessary information can be even more damaging than revealing unnecessary information. A clear line of communication is essential to avoid misunderstandings based on different priority systems, cultural gaps, etc. Certain facts should not be mentioned at the outset but only at a later point in the *shidduch*.

⇜ 31 ⇝

לשון הרע בשידוכים:
חילוקי דינים לפי שינויי מצבים
Shemiras Halashon for
Shidduchim: Varying Situations

6 Sivan	6 Tishrei	6 Shvat

Taking All Factors "Asher, I'm taking the phone off the hook," Perel
into Consideration said with exasperation. "That was the fifth *shidduch*
inquiry in the last half-hour. Nobody told me that
when I became a seminary teacher, my evening sideline would be giving
people information about my students. I think I'm going to start saying
that I just don't answer such questions. I've heard of some teachers who
do that."

"I'm not sure that's the right thing to do, Perel," Asher ventured. "Taking
the phone off the hook so we can eat supper — well, that's all right. But
to refuse to help out people who are dependent on you for information?
I don't know..."

"But I'm always walking a tightrope. Not every girl is the top student
and the future Sarah Schenirer of her generation. It's not easy coming on
positively about each one. And if the person calling me has already called
to ask about other girls, I know that she's comparing my every word, trying to figure out what I left out or added this time."

"I agree that it's not easy. But you play an important role. You can make
a *shidduch* or break it. Sometimes you have to know to be quiet about a

373

particular detail, and other times you have to speak up, or you'll be wrong-
ing the other party. I suggest we go to the Rav and ask him for some
guidelines, so you can play this involuntary role of yours to the hilt — as a
great *mitzvah*, and without slipping into *issurim*. But first, let's finish supper...."

Brrring... "Oh, I knew I should have taken it off the hook..."

A WIDE VARIETY of factors will affect the question of whether we are
forbidden or obligated to reveal derogatory information for *shidduch*
purposes, as well as the time and manner that is best to reveal it. Among
these factors are: the extent of the flaw, the importance it will be given
by the other party, the question of how receptive they will be to our
information, and much more. While in other areas, when there is a
doubt, the ideal solution is to "sit by and do nothing," in this area we
cannot always evade the question by remaining silent, because in many
cases, not only are we permitted to divulge the information, we are
obligated to disclose it; if we do not do so, we will have violated our role
in our obligation to the other party and we will be responsible for any
results that follow.

In this chapter we will discuss some of these varying factors and
how the distinctions between them may affect the relevant *halachah*.
(*Mishpetei Hashalom* 20:12)

7 Sivan	7 Tishrei	7 Shvat

Serious   A SMALL NUMBER of flaws would be considered serious
Deficiencies deficiencies in any *shidduch*, and we would be required
               to divulge the information even if we were not asked
about it:

▫ *Apikorsus* — If either the *chassan* or *kallah* has even a very slight
  tendency toward heretical thought, for example, if they do not
  believe in one of the thirteen fundamentals of faith, or if they
  deny even one aspect of the Torah — even a single *gezeirah shavah* (principle of deducing a law of the Torah through different
  citations of similar language), we must inform the other party.
  Included in this area would be someone who denigrates *talmidei*

chachamim, scorns the words of *chachamim* or reads heretical texts.

▫ **Immodest background** — If either one comes from a household of *pritzus*, immodest behavior, this must be revealed.

▫ **Serious illness** — If either one suffers from an illness that could become life-threatening or could prove disruptive to their day-to-day lives, we cannot keep it to ourselves. Examples would include: cancer, diabetes, epilepsy, a missing limb, depression or other mental/emotional illnesses. Infertility would also fall into this category.

▫ **Negative traits** — If either party exhibits negative character traits to such an extent that it would make it difficult to live with him or her, it would be wrong to withhold this information. Examples would include a person who is hot-tempered, miserly, cruel, over-exacting, excessively strict or constantly critical.

▫ **Adopted** — If the candidate is adopted, according to the *poskim*, this too must be revealed.

When it comes to *apikorsus* and *pritzus*, the Chofetz Chaim ruled that we should speak up even if we only heard a rumor that the *chassan* or *kallah* has a flaw in these areas, as long as we do not present it as a proven fact, but rather say, "I heard that…" However, if we do know the information definitively, we are obligated by Torah law to speak up, in keeping with the *mitzvah* of *lo saamod*, whereas if we know it only through hearsay, we are not unequivocally obligated to say it. In contrast, in the case of serious illness, we should mention it only if we are very familiar with the situation, not if our knowledge is based on flimsy secondhand information. (*Mishpetei Hashalom* 20:12–13)

8 Sivan | 8 Tishrei | 8 Shvat

Exaggerating a Serious Deficiency WHEN A SERIOUS deficiency exists, it is vital to prevent the *shidduch* so as to forestall a tragic outcome. Therefore, if, for example, we know that the person in question shows some signs of *apikorsus*, we are permitted to exaggerate the situation in order to make sure that the asker will fully understand the seriousness of its effect and drop the *shidduch*.

The same is true in the case of the other deficiencies mentioned. If presenting the dry facts will not depict the situation in all of its severity, we can exaggerate a bit in order to get the message across so that the listener will accept and act on our information. For example, if we know that the subject suffers from depression, and we sense that the listener will brush off our report of the facts and deduce that the candidate is merely a bit sad at times, we may present the situation as worse than it is and say that he suffers from severe depression, to ensure that the listener will take heed. However, we may not fabricate a deficiency that does not exist at all — such as by saying about someone suffering from depression that he has cancer, or that someone who shows signs of heresy is diabetic.

Some opinions maintain that certain indecent behaviors in our times would be given the same status as *apikorsus* in the times of the Chofetz Chaim, permitting us to inform the listener about them even if not asked, and permitting us to exaggerate the situation if necessary. For example, taking drugs or improper use of the Internet can easily become an addiction that can ruin a person's life physically and spiritually. If we know that the subject is involved in such activities, we should certainly report it to someone inquiring for a *shidduch*.

When there is definite danger that a *shidduch* will go through with someone who has a serious deficiency, we may be required to tell an outright lie if that is the only way the listener will be persuaded to back off from the *shidduch*. In all questionable cases a Rav should be consulted for guidance. (*Mishpetei Hashalom* 20:14)

| 9 Sivan | 9 Tishrei | 9 Shvat |

"Had He Known …" IN DISCUSSING THE subject of "serious deficiencies," the Chofetz Chaim adds an important explanatory phrase: "**Had he known about this deficiency, he would not have agreed [to the *shidduch* in the first place].**" It is clear that most people would indeed not agree to a *shidduch* that displays the serious deficiencies that the Chofetz Chaim mentioned — *apikorsus*, serious illness and immodest behavior. The same would be true of a *shidduch* with someone who has a very bad nature or extremely negative character traits, even though the Chofetz Chaim did not mention them explicitly; therefore, if we do not inform the other party of such qualities, and later he must suffer from the results of our reticence, we will be guilty of violating the *issur* of *lo saamod*. Some explain that in the abovementioned directive the Chofetz Chaim meant to stipulate that if we have strong reason to believe that the asker *would* go ahead with such a *shidduch* anyway, then we may not reveal the information to him.

However, it appears that the Chofetz Chaim was implying an additional *halachah*: that even in the case of other, lesser deficiencies — such as physical weakness, poverty, simple-mindedness, derogatory information about ancestors and other, similar issues — the decision of whether they must be mentioned or not depends very much on the individual circumstances. If for this particular person such a deficiency would be reason to regret having gone into the *shidduch*, then it takes on the status of a serious deficiency, with all that the definition implies.

For most people, the question of how the candidate's great-grandparents conducted their lives may not affect the success of the *shidduch* in the least. But if the asker is known to be very particular about *yichus*, then for *him*, derogatory information about ancestors may be extremely significant. Or, if the family is comprised of all *talmidei chachamim*, then they may not be able to welcome a simple-minded person into their midst; for someone from that family it would be important to know of the candidate's mediocre intellect. It may be that the asker is extremely fearful of a life of poverty; for him it is vital to know if the other party is in dire financial straits. Or the asker may be unusually particular about matters of health and genetic conditions. In each of these cases, the principle of "Had they known, they would not have agreed in the first place" would apply, and we would have to divulge this information to them, because in their particular case these generally minor deficiencies turn into serious deficiencies.

The principle is: If the *shidduch* looks like it has a good chance of succeeding despite a particular flaw, we should not reveal the deficiency unless we are asked about it specifically. But when the standard of the *shidduch* falls far below what the inquiring party expects in areas that

we know are important to him, and because of which we can be quite certain that he would regret having gone into the *shidduch*, then we are required to disclose the information relevant to those areas, even if he does not ask about them specifically. (*Mishpetei Hashalom* 20:15)

Depending on Who Is Asking WHEN WE ARE uncertain about the facts regarding a particular deficiency in the subject, we may give the information with the stipulation that we only know the information secondhand: "I heard that..." However, we may do so only if we know that the person inquiring is knowledgeable in the *halachos* of *shemiras halashon* and will not accept our report at face value, but rather will investigate the matter further. (Even though, as we mentioned earlier, in a case where there is doubt, we are not obligated to speak up as far as the *mitzvah* of *lo saamod* is concerned, we might still be obligated to do so under the principle of "returning lost objects" — that is, saving a fellow Jew from a possible loss.)

If the inquirer is not familiar with the necessary *halachos*, then we should simply answer that we do not know about the deficiency in question, since in a case where there is doubt, we are not permitted to risk violating the *issur* of *lashon hara*. (*Mishpetei Hashalom* 20:16)

Permission to Speak Withdrawn IN CERTAIN SITUATIONS, we are not permitted to report a deficiency to the inquiring party, since our beneficial purpose will not be served by speaking up, in which case the *issur* of *lo seileich rachil* is applicable:

◻ If the inquiring party **will not accept** our report, for whatever reason, then there is no *heter* to say the information. This may be the case if there is a lack of communication between the inquirer and the one being asked, or if the inquirer possesses the same flaw and will not perceive it as something negative. Alternatively, the asker may simply not trust the speaker's opinion or may not rely on his report, or may dismiss his words because the speaker does not have the same priorities as he does.

❏ If there is reason to believe that we will be **harassed** by the other side if word gets out at some later point that we were the ones who revealed the information, we are not required to reveal it.

❏ If we are quite sure that the report **will not cause the other side to break off** the *shidduch*, then there is no *heter* to tell them the information. We often find this situation when the other party is already enthusiastic about the *shidduch* because of the many positive qualities of the *shidduch*-candidate, or when the boy and girl have already met and there is some kind of emotional bond between them. In either case, when one feels confident that hearing the derogatory information will not change anyone's mind, the report may not be said.

❏ If one of the sides in a *shidduch* is asking for information just out of **curiosity**, when the information is not really necessary for the *to'eles* of helping them make their decision, then we may not reveal the derogatory report.

❏ If the deficiency **will not affect their lives in any negative way** at all, and there is no indication that knowledge of the deficiency would cause them to break off the *shidduch*, for example, when the boy's side is "digging" for flaws so that he can negotiate a higher dowry, we may not reveal it to him.

❏ If the inquiring party **also possesses a serious deficiency**, or

❏ If we know that there is some kind of **deceit** present — whether by the young people themselves, by the parents or *shadchanim* — we may not reveal the information to the side that is being deceitful.

The Chofetz Chaim warns that if we reveal derogatory information in such situations, it will boomerang back when the couple gets married anyway and they have their first fight. More than likely, in the heat of the argument one will tell the other, "So-and-so was right when he told me that you…" Obviously, therefore, not only is revealing derogatory information under these circumstances of no benefit, it is also a clear violation of *lifnei iveir*, since it enables the couple to later violate the *issur* of *rechilus*. (*Mishpetei Hashalom* 20:17, 35)

Not So "Reb Sholom? This is Mordechai Alster on the line."

Serious "*Shalom aleichem*, Reb Mordechai. I've been waiting for your call. So what does your son have to say at this point, after the second meeting?" the *shadchan* asked with eager interest.

"Shmuli is quite impressed, and he is interested in continuing. But I was disturbed by something that came up. When they were talking last night, the girl mentioned something about having suffered from some asthma as a child. My wife and I were a bit taken aback. Reb Sholom, I trust you as a *shadchan*. Why didn't you mention that to me before?" Mordechai seemed offended.

"Tell me, is Shmuli — or your wife, for that matter — planning to break things off because of the girl's childhood medical history?"

"Well, no … she's too much of a prize, I must admit," Mordechai conceded.

"Well, there's your answer," the *shadchan* asserted triumphantly. "Childhood asthma is so common, it's almost like having an annual flu. If I'd mentioned it before, you just would have gotten your defenses up and maybe even let this jewel slip through your hands. But at this point, you see that it's not so significant. And besides, for the same reason, I didn't tell the other side about Shmuli's skin condition. Nu, you still trust me, Reb Mordechai? I'll pass on your answer to the other side, and I'll get back to you as soon as I can."

MANY POSSIBLE DEFICIENCIES might exist in a *shiddush* candidate that would not be likely to have a serious, deleterious effect on the couple's married life, nor would they be reason for either side to regret having gone ahead with the *shiddush* on the principle of "Had he known, he would not have agreed." Flaws that would fall under this category include:

- **Medical conditions** that are not life-threatening, such as eczema, migraines, light asthma, allergies, or a susceptibility to colds and infections. Also included would be internal illness suffered during childhood from which the subject has fully recovered, as long as there is no risk of recurrence and there are no lingering side effects. (In a case of uncertainty over whether the illness may recur, one should verify the matter carefully or say "I don't know.")

- ❏ **Character weaknesses**, such as bad *middos* that are not so difficult to live with, an excessively quiet or loud personality, exceptional naïvete, being less of a *talmid chacham*.
- ❏ **Bad habits**, such as sloppiness and sleeping late.
- ❏ **Assorted objective statistics**, such as age, height, financial situation, difficult family background.
- ❏ **Religious observance** to either extreme — being either too easy-going or overly stringent in keeping *halachah*.

In each of these cases, since there is no definite damage that is imminent if the *shidduch* goes through, we are not permitted to reveal these points unless the inquirer asks about them specifically. The assumption is that if the point was of particular importance to the person inquiring, he would have asked. Therefore, when giving a report on a *shidduch*-candidate, it is important to offer information in a general way and answer in detail only the specific questions asked, without adding any additional information regarding flaws or personal opinions that were not asked for.

Even when we are asked specifically about certain minor deficiencies and are required to answer truthfully, we should still try to say as little as possible about the flaw and to balance out the negative report with good qualities. We might suggest that the other party be advised to overlook the deficiency in light of the subject's many good points.

In addition, we can try to play down the flaw as much as possible. For example, if the boy gets up late, we might point out that he learns until very late at night and that he is always careful to *daven* with a *minyan*. If he is rather quiet, we can point out that he has no trouble carrying on a conversation with his close friends and is very well-liked and accepted socially, despite his quiet nature. (*Mishpetei Hashalom* 20:18, 20)

| 13 Sivan | 13 Tishrei | 13 Shvat |

Self-Inflicted Damage   IN THE CONTEXT of giving information about a subject's level of Torah erudition, the Chofetz Chaim cites the principle of "causing oneself a loss." Since the father who is inquiring could have had the young man tested by a *talmid*

chacham to verify his level of learning and did not do so, the Chofetz Chaim asserts, we need not reveal the boy's lack of Torah knowledge, since the father caused his own loss by his negligence.

However, in many cases, this principle does not apply. For example, if the situation falls into the category of "Had he known, he would not have agreed" — that is, when we are certain that this factor is crucial to the asker, such as in the case of the daughter of a renowned *talmid chacham*, or of a layman who is offering a hefty dowry in order to find a son-in-law who has a glowing future in the Torah world — then the principle of "he caused his own loss" does not apply. In such a case we would be required to reveal the information to the inquirer, and failing to do so would be a violation of *lo saamod*.

Nor would the principle of "causing his own loss" be sufficient to defend the boy's side against the other side's claim that there was a *mekach ta'us* — a transaction based on a major error — in which case the marriage or the dowry obligation could be nullified. Whenever it is clear from the situation — from the character of the family or from previous *shidduch*-dealings with them — that the information is vital to them, this principle does not allow us to refrain from disclosing negative information about the boy's level of learning.

Moreover, while in the Chofetz Chaim's time it was common to take a *shidduch*-candidate to a great *talmid chacham* to be tested, this is not the usual practice in our times; therefore, not doing so is not sufficient reason to say "he caused his own loss." In any case, it does not make sense to say that a girl who is seeking to marry a budding *talmid chacham* should suffer a great lifetime loss just because her parents were negligent in their inquiries.

The only time the principle applies, as the Chofetz Chaim stipulates, is when we can be reasonably certain that the inquirer's failure to make the necessary effort to investigate the matter is a clear indication that this aspect is not so important to either him or his daughter.

Therefore, even if the parents were lax in doing their job, we are still required to inform the prospective *chassan* and *kallah* of a deficiency, wherever it is permitted or required according to the rules we have set forth. (*Mishpetei Hashalom* 20:19)

14 Sivan | 14 Tishrei | 14 Shvat

"Why Prefer One Side Over the Other?" The bachur was ushered into the simple quarters of the Chazon Ish, and he presented his question briefly. Describing the *shidduch* suggestion that had been presented to him, he asked the *gadol* how to proceed.

"Yes, yes," the Chazon Ish nodded enthusiastically. "I highly recommend that you go ahead with it."

The *bachur* relayed his answer to the *shadchan*, who passed it on to the girl's side. The girl's father went promptly to the Chazon Ish to ask his opinion on the *shidduch*.

"Nu, nu. Perhaps you should wait for something a bit better," was the *gadol*'s reply.

When the close disciples who were present questioned him about the seemingly contradictory responses, the Chazon Ish explained, "The Torah obligates me to give each one the advice that is best for him — and that is exactly what I did..."

ANOTHER FACTOR THAT might limit our right to reveal deficiencies that are not serious is the concept of "*mai chazis*" — "Why should we favor one side over another?" If Reuven wishes to make a *shidduch* for his daughter with Shimon, and we know that Shimon possesses some minor deficiency, then we are in a dilemma. If we reveal the flaw to Reuven, then Reuven will have an advantage in the *shidduch*, while if we keep the information to ourselves, then Shimon will have an advantage in the *shidduch*.

In such a case, there is no *mitzvah* of *hashavas aveidah*, since protecting one party from a loss will simply cause a loss to the other. Under the circumstances, the principle of "Better to sit and do nothing" applies; as long as Reuven does not come to ask us information about this point, we should not speak up.

However, the moment Reuven addresses his inquiry to us, the situation shifts, and we are then obligated to reveal the derogatory information, for a number of reasons: a) the obligation of *lo saamod* applies, since by asking, Reuven demonstrates that this is important to him, and "if he would know, he would not agree"; b) the obligation of *hashavas*

aveidah — protecting Reuven from a known loss; c) the *issur* of *lifnei iveir* — not giving another Jew bad advice. (*Mishpetei Hashalom* 20:21)

15 Sivan   15 Tishrei   15 Shvat

Revealing Information Even When Not Asked

THERE ARE A number of special situations in which we would be obligated to give derogatory information about deficiencies that are not serious, even when we have not been asked about them specifically:

- **Rav** — When the girl's side asks information from the boy's Rav and seeks his counsel, perhaps even asking him to test the boy's level of learning, the Rav is obligated to reveal to them everything pertaining to the boy in question, including his own opinions and views, to the best of his ability and as he understands will be for the benefit of the *shidduch*. The same would apply to any individual who is close enough to the situation to see clearly that there will be incompatibility and certain loss if he does not disclose information.

- **Total reliance** — When the person being asked is clearly being relied upon as the only source of information for the *shidduch*, he would be obligated to reveal even deficiencies that are not serious. An example of this would be if the father of the girl approaches the local Rav to ask him to test the boy and to seek counsel on the matter, where no other source is available. Even a young *bachur* may fall into this category, if he is the only connection the girl's family has with the boy or with his yeshivah, neighbors or friends. As long as the responder senses that the family is relying totally on his report, he has to reveal whatever he knows that would be relevant to the success of the *shidduch*.

- **Uncommon deficiency** — Sometimes we are aware of a deficiency of the other party that is so uncommon that it would never occur to the inquiring party to ask about it. Even if this deficiency is not generally perceived as very serious, if we can reasonably assume that the other side would regret having gone into the *shidduch* were they aware of it, we must reveal it even without being asked about it explicitly.

▫ **Shadchan** — The *shadchan* who is suggesting and promoting the *shidduch* is considered an "adviser" and must be careful not to violate the *issur* of offering unsound advice. Therefore, he is obligated to reveal to the parties any detail, however small it may be, that he feels would affect his decision were he in their position.

It would appear that anyone inquiring about a *shidduch* could ask for advice, and then the person who is advising him could fall into the category of s*hadchan*: "What would you do about this *shidduch* if you were in my position?" Then, the person being asked would be permitted — and obligated — to disclose all the details that would have affected his own decision, revealing even deficiencies that are not serious and noting even the most remote doubts, since he is compelled to give good advice, as is the rule for the *shadchan*.

▫ **Deceit** — As we mentioned earlier, whenever someone is certain that there is deceit involved or that one side is being misled in some way, he is required to reveal the deceit to the other side, in order to avoid violating the *issur* of *lifnei iveir* — misleading another Jew with bad advice. (*Mishpetei Hashalom* 20:22, 24, 26)

16 Sivan	16 Tishrei	16 Shvat

Obligation to Relatives ANOTHER CASE IN which we might be required to reveal a deficiency that is not serious, even if we were not asked about it explicitly, is when we are asked for information by a relative, since we have an added obligation toward them of "*Mibesarecha lo sisalem* — Do not ignore your own flesh and blood."

Close friends would also fall into this category, provided they are so close that we would feel their sorrow as our own or that they would subsequently have complaints against us if we did not volunteer such information; in either case, it is considered as if we are revealing the information for our own benefit. Even if the inquirer is not a lifelong dear friend, as long as the bond is close enough that it would obligate each side to take special interest in the welfare of the other, that person becomes a "relative" for this purpose. Some opinions maintain that the same obligation exists toward any *talmid chacham* who inquires of us.

This *halachic* preference in revealing information to relatives and close friends applies only where there is a *to'eles* — a permitted beneficial purpose to speak up. But where there is an *issur* of *lashon hara*, there is no *heter* to say the prohibited words to a relative any more than one could say them to anyone else. (*Mishpetei Hashalom* 20:23)

Obvious Incompatibility   AT TIMES, WHEN we are familiar with both sides of a suggested *shidduch*, it may be crystal-clear to us that the *shidduch* is not appropriate. We may perceive a wide chasm between the two, due to extreme differences in their temperaments or lifestyles, that would clearly interfere with the smooth running of their home after marriage. For example, the boy might be notably critical and negative and the girl highly sensitive and easily offended, breaking down in tears at the slightest critical comment. Or we might know that the one side is scornful of matters that the other side considers to be of utmost importance.

In such a case, where there is obvious incompatibility and long-term damage seems inevitable, even though the flaws are not in the category of serious deficiencies, the two could suffer from the situation for the rest of their lives if the *shidduch* goes through. Therefore, we would be required to reveal the problem, because of our obligation of *lo saamod*.

Nevertheless, we should not be too quick to determine that a difference in temperaments is bound to lead to failure. Quite often we find that, amazingly enough, people with contrasting personalities do not clash but rather complement each other, build fine Jewish homes together and bring up wonderful families. As long as we see even a small chance that the marriage could succeed, we revert back to the basic rule — not to reveal any deficiency that is not considered serious unless we are asked about it specifically. When in doubt, a Rav should be consulted. (*Mishpetei Hashalom* 20:25)

Well-Known   WHEN A DEFICIENCY is well-known, there is no pro-
Deficiencies   hibition to mention it. On the other hand, the *poskim*
imply that we are nevertheless not obligated to reveal
it. Since the flaw is public knowledge, it can be assumed that the other
side is aware of it. If they are not, that is an indication that they have
not done the minimal research, evidently because they decided that
this point is not important to them, and they are responsible for their
own loss.

However, if they are from a different city and do not have close acquaintances in the city where the proposed *shidduch* lives, and therefore
it is likely that they will not hear this detail, despite its being public
knowledge, until after the *shidduch* is settled, we should inform them
of it.

Even in the case of a well-known deficiency, the advisable practice is to be open and mention the flaw, perhaps after a few meetings.
Otherwise, when the other party does hear about it they will feel they
have been deceived and might claim that had they known the fault in
advance they would never have proceeded with the *shidduch*. Then there
is a risk that they will call off the engagement after it was announced,
or, if the wedding has already taken place, they may even demand that
the marriage be annulled because it was based on a *mekach ta'us* — a
transaction based on error.

Examples of well-known deficiencies include: a father who was
once imprisoned or who went bankrupt or who has a bad reputation;
a family that lacks Torah knowledge or whose members are naïve and
easily taken in. Included also are all well-known deficiencies that are
not considered serious and would not be likely to affect the marriage,
but that the other side may be particular about.

By the same token, when we are aware of the subject's good qualities,
then even if those good qualities are obvious and well-known, we should
make sure to mention them to the person asking information, since he
will certainly enjoy hearing them repeated, and our praise might be just
the thing needed to give the *shidduch* the push to get moving. (*Mishpetei
Hashalom* 20:27–29)

Deficiencies That Will Become Known

SOME DEFICIENCIES MAY not be public knowledge but will certainly become known to the couple in the course of their knowing one another, either because the subject and his family are simple, straightforward people who would not know how to conceal such a flaw, or because they are very open and can be counted on to reveal the deficiency on their own. In that case, we do not have any obligation to mention this deficiency in advance. Concealing these flaws at the stage of the inquiry is not a breech of the *mitzvah* of *ve'ahavta lerei'acha kamocha*, because we ourselves would not feel deceived if we were not informed of some detail that is open and well-known.

Sometimes, however, if we have important information and we are not sure that the other side revealed it on their own, as we might have expected them to do, we should check to make sure that the necessary information has indeed been disclosed. (*Mishpetei Hashalom* 20:30)

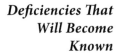

| 18 Sivan | 18 Tishrei | 18 Shvat |

Visible External Defects

"Moishe, I thought you were a friend," Refael said bitterly to his roommate.

"Uh-oh, I guess the date was a flop," Moishe surmised.

"Well, what do you think? You know I'm not looking for a beauty queen, but when I asked you for a general idea of how the girl looks, all you said was that she had brown hair and blue eyes and looked okay. Why didn't you tell me she's obese and cross-eyed?! Then I could have decided whether to go ahead or not. I would have been prepared. I almost sank into the floor when I saw her. She must be twice my weight. I had planned to go for a walk, but instead I found a quiet table in the corner of the lobby and we stayed there — for the absolute minimum time I could get away with."

"Uh, I figured you'd see for yourself," Moishe mumbled.

"Thanks a lot. Didn't you think about how I would feel? And for this I missed my night *seder*? What a waste of time — and emotional energy," Refael sighed.

REGARDING DEFECTS THAT are clearly visible, we are permitted to describe the situation as it is but have to be very careful to present only the facts, without adding our own commentary. For example, we can give the girl's height, build, hair color, etc., but should not volunteer our

opinion as to whether she is pretty or not, since that is purely a matter of personal taste. Examples of visible defects are: unusually tall or short, noticeably heavy, a birthmark, acne or a visible scar, very thick glasses, unkempt beard, cross-eyed, stuttering or other speech defects, squinting, spasms or nervous tics.

While we should not exaggerate the problem or give our opinion, we also have to be sure not to conceal a detail that is likely to immediately turn off the other party, since in many cases the date will not only be a waste of time but might also be insulting and upsetting, making us responsible for a violation of *ona'as devarim* — hurting others (as well as causing the boy to socialize with a girl unnecessarily, waste time that could have been spent learning Torah, and spend money unnecessarily, besides the aggravation involved).

This is especially important in circles where the meetings between the boy and girl are very limited, and they themselves might not notice even visible deficiencies during their brief meetings, due to their own modesty and nervousness. In that case, they rely heavily on the person they are asking for information, and we are obligated to reveal what they might need to know, but we should do so in a delicate, matter-of-fact way, cushioning it with an emphasis on their good qualities. ("She's a little overweight, but she dresses well and always looks good.")

Where there are visible deficiencies, we are obligated to speak up even if the inquirer asks about the candidate in a general manner, as long as the detail is one that would likely cause the other party to discontinue the *shidduch*. Revealing the necessary information is also important when the parents involved are concealing these flaws from their children, who rely exclusively on them for information, and when the boy and girl may not have the opportunity to notice the flaws on their own. (*Mishpetei Hashalom* 20:31–33)

19 Sivan	19 Tishrei	19 Shvat

A Case of Deceit IF BOTH THE boy and the girl have serious deficiencies, and we know for a fact that one side is deceiving the other and concealing the flaw, we do not have to reveal to them the other side's serious deficiency. This principle certainly applies when

both have the same flaw — such as if both secretly make improper use of the Internet, and also when they have flaws of equal severity — such as if one side conceals signs of *apikorsus* while the other conceals her *pritzus*.

When the deficiencies are of different types — as if one side is hiding a serious illness while the other is concealing *apikorsus*, or one side is deceiving regarding financial issues while the other is hiding information about a serious illness — it is not clear how we should act. The same doubt exists when one side hides a major fault while the other conceals a small defect.

These rules apply whether the deceiving is being done by the boy and girl themselves, by the parents or by the *shadchanim*, since the moment one side engages in dishonest practices, we no longer have an obligation of *lo saamod* — "not standing by while your friend's blood is spilled" — and we do not have to reveal the information to them. (*Mishpetei Hashalom* 20:34)

Unwarranted   IN CHAPTER 29 we cited the seven conditions enumer-
Damage   ated by the Chofetz Chaim that give us license to say *lashon hara leto'eles* — for a constructive purpose. We will discuss a number of these conditions to explore how they are affected by varying situations.

One of the seven conditions necessary to enable us to say *lashon hara leto'eles* is that in relating the information, we will not cause more damage than the *din* would sanction had the two sides gone to *beis din*. Speaking up when such damage might result would make the speaker liable to punishment according to *dinei Shamayim*, since he was the indirect cause of the other person's loss. We are not permitted to help one person if doing so will cause undeserved damage to someone else.

Therefore, if the person asking information is known to be a gossip-monger by nature and will wrongfully publicize the derogatory report, we may not reveal it to him. Nor should we give information if it might lead to *machlokes* — arguments between people. In these cases, we can sometimes accomplish our purpose of protecting the parties involved in other ways, such as by approaching the person's Rav or close confidante and asking him to advise the inquirer against continuing the *shidduch*. But under no circumstances may we reveal the information to an irresponsible listener, which could cause untold damage to the subject.

If we ourselves stand to suffer a loss if we give the information — either a monetary loss or some other kind of suffering due to the other side harassing us for divulging the information — then we are not obligated to reveal what we know. However, if we stand to lose in a minor way, while the potential loss of the asker would be much greater, the right thing to do would be to go beyond the letter of the law and speak up, even if it means suffering some minor damage, similar to the *halachah* in cases of *hashavas aveidah* — returning a lost item.

If the couple is already engaged and, as a result of the information, one side will dissolve the *shidduch* in a manner that would not be in keeping with the *halachah*, then it is forbidden for us to reveal the information. (*Mishpetei Hashalom* 20:36)

20 Sivan | 20 Tishrei | 20 Shvat

Where Feelings of Hatred Exist   Ever since his neighbor, Meshulam Strauss, had refused to sign a paper authorizing him to build a porch onto his apartment, Yosef Meir Kahn could not rid himself of the hostile feelings that bubbled in his heart. True, the porch would have darkened the Strauss' living room a bit, but it would have been such a help to the Kahn family, both for Sukkos and all year round.

With great effort Yosef Meir managed to maintain a cordial relationship with Meshulam, helping out as any neighbor would and giving him a cheery "Good morning" as they passed in the stairwell. But he could not eradicate the hatred that lay dormant in his heart.

"Hello, Reb Yosef Meir," said the voice on the phone. "This is Shalom Ribner, your son Yankie's rebbe from last year. I understand you are a neighbor of the Strauss family. We're looking into their daughter for a *shidduch* for my son, and I wanted to hear what you had to say about the family, specifically the father — *leto'eles*, of course."

Yosef Meir's heart jumped. He certainly had what to say about his neighbor — and now it would be *leto'eles*, so it would be allowed. Ah, it would be a pleasure to give that Meshulam a taste of his own medicine. But as he

was about to speak, a little voice in the back of his mind seemed to chide him, "Not so fast, Yosef Meir. Are you sure you're qualified to speak about your neighbor, considering how you feel about him?" Yosef Meir hesitated. That voice had a point…

"Hmmm. Rabbi Ribner, maybe you could leave me your phone number. I'm on my way out, and I'd rather get back to you tomorrow. I hope I'll be able to help you out then." He had some work to do on himself before tomorrow…

ANOTHER CONDITION THAT must be met to enable us to say *lashon hara* for a beneficial purpose is that our intentions be totally for the positive *to'eles*, not tainted by our own feelings of animosity toward the subject. The Chofetz Chaim stipulates that when we harbor even a trace of hatred in our hearts and cannot avoid having that hatred color our intentions when we speak, then we are not permitted to reveal the derogatory information at all. Ideally, we should work on ourselves intensely to uproot the hatred so that we can convey the necessary information. However, if we cannot do so no matter how hard we try, then our report will certainly be a violation of the *issur* of *rechilus* and of *lo sisna*. In that case, even though refraining from giving the report will automatically cause us to violate the *issur* of *lo saamod* — "Do not stand by while your friend's blood is spilled" — in this case it is preferable to "sit and do nothing."

The basis for this *halachah* is the rule that we may not violate *issurim* in order to save others from a loss — for example, we are not permitted to steal or to wear *shaatnez* (a forbidden mix of wool and linen) in order to save someone else from damage. Since the foundation of *lashon hara* and *rechilus* is the *issur* of saying derogatory or damaging information that emanates from corrupt *middos* and negative feelings toward the subject, giving such a report when hatred exists is prohibited, even to save another person damage.

| 21 Sivan | 21 Tishrei | 21 Shvat |

Thus, when we possess important information but cannot uproot the hatred in our hearts, we are in a difficult position. On the one hand, we have on our conscience the unfortunate young person we may be dooming to a life of suffering if we do not speak up. On the other hand, the *issurim* of *lo sisna*, *lo seileich rachil* and *lo sikom* will be violated if we speak. That is why it is preferable to remain silent.

However, some *poskim* understand the words of the Chofetz Chaim a bit differently. They maintain that in *all* cases of real potential damage, we are required to disclose necessary information because of our obligation of *lo saamod*. The *halachah* demands that we do our utmost to wipe out the hostile feelings before we speak, but even if small traces of hatred remain, "the Torah was not given to angels"; we are only human, and as long as we have tried our best, we have fulfilled our requirement.

This viewpoint is supported by the reasoning that the *issur* of blending even a trace of hatred into our report applies only to *lashon hara* where there is a vague, non-immediate constructive purpose at stake — such as publicizing the deeds of *resha'im*. When there is a specific, practical, constructive goal, such as saving someone from a potential theft or preventing a disastrous *shidduch* or a damaging partnership from going through, then even if there is a bit of hatred blended in, we are obligated to speak up.

According to this opinion, our understanding of the *halachos* of *lashon hara leto'eles* would be somewhat altered. This viewpoint would seem to imply that once there is a specific, constructive purpose for the speech, then even if there still remain some feelings of hatred, the report no longer falls under the category of prohibited gossip, and not every one of the seven conditions enumerated by the Chofetz Chaim necessarily has to be met in order to permit speaking up. As long as some of the conditions are adhered to, others may be waived if necessary.

The same would apply in a situation where there is a specific, constructive purpose in speaking up, but disclosing information could possibly cause more damage than the *din* would require.

In practice, we should not be hasty in dispensing with any of the necessary conditions without consulting a Rav, since each situation must be judged according to its particular context. (*Mishpetei Hashalom* 20:37)

Doubtful ANOTHER CONDITION CITED by the Chofetz
Derogatory Report Chaim to allow us to speak *lashon hara leto'eles*
is that we either saw the derogatory act being
done ourselves or have clarified that it is definitely true. For this condition, there would be no *heter* to reveal the information if we heard it
secondhand, unless we feel certain that the person we are speaking to
is knowledgeable and meticulous in the laws of *lashon hara* and will
definitely not take our report as absolute truth. Even then, in a situation where some doubt exists, we are not bound by the obligation of
lo saamod to speak up (although we might still have an obligation of
hashavas aveidah — restoring the person's loss).

Therefore, if, for example, the subject of the inquiry once stole as
a young boy, we may not report this information years later unless we
know for certain that he is still dishonest; chances are that he has since
grown out of it and done *teshuvah* and is today an upstanding citizen.
Besides, there might be similar stories going around about the other
side.

The same would apply if the subject was once guilty of *chillul
Shabbos* or acted in an immodest manner. Young people often do irresponsible things because of their immaturity or because they are
momentarily taken in by some wild "spirit of madness." As long as
their current behavior exhibits no sign of the past *aveirah* and there is
no reason to believe that they will go back to it, we are not permitted
to mention it.

If we are asked explicitly about the past misdeed, we can brush the
concerns aside: "Yes, there were rumors to that effect, but you don't have
to believe everything you hear. Check out how much truth there is to it,
perhaps by the local Rabbanim" (and make sure not to give the name of
a Rav who was vehemently opposed to the act at the time).

However, when we know that the subject changed his religion at one
time, or was guilty of immoral acts, or gained a reputation for doing
despicable acts, especially if the matter was public at the time, this is
considered an intrinsic blemish, not a passing lapse. Even if he appears
to have done *teshuvah* and shed his past, we have to give much thought

and consult a Rav to know how to respond to inquiries about him for *shidduchim*. (*Mishpetei Hashalom* 20:38)

Uncertainty Over IT IS NOT sufficient to be certain that an act took
Whether the Act place before reporting it *leto'eles*; an additional
Was Prohibited condition requires that we be certain that it was
a wrong act according to Torah law and, when
answering a *shidduch*-inquiry, that we be certain that it is an act likely
to have a detrimental effect on the marriage (as we discussed in the
case of minor deficiencies). The rule to keep in mind is: "Do not do to
others what you would not want them to do to you were you in their
position."

Sometimes we jump to conclusions and assume an act is halachically
wrong when it is not. For example, a non-Jew agrees to sell his house
or land to Reuven. Before the transaction is finalized, Shimon comes
along, offers a better price or more favorable conditions, and makes the
purchase, pre-empting Reuven's purchase. It seems obvious to us that
such conduct is corrupt and lowly and is a violation of *halachah*.

But if we investigate the topic, we will find that according to
Tosafos and many *Rishonim*, the *issur* of *ani hamehapeich bechararah* — grabbing someone else's business — does not apply in a case
where the object would not be easily available elsewhere. The Rama is
of the opinion that land that is hard to acquire would also have this *din*
and would not be subject to restrictions in acquiring it. Therefore, in
the case cited above there would have been no violation of *din Torah*,
and therefore we would not be authorized to mention it in a derogatory report. Our purpose here is not to sanction or even justify such
behavior by any means; however, once there is an opinion permitting
it, the *heter* to mention it *leto'eles* no longer applies. If, however, there is
a *takanah* — a regulation of the Rabbanim or the town committee — to
prohibit such conduct, then it is considered a violation of *din Torah*
and we are permitted to say it.

If the act is so lowly that had the inquiring party known about it

he would not have agreed to the *shidduch* to begin with, then even if no Torah law has been violated, it is no worse than any other minor deficiency that is significant to the asker, and here too, concealing the fact would be a violation of *lo saamod*. (*Mishpetei Hashalom* 20:39)

Remaining Conditions "Mimi, can you tell me about your cousin Menachem Reisner? I have my eye on him for a *shidduch* for my daughter," Dina asked her coworker.

Oh, no, Mimi thought to herself. *I know that Menachem is nowhere near her daughter's level in* yiras Shamayim *and* mitzvah-*observance. But I don't want to besmirch his reputation if I don't have to. What should I say? Ah, I've got it!*

"I don't think Menachem would be the right one for your daughter. You're always telling me how important music is in her life — singing, playing instruments, conducting bands and choirs … Menachem has no affinity for music at all. He doesn't even sing *zemiros*; he just says them."

"Oh, you're right, Mimi. She could never cope with that kind of husband. Thanks so much for tipping me off."

AMONG THE REMAINING conditions permitting *lashon hara leto'eles* is the requirement to use other means to accomplish our constructive purpose whenever possible before resorting to reporting the derogatory information. This can often be accomplished in responding to a *shidduch* inquiry, if we will use our imagination to find other ways to show the inquirers that the candidate is not right for them without relating outright derogatory information. However, we have to be careful not to fabricate imaginary reasons in order to accomplish this purpose.

There is also the condition requiring us to reprove the sinner before revealing his wrongful behavior. This is generally not applicable in the case of a *shidduch* inquiry. (*Mishpetei Hashalom* 20:40)

When the Shidduch Is Off IF AN ENGAGEMENT is broken, the side that decided to terminate the *shidduch* should not reveal his reasons to others if there is derogatory information involved. On the other hand, the side that was not responsible for the break-up can say, "I did not break the *shidduch*" as long as they do not say explicitly that the other side did so. However, it is *middas chassidus* — a commendable level — to avoid saying even that much, if he can do so without incurring too much of a loss.

When one side is not interested in continuing the *shidduch* with another meeting, and the *shadchan* inevitably asks, "What is the problem?" we sometimes have to reveal our reasons even when they contain derogatory information. This is because the *shadchan*'s whole function is to work out compromises, emphasize the positive side and play down the negative aspects; perhaps he will indeed be able to help smooth things out to the benefit of both parties.

However, when one side has decided, leaving no room for doubt — such as after having consulted with a *Gadol* — not to continue, then they may not reveal any derogatory information that will not be of specific benefit to the *shadchan* or to anyone else, even for the purpose of saving themselves from an embarrassing situation or from pressure to continue.

25 Sivan	25 Tishrei	25 Shvat

Severity of Misusing the Situation SHADCHANIM AND ANYONE else involved in these matters must be extremely careful not to let any words that are not *leto'eles* escape their lips. Just because they are involved in helping people does not authorize them to exchange information freely for no justifiable reason. This is a very serious matter, because every derogatory word that is spoken without the necessary conditions having been fulfilled, and certainly when there is no constructive purpose at all, is a serious *aveirah* and a violation of numerous *mitzvos* (see chapter 28).

On the other hand, if we are careful to speak in accordance with *halachah*, without violating any of the *issurim* of *lashon hara*, and then others unpredictably misuse our information to cause damage or pain to people in violation of *din Torah*, this is not our concern and we are not held responsible. "The paths of Hashem are straight; *tzaddikim* walk on them, and sinners stumble on them." (*Mishpetei Hashalom* 20:41–42)

In summary: Varying factors in a *shidduch* will affect the halachos involved. Serious deficiencies in a *shidduch*-candidate must be revealed, and exaggerated if necessary, even if we are not asked about them. Lesser deficiencies should be mentioned only if explicitly asked about, or if we can assume that such a flaw is so significant to the inquirer that he would have regretted becoming involved in the *shidduch* had he known about it. We are not permitted to provide information if the listener is not careful in *hilchos shemiras halashon* and is likely to believe our words, if he will go ahead with the *shidduch* anyway, if there is deceit on the part of the party requesting information, and in a number of other cases.

Certain circumstances require us to be more open — such as if we are the only ones being relied on for information, if the person asking is a relative or close friend, or if the inquiry comes in the form of a request for our advice. Specific rules govern revealing well-known deficiencies or visible external defects. Permission to speak may be complicated by the presence or absence of the required conditions — where unwarranted damage may be incurred, when we harbor hatred toward the subject, if we are doubtful about whether the derogatory information is accurate or whether it was a violation of *din Torah*, or if we have other ways to accomplish our purpose. Other specific rules apply in regard to revealing derogatory information to the shadchan during the course of the *shidduch* or after we have decided to terminate it, as well as when an engagement has been broken off.

All the *halachos* we have outlined here apply not only to *shidduchim* but to all areas of life where exchanging information about individuals is involved.

⬚ 32 ⬚

כיבוד אב ואם
Honoring Parents

| 26 Sivan | 26 Tishrei | 26 Shvat |

To Honor and to Revere "Are you also waiting to speak to the *mashgiach*?" Nachum asked Betzalel, who had just joined him in the hallway outside the *mashgiach*'s room. "He's usually here at this hour."

"I'm not sure if we'll be able to talk to him now," Betzalel commented. "As I came from the dorm, I saw him outside giving a very warm welcome to an older man who was getting out of a taxi. It must be one of the yeshivah's donors or something like that; the *mashgiach* was so enthusiastic when he spoke to him."

"I wonder who it is. I hope the mashgiach won't be spending too much time with him. I had something important I wanted to discuss," Nachum fretted.

Just then the *mashgiach* walked up to his room holding the elderly gentleman's arm. The man he was escorting so graciously looked so … ordinary — neither an honored *talmid chacham* nor a pompous philanthropist. The bachurim were struck immediately by the way the *mashgiach* gave him such solicitous attention.

"I'm sorry, boys. I won't be available for at least the next hour," the *mashgiach* apologized gently to the boys who were hovering at the entrance to his room. Then he ushered in the guest and closed the door.

399

"Who could that have been? The *mashgiach* acted as if he was hosting the king of England!" Nachum commented.

"Who — the man he just brought in to the room?" asked their friend Yankie, who had overheard Nachum as he walked down the hall. "That's the *mashgiach*'s father! To the *mashgiach*, that's much more important than hosting the king of England!"

THE TORAH TEACHES us how to relate to parents in two separate *mitzvos*: "*Kabeid es avicha ve'es imecha* ... — Honor your father and your mother, that you may live a long life on the land that Hashem gave you" (*Shemos* 20:12), and "*Ish imo ve'aviv tira'u* — Each person should revere his mother and his father" (*Vayikra* 19:3). From these *pesukim* we learn that every person should behave toward his parents as he would behave toward someone before whom he stands in awe and whom he respects deeply. He should indeed perceive his parents as a king and queen, and in his every interaction he should be careful to give them the honor and reverence he owes them.

One of the underlying foundations of these *mitzvos* is the basic human quality of *hakaras hatov* — the gratitude we should feel toward the people who brought us into this world and who did so much for us throughout our lives. Even the nations of the world recognize the need to respect parents, as a matter of common human decency. There are few qualities more despicable than ingratitude toward those who have been kind to us. By fostering this sense of appreciation, we will achieve a deeper understanding of our debt of gratitude toward Hashem for all that He does for us every moment of our lives.

However, our obligation remains even when the aspect of gratitude is not so evident. We are required to honor our parents even if they did not teach us Torah and did not provide for us in any way — as we learn from the Jews in the time of *matan Torah*, who spent forty years in the *midbar*. They were provided with all their needs, spiritual and physical — Torah, food, clothing — directly from Hashem, yet still they were expected to fulfill these *mitzvos*. Likewise, a child who was adopted as an infant and was raised by others is still obligated to respect his biological parents.

The significance of this *mitzvah* is evident from the words of *Chazal*,

who point out that the Torah equates honor and reverence for parents, and the *issur* of cursing them, with those same obligations toward Hashem. When we fulfill these *mitzvos*, *Chazal* add, the *Shechinah* abides among us, and if, *chas veshalom*, we neglect them, we cause pain, so to speak, to the *Shechinah* and banish the *Shechinah* from our midst. (*Mishpetei Hashalom* 21:1–2)

27 Sivan	27 Tishrei	27 Shvat

Who Is Obligated? THE *MITZVOS* OF honoring and revering parents, as well as the *issurim* of cursing and striking parents, apply in all places and at all times, and these *mitzvos* apply equally in our relationships with both father and mother, although in some cases, when both need our attention simultaneously, the father may be given precedence. Both sons and daughters are obligated; however, after marriage the daughter's obligation may undergo some change, as we shall discuss. (For the sake of brevity, in this chapter we will often write "son" and "father" when the same *halachah* would apply equally to a daughter and mother.)

Since the reward for this *mitzvah* is spelled out in the Torah, the *beis din* does not have to pressure people to fulfill it, as it does for other *mitzvos* (for instance, in the case of *tzedakah*), although they may use minimal force to enforce it where necessary. Certainly if a child actually disgraces his parents, an authorized *beis din* may take action by giving him *malkos* — a flogging — or punish him in some other way. Also, if a parent cannot support himself and his children have the wherewithal to support him, the *beis din* can compel them to do so.

Children should be trained in this *mitzvah* from an early age. It is important to convey to the child that we are training him in a *mitzvah*, not just seeking our own benefit. Ideally, the father should insist that the children respect their mother, and the mother should insist that the children respect their father, when the situation allows for it, so that the child will not misinterpret the parents' efforts to train them as attempts on the parent's part to assert his own power. (*Mishpetei Hashalom* 21:2, 7, 74)

Disgracing, Cursing and Striking   IN ADDITION TO the positive commandments we have mentioned, we have to be exceptionally careful not to do anything that would detract from our parents' honor.

Anyone who belittles his parent, even using words alone, or even by implication, whether in the context of light banter or as an intentional barb, is subject to Hashem's curse, "*Arur makleh aviv ve'imo* — Cursed is the one who disgraces his father and mother" (*Devarim* 27:16). The Ibn Ezra adds that this *arur* applies even if he belittles his parent in private. In any event, the *beis din* should give *malkos* and punish him for this *aveirah*, when authorized to do so, to the extent it deems necessary.

Therefore, we have to be extremely careful not to speak or believe *lashon hara* or *rechilus* about our parents, not to speak to them with chutzpah, and certainly not to cause them shame. Even if we may have had good reason to place them in a shameful position, the *aveirah* is still very grave. According to some opinions, these rules apply not only to parents but also to stepparents and older siblings.

Cursing a parent is an even more severe transgression. In the times of the *Sanhedrin*, if a son or daughter cursed a parent using one of the sacred Names of Hashem, even after the parent's death, in front of witnesses and after having been warned, he or she was sentenced to death by *sekilah* — stoning. If a *kinui* — a substitute Name of Hashem — was used, then the curse is a transgression of the general *issur* of cursing another Jew (see Volume I, chapter 8).

Similar in severity is the prohibition to strike a parent. In the times of the *Sanhedrin*, if a son or daughter struck a parent in front of witnesses and after having been warned, causing the parent even the slightest wound or bruise, he or she was sentenced to death by *chenek* — strangulation. This applies even if only a capillary was broken, causing bleeding only beneath the skin. If the blow did not result in a bruise at all, then he transgresses only the general *issur* of striking another Jew (see Volume I, chapter 7).

Since these matters are so serious, if a child under bar- or bas-mitzvah strikes a parent, even though he does not really need *teshuvah*,

it is advisable that he accept upon himself some form of atonement at a later point. (*Mishpetei Hashalom* 21:3–7)

| 29 Sivan | 29 Tishrei | 29 Shvat |

From Heart and Mind to Action As Nachum and Betzalel walked back to their dormitory rooms, Nachum confided to his friend, "You know, the *mashgiach*'s attitude toward his father struck a guilty chord in me. You see, my family is not exactly Torah-oriented. We were always *shomer Shabbos*, and I went to a religious school, but Torah learning was not an integral part of the family experience, and my father doesn't open a *sefer* very often. *Baruch Hashem*, I ended up where I am, learning Torah in a yeshivah. I try to honor my father — speak to him respectfully, call home regularly, things like that…"

"So what's the problem?" Betzalel asked, genuinely puzzled.

"When I saw how the *mashgiach* related to his father, I realized that I'm missing the point. I'm just paying lip service to my obligation of *kibbud av*, but I have to admit that deep down I don't really respect my simple, unlearned father. I'm just going through the motions, when the truth is, I sort of look down on him."

"I see your problem," said Betzalel. "You're right to feel guilty. But you can develop an awe and respect for your parents in the things that make them special."

"Hmmm. That's right. They really are special people. My father is unbelievably honest in all his dealings. He's also very generous when it comes to giving *tzedakah*, without expecting any recognition for it. My mother is so full of good *middos*, I don't even know where to start. You're right. Even if I can learn a *blatt Gemara* better than my father, there's more than enough reason for me to feel a genuine respect in my heart for my parents."

THE PRIMARY FULFILLMENT of the *mitzvos* to honor and revere our parents takes place in our hearts and minds. Even if the world at large does not perceive them as particularly important, the child should view his parents as great and distinguished individuals. Nevertheless, attitude alone is not sufficient; our behavior must reflect what is in our hearts.

Chazal defined for us the practical application of *kavod* and *mora*, and we will present the *halachos* that are derived from their definition in the sections that follow. (*Mishpetei Hashalom* 21:8)

Mora Av —
Reverence for
a Parent

IF A FATHER has a special place where he stands to discuss important matters with his respected contemporaries, his son may not stand in that place even when no one is consulting his father there, since it may appear as though he considers himself to be his father's equal. Nor may a son sit in his father's regular place in shul, or in his father's seat at the table at home, even if the father is not present and even if the son is not sitting down to a meal. The same *halachah* would apply regarding a mother's regular seat at the table or in the *ezras nashim*, the ladies' section in shul.

If the parent is not particular about this and grants the child explicit permission to sit or stand in these places, then the child may do so. However, traditionally the father's place at the table at home is kept exclusively for the father, in order to train the children in this *mitzvah*, and it is therefore not advisable for the father to be *mochel* (to forgo his own privileges) when it comes to this particular *halachah*.

When the father is eating at the home of his married son, the accepted practice is not to seat the father in the son's place at the head of the table, but rather to seat him at the side. However, the father should be the first to wash for the meal and the first to be served, and he should be shown respect in every other way.

A child may not contradict his parent; he may not even "be *machria*," that is, to appear to give his approval, to his father's words or opinion in his father's presence. For example, if his father is discussing a matter with someone else, the child may neither contradict him by saying, "The other fellow's words appear to be right," nor may he judge his father's words positively by saying, "My father's words seem to be more correct," since this would again imply that he is placing himself on the same level as his father to be able to judge his words, even favorably. This *halachah* applies whether the matter being discussed relates to *divrei Torah* or to mundane matters.

The prohibition of contradicting or confirming a father's words applies only when the child makes a definitive statement. However, a son is

certainly permitted to have a lively exchange in learning with his father, bringing up questions regarding his father's points and offering his own explanations. And if his father explicitly asks his son's opinion on any matter, the son may even directly contradict his father's words.

When his father is not present, the son is permitted to be *machria* his view; in this case, defending his father's stance in his absence is an honor for him. According to some opinions, when discussing *divrei Torah* a son may respectfully contradict his father's opinion, at least when his father is not present; the source for this approach is the disputes between Rebbi and his father Rabbi Shimon ben Gamliel, and those between the Tur and his father the Rosh. Even though other authorities are stringent and prohibit contradicting a parent even when not in his presence, the accepted practice is to follow the lenient opinion when it comes to Torah learning. This is because the importance of attaining a true and clear understanding of Torah does not allow us to doctor up a wrong perception for the sake of the honor of another person — even a father.

When a child is reproved by his father, even if the criticism is made in error or is unjustified, the child should be careful not to defend himself in a manner that contradicts his father's words. This is true regarding both *divrei Torah* and mundane matters. If he is concerned that he will have to suffer unwarranted punishment or other negative consequences, he is permitted to clarify his standpoint, but he should do so in the most delicate and respectful way possible.

Children should also be careful not to interrupt their parents. If the parent is asked a question in the children's presence, they should not jump to answer before the parent, since this too is a sign of disrespect, as we see from Lavan, who stepped in brazenly to answer the question Eliezer posed to his father Besu'el. (*Mishpetei Hashalom* 21:9–11)

2 Tammuz	2 Cheshvan	2 Adar

The Parent's Name   A SON MAY not call his father or mother by name, even in their absence, whether during their lifetime or after their death. Instead, he should address them with names such as Abba, Tatte, Pappa, Father, etc., and as Ima, Mama,

Mother, etc. When speaking about his parents when he is not in their presence, a child should refer to them in terms such as *avi mori* and *imi morasi* — "my father/mother, my teacher," and when asked his parent's name, he should preface the name with a respectful title, such as Rabbi, or Mr. ____, and Rebbetzin, or Mrs. ____, for example. The same *halachah* applies when writing the parent's name. However, when filling out an official document that does not allow for titles, it is permissible to write the parent's name as is. When a son davens for a parent, the *minhag* is to say only the name, preceded by *avi* or *imi*, without mentioning any further titles.

When a son needs to address someone who has the same given name as his parent, it could be problematic, as the parent or others present may infer that he is calling to his parent using the parent's first name. There are varying opinions among the *poskim* regarding the correct conduct under such circumstances. Many are of the lenient opinion, which maintains that if the name is a common one, such as Moshe or Sarah, there is no problem with the son's calling that person by name even in his parent's presence, while if the name is an uncommon one, such as Paltiel or Chulda, then it would be prohibited to use the name in the parent's presence. Nowadays, since we can generally assume that the parent is not particular about this point, the prevalent practice is to abide by this lenient opinion. (*Mishpetei Hashalom* 21:12)

Extent of the Obligation of Mora Av IN TODAY'S AGE of "democracy," when, unfortunately, the general populace sees parent/children and teacher/student relationships as almost a bond between friends or equals, we have to be careful not to forget the stringency of our obligation to revere parents. The *Shulchan Aruch* outlines the extent of that obligation in no uncertain terms, through the following scenario: The son, a respected public personage, is sitting at the head of an honored gathering, clad in expensive finery, when his father or mother enters, rips his clothing, strikes him on the head and spits in his face. What should his reaction be? "He should not shame his parent in any way; rather he should remain silent and fear the King of all kings who commanded him to do so" — that is, to treat his parents with the utmost awe and reverence under all circumstances.

(Of course, the son can take steps to prevent his parents from acting in this way to begin with, as long as he can do so through an agent and in a way that will not disgrace his parent. Similarly, if the parent causes his child a monetary loss, the child can claim the compensation that is due him.) (*Mishpetei Hashalom* 21:13)

3 Tammuz	3 Cheshvan	3 Adar

***Kibbud Av —
Honor for a
Parent***
"I don't understand it," Leah told her husband Dovid. "I asked Tatte about coming to us for Pesach, and he tried to evade the question. Then he mumbled something about how hard it is for him to get used to different places at his age, and that he preferred to stay with Dina."

"That's too bad. The children will be disappointed," Dovid commiserated.

"But Dina's house is so tiny," Leah continued. "Tatte doesn't even have his own room there. He shares it with two of Dina's children. And they're on the third floor, so he hardly ever gets out. Why shouldn't he want to come to our big, comfortable home for one Yom Tov a year?"

"Leah, I'll tell you what I think, if you promise that you won't be insulted," Dovid said cautiously. "Do you ever observe closely how Dina sees to your father's needs? She makes him feel as if he's doing her a favor by allowing her the pleasure of serving him. Even when she's busy or upset about something, as soon as Tatte needs something, she puts a genuine smile on her face and runs to get him what he needs."

"I'll get Tatte whatever he needs, too — but with a grouchy expression and a lot less patience," Leah admitted sheepishly, saving Dovid the unpleasant experience of saying it himself. "I think you're right. That must be what's holding him back. Maybe if I would polish up my style and upgrade my attitude, Tatte would enjoy spending time here too."

AS WE MENTIONED, the primary aspect of *kibbud av* is the respect we feel in our hearts for our parents. However, fulfilling this *mitzvah* requires that we honor them in action as well: taking care of our parents' needs, providing them with food, drink, clothing and other necessities, and escorting them wherever they have to go, such as to and from shul or a shopping trip. If the parent is ill or infirm, the son should help him eat and get dressed, and should take him around in his wheelchair.

The son should serve his parent devotedly, as a personal attendant serves his master; no task should be too menial for him. The *Tanna'im* and *Amora'im* went to extreme lengths to honor their parents, despite their lofty positions. Even when Rav Avdimi had five children of his own, who were all ordained Rabbis, if his father knocked, he would run to open the door himself, calling, "I'm coming!" until he reached his father. Once his father asked for water, and by the time he returned with the water, his father had dozed off in his chair. Rav Avdimi remained bent at his side until he awakened. Rabbi Tarfon would crouch beside his mother's high bed to serve as her stepping stool. And Yosef Hatzaddik, despite his exalted status as viceroy to the king, accorded tremendous respect to his father Yaakov Avinu, both during his lifetime and after his death, in arranging his burial.

Equally important is to provide service to our parents "with a smile"; as *Chazal* say, one child may serve his father the finest delicacies with a sour expression on his face and be punished for his efforts, while another may put his father to work grinding wheat [to spare him from a more difficult task], yet do so with such sincere words of appeasement, explaining to the parent that it is for his benefit, that he earns a portion in *Olam Haba* for his actions. (*Mishpetei Hashalom* 21:14, 47)

4 Tammuz	4 Cheshvan	4 Adar

Footing the Bill WHILE THE PHYSICAL exertion involved in seeing to a parent's needs is the responsibility of the child, the monetary expenses are the parent's responsibility, as long as he has adequate funds to cover those costs. If the parent does not have sufficient means and the son has more than enough to cover his own personal expenses, the son should pay as much as he can afford (even if that sum will not cover the full cost of his father's care). If the son refuses, the *beis din* can compel him to pay.

If the son does not have enough money of his own, he is not obligated to go collecting door-to-door for money to support his parents. Although he is obligated to exert himself physically to serve his parents, the exertion of collecting money for them is not a direct fulfillment of the *mitzvah* of honoring them. It is only a preparatory step in serving them their needs, and the Torah does not obligate a son to do this.

A son is required to exert himself physically to care for his parents and serve them, even if that requires him to take time off from his job. This applies as long as he has earned enough to pay for his food for that day, even if as a result he will later use up his last penny and will be forced to go begging the next day.

Some authorities maintain that the son is obligated to support his needy parents from his own resources only to the amount he would have been required to give as *tzedakah*. In the order of priorities that govern the disbursement of a person's own *tzedakah* funds, a parent takes precedence over every other poor person, even one's children (over the age of six), and if the father is a *talmid chacham*, he precedes even one's *rebbe muvhak* — his primary Torah mentor; therefore, the son may not give *tzedakah* to anyone else until he has provided adequately for his parents. If he has enough money, he should give even more than the maximum fifth of his resources to support them, since in addition to the basic *mitzvah* of *tzedakah*, there is the additional aspect of *kibbud av ve'eim*.

5 Tammuz	5 Cheshvan	5 Adar

A person who has the wherewithal should provide for his parents from his personal funds, since *Chazal* cursed those who can afford to support their parents freely and yet provide for them from their allotted *tzedakah* funds. If the needy father has a number of sons, they should calculate how much each one can afford, according to his financial position, and each should contribute his part. (*Mishpetei Hashalom* 21:15–16)

Gestures of Respect   A SON SHOULD take every opportunity to increase his father's honor in his own eyes and in the eyes of others. Therefore, if the son needs a favor, and he knows the person involved would fulfill the request in deference to his father, then he should not say, "Do this favor for my sake," even if that would be equally effective. Instead, he should make a point of asking that the favor be done for his father's sake, since this enhances his father's honor (assuming that is in fact the case).

Needless to say, if the person he is approaching is not on good terms with his father, and if he mentions his father's name the request would likely be denied, he should request it on his own behalf. In this case, bringing up his father's name would only lead to his father's dishonor. When in doubt, he may make the request any way he likes.

The accepted *minhag* is to mention in the *birkas hamazon* — the blessing after meals — a special *brachah* for the welfare of one's parents: "*HaRachaman Hu yevarech es avi mori ve'es imi morasi*" — May the Merciful One bless my father, my teacher, and my mother, my teacher. (*Mishpetei Hashalom* 21:17–18)

| 6 Tammuz | 6 Cheshvan | 6 Adar |

Standing Up for Parents A PERSON IS obligated to stand up for his parents, when they are in the same area as he is, as soon as they come into sight. Some maintain that he should stand up as soon as he hears their footsteps. The Rama is of the opinion that he must stand up for them only once in the morning and once in the evening; however, if there is someone present who may not know that he already stood up earlier, he should do so once again, to avoid suspicion. After getting up, he should not sit down again until the parent has sat down or walked on until he is out of sight (as in the case of a *rebbe muvhak*).

If the parent lives in the son's home, then the son does not have to stand up each time the parent enters the room, but only when the parent enters the house after having been out. If the parent walks in just before the child has to get up to leave, the child should first rise from his place and sit back down again, to make it clear that his rising was in honor of his father, and only then should he get up again and go on his way.

This obligation applies for a blind parent, even though he cannot see his child standing up, as well as to a blind child, even though he cannot see the parent walk in. The obligation applies equally to sons and daughters.

Many people today are not accustomed to standing up for parents, perhaps because most parents nowadays choose to forgo their honor. However, it is preferable for the parent to state explicitly that he waives the honor, so as to free the child from his obligation. (Perhaps it would be better, though, to reinstate the practice of standing up for the parent, which does much to enhance *kibbud av va'eim* in the household.)

If the father is a *talmid* of the son, they have a complex situation in which each one is obligated to rise before the other. In such a case, each one is entitled to waive the honor that is his due. However, if the son is a *Gadol baTorah* — a great Torah leader — and the people of the area are not familiar with his father, then the son may not waive his honor publicly, as this would be a dishonor for the Torah. Therefore, it is best that they keep their distance from one another so as to avoid either one's inadvertently belittling the honor of the other. (The *poskim* point out that when the Maharam of Rottenberg became a Torah leader, he refrained from visiting his father and asked his father not to visit him, in order to avoid complications resulting from the obligations of *kavod haTorah*.) (*Mishpetei Hashalom* 21:19–20)

7 Tammuz	7 Cheshvan	7 Adar

Accepting the Services of a Parent   "Shaya'le, sit down. I'll bring you a cup of coffee and some of my fresh kokosh cake. No, no, don't get up. When my baby comes to visit from yeshivah, I shouldn't pamper him a little bit?" Mrs. Rubinstein fluttered around her youngest son like a mother hen. Despite the fact that he was over six feet tall, Shaya would always be her "baby."

"But Mama, it's *erev Shabbos*, and you're so busy," Shaya pleaded. "Please, maybe you could sit down for a minute, and I'll get *you* a cup of coffee?" Each time he came home for Shabbos, he resolved that this time he would not let his mother fuss over him; after all, the *mitzvah* of *kibbud eim* required that he serve his mother, not the opposite.

"I've told you before and I'll tell you again, Shaya'le," his mother said, waving a finger at him playfully, "serving you is my greatest pleasure, and I won't let you take it away from me, not even for a *mitzvah* …"

WHEN A PARENT wants to serve the child who is so beloved and precious to him, the child is permitted to accept the parent's ministrations, since "a person's wish is his honor." However, if the father is a *talmid chacham*, the son should not allow his father to serve him, since the fact that his son accepts his service may still cause the father distress; it demonstrates that the son does not appreciate the honor that is due his father.

The Gemara (*Kiddushin* 45b) states that a person would not have the gall to send his father as an emissary to be *mekadesh* — to betroth — a woman on his behalf. It would be a blatant act of chutzpah to demand of a parent that he or she run an errand or do some other service for us, even if it is for the purpose of a *mitzvah*.

Therefore, a child should be extremely cautious about how he words his requests when he asks a parent to pass him an item, or to take care of something for him — such as if he asks his mother to prepare food for him or do his laundry. Ideally, he should mention what he needs done and then let the parent take the initiative to do it without having been explicitly asked. In that case, when the parent does so on his own, it is clear that he forgoes his honor. Naturally, if the parent is happy when the child informs him of what he lacks, because he wants to take care of the child's needs, then making the request would be a fulfillment of the *mitzvah* of kibbud. (*Mishpetei Hashalom* 21:21–22)

| 8 Tammuz | 8 Cheshvan | 8 Adar |

Extent of the Obligation of Kibbud Av — Loss vs. Preventing Profit

THE OBLIGATION OF *kibbud av va'eim* is at times easier to fulfill, while at other times it is a distinct challenge; it is obviously simpler to honor a young, healthy parent by serving him some cake and tea than to honor an elderly, infirm parent who requires a great deal of physical assistance and is not always in a state of being able to appreciate the help he is given. Our obligation remains unchanged, however, even under the most trying circumstances.

The *Shulchan Aruch* offers the following scenario as an extreme example: A parent takes a wallet full of his son's gold coins and, as the son watches, tosses the valuable wallet to the depths of the sea. What should be the son's reaction? "He should not shame him, cause him anguish or become angry with him; rather, he should accept the decree of Hashem and remain silent." If our obligation of *kibbud av va'eim* extends even to such extreme circumstances, it goes without saying that we should not show a parent anger simply because we do not see eye to eye on some issue.

As we mentioned earlier, in the case of *mora av*, a person may prevent his parent from taking action to cause him a loss, if he can do so through an agent and without causing his parent embarrassment. If one's money was indeed lost because of his parent's actions, the son can reclaim his loss through *beis din*. Some maintain that he may even take such measures to prevent the father from throwing his own (the father's) wallet into the sea, to prevent a violation of *bal tashchis* — pointless destruction of property.

These rules apply, however, only when a loss may be incurred or has already taken place. In a case where a parent is not causing a loss but is only preventing us from making a profit of some kind, we may not cause him anguish, even if as a result we will lose out on large potential profits. For example, if it would be necessary to rouse the parent in order to get the keys to a shop for the purpose of making a very profitable deal, we are not permitted to wake the parent from his sleep.

9 Tammuz	9 Cheshvan	9 Adar

If, however, the potential business deal is for the parent himself, and it is clear to us that he would be happy to be woken up for such a purpose, or if we know that he would want to be woken to prevent his son from losing out on a business opportunity, it is a *mitzvah* to wake him, so that we will not cause the parent anguish because of a lost opportunity. Similarly, we may rouse a parent from sleep if he wants to get to shul on time or for a *devar mitzvah* for which the time limit will soon pass, since both the parents and the child are equally obligated to honor Hashem.

In both of the above cases — for a potential profit and for a *devar mitzvah* — it is always preferable to wake the parent through a third party, as long as this will not prove embarrassing for the parent. (*Mishpetei Hashalom* 21:23–24)

Honoring Parents in Their Absence IN DISCUSSING A number of the *halachos* mentioned earlier in this chapter, we stated that some apply even when the parents are not present (such as the prohibition to contradict a parent). Regarding our obligation to fulfill a parent's requests if they are not for the parent's own personal, direct benefit — for example, when a parent instructs his son to go on a diet or to stop smoking — the *poskim* differ in their opinions.

Some authorities maintain that failing to fulfill such a request would be considered a violation of *mora* and "contradicting the parent's words," but only when it is done in the parent's presence. However, certain types of requests would be considered to have been violated "in their presence" even when the parent is not there — such as if a parent asks his son to shave his beard or to grow a beard, to wear a certain type of clothing, not to live in a certain place, or not to travel through a dangerous area.

Other authorities state that when there is significant financial loss, excessive bother or distinct anguish involved in fulfilling such a request, these are grounds for leniency. However, since this is a Torah prohibition, one should not take the liberty of being lenient in such a matter without first consulting with a *halachic* authority. (*Mishpetei Hashalom* 21:25)

10 Tammuz	10 Cheshvan	10 Adar

Honoring Parents After They Have Passed Away

"I feel as if I'm missing a limb," Dina told her sister Leah on the day they got up from *shivah* for their elderly father. "After scheduling my whole day around Tatte for so long, especially these past few months, when he was in the hospital, I hardly know what to do with myself now that he's no longer with us."

"Maybe we could do something special for Tatte even now — some special *mitzvah le'ilui nishmaso*," Leah thought aloud. "What if we would open a *gemach* of some kind — one branch in your house and another in mine. Then, every time someone would come to borrow an item, we would be doing another *chessed* for Tatte and moving him up a notch higher in the *Olam Ha'elyon*."

"Leah, that's perfect! Let's start thinking what service our neighborhoods need..."

THE OBLIGATION TO honor parents applies even after they have left this world. Therefore, when a son mentions his deceased parent — such as

when he quotes a *devar Torah* he heard from his father — he should say, "*avi mori [state the father's name] zichrono livrachah [lechayei ha'Olam Haba]* (or "*imi morasi ... zichronah livrachah ...*") — My father [or mother], my teacher, so-and-so, of blessed memory [in the World to Come]." During the twelve months of mourning after one's parent's death, after mentioning his parent's name, a person should say, "*Hareini kapparas mishkavo* — May I be an atonement for any bad that should have befallen my parent in the afterlife." Some say that one may say *zichrono livrachah* during the first twelve months, but one may not say *hareini kapparas mishkavo* after that twelve-month period, since twelve months is the limit of the time of punishment in *Gehinnom*.

When mentioning a parent's name in writing, some say that even within the twelve months of mourning, one should write *zichrono livrachah*, and not *hareini kapparas mishkavo*, since the written word remains even after the year is over. Others disagree and insist that *hareini kapparas mishkavo* should be written nonetheless.

All of the above applies equally whether it is a father or a mother who passed away.

11 Tammuz	11 Cheshvan	11 Adar

There are other *minhagim* through which the mourner is able to honor his parent after the parent's passing, such as for the sons to say *Kaddish* for the parents, to be called up for *maftir* when possible, and to act as the *shaliach tzibbur* throughout the first eleven months following the parent's *petirah*. When the son is capable, he should try to be a *shaliach tzibbur* for all of the weekday *tefillos*, since this is even more beneficial for the *niftar* than *Kaddish*.

Within the twelve months of mourning for a parent, the son's leading the *davening* is especially auspicious for *tefillas Maariv* on *motzaei Shabbos*, since that is the point when the *neshamos* of the deceased return to *Gehinnom* after their "break" for Shabbos. When the child serves as *shaliach tzibbur* at that point and publicly sanctifies Hashem's Name, his parent is redeemed from *Gehinnom*.

The reason these *minhagim* apply for only eleven months is that this is the extent of the judgment of ordinary people in *Gehinnom*, as opposed to the judgment of *resha'im*, who suffer for a full twelve months. A person should say *Kaddish* for his mother even if his father is still alive, and the father has no right to object; likewise, he should say *Kaddish* for his father even if his mother is alive.

Even after the first eleven months have passed, the son continues to honor the deceased parent by observing the *yahrtzeit* every year. There is a *mitzvah* to fast on that day, to be the *shaliach tzibbur* and say *Kaddish*, and to be called up to the Torah. Other *minhagim* to uplift the soul of the *niftar* on the *yahrtzeit* include: learning *mishnayos*, having a public *shiur*, quoting the parent's *divrei Torah*, developing new Torah insights or dedicating a Torah publication for the parent's merit, giving *tzedakah*, lighting candles, or arranging a meal to commemorate the *yahrtzeit*. Some children set up a loan fund or other *gemach* (lending items free of charge), or undertake to have a *sefer Torah* written for their parent's merit.

If someone does not know the exact date of his parent's death — which was a common occurrence after the Holocaust — he may choose a date arbitrarily and set it as the *yahrtzeit*. (*Mishpetei Hashalom* 21:26–27)

12 Tammuz | 12 Cheshvan | 12 Adar

Unfinished Business THE HEIRS HAVE an obligation to pay off the parent's debts after his passing, using the money from the father's estate. If they did not inherit any money from the parent, then according to the *Shulchan Aruch* they are not bound by this obligation; nevertheless, it would be *middas chassidus* — a higher level of piety — for the children to repay the debts from their own resources.

The children should do whatever is in their power to spare the deceased parent disgrace. Thus, for example, if the father had, contrary to the *halachah*, taken interest on a loan, in the form of an item clearly identifiable as belonging to the borrower, then if he repented and requested that the item be returned to its owner, the children are obligated to return it.

The Gemara mentions in a number of places that there is a *mitzvah* to carry out the will of the *niftar*, such as to give gifts to particular people, and the heirs can be compelled to do so. Certainly, if the parent wrote in his will or verbally enjoined his children to give *tzedakah*, to perform acts of justice and to follow the paths of righteousness, then carrying out their parent's words will bring an elevation to the parent's soul, since a person's acts bring merit to his parents.

In the event that the father asks his offspring to do things that are unreasonably difficult, such as going to visit a distant grave every year, the child should consult with a Rav to determine the extent of his obligation in that case. (*Mishpetei Hashalom* 21:28–30)

<table>
<tr><td>13 Tammuz</td><td>13 Cheshvan</td><td>13 Adar</td></tr>
</table>

Infirm Parents   WHEN A PARENT suffers from mental deterioration or the symptoms of senility, the children should try to relate to him as respectfully as the parent's condition permits and to please him in accordance with his current needs, *davening* constantly that Hashem should show him mercy and that the situation should improve. If someone sees that he cannot cope with caring for his parent on his own, because the parent's condition has deteriorated so drastically, he may arrange for others to tend to the parent's daily needs in a dignified manner, such as in an institution for the aged that provides high-quality care, or in the home of the parent or child with the help of a live-in attendant. However, the child should not divest himself of responsibility altogether; he should strike a balance, seeking the guidance of a Rav.

When deciding on what arrangements should be made for caring for for an infirm parent, each child must honestly evaluate his own abilities to cope. In theory, caring for parents directly may be the most ideal way to fulfill the *mitzvah*, but if the child does not have the emotional or physical stamina to deal with such a responsibility, or when he is struggling with raising his own children and earning a livelihood, this may not be a practical option.

Often, the parents themselves stipulate that they would prefer to move into an institution that offers professional care for all their needs.

Before taking the step of placing them in such an institution, however, the child should consider the risks to the elderly parent's health that may result from the loss of independence, a possibly depressing environment, severe boredom, and other factors. When it is possible to arrange for adequate, affordable in-house help and to keep the parent in the environment he is accustomed to, surrounded by family members who are happy to cater to all his needs, this is often an excellent compromise.

14 Tammuz   14 Cheshvan   14 Adar

As we discussed in chapter 23, when a parent needs some kind of medical attention that may result in bleeding, such as removing a thorn or splinter, the child should not do it, since he may cause an injury to his parent, which is a very severe offense. If the child is a physician, he should not draw blood from his father, nor should he perform surgery on him, even though he is doing so for medical purposes. Giving injections, setting up an intravenous line and the like would also be included in this *issur*.

Of course, this *halachah* applies only when there is someone else available to give the necessary treatment. If there is no one else who can do it, and the parent is in pain, the son can do whatever is necessary for the sake of his father's health and comfort. This question often comes up for those with ill or aging parents, who need frequent medical procedures done to them. In many cases, while it might be possible to arrange for someone else to administer the treatment, the arrangement would be inordinately expensive or greatly inconvenient, or it might cause the parent embarrassment. In such cases, there may be grounds to say that this is equivalent to having no one else available, and the child would be permitted to do it himself. However, we should not decide to tend to our parents ourselves without consulting a competent Rav on our particular question.

If an ailing parent is under doctor's orders to abstain from certain foods or drinks, then even if the parent, with full understanding, demands one of those foods or drinks, the child is not permitted to give it to him. According to some opinions, this would apply only if the food is actually life-threatening; if it is only harmful, but not dangerous, the child may give it to a parent who insists.

Sometimes it is necessary to conceal from an ill parent just how serious his situation is, so that knowledge of his condition will not cause him to fall into despair and have a deleterious effect on his health. Here too, a Rav should be consulted before deciding what to tell a parent and what not to tell him. (*Mishpetei Hashalom* 21:31–33)

15 Tammuz | 15 Cheshvan | 15 Adar

Relating to a Father Who Transgresses   PARENTS ARE HUMAN, and they too may err. If a child sees his father transgressing a Torah prohibition inadvertently or out of ignorance of the *halachah*, he should be careful not to say bluntly, "You violated a *mitzvah* of the Torah!" Rather, he should ask, tactfully and in a non-accusatory way, "Doesn't the *passuk* say …?" and quote the relevant *passuk*. When the parent hears the *passuk*, he will understand the implied rebuke on his own and will be able to correct his mistake without undue embarrassment.

Similarly, if the father repeats a *devar Torah* incorrectly or even makes a mistake in a *halachic* ruling, his son should not react by saying, "You're mistaken!" or, "That's not the way to learn it!" Instead, he should say gently, "Father, didn't we learn it *this* way?"

If the father or mother are absolute *resha'im* who have made no move to do *teshuvah*, the children are still not allowed to strike or curse them. Even if the parent has been sentenced to *malkos* or *nidui*, the son may not act as the *shaliach beis din* — the court representative — to carry out the punishment. (The only exception is in the case of a parent who is a *meisis umeidi'ach* — who methodically incites others to sin. Regarding such a sinner, the Torah tells us, "Do not have mercy and do not cover up for him" [*Devarim* 13].)

Regarding the positive *mitzvos* of *kibbud* and *mora* toward a parent who sins repeatedly, the matter is not so clear. The Rambam rules that even if the parent is a *rasha*, who sins regularly and has not done *teshuvah*, the child is still obliged to revere and honor him. However,

several sources in the Gemara seem to state otherwise, leading the Tur
and other *Rishonim* to disagree with the Rambam's ruling.

Therefore, a difference of opinion remains as to whether a *mamzer* —
a child born of a relationship forbidden by the Torah — needs to honor
his father who has not yet repented. The *Shulchan Aruch* rules according
to the stringent view of the Rambam that the son must honor such a father, while most *poskim* are lenient and rule to the contrary. In practice,
since a Torah commandment is at stake — *kibbud-* and *mora av* — we
should abide by the stricter ruling of the *Shulchan Aruch*, unless the
parent is a deliberate and purposeful sinner, a *meisis*, or an *apikores*. In
any case, the difference of opinion relates only to positive acts of honor
and reverence. According to all views, the son is not permitted to cause
anguish to his father.

| 16 Tammuz | 16 Cheshvan | 16 Adar |

Even according to the Rambam, who maintains that we must honor
a parent who is a *rasha*, we do *not* have to honor him in matters relating
to the sin itself, until he has done *teshuvah*. Certainly, at the moment he
is transgressing, the children have an obligation, as does anyone else,
to reprove him and to actively prevent him from continuing in his sin,
preferably through the agency of a third party. When this is not possible, they should consult a Rav to ask how best to proceed.

In the situation most commonly encountered by *baalei teshuvah*,
the parents are not Torah observant because they were never educated
in the Torah way. When the parent is considered a *tinok shenishba*, the
children should certainly be meticulous about showing him respect and
treating him with reverence. Besides being a fulfillment of this *mitzvah*,
it is also a great *kiddush Hashem* and one of the most effective ways of
drawing the parents closer to *Yiddishkeit*. (For a more complete discussion of *tinok shenishba*, see Volume I, chapter 18.)

When the parent is not a *rasha* but has a repulsive character, conducts himself in a lowly, despicable manner or is a drunkard, it is advisable that his children keep their distance from him. Likewise, when a
parent and child are not on good terms and are constantly quarreling
with one another, even if the son is the one suffering the most, it is best

that they separate and live apart from one another, since they cannot tolerate each other's company. When constant tension and frequent misunderstandings cloud their relationship, the children will often find it easier to honor the parent properly when they are not living in such close quarters. Here too, one should seek the counsel of a Rav before distancing oneself from one's parent. (*Mishpetei Hashalom* 21:34–38)

17 Tammuz	17 Cheshvan	17 Adar

A Parent's Request *That Entails a Torah Violation*

"Stanley, eat something. I especially went out and bought fish to broil for you, since I knew you wouldn't eat our meat," Mrs. Styne prodded her son.

From the moment Stanley walked into the house, bursting with good intentions, he seemed to be running into conflicts at every turn. It was his first visit home since he had become a full-fledged *baal teshuvah*, and he wanted so much to give his parents a good impression so they would accept him for what he was and have a positive opinion of religious life.

"Looks delicious, Mom. But, uh, I'm really not too hungry." Stanley hoped that would satisfy her. Actually, he was famished — but not for a piece of catfish…

"I thought the one thing they taught you in that school was how to respect your parents," Mr. Styne snapped at his son. "Mom worked so hard, and that's the thanks she gets?"

"I'll … I'll help Mom clean up. And I'll take out the garbage. And I'll do the shopping tomorrow. Here, let me pour you a drink of water, Dad. I do want to give you all the respect in the world. But I can't eat something that the Torah says is forbidden…"

ATHOUGH WE ARE obliged to honor our parents with true devotion, there is one place where the line must be respectfully drawn. The Torah tells us, "*Ish imo ve'aviv tira'u … Ani Hashem* — Each person should revere his mother and his father … I am Hashem." Both you and your parents are equally obligated to honor Hashem and to follow His will. Therefore, if a parent tells his son to violate a *mitzvah*, the son may not obey him. This *halachah* applies whether the parent orders his child to abstain from doing a positive *mitzvah* or to transgress a negative *mitzvah*, and is applicable even if it is only a Rabbinically ordained *mitzvah*, and even if there is no action involved in the violation and all it entails is sitting and doing nothing.

Consequently, if a parent tells his son to be *mechallel Shabbos*, to steal, to eat something that is not kosher, to refrain from returning a lost item to its owner, or, for a *kohen*, to go into a cemetery, or to do any other such *issurim*, the son may not obey him. Similarly, if the parent tells him not to do a positive *mitzvah* — such as not to put on *tefillin*, say *Krias Shema*, *daven*, learn Torah or get married — the son may not listen to him. The same applies if the parent wishes to stop him from observing a Rabbinical injunction — such as lighting Chanukah candles or making an *eiruv tavshilin*.

If a parent instructs his son not to be on speaking terms with some-one and not to forgive him until a certain amount of time has elapsed, and the son would really like to patch things up with that person im-mediately, then he should go right ahead and make peace with the person. He need not be concerned about his father's request, since by instructing him to prolong the enmity, the father is demanding that he violate the *issur* of *lo sisna* — "Do not hate your brother in your heart." (If, however, the person in question is a *rasha* whom it is a *mitzvah* to hate, then he should obey his father's request.) Similarly, if a father tells his son not to say *Kaddish* for his deceased mother, the son should not listen to him, since the father's request is a violation of *ve'ahavta lerei'acha kamocha*.

When a father wants his son to go to university to learn a profession, the son does not have to listen to him, for two reasons: First, Torah learning takes precedence, and second, going to university poses a genuine risk to his spiritual level. Nor does the son have to obey if the father tells him to do something that poses a physical danger to him, or if he asks him to do an abominable or foolish act.

If a son knows that his parents are distressed when he fasts, he should not fast in their presence on any days when fasting is not obliga-tory. From this *halachah* we can extrapolate that any stringent conduct that is not required by *halachah* or *minhag* should not be done in the presence of one's parents if the person knows that it would upset them.

If the child wishes to move to Eretz Yisrael and his parents wish to deter him, he does not have to listen to them. On the other hand, the son is permitted to leave Eretz Yisrael for the purpose of fulfilling the *mitzvah* of *kibbud av va'eim*. (*Mishpetei Hashalom* 21:39–43, 48)

To Forfeit a Mitzvah or Not? WHEN THE PARENT makes a request — such as, "Give me a drink of water" — and fulfilling that request will cause the son to miss out on an opportunity to fulfill a *mitzvah* that he will not be able to fulfill at a later time, such as burying a *niftar* or attending a funeral, then the *halachah* is as follows: If there is someone else available to do the other *mitzvah*, then the son should forfeit the *mitzvah* and focus his attention on honoring his parent. If there is no one else available to do the *mitzvah*, then he should set aside his obligation of *kibbud av* for the time being and deal with the *mitzvah* at hand, since both he and his father are equally obliged to honor the One Who commanded that *mitzvah*. However, if the *mitzvah* is one that he could just as well do at a later time, then he should give precedence to honoring his parent and do the *mitzvah* later.

If a person had already begun to do a *mitzvah* before his parent made a request of him, then even if the *mitzvah* will still be there for him to complete later, he should first finish what he had started. For example, if the request is made when he is in the middle of saying *Krias Shema*, he should first finish *Krias Shema* before responding. This is because of the principle that "a person who is involved in one *mitzvah* is exempt from the obligation to perform another *mitzvah*." (However, if he already said the *brachah* of *hamapil* before sleeping, after which, ordinarily, he would not speak, and then his father calls to him, he *should* respond to his father.) (*Mishpetei Hashalom* 21:44)

Interrupting Torah Learning TORAH LEARNING IS considered equivalent in importance to all the other *mitzvos* combined. Whenever a person has to choose between doing a *mitzvah* and continuing his Torah study, as long as the *mitzvah* can

be performed by someone else, he should not interrupt his learning. If there is no one else available, he should do the *mitzvah* and then resume his learning immediately.

When a parent asks his son to do something, carrying out that request is a fulfillment of the *mitzvah* of *kibbud av va'eim*; therefore, the same rule applies: If it is something that no one else can take care of, then he is obligated to interrupt his learning in order to fulfill his parent's request. However, if he was not asked, but wishes to do something for his parents of his own accord, usually he should not do so if it will take away from his Torah-learning time. An exception would be meeting his parents who have arrived in town — for that purpose, he should interrupt his learning even if they did not ask him to go out to welcome them.

The same would apply, in many cases, to girls who are in school. Even though the *mitzvah* of learning Torah is not an obligation for women, they are still required to learn what they need to know in order to observe the Torah properly, including necessary *halachos* and other Torah studies that will strengthen their *emunah* and *yiras Shamayim*. When a girl misses school, she may well be left with gaps in her *halachic* knowledge or spiritual inspiration that cannot easily be filled. Therefore, a parent should think twice before taking a daughter out of school to help him or her, unless there is no alternative.

A father is bound by a positive *mitzvah* to teach his son Torah. At the same time, he himself is obligated to learn Torah. If there is enough money to allow only one of them to study, then, as long as their intellectual abilities are about equal, the father's Torah learning takes precedence, and the son should manage on his own. If, however, the son is very bright and would be able to achieve greater success in his learning than his father would, the son's Torah learning takes precedence, and the financial support should be given to him. Needless to say, the father should not neglect his own Torah learning entirely; he should still find time to learn regularly.

Of course, there will be times when the son will have to interrupt his learning in order to pitch in and give his father a break from his work, even if the father is an ignorant person. On the other hand, at times a father may feel it right to interrupt his own learning to allow his son to

take a hiatus from his work. Each situation should be judged individually, based on the circumstances.

Even though, as we mentioned earlier, the great *Tanna'im* and *Amora'im* were extremely careful to honor and serve their parents in the best way possible, Torah learning is a greater *mitzvah* than *kibbud av va'eim*. Therefore, a son may leave his parents' town in order to learn at a particular yeshivah or with a specific rebbe, even though as a result of that move he will be unable to serve his parents on a daily basis, as long as there is someone else available to tend to their needs. However, when he is in town, he should serve his parents himself whenever possible, and then resume his learning.

Sometimes, the son may feel that if he goes to another town to learn under a specific Rav, his learning will be crowned with greater success, but his parents object because they are concerned for his safety. They may be afraid that the anti-Semites in that town will cause trouble and harm their son, or they might be concerned about some other danger. In such a case the son is not obligated to refrain from going because of their worries; however, he should keep in touch with them to reassure them of his well-being, so they will not be anxious. (*Mishpetei Hashalom* 21:45–48)

| 20 Tammuz | 20 Cheshvan | 20 Adar |

Parents and Shidduchim   "Mrs. Bromberg, I just had to speak with you." Ilana slipped into the chair opposite her seminary teacher. "I don't know what to do!"

"I'm always here for you, Ilana. Let's hear what's on your mind," Mrs. Bromberg said, urging her on.

"I'm leaving *Eretz Yisrael* tomorrow, and my parents have already told me that they have a *shidduch* lined up for me. They're very excited about it. But they don't realize how I've grown this year. I want to build a Torah home, to marry someone who will learn all day, at least for a few years. They found a *shidduch* that's right for the 'old me'—a nice boy who's in law school, maybe goes to a *shiur* once or twice a week..." Ilana felt the tears coming to her eyes.

"Did you try explaining the situation to your parents?" Mrs. Bromberg inquired gently.

"I tried, but they're convinced that I'm just floating now, and that when I come back down to earth, I'll return to my senses. I've always trusted them; I know they want what's best for me. But in this case, I know that they don't understand where I am. I'm afraid I'll end up in a marriage I'll regret fo the rest of my life," Ilana sobbed.

"Listen, Ilana," Mrs. Bromberg took Ilana's hand in hers. "*Kibbud av va'eim* is a great *mitzvah*, and you should do whatever you can to honor your parents in every way. But when it comes to a *shidduch*, your needs supersede your parents' wishes. Remain firm in your aspirations, explain your position respectfully, and in time, your parents will realize what is really best for you. And make sure to let me know when there's a *mazal tov!*"

WHEN PARENTS OBJECT to their child's marrying the person he wishes to marry, and certainly if they do not want him to get married yet at all, even though he feels he is ready — he does not have to listen to them. Nor is he obligated to marry someone they recommend if he is not interested in that person — for example, if his parents want him to marry someone who is not such a fine person, just for the sake of her money, he certainly does not have to agree. Getting married is a *mitzvah*, and if his parents interfere with his ability to marry the right person, that is equivalent to preventing him from fulfilling a positive commandment in the best way; as we discussed earlier, in such a case he does not have to obey them.

Furthermore, the main purpose of *kibbud av va'eim* is to bring benefit to the parent. In a case where the act is not of direct benefit to the parent, and will cause the child loss or anguish, which will certainly be the case if he will subsequently suffer from an unhappy marriage or settle for a lower spiritual level in his home, then obeying his parents in this matter is not in the category of *kibbud av va'eim*.

Needless to say, the child should take into consideration the fact that his parents have a lot of experience and generally have his best interests in mind. He should not be so quick to disregard their advice, which most likely flows from their love for him. Nevertheless, if the parents are pushing a *shidduch* that he feels is not for his benefit, then it is his prerogative to refuse.

The same rule applies regarding other *mitzvos*. If the son wishes to *daven* in a shul where people *daven* with greater *kavanah* and where he finds the _tefillah_ more uplifting, then even if his parents object, he does not have to listen to them. At the same time, the child must tread with caution in such areas, since in most cases, despite the way it appears to the child, his parents are not really treating _mitzvos_ lightly. On the contrary, most of the time, the parents know better than the child himself what is best for him, both in the material and in the spiritual realms, and they are generally acting _lesheim Shamayim_. "_Setiras zekeinim binyan_ — Even when the older generation appears to be destroying, they are actually building." Each situation should be judged individually, and a Rav should be consulted. (_Mishpetei Hashalom_ 21:49–50)

21 Tammuz | 21 Cheshvan | 21 Adar

Court Cases   AS UNPLEASANT AS it may be, there are times when a father and son have to handle their issues with each other in _beis din_.

Yet even though the two are on opposing sides for the purpose of the _din Torah_, the son must still act in accordance with certain _halachos_ that ensure that he will fulfill his obligation of _mora av_:

Generally, when the two litigants are not in agreement on the question of which _beis din_ should judge their case, they are to bring their case to the place that the defendant prefers. However, when the litigants are a father and son, then even when the son is the defendant and he lives in another city, he is obligated to come to the _beis din_ his father chooses, as a gesture of respect; however, the father has to pay the expenses incurred by his son's traveling and loss of time.

When it is necessary for the father to take an oath, the son may have him take only an oath that is not worded in the form of a curse. In addition, the son must be extremely careful not to say an extraneous word in presenting his case, nor should he belittle his father's words in any way. Rather, he should speak to his father with the utmost respect, despite the uncomfortable situation in which they find themselves. If possible, he should have someone else represent him in his claim, so that he will not have a direct legal encounter with his father. According to some opinions, bringing a mother to _beis din_ leads to such embarrassment that it is not permissible at all.

כיבוד אב ואם

Although the *halachah* permits suing a father, the *middas chassidus* — exemplary behavior — would be never to sue or press charges against a father. In fact, even if one's father has a claim against someone else, it is preferable that the son go to *beis din* in his father's stead, to spare his father the demeaning position of appearing in court. (*Mishpetei Hashalom* 21:51)

22 Tammuz	22 Cheshvan	22 Adar

Parents — Doing THE *MITZVAH* OF *kibbud av va'eim* is a demand-
Their Part ing one, and the dangers of violating it are great.
Parents should do whatever they can to make it easier for their children to fulfill their obligations properly. Some say that a parent should relate to his grown children as if they were his brothers, so that they will have an easier time getting along and maintaining a peaceful relationship.

A father should not rule his home with a heavy hand, nor should he be overly particular about his own honor, since this is likely to cause his children to fall short in fulfilling their obligations of *kibbud av va'eim*. Rather, he should overlook their slips and forgo his honor, since "if a father is *mochel* — if he forgoes — his *kavod* or his *mora*, these [shortfalls] are forgiven." That means that if the child fulfills his obligations properly, he will be rewarded, but if he fails to do so in areas where the parent was *mochel*, he will not be punished.

If there is reason to be concerned that others will learn to be lax in their *kibbud av va'eim* when they see that the parent forgoes an honor due to him, he may not be *mochel* in that case. A parent is certainly not permitted to make allowances for a child's hitting or cursing him, and some *poskim* maintain that a parent may also not be *mochel* the child's shaming his parent or causing him anguish.

A parent may retract his *mechilah* at any time. For example, if he was *mochel* and allowed the children to sit in his place, and then decided against it, he can retract his *mechilah* and prohibit their sitting there from that point on. When the parent is *mochel* an honor, the *poskim* differ on the question of whether he has to inform the child of his *mechi-*

lah, and whether his *mechilah* is effective if the child is not aware of it.

A parent who strikes his grown son or daughter violates the *issur* of *lifnei iveir* — causing others to sin — since the child may not be able to resist his *yetzer hara* and may raise a hand against his parent, curse him or make a disrespectful retort, all of which would constitute serious violations of the *mitzvah* of *kibbud av va'eim*.

The *halachos* of *chinuch* of children are explained in Volume I, chapter 13, and the *halachos* of striking children are discussed in Volume I, chapter 7. (*Mishpetei Hashalom* 21:52–54)

23 Tammuz | 23 Cheshvan | 23 Adar

Distinctions Between Father and Mother ALTHOUGH THE CHILD'S obligation of *kavod* and *mora* applies equally to father and mother, in some situations one takes precedence over the other, as we shall explain.

When, for example, both the father and the mother ask for a drink, the child should momentarily set aside his obligation to his mother and serve his father first. This is because his mother, too, is obligated to honor his father, since he is her husband. If his parents are divorced, however, the mother is no longer bound to honor the father, and therefore the child's obligation toward the two is equal and he can give precedence to whichever parent he chooses.

The child of divorced parents is often cast into difficult situations. For instance, his father may tell him to do one thing while his mother demands that he do the opposite. Often, even if one party is in the right, the circumstances may demand that he follow the other. At times, "sit and do nothing" is the best solution, but that is not always an option. Since the slightest wrong move in such a situation may ignite explosive fury, the child has to proceed with great caution and give each action much thought, so that he not cause more harm than good in his zeal to perform his *mitzvah* of *kibbud*. It is best to consult with a Rav in such cases.

If the father has passed away, and the mother tells the child to do something that contradicts the will of his deceased father, some say that he should obey his mother, since respect for the living takes precedence over respect for the deceased; however, other authorities disagree with this ruling.

Another difficult situation may arise when one parent tells the child to do something, then the other parent asks him what the first one said, and the child knows that revealing this information will cause this parent to be angry at the other parent. For example, the father tells his son to go buy him a certain item in the store, and the mother will be angry if she hears about it, since she feels that the father wastes money on unnecessary purchases. In such a case, the child is allowed to bend the truth in order to preserve peace, even if as a result one of the parents will become angry at the child. (*Mishpetei Hashalom* 21:55–58)

| 24 Tammuz | 24 Cheshvan | 24 Adar |

Distinctions Between Son and Daughter A SON AND daughter are equally obligated in *kavod* and *mora* of their parents. However, when a daughter marries, she has a *mitzvah* to respect her husband, and her first obligation is to him and his will. Therefore, if her husband objects to her serving her parents in ways that will interfere with his needs, there are things she will not be in a position to do for her parents; in these areas, she is exempt from her obligation of *kibbud av va'eim*. However, her obligation of *mora* remains unchanged, and she is certainly not allowed to shame her parents or cause them anguish.

Some authorities maintain that the woman must give precedence to her husband only in matters relating to *kavod*, but not in matters relating to *mora*. Sometimes there is a conflict between the will of the father and that of the husband, and it is unclear whether we are dealing with a question of *kavod* or *mora*. For example, the father may tell his daughter not to wear a certain head covering, while the husband insists that she wear it. If she wears that head covering in her father's presence, this may be more than a question of *kavod*; it might be considered a violation of the *issur* of causing her father anguish. On the other hand, the choice of head covering might be considered exclusively the husband's domain. The father may have no right to make such a demand, and therefore he would actually be causing anguish to himself. In such delicate cases it is vital that she ask a Rav how to conduct herself.

Ideally, a parent should not ask his married daughter to tend to him when she is busy tending to her husband's needs. At the same time, a husband should urge his wife to give precedence to her father's request. Situations in which these matters come up commonly occur when one is being hosted by the other. With a bit of goodwill, conflicts can be avoided and a positive, respectful atmosphere maintained.

When a woman is either divorced or widowed, or even when she is married and her husband does not mind that she serves her parents, her obligation is equal to that of a man. For a single girl as well, the obligation of _kavod_ and _mora_ for her parents is equal to that of a man. (_Mishpetei Hashalom_ 21:61–62)

25 Tammuz | 25 Cheshvan | 25 Adar

Parents Come First

Shimon kept his eyes glued to the door, waiting to see his parents emerge after their long plane trip. Many of the passengers that were on his parents' flight had already come out. _I guess their luggage must have been the last to deplane_, he thought to himself.

Suddenly, he saw a different familiar face — that of Mr. Moskowitz, his elderly neighbor from down the block. Seeing that he was on his own, Shimon rushed over to help Mr. Moskowitz maneuver the wagon carrying the heavy suitcases, looking over his shoulder all the time. When he reached the taxi-stand, Mr. Moskowitz asked if he could wait a few minutes while Mr. Moskowitz searched for a letter he had brought from overseas to mail.

"Sorry, Mr. Moskowitz, I can't help you any further. I see my parents coming out, and I have to help them with their load."

Mr. Moskowitz understood. "Of course, of course. Thank you for the help you were able to give me," he added as Shimon rushed over to greet his parents.

IN A NUMBER of _mitzvos bein adam lechaveiro_, a parent takes precedence. This applies when it comes to returning a lost item, loading and unloading a heavy burden, redeeming captives, saving a life, and many

other *mitzvos bein adam lechaveiro*; in all these areas, when we have the choice of helping someone else or helping our parent, the parent comes first. However, our own loss precedes a father's loss. Therefore, as we discussed in chapter 22, if a person comes across his own lost item as well as that of his father, and he cannot retrieve both of them, he should give precedence to his own. The *passuk* says (*Devarim* 15), "*Ki lo yihyeh becha evyon* — There shall not be a needy person among you," and the Gemara (*Sanhedrin* 64b) derives from here that "Your lost property takes precedence over anyone else's, because you have a responsibility to avoid bringing yourself to a state of poverty."

Nevertheless, if the loss to one's father will be major or imminent, and one's own loss is minor or improbable, then the proper response is not to be so particular, but rather to go beyond the letter of the law and to retrieve the father's loss first. (The *halachos* regarding giving precedence when presented with one's father's loss and one's rebbe's loss, as well as redeeming one of them from captivity in a case where both need to be redeemed, are discussed in chapter 33.)

When both parents have been taken captive, the obligation to redeem one's mother takes precedence. The same holds true when they both need to be supplied with food or clothing. However, if they are both drowning, and it is not possible to save both of them, a father comes first. In the case of lost items, the father's loss precedes the mother's loss. (*Mishpetei Hashalom* 21:59)

26 Tammuz	26 Cheshvan	26 Adar

Special Situations A *SHTUKI* IS a child who knows who his mother is but whose father's identity is not known. The *shtuki* is held accountable for striking or cursing his mother, but he is not held accountable for striking or cursing his "father" — that is, the person who claims to be his father, even if his mother tells him that he is that person's son. If there seems to be some basis for her claim, then he should be concerned for the possibility that it is true and should act stringently; still, he would not be punished based on her words alone.

A person whose father is Jewish and whose mother is not Jewish is not obligated to honor his parents, even if his mother has since converted to Judaism, and even if she did so between the time when he was conceived and the time when he was born.

A person whose mother is Jewish and whose father is not Jewish is not considered to be related to his non-Jewish father — even if the father subsequently converted to Judaism — and therefore he is not obligated to honor his father, even as a gesture of _derech eretz_ (refined behavior). However, if after the father's conversion he brings the child up in his home, the child is obligated to honor him no less than any adopted child would have to honor his adoptive father (see below).

A _ger_ — a convert to Judaism — may not curse or strike his non-Jewish father, nor may he degrade him. Rather, he should treat his father with a certain amount of respect, so that _geirim_ should not come to say, "We have come down from a higher level of _kedushah_ to a lower level" (since non-Jews generally observe this aspect of ethical behavior).

Children who are adopted are obligated to observe all of the _halachos_ of _kavod_ and _mora_ toward their biological parents, as well as all the _issurim_ of striking, cursing or disgracing their biological parents. It is also proper for them to honor their adoptive parents who raised them, for reasons of _hakaras hatov_ — basic gratitude — and also in order not to upset the smooth-running patterns of their adoptive home. _Chazal_ say that someone who raises a child in his home is considered to have given birth to him, even if the biological parents are still alive, so it is self-evident (ethically, even if not halachically) that adoptive parents should be treated with the requisite honor and reverence. (_Mishpetei Hashalom_ 21:63–67)

| 27 Tammuz | 27 Cheshvan | 27 Adar |

Kavod for Stepparents WHEN ONE PARENT has passed away and the surviving parent wishes to remarry, the children often have mixed feelings about the remarriage. They may perceive it as an insult to the memory of the deceased parent and might be hesitant to encourage remarriage. However, the Torah does not view it that way at all. In fact, if we are obligated to help every other Jew marry, then our obligation to a parent, who is often lonely and disconsolate in widowhood, is even greater. The same applies to helping a divorced parent remarry. This is the case even though it happens very often that the new partner is very different from what the children hoped or expected he or she would be like. Also, often there are very painful changes that the parent might have to make in order to accommodate his or her new spouse. This does not change the *halachah*, and children are obligated to respect the new parent in any case.

A person is obligated to honor his father's wife as long as his father is alive, even though she is not his mother, and likewise to honor his mother's husband, as long as his mother is alive. After his parent's death, he is no longer obligated halachically to honor the stepparent; however, it is proper to continue to do so even after the parent has passed away.

Certainly, a child's honor for his father or mother should not diminish after his parents have divorced and remarried, even if the remarriage has caused the children much anguish. On the contrary, as we mentioned, the children should do whatever they can to help their divorced or widowed parents in all matters, including finding a *shidduch*. If a divorced parent instructs the child not to help the other parent, the child need not obey him, since this is a command that involves violation of a *mitzvah*. (*Mishpetei Hashalom* 21:68)

28 Tammuz	28 Cheshvan	28 Adar

Honoring In-Laws A MAN IS obligated to honor his in-laws in the manner that he would honor any esteemed older people. A woman is likewise obliged to honor her in-laws; in doing so she is also honoring her husband. The proper way to address in-laws is "*Abba*" or "Father," and "*Ima*" or "Mother"; however, if this upsets one's own parents, a different title can be used.

Ideally, when each spouse treats his/her in-laws with love and respect, a harmonious relationship should ensue. Unfortunately, however, this is not always the case. When the husband feels that his parents-in-law or siblings-in-law are interfering with the peaceful functioning of their home, he may request that they restrict their visits to special

occasions, while his wife should go to visit them at their home regularly. The same applies if the wife feels strongly regarding the presence of her husband's parents or siblings in their home.

The relationship with in-laws is a very delicate one. When a rift forms between a person's wife and his parents, he has to weigh his actions and responses very carefully to avoid making matters worse. At times he should conciliate his wife and urge her to give in even when she is in the right; in other cases, he needs to keep a distance from his own parents even when they are right, in order to preserve the peace in his own home. In these matters, it is absolutely crucial that one consult a Rav and follow his counsel.

Although in principle, the obligation to honor one's parents precedes one's obligation toward in-laws, in certain areas there may be local custom that will dictate otherwise. For example, in many circles a newlywed couple traditionally spends the first Pesach with the wife's family, and the name for the first child born to the couple is chosen from the wife's side.

If parents tell their son not to visit his in-laws or to treat them with disrespect in some other way, he does not have to listen to them, since this is a request to violate a _mitzvah_ and is considered void. (_Mishpetei Hashalom_ 21:68)

| 29 Tammuz | 29 Cheshvan | 29 Adar |

Other Relatives   AN EXTENSION OF the _mitzvah_ of _kibbud av va'eim_ is the obligation to honor an older brother or sister. This _halachah_ applies even to a half-brother, and even when the younger brother is a greater _talmid chacham_ than his older sibling is. When a person speaks _lashon hara_ about an older sibling or transgresses any other of the _mitzvos bein adam lechaveiro_ toward him, in addition to the other violations, he also violates this _issur_.

The _poskim_ differ regarding certain details of the obligation toward an older sibling. Some say it applies only as long as the parents are alive, while others say that it continues even after the parents have passed away. Some are of the opinion that one must honor only the oldest

brother in the family, and not the other older siblings. Another limit set by some *poskim* is to restrict the obligation to *kavod*, while the *halachos* of *mora* — such as not sitting in the brother's place — would not apply. Similarly, the *Minchas Chinuch* points out that one may call his brother by name, which is not permitted for a parent.

If someone degrades and disgraces his younger brother who is a *talmid chacham*, it would be correct for the younger brother to put his older brother in *nidui*. Since the older brother does not respect the Torah, his behavior does not reflect the spirit of the Jewish people, and his younger brother does not owe him any honor.

A person is obligated to honor his father's father and mother; however, honoring his father is a greater obligation and takes precedence. Some *poskim* extend this *mitzvah* to include the mother's father and mother as well.

Consequently, if a person does not have sufficient resources to support his father, but his son — the grandson of his father — can afford to do so, the grandson can be compelled to support his grandfather. (*Mishpetei Hashalom* 21:69–72)

| 1 Av | 1 Kislev | 1 Nisan |

Unlimited Mitzvah — Unlimited Reward ONE OF THE reasons we do not make a *brachah* on the *mitzvah* of kibbud and *mora av va'eim* is that it is not a *mitzvah* that distinguishes us as Jews, since non-Jews generally observe some aspects of it as well. Nevertheless, when we honor our parents, we should not do it simply as an expression of human ethics or social mores; nor should our intentions be for the inheritance or other compensation we may gain from our parents. Rather, we should have in mind that we are doing a *mitzvah* and fulfilling the Divine Will.

The *mitzvah* of *kibbud av va'eim* has no upper limits; we can always enhance the honor we show our parents and bring it a notch higher. When we fulfill this *mitzvah* we enjoy its fruits in this world, while the principal reward remains intact for us in the World to Come. The more meticulous and enthusiastic our fulfillment of this *mitzvah*, the more praiseworthy it is. (*Mishpetei Hashalom* 21:73, 75)

In summary: We are obligated to both honor and revere our parents, and to refrain from cursing, striking and disgracing them in any way. These *halachos* are incumbent on sons and daughters toward fathers and mothers, and young children should be trained in them as well. While the main fulfillment of this *mitzvah* is in the heart, there are numerous *halachos* that guide us in applying it in words and deeds: *Mora* — reverence — includes such things as not sitting in a father's place, not contradicting his words and not calling him by name. *Kavod* — honor — includes actions such as standing up for the parent and providing him with food and clothing. The cost of providing for these needs should come from the parents' funds. If they are lacking, the child is obligated to support them. The child may act to prevent or retrieve damage caused by a parent, but may not do so in a case where the parent is merely preventing him from making a profit.

A child has special obligations to enhance the honor of a deceased parent, such as by saying *Kaddish* and leading the *davening*. In caring for an ill parent, the child must do what is best for the parent within the realm of his abilities. Special *halachos* guide our conduct toward parents who are sinners or who are of objectionable character. A child need not obey a parent who instructs him to violate a *mitzvah*. However, he may at times need to forgo a *mitzvah* or interrupt his Torah learning in a case where *kibbud av* takes precedence. A child is not obligated to heed a parent regarding a *shidduch*, or in a case where his spiritual growth is at stake. Parents should make it as easy as possible for their children to honor them.

There are a number of distinctions between the obligations one has toward a father and those toward a mother, and between the obligations of a son and those of a daughter. There are specific *halachos* that apply to special parental situations, such as adoptive parents and stepparents. In-laws must also be honored to an extent, as well as an older brother and grandparents. There are no limits when it comes to observing the *mitzvah* of *kibbud av va'eim*, and fulfilling this *mitzvah* brings with it the promise of great reward in this world and the next.

"There are three partners in [the creation of] a person: Hashem, one's father and one's mother; when a person honors his father and his mother, Hashem says, 'I consider it as if I Myself lived among them and they honored Me'" (Kiddushin 30b).

כבוד אב ואם

33

כבוד חכמים וזקנים
Honoring Torah Scholars and the Elderly

2 Av	2 Kislev	2 Nisan

Honoring Hashem by Honoring His Representatives

"This is my first encounter with such a crowd," Tal confided to his friendly seatmate at the grand *Siyum HaShas.* The tall, swarthy fellow, his obviously new *kippah* perched precariously on his mass of black curls, seemed a bit ill at *ease.* "I actually just joined the *shiur* in the Tel Aviv *Beit Knesset* near my job a few months ago. I had to say *Kaddish* for my father, and when I began to appear there regularly, the Rav roped me in for his *shiur.*"

"I'm sure you'll find the gathering very inspiring, even if you haven't finished *Shas*—yet…" the *avreich* assured him with a wink.

Suddenly there was a growing rustle as all those present jumped to their feet.

"What happened?" Tal asked with concern as he too stood up. "Is there a '*chefetz chashud*'—a suspicious object? Could it be a bomb?"

"Calm down; it's nothing of the sort," his neighbor assured him with a smile. "That was only an 'explosion' of honor for the King's representatives."

"King? What king?" Tal was confused.

"The *Gedolim*—the great *talmidei chachamim* of our time—just

stepped into the hall. These spiritual giants, who teach our generation Torah, are the representatives of Hashem, the King of Kings. Isn't it appropriate that we accord them the honor that is due them?"

THE MAIN PURPOSE of Man's creation was so that he should honor and
sanctify Hashem, and the primary means for ensuring the service of
Hashem — fearing Him and fulfilling His *mitzvos* — are the Torah scholars, who uphold this purpose throughout the generations. By honoring
talmidei chachamim, we proclaim our awareness of and appreciation
for *avodas Hashem* — Hashem's service. Conversely, if, *chas veshalom*,
we show a lack of respect for *talmidei chachamim*, or despise them, such
reprehensible conduct goes far beyond the mere violation of the *mitzvah*
of honoring these individuals.

There are several *mitzvos* associated with this topic: honoring
talmidei chachamim; standing up for them — an obligation that we must
fulfill toward all elderly people as well; the prohibition of degrading
or despising a *talmid chacham*; and the positive *mitzvah* of clinging
to a *talmid chacham* and benefiting him in various ways. (*Mishpetei
Hashalom*, chapter 22: Preface)

Reverence   THE TORAH TELLS us, "*Es Hashem Elokecha tira* — Fear
and Love   Hashem, your G-d" (*Devarim* 6:13). From the seemingly
              extraneous word "*es*" (which often means "with" or "in ad-
dition to"), *Chazal* derive that *talmidei chachamim* are also included; there
is a *mitzvah de'Oraisa* to fear and revere them, just as we fear Hashem.

According to the *Sefer Hachareidim*, the same reasoning would require us to love *talmidei chachamim*, since the *passuk* tells us, "*Ve'ahavta
es Hashem Elokecha* — Love Hashem your G-d" (*Devarim* 6:4), using the
same word "*es*."

These *mitzvos* apply at all times and in all places and are incumbent
upon men and women alike. Children should be trained in honoring
talmidei chachamim from a young age. Traditionally, whenever a great
talmid chacham would come to town, the pious fathers and mothers
would bring their children, even toddlers, to get a glimpse of his holy
face and absorb the aura of reverence accorded to Torah scholars.
(*Mishpetei Hashalom* 22:1)

Varying Levels THE DETAILED *HALACHOS* of these *mitzvos* vary, depending on the nature of our relationship to the *talmid chacham*, and also depending on the level of the *talmid chacham* himself:

- A *rebbe muvhak*, defined as our principal mentor, from whom we have attained most of our knowledge in any particular area of Torah.

- A *rebbe* from whom we have learned even a minimal amount.

- Any *talmid chacham*.

- Our **Torah colleagues**.

- Our **students and disciples**.

- A **scholar who has forgotten his Torah knowledge**. *Chazal* say that we must be careful with such a person's honor even after he has lost his *chochmah*, as we learn from the fact that the broken *luchos* were placed in the *aron* alongside the whole, second set of *luchos*.

- Even if a ***talmid chacham* has become corrupt**, we may not disgrace him in public.

- A ***Gadol Hador***, who is recognized as being greater and more knowledgeable than the other Rabbanim of his generation, falls into the category of a *rebbe muvhak*, even if we did not personally learn anything from him. Thus, for example, we may not contradict his words. (*Mishpetei Hashalom* 22:2)

Honoring and Retrieving His Lost Item SOME OBLIGATIONS TOWARD a rebbe exceed those toward a parent, since a parent brings us into this world, while the rebbe brings us into the Next World. *Chazal* advise us (*Avos* 4:12) that the fear we feel toward a rebbe should be comparable to our *mora Shamayim*, our fear of Heaven.

One application of the above principle is in the order of precedence we are to give in fulfilling the *mitzvah* of *hashavas aveidah*, returning a lost item. If we come across a lost item of our own along with an item belonging to a parent and another belonging to our rebbe, and

circumstances do not allow us to retrieve them all, then retrieving our own item takes precedence, as the Gemara derives from a *passuk*. However, if we encounter one item belonging to our father and one belonging to our rebbe and cannot retrieve both, then our rebbe's item comes first, unless the father is an equally great scholar, in which case the father's lost item would take precedence.

Similarly, in a case of redeeming captives, the rebbe should generally be redeemed first; however, if the father is a *talmid chacham* as well, even if he is not on a par with the rebbe, we must redeem our father first. According to most opinions, the same applies in a case of assisting with loading or unloading, when both are carrying a burden. Since there is physical strain involved, the learned father takes precedence, even if his level of knowledge does not exceed that of the rebbe.

In all of these cases, some opinions maintain that precedence is given only to a Rebbe who teaches free of charge, but if the father pays the rebbe to teach his son, and the rebbe would not have learned with him otherwise, then the father is, in essence, the one to take credit for his son's Torah-learning, and he takes precedence in all situations. Some even go so far as to say that an unrelated individual who undertakes to pay the rebbe would be given precedence over both the parent and the rebbe when it comes to returning his lost item, as well as in all the other *mitzvos* we have discussed above. (The *poskim* speak very highly of those who cover the cost of tuition to enable poor children to learn Torah; some people do not realize that such support is considered even more important than building shuls.) (*Mishpetei Hashalom* 22:3–5)

| 4 Av | 4 Kislev | 4 Nisan |

Reverence for One's Rebbe THE OBLIGATION TO revere one's rebbe is not just a matter of attitude; as we saw in *kibbud-* and *mora av*, here too, our behavior must reflect that attitude. A number of *halachos* guide us in shaping our conduct toward the rebbe.

It should be noted that while some of the gestures of respect we will mention apply to any rebbe, many of those gestures enumerated here are applicable only to a *rebbe muvhak*, someone from whom we have attained most of our knowledge in any particular area of Torah, be it in the written Torah, in Mishnah or in Gemara. In our times, this definition does not apply to the one who taught us *pilpul* and *chilukim* — engaging in challenging and stimulating mind exercises in comparing and contrasting different sources in Gemara. Rather, it would refer to the one who taught us *halachah* and gave us a deep comprehension of the Gemara, putting us on the path of straight and true Torah understanding, or the rebbe who taught us how to derive the correct *halachah* from the source.

Some opinions maintain that in our times, the concept of a *rebbe muvhak* does not exist at all; others state that a person may have more than one *rebbe muvhak*. In any case, as we have mentioned, a *Gadol Hador*, who towers above those of his generation in his Torah knowledge, is to be regarded by everyone as a *rebbe muvhak*, and all the relevant gestures of respect apply.

If someone argues with his rebbe, complains about him, or even entertains doubts about him, it is considered as if his actions or thoughts were directed toward the *Shechinah*.

A *talmid* may not establish a *yeshivah* for the purpose of lecturing, teaching or making *halachic* rulings, even in another country, unless he obtains his rebbe's permission. Never may the *talmid* give a *halachic* ruling in his rebbe's presence, unless there is an urgent need to stop someone from committing an *aveirah*. However, the *talmid* may respectfully differ with his rebbe regarding a particular ruling or teaching if he has a sound basis for his opinion.

A *talmid* may not confer *semichas Rabbanim*, rabbinical ordination, on his own students in the presence of his rebbe. (The complex *halachic* details relating to this issue are elaborated on in *Yoreh Dei'ah* 242.)

A *talmid* may not call his rebbe by his first name, even after he has passed away. Nor should he call others by their first names in front of his rebbe if their name is the same as that of his rebbe. If the name is an uncommon one, he should not call others by that name even when his rebbe is not present.

When not in the rebbe's presence, the *talmid* may say "*rabbi umori ploni* — my rebbe and my teacher, so-and-so [using his first name]," but in front of the rebbe, even that is not permitted; he should simply say,

"Rebbe." If the rebbe is his father, some say that he is permitted to call him Abba.

When we greet our rebbe, we should not speak in the same informal tone we would use with anyone else. Rather, we should greet him respectfully and with a tone of reverence. When dining with him, we should conduct ourselves as if we were sitting at a table with the king. *Tefillin* should not be removed when we are facing our rebbe, since it would be considered disrespectful to stand bareheaded before him; rather, we should turn aside and remove our *tefillin* some distance away from him.

When *davening*, we should not stand directly in front or in back of our rebbe, or even within four *amos* (about six feet) of his side. Nor should we enter a bathhouse or *mikveh* together with the rebbe unless we are needed there to assist him.

We should not take a seat in the rebbe's presence, nor should we get up when we have been sitting, without the rebbe's permission. When departing from him we should not turn our back in his direction but should rather face the rebbe while backing away humbly. If we need to leave town, we should first request permission from our rebbe. (*Mishpetei Hashalom* 22:6–9, 13)

5 Av	5 Kislev	5 Nisan

Additional Applications of Mora

WHEN WE WALK with our rebbe, we should not walk either right alongside him or directly behind him, but rather slightly after him at a diagonal. When two disciples accompany the rebbe, the more important one should be to his right and the lesser one to his left. When a *talmid* walks alone with his rebbe, the rebbe should be at the right and the *talmid* at the left. Some opinions say that this applies when walking with anyone who is greater in Torah stature than us, not only our rebbe. When we reach a doorway, the rebbe or greater person should walk in first.

We may not sit in our rebbe's place, nor contradict him, nor even pass favorable judgment on his words in his presence; these *halachos* apply to our rebbe just as they do to our parents, as we discussed in the chapter on honoring parents (chapter 32). If we see our rebbe doing an act that is definitely contrary to a *mitzvah* of the Torah, or that is even a violation of a Rabbinical prohibition, we should say delicately, "Rebbe, you taught us such and such…" When the rebbe is doing something that we suspect may be prohibited, but we are not certain about it, then our reaction depends on the severity of the prohibition: If a Torah *issur* is involved, we should stop the rebbe and question him before he goes ahead with the possible transgression. However, if the prohibition is a *deRabbanan* — a less severe Rabbinical one — then our Torah obligation of reverence demands that we first allow him to go ahead with the dubious act, and only afterward ask questions.

6 Av	6 Kislev	6 Nisan

A *talmid* should serve his rebbe as a servant serves his master. A rebbe who prevents his *talmid* from serving him deprives him of an opportunity for *chessed* and undermines the *talmid*'s *yiras Shamayim*. A *talmid* who belittles any aspect of the honor that is his rebbe's due causes the *Shechinah* to depart from *Klal Yisrael*, and if the *talmid* is so lowly as to spit before his rebbe, he falls into the category of an adversary of Hashem, of whom it is said, "All who hate Me love death" (*Mishlei* 8:36).

A rebbe — even a *rebbe muvhak* — may be *mochel* — forgo — all or some of the gestures of respect that are his due, relieving one particular *talmid*, or all of them, from these obligations. However, even if the rebbe was *mochel*, the *talmid* should still stand up for him and should certainly not disgrace him. *Chazal* said that we should honor even a *talmid*: "Your *talmid*'s honor should be as dear to you as your own" (*Avos* 4:15). How much more should we honor our rebbe, even if he has excused us from the requisite gestures of *kavod*.

Even the rebbes who taught us *alef-beis* and *Chumash* are deserving of our respect. Similarly, a *talmid chacham*, though he may long since have surpassed his mentors in all areas of Torah, should still treat even his early rebbes with some gestures of respect, even though they do not by any means fall into the category of *rebbei'im muvhakim*.

A *talmid* who lives far away should make a point of visiting his rebbe every Yom Tov. If his place of residence is not so distant, he should visit the rebbe once a week or once a month, and if they live in the same town he should make a point of seeing his rebbe every day. (*Mishpetei Hashalom* 22:10–12, 14–16)

| 7 Av | 7 Kislev | 7 Nisan |

"Mipnei Seivah Takum, Vehadarta Penei Zakein"

"Shloimy, come here," Shauli called softly to his friend as he walked down the aisle of the bus. "I saved a seat for you."

"Thanks, Shauli." Shloimy sank gratefully into the seat. "I'm really exhausted. What a test that was! I thought my hand would go numb, writing for an hour-and-a-half straight."

Moments after sitting down, Shloimy jumped to his feet. Shauli opened his mouth to ask what happened when he saw an older gentleman sliding into the seat Shloimy had vacated.

A few stops later the two boys got off the bus. As they walked home together, Shauli asked, "Shloimy, why did you get up for that man? You yourself told me how tired you were. And I'm not even sure that fellow is *shomer Shabbos.*"

"It's true that I'm really knocked out," Shloimy agreed. "But my father once told me that as long as I don't know for a fact that the older person is a deliberate *rasha* — and that's hardly ever the case — I should stand up for him, especially in a public place, where other people are watching. If he takes the opportunity to sit in my seat, that's all right; I can manage to stay on my feet for a few more minutes, till I get home. It's better than staying in my seat and maybe missing a *mitzvah* of '*mipnei seivah takum*' — and maybe even causing a *chillul Hashem, chas veshalom!*"

THE TORAH TELLS us, "*Mipnei seivah takum, vehadarta penei zakein* — Rise before an elderly person, and honor the presence of a *zakein*" (*Vayikra* 19). *Chazal* explain the word "*zakein*" as an acronym for "*Zeh sheKaNah chochmah*" — one who has acquired wisdom. From this *passuk* we learn that there is a *mitzvah* to stand upright out of respect before every *talmid chacham*, even if he is very young and even if we have not learned anything from him directly; we have to stand up for him simply because he is more knowledgeable in Torah than the average person, and there is much that we can learn from him.

The wife of a *talmid chacham* is known as an *aishes chaveir*; since she is an inseparable partner in her husband's Torah, we are obligated to rise for her as long as her husband is alive. Even after his death, we should still show her a certain amount of respect.

Girls should stand up for their *limudei kodesh* teachers and accord them the necessary respect. Though they may not bear the title of "*talmidei chachamim*," they are certainly more knowledgeable in Torah than their students and are a source of Torah wisdom and inspiration for the girls.

8 Av	8 Kislev	8 Nisan

There is a separate positive *mitzvah* to stand up for the elderly, including any man or woman age seventy or over, even if he is an ignorant person, as long as he is not a *rasha*. Likewise, we are obliged to honor him, and to speak to him kindly and with respect. Present-day *halachic* authorities say we are not obligated to honor an elderly man whom we know does not put on *tefillin* or *daven* every day. If we wish to show him respect, however, we are allowed to do so, unless he is a deliberate sinner who transgresses for no apparent personal benefit, in which case we may not accord him any respect at all.

Even an elderly gentile deserves a degree of respect, since the years have given him a wealth of experiences, much suffering, many miracles and much knowledge. Therefore, we should speak to him respectfully, offer him an arm to lean on and show him other such gestures. (*Mishpetei Hashalom* 22:17–18, 29)

Standing Up — When and How   THE TORAH OBLIGATION to stand up out of respect requires us to rise to our feet as a gesture of honor and to remain standing until the person either sits down or moves out of our *dalet* (four) *amos*. This does not include any obligation to give a *talmid chacham* or an elderly person our seat on a bus, for example. (Of course, since in any case we have to remain standing until the person sits down, and our seat is likely to be the closest available one, his taking our seat would often be the outcome of our standing up for him.) In any case, though giving up our seat is not part of the core obligation of "*mipnei seivah takum,*" it is certainly a fulfillment of the general requirement to show these people respect, and it is also an act of *gemilus chessed.*

When in public, where there is the risk of causing a *chillul Hashem,* we should certainly go beyond the letter of the law and give our seat to the *talmid chacham* or to the elderly person, and we should also do so for a woman who is expecting or a disabled person, if only out of *derech eretz* and basic decency.

9 Av	9 Kislev	9 Nisan

The obligation to stand up begins when the person comes within our *dalet amos* — a distance of about six feet — and not before that, since only then is it clear that we are getting up in his honor. However, when a *talmid chacham* enters a large hall, the *minhag* is that everyone rises together, without waiting until the *talmid chacham* is within his immediate area, since remaining seated when others are rising might be perceived as a slight to the *talmid chacham.* We should not sit down again until the person is no longer in front of us. When the person is riding on a bicycle or being wheeled in a wheelchair, then even though he is in a sitting position he is considered as one who is walking, and we are obligated to stand up for him.

Regarding a *rebbe muvhak* or a *Gadol Hador,* it is not enough to wait until he has passed by; we should remain standing as long as we can still see him, or until he has taken a seat. The same applies for the town's Rav in his town, and for the *Rosh Yeshivah* in his *yeshivah.*

The *passuk* that requires us to stand before a *talmid chacham* and the elderly concludes with the words "*Veyareisa mei'Elokecha* — You shall fear Hashem." From here we learn that we may not close our eyes and pretend we do not know he is there before the person comes within our *dalet amos,* in order to avoid the need to stand up for him. "Fear Hashem" — Hashem knows our intentions in closing our eyes and will hold us responsible for evading the *mitzvah.* In any case, if we know that a *talmid chacham* or elderly person is coming, closing our eyes does not excuse us from standing up, since even a blind person must stand up for such people. (*Mishpetei Hashalom* 22:17–20)

Limitations of ACCORDING TO SOME opinions, students in a *ye-*
the Obligation *shivah* have to stand up for their rebbe only once in
the morning and once at night. However, if there are
others present who may not know that they have already stood up, the
students should rise for the rebbe again.

When they are each in a different *reshus* — a halachically separate
area, such as in another room or even at the *bimah* in shul when it
is fenced off by a railing that is 10 *tefachim* (approximately 3 feet)
high — the *talmid* does not have to stand up for his rebbe, and certainly
not for a different *talmid chacham*.

10 Av	10 Kislev	10 Nisan

In the bathroom or bathhouse, we do not stand up for a *talmid
chacham* or an elderly person, since the reason for rising is to accord
him respect, and there is nothing respectful about standing up for him
in such a place. However, in an outer chamber of these rooms, where
people are fully clothed, we would be required to stand up.

When someone stands up for us, we may tell him "*Sheiv* — Be seated."
However, if the person who got up is a mourner or is sick, we should not
use such a phrase, since it could imply, "Sit and remain in your mourning," or "… in your illness." Actually, the mourner or the sick person is
not obligated to get up at all, even for a great leader of *Klal Yisrael*.

Some say that we are not obligated to stand up for our rebbe on
Tishah B'Av; however, the latter *poskim* disagree and assert that the
prevalent *minhag*, both in Eretz Yisrael and elsewhere, is to stand up
for *Rabbanim* and *talmidei chachamim* on Tishah B'Av, just as we would
on any other day. Some opinions maintain that a person holding a *sefer
Torah* need not stand up for his rebbe. (*Mishpetei Hashalom* 22:21–23)

Loss of Income and SELF-EMPLOYED WORKERS WHO are busy with
Tircha Detzibura their work — such as diamond cutters, *sofrim* or
barbers — are not obligated to stop their work to
stand up for someone if they will suffer a loss as a result. This is because the same principle applies here as it does for *kibud av*: We are not
required to lose money in order to fulfill this *mitzvah*. If such workers

wish to, however, they may be stringent and stand up. But if the worker is an employee, he is not permitted to stop his work and stand up, since he will be causing an illegitimate loss to his employer. However, when a person is learning Torah, he should interrupt his learning to stand up for a *talmid chacham*.

The *talmid chacham* himself should try to avoid *tircha detzibura* — troubling a crowd to stand up for him. Therefore, when he has to pass through an area where people are sitting, he should take the shortest route so as to minimize the bother that the people are caused. If he can take a roundabout route that will not pass by the people at all, it would be commendable for him to do so in order to spare the people the inconvenience of standing up for him.

11 Av	11 Kislev	11 Nisan

Talmidei chachamim may go in and out of their seats to serve public needs — such as to go to deliver a *shiur* or to take care of a *devar mitzvah* — even though this will entail troubling the crowd to stand up for them as they pass. Likewise, a *talmid chacham* may leave his place if necessary in order to relieve himself; these are situations that cannot be avoided. However, he should make every effort not to arrive late at a function, after everyone has been seated, since this will inevitably upset the decorum by requiring all those seated to rise so that he can gain entrance.

Talmidei chachamim and elderly people may forgo the honor of having people stand up for them; even if they do, however, we should still honor them and rise slightly, out of respect for them. (*Mishpetei Hashalom* 22:24–27)

Family of the CHILDREN OF COMMUNITY leaders, public speak-
Talmid Chacham ers or the elderly may accompany their parents to their places of honor, remain with them to be available to attend to their needs, and go in and out of their places as necessary for that purpose. However, *talmidei chachamim* who do not hold a public position may not seat their children in the honored section at their side.

When two brothers are both engaged to be married, we should not schedule the younger brother's wedding before that of the elder, even if the younger one is a greater *talmid chacham* than his older sibling. However, when the older brother is delayed in finding a *shidduch*, whatever the reason, and especially when it is because of his own excessive choosiness, he may not stop his younger brother from marrying first. Nevertheless, this is a very delicate matter, and circumstances may differ. Therefore, the question of when to pass over the older sibling should always be brought before a competent Rav. (*Mishpetei Hashalom* 22:28–29)

12 Av	12 Kislev	12 Nisan

A Talmid Chacham and WHEN BOTH A *talmid chacham* and an
an Elderly Person — elderly person are present, or when two
Who Comes First? people of similar stature are in the same
place, the question of who takes precedence becomes a bit more complex. The basic guidelines are as follows:

◻ A young person who is a *talmid chacham* should stand up for an elderly person who is equal to him in wisdom. However, if the younger person is more learned than the older one, he need not rise to his full height; it is sufficient to rise slightly, as a gesture of respect.

◻ Two *talmidei chachamim* or two elderly people do not have to rise to their full height before each other. However, they should rise slightly for one another. A Rav may rise slightly, out of respect for any *talmid*.

◻ Even an extremely knowledgeable *talmid chacham* is permitted — and some say even obligated — to stand up for a *baal maasim* — someone who is known for his extensive good deeds; but the *talmid chacham* may not belittle his Torah by standing up for anyone who is not learned, other than a *baal maasim*.

◻ When an extremely learned young person and a slightly learned elderly person are in the same place, then the *halachah* differs, depending on the milieu: If they are sitting together at a Torah gathering (such as a Torah lecture, a *halachic* discussion or a meeting of *beis din*), then the honor of the *talmid chacham* takes precedence; he should sit at the head of the table and be given the privilege of speaking first. However, at a social gathering, such as a wedding meal or some other festive *seudah*, the elderly person takes precedence.

□ If the *talmid chacham* is exceptionally learned and the elderly person is not extremely old, the *talmid chacham* is always given preference — both at a Torah assemblage and at a social gathering. If the older person is truly aged, and the *talmid chacham* is not exceptional in his wisdom, then the elderly person is always given first honors, as long as he is slightly learned.

□ When neither of them is either extremely old or exceptionally knowledgeable, the elderly person who is even slightly learned takes precedence in every situation, even if the young *talmid chacham* is more knowledgeable than he is. However, there are differing opinions on this last point; some maintain that in Torah gatherings the ordinary *talmid chacham* would still come first. (*Mishpetei Hashalom* 22:30–35)

| 13 Av | 13 Kislev | 13 Nisan |

Exemption from Community Taxation   TALMIDEI CHACHAMIM WHO are in the category of *Toraso umanuso* — occupied in full-time learning — are halachically exempt from all kinds of community tax levies, both general and personal. Even if the town ruler specifically sets a head tax on the *talmid chacham*, the community is obliged to pay it on his behalf. However, the *talmid chacham* is responsible to contribute his part for city services, such as water supply, drainage, road construction, street lighting, etc. This is true, however, only when the community contributes money, and workers are hired to do the actual labor. When the residents of the city personally take their turns at these jobs, the *talmid chacham* is exempt from participating. The one city service toward which the *talmid chacham* need not contribute is the cost of security, since *talmidei chachamim* are protected by their Torah and do not need guarding.

A *talmid chacham* who is lightly involved in a trade, profession or business as a means of support is still eligible for an exemption from taxes, as long as:

1. The work is not for the purpose of making him rich but just to ensure that he has an adequate livelihood.
2. When he is not involved in his business, he does not fritter his time away in idle occupations but rather immediately resumes his diligent learning.

In such a case, it is obvious that Torah study is the main focus of his day, and we consider it as *Toraso umanuso*, despite his side-occupation.

Even if a person does not hold a Torah position, such as community Rabbi or *yeshivah* teacher, as long as he is recognized among the people of the community as a *talmid chacham* with an ability to carry on a Torah interchange, and he has a fair level of understanding in most of the Talmud and commentaries and in the *poskim*, he is considered a *talmid chacham* for these purposes. Nowadays there are varying customs related to this topic; however, in most communities, a Rav or *dayan* who is provided for by the community, or any other *talmid chacham* who is totally involved in Torah learning and is supported by his wife or by someone else, would be exempt from taxes. (*Mishpetei Hashalom* 22:36–37)

| 14 Av | 14 Kislev | 14 Nisan |

Precedence to the Talmid Chacham

It was a frigid, gray winter morning, so it came as no surprise to Mrs. Fried that the waiting room at the doctor's office was packed to the gills. Dr. Weinstein worked on a first come, first served basis in the mornings. That saved patients the trouble of trying to get through to the office to make an appointment, but on a day like this, it could mean as much as a two-hour wait.

As efficient as the well-meaning secretary tried to be, there were inevitable clashes. "Don't you hear how my baby is wheezing? You must let us go ahead!" "Why did he go in first? I've been waiting here much longer than he has!" The secretary made a vain attempt to explain that the other

patient had been at the door of the clinic even before it was opened; she had sent him home to rest until his turn, because he was dizzy with fever. Other complaints arose in the course of the long waiting period, interspersed with frequent coughs and sneezes.

There was only one incident that went by without a peep on anyone's part: The door opened at 11 a.m. and in walked Rabbi Rosenfeld, the revered *Rosh Yeshivah*. Everyone rose in his honor, and a seat was quickly arranged for him. The next time the doctor's door swung open, the secretary ushered Rabbi Rosenfeld in, and amazingly enough, not a single complaint was voiced; everyone knew that a *talmid chacham* should not have to wait!

IN THE DAYS when community leaders had control of the market, they would not allow anyone to sell merchandise until the *talmidei chachamim* had successfully sold all of their stock. Nowadays there is no such control over the market; therefore, such a rule would not benefit the *talmid chacham*; it would just cause a loss to the other vendors.

Precedence is given to the *talmid chacham* in disbursement of *tzedakah*, as well as in *matnos kehunah* — the allotments set aside for the *kohanim*.

A *talmid chacham* is also given precedence in the *beis din*. If he arrives for a *din Torah* with someone else, his case is pushed ahead of other cases that may have arrived at the *beis din* before his. Other privileges are also given to the *talmid chacham* in court; for example, he may remain seated during the judgment or when taking an oath, while others are required to stand. Of course, this requires a delicate balance since, on the one hand, we have to be careful not to distort the *din* by our preferential treatment of the *talmid chacham*, and on the other hand, we are required to accord him the requisite honor.

Likewise, in all situations where there is a queue, whether at the home of the Rav to ask a question in *halachah*, at the doctor's office or at the butcher shop, a *talmid chacham*, or even his emissary, should be given a turn before everyone else. At the Torah reading the *talmid chacham* should be given an *aliyah* that bears more honor.

Other areas of precedence, such as in *bentching* and in leading the *davening*, are discussed in the next chapter. (*Mishpetei Hashalom* 22:38–39)

Severity of Degrading a Talmid Chacham DEGRADING OR DESPISING a *talmid chacham* is an extremely severe transgression. Someone who degrades a *talmid chacham* is considered an *apikorus*, loses his portion in the World to Come and is almost beyond hope of correction. "*Ki Devar Hashem bazah* — He has disgraced the Word of Hashem" (*Bamidbar* 15:31) and violated the positive *mitzvos* of *es Hashem Elokecha tira* (*Vayikra* 19:32) — fearing Hashem, and *vehadarta penei zaken* (ibid.) — honoring the presence of a *talmid chacham*. Yerushalayim was not destroyed until the people became guilty of disgracing *talmidei chachamim*. Considering the severity of the matter, we have to be exceptionally careful not to speak with chutzpah toward our Rabbanim and Torah teachers, and not to shame them in any way; such an act toward any Jew is an *aveirah*, but it is even more serious when done to a *talmid chacham*.

As we have mentioned, a *talmid chacham* who has forgotten his Torah knowledge should still be treated with respect, and even a *talmid chacham* who has become corrupt may not be degraded publicly.

Even if we do not say a word against the *talmid chacham*, if we hear someone else speak against him and remain silent, without voicing our protest, the punishment for such silence is very severe.

If we speak or hear *lashon hara* or *rechilus* about a *talmid chacham* or an elderly person in his presence, or if we hurt him with our words or engage in a quarrel with him, and certainly if we strike, curse or degrade him, then in addition to all of the relevant *mitzvos* violated, we also violate the positive *mitzvah* of *vehadarta*, since if we belittle or hurt him, we obviously cannot be honoring him at the same time. If the victim is both elderly and a *talmid chacham*, then we commit a double violation. If these violations are done when we are not in the person's presence, they are still serious *aveiros*.

In earlier generations, anyone who shamed a *talmid chacham* was heavily fined, in the amount of a certain weight of gold. Nowadays the *beis din* sets the fine, depending on who is the one who shamed the other and who has been shamed. This is only in a case where the *talmid chacham* did not initiate the argument or shame the other person,

leading the victim to react against him. Nevertheless, even if the *talmid chacham* instigated the quarrel in some small measure, the other person is not permitted to respond with chutzpah. The *beis din* has to consider the circumstances and set or nullify the fine accordingly.

When witnesses have testified that someone degraded a *talmid chacham*, even with words alone, and even in his absence or after his death, that person is put into *nidui* until he has conciliated the *talmid chacham* and done *teshuvah*. The *talmid chacham* himself can put an ignoramus who offended his honor into *nidui*, even without witnesses and a prior warning. On the other hand, he may forgo his honor and forgive the offense — and it is commendable to do so — as long as the incident took place in private. However, if the offender degraded him in public the *talmid chacham* may not forgo his honor. He should be "as vengeful as a snake" for the sake of *kavod haTorah*, until the offender asks his forgiveness; at that point, he should be quick to forgive and forget. (*Mishpetei Hashalom* 22:40, 43–45)

16 Av	16 Kislev	16 Nisan

Using the Services of a Talmid Chacham

ASKING A *TALMID CHACHAM* to do a menial task on our behalf distracts him from his learning and is disrespectful of his position and is therefore forbidden. Some opinions maintain that if the *talmid chacham* wishes to do this task for his own benefit, or if he does so for a livelihood, it is permissible to use his services; otherwise, it would appear that his Torah learning is working against him. Even if he forgoes this honor and insists that we should feel free to call on him for his services, we should not do so, unless he comes forward of his own accord to help.

Therefore, when a *talmid chacham* comes to a place where people do not know him, he may inform them of his Torah stature to prevent them from transgressing by inadvertently offending his honor or using his services. This is not considered "taking advantage of his Torah," even though the outcome will be that they will honor him as a result of his declaration. However, if they know who he is and there is no need to make a point of his scholarship, he should not flaunt his knowledge,

as we learn from the *passuk*, "*Yehalelucha zar velo ficha* — Let another person sing your praises, and not your own mouth" (*Mishlei* 27:2). Furthermore, in spite of the honor accorded the *talmid chacham*, he should be careful not to boast, act in a superior, lording manner, or belittle the ignorant. (*Mishpetei Hashalom* 22:41–42)

17 Av	17 Kislev	17 Nisan

Beneath His Dignity IN CERTAIN CASES, a *talmid chacham* and an elderly person would be exempt from a *mitzvah* if fulfilling it would be beneath their dignity. If, for example, a *talmid chacham* or an elderly person comes across a lost article that he would be embarrassed to be seen with, like a trash bag or a sock, he has to honestly assess the situation: If he is sure that, had the item belonged to him, he would have forgone his honor and retrieved it, he should do so for others as well. If he would have opted to give up on the item rather than retrieve it personally, he is exempt from returning it to someone else.

This is the basic *halachah*; however, a person should go beyond the letter of the law and return every lost item that he finds, even when it may be beneath his dignity. There are two opinions in this matter:

1. The Rambam applies this *din* to both the *talmid chacham* and the elderly person.

2. The Rosh applies it only to an elderly person or other dignified gentleman. In regard to the *talmid chacham*, however, the Rosh stresses that once the Torah exempted him from the obligation, he has no right to belittle the Torah's honor and return the lost item. On the other hand, he shouldn't just walk on and callously ignore his friend's loss. Rather, he should take money from his own pocket and compensate the person for his loss, so that the person who lost the item will not suffer damage. For example, if he wishes he can purchase the item from the person who lost it, and if he doesn't need it, he may then declare the item *hefker* — ownerless.

The same *din* applies in the *mitzvah* of loading and unloading, and in other *mitzvos* dealing with the money and property of others, where

the obligation flows from the general *mitzvah* of *ve'ahavta lerei'acha kamocha*. Since this is the root of the obligation, the Torah exempts the *talmid chacham* from doing anything for his fellow that he would not have done even for himself.

However, when it comes to a *davar shebikdushah* — such as building a sukkah, drawing water for matzah baking or making preparations for Shabbos — the *talmid chacham* may forgo his honor and perform tasks that are beneath his dignity, for the sake of the honor of Hashem.

The same may be applied to *mitzvos bein adam lechaveiro* that do not involve money, such as visiting the sick, burying the dead and gladdening the *chassan* and *kallah*. Throughout the generations, the greatest of our Sages have lowered their own dignity in order to fulfill these *mitzvos*, bolstered by the principle that whoever treats his own honor lightly in order to do a *mitzvah* and honor Hashem is worthy of praise. *(Mishpetei Hashalom 22:46–48)*

18 Av	18 Kislev	18 Nisan

Attaching Ourselves to Talmidei Chachamim

"Yossi, I see you're making the rounds again. Who is it this time?" Dovid asked his friend, whom he noticed sitting at the wheel of his parked car, obviously waiting for someone.

"Ah, this week I have the *zechus* of accompanying Reb Baruch, from Yeshivas Ohr HaTorah in Yerushalayim." Yossi sounded like he felt as fortunate as if he had won the grand lottery.

"But tell me, Yossi — how can you walk out on your business for hours at a time to accompany these assorted *talmidei chachamim* on their collection rounds? Even with your dedicated employees taking your place, I'm sure the business suffers from your frequent absences. Why don't you let them take a paid driver?"

"What? And lose the opportunity of spending hours in the company of these great people, basking in their Torah and gaining from their every word? My business will manage; more important to me is the business of associating with *talmidei chachamim*!"

THERE IS A positive *mitzvah* of the Torah to cling to *talmidei chachamim* and their *talmidim* in order to learn from their ways, as the *passuk* states, "*Uvo sidbak* — Cling to Him" (*Devarim* 10:20 and 11:22). *Chazal* ask: "How can we possibly cling to the *Shechinah* itself?" When we cling to a *talmid chacham*, they conclude, it is as if we are clinging to the *Shechinah*.

Therefore, we are obligated to take every opportunity to associate ourselves with *talmidei chachamim*: to marry the daughter of a *talmid chacham*, to take a *talmid chacham* as a son-in-law, to eat and drink with *talmidei chachamim*, to do business with them and on their behalf, and to attach ourselves to them in every possible way. *Chazal* tell us (*Avos* 1:4) to "sit in the dust of their feet and drink in their words thirstily." We should foster a love for them in our hearts and do whatever is in our power to benefit them in every way, since they are the ones who uphold Torah and serve as the firm foundation for the redemption of the souls of all of *Klal Yisrael*, and through the conduit of their Torah, we can learn how to follow the ways of Hashem.

We should make every effort to receive *talmidei chachamim* who arrive in town and to be at their service, since *Chazal* teach us that serving a *talmid chacham* — which enables us to imbibe the *talmid chacham*'s ways — is even greater than learning Torah from him directly. For the same reason, we should try to raise our children in the environs of a *talmid chacham*, so that this will influence their spiritual growth.

Great care should be taken not to cause pain or discomfort to a *talmid chacham*, even in error. Our love for the *talmid chacham* should be as intense as the love of a father for his child. The Sages say that one who loves a *talmid chacham* merits children who are *talmidei chachamim*. On the other hand, as we mentioned earlier, there is a particular *issur* to hate *talmidei chachamim*.

When we are faced with two groups of people — one comprised of *talmidei chachamim*, and the other of people engaging in idle talk about the latest news or speaking *lashon hara* and engaging in other forbidden talk — we should make a point of associating with the group of *talmidei chachamim*. If we deliberately choose to join the other group, then, in addition to the other *aveiros* we are likely to commit, we will also have violated the positive *mitzvah* of *uvo sidbak*.

This *mitzvah* applies at all times, in all places, for men and for women, who are commanded to heed the words of *chachamim* in order to learn how to serve Hashem. Children should be trained in this *mitzvah* from a young age. Needless to say, a child should never hear his parents criticizing a *talmid chacham*; on the contrary, he should absorb his parents' eagerness to come to the aid of *talmidei chachamim* and drink in their words of wisdom. *(Mishpetei Hashalom 22:49–50, 52)*

19 Av	19 Kislev	19 Nisan

Value of Clinging to Talmidei Chachamim and Its Reward

THE SAGES ESPECIALLY praised those who carry on business on behalf of a *talmid chacham*, investing his money for him so that he can have ready income and be free to study Torah undisturbed. When someone assists a *talmid chacham* in such a way, it is considered as if he has attached himself to the *Shechinah*. Similarly, *Chazal* say that someone who supplies a *talmid chacham* with profitable merchandise that can provide him with an easy income merits to sit in the "Heavenly Yeshivah" in the World to Come.

We have much to learn even from the casual conversation of a *talmid chacham*, and if we make an effort to understand their "small talk," we will eventually be able to comprehend their *divrei Torah* as well. *Chazal* say that when a person brings a gift to a *talmid chacham* it is as if he brought *bikkurim*, and if he hosts the *talmid chacham* in his home and allows him to benefit from his possessions, it is as if he brought a *korban tamid* — the daily offering in the *Beis Hamikdash*. In contrast, someone who does not endow the *talmid chacham* from his possessions will never see a blessing in his endeavors.

In addition to the obvious benefit that we derive from clinging to a *talmid chacham* — seeing his fine ways, sterling qualities and positive habits, and learning to follow in his footsteps — we will also enjoy the fruits of his company: We will be blessed along with him in this world and will share in his merit in the Next World.

When a person cannot learn on his own — either because he does not know how to learn or because he is preoccupied with other needs — but he has the available resources, he should use his money to support others who are learning; it will then be considered as if he himself learned Torah. We can even draw up an official agreement with

a *talmid chacham* by which we obligate ourselves to provide fully for the *talmid chacham* while he devotes himself to learning, and he agrees to share the rewards. This kind of setup is known as a Yissachar-Zevulun arrangement. (*Mishpetei Hashalom* 22:51, 53)

20 Av	20 Kislev	20 Nisan

The Unworthy Talmid Chacham   A PERSON WHO is learned in Torah but who belittles *mitzvos* and lacks *yiras Shamayim* has placed himself in the lowest category of society, and we are not permitted to honor him in any way. The Gemara says that a *talmid chacham* whose Torah is only skin-deep is not a *talmid chacham* at all; he is called *nis'av* — repulsive — and is worse than someone who never learned Torah at all.

Even though, as we mentioned, the general rule is that a *talmid chacham* who became corrupt should not be humiliated publicly, at times it is necessary to do so in order to prevent the masses from being drawn after him and punished along with him, or in order to prevent him from desecrating the honor of the Torah and detracting from service of Hashem.

Similarly, a *talmid chacham* who is known to be argumentative and to stir up trouble and instigate *machlokos* that are not for constructive purposes does not deserve the honor of our standing up for him. A Rabbi appointed by the government who is not a *Gadol baTorah* is not entitled to put someone in *nidui* for belittling his honor. Needless to say, we have to proceed carefully and ask guidance from respected Rabbanim when relating to such a "Rabbi," who may be ignorant and unworthy of a leadership position but may nevertheless be invested with power to harm those who oppose him. (*Mishpetei Hashalom* 22:54–55)

Consulting with a Talmid Chacham   A TALMID CHACHAM, even if he has clear and accurate opinions, should not speak up before someone who possesses greater Torah knowledge than himself, even if he has never learned anything from that person. Once a Rav has ruled to permit or prohibit something, the ruling stands and we are obligated to carry it out; another Rav may overturn the ruling

only when adhering to a tight set of stringent guidelines. Therefore, in a case when the asker is concerned that a mistake has been made, or when he does not understand the *pesak*, and there is no possibility of his returning to the original Rav, then when he approaches a different Rav, he must inform him that he has already received a ruling on this question.

When a *chacham* arrives, the *talmidim* should not barrage him with questions the moment he walks in. Rather, they should wait until he has seated himself and has had a chance to settle his mind; only then should they approach him, one at a time. A person who enters in the middle of a Torah discussion should not interrupt or express an opinion until he has first listened and understood just what they are discussing and where they are holding.

When a particular *masechta* is being discussed, a *talmid* should not ask about a different *masechta*, as this could confuse the speaker and cause him embarrassment. Similarly, any time the *talmid* suspects that the Rav will not be able to answer his question, he should not ask it, especially in the presence of others. Of course, in some cases the Rav may encourage his students to pose sharp questions; however, this is usually done when everyone is involved in clarifying the same topic together, in a constructive, positive manner, so as to arrive at the true understanding. It must never be done as a sinister way to "trip up" the teacher.

21 Av	21 Kislev	21 Nisan

Generally, the *talmid* should sit when asking a question and the Rav should sit when responding. However, some opinions maintain that when posing a *halachic* question we are required to stand. We should not ask a question from a high place, from a distance, or from behind the heads of elderly people.

When two people come at the same time to ask their questions, the rules of precedence are as follows:

- When one is a *chacham*, or any learned person, and the other is an ignorant person, the *chacham* or learned person comes first.
- Even a *talmid chacham* who is of illegitimate heritage precedes a *kohen* who is an ignoramus.

- If the two are equal in Torah stature, but one has a question of immediate relevance, while the other is asking something that is not of immediate relevance, we give precedence to the former.
- If one is asking a practical question, and the other a theoretical question, the practical question comes first.
- Asking about a *halachah* precedes asking about a *midrash*, and a *midrash* precedes an *aggadah*.

These laws are dealt with at length in *Shulchan Aruch Yoreh Dei'ah* 246.

A *talmid chacham* should not speak in the presence of someone who is greater than he is in wisdom — as we have mentioned. He should not interrupt another's words, nor should he answer impulsively. His questions should be relevant to the subject, and his responses should be accurate. When asked a number of questions, he should relate to first things first and last things last. If there is something he does not know, he should not hesitate to say, "I don't know," and if he errs he should admit it.

The *talmid chacham* bears great responsibility in his words and even in his silence. His words should be phrased in a clear, concise and simple manner. He should make sure to choose his words carefully, so that his answer will not be misunderstood, and he should make sure that no one infers from his silence or from his actions that one should be lenient about any prohibition. When necessary he should explain his actions to those present, so as to avoid their jumping to conclusions about the implications of what he did. (*Mishpetei Hashalom* 22:57–60)

| 22 Av | 22 Kislev | 22 Nisan |

Final Respects ALTHOUGH THERE IS a great *mitzvah* to give a *hesped* — a eulogy — for every *niftar* as he deserves, we have to be especially careful when eulogizing a *talmid chacham*, since there is a specific injunction not to be neglectful about his *hesped*.

There are many joyous days in the year when we may not eulogize a layman but would be required to eulogize a *chacham*. Similarly, a *hesped* may be delivered for *talmidei chachamim* and their wives in a shul or in a *beis medrash*, whereas we may not deliver a *hesped* for others in these places. (For further details on *hesped* and on interrupting Torah learning for the funeral of a *talmid chacham*, see chapter 24.)

> **In summary:** The Torah obligates us to revere and love *talmidei chachamim*, according to the level of their *chochmah* and according to our relationship to them. The Rav is given precedence when it comes to *hashavas aveidah* and redemption from captivity. Applications of our obligation to honor a *talmid chacham* include, among other things, not contradicting his words, not ruling in his presence and not calling him by name. There is an additional *mitzvah* to stand up for a *talmid chacham* and for an elderly person, from the time they enter our four *amos*, until they either pass or sit down. A *talmid chacham* is exempt from community taxes and is given precedence when waiting in line, in *beis din* and in other circumstances. Belittling a *talmid chacham* is a very serious transgression. We may not use the services of a *talmid chacham* unless it is for his benefit. A *talmid chacham* and an elderly person are exempt from certain *mitzvos* when fulfilling them are beneath their dignity. We should try to associate with *talmidei chachamim* and help them in any way possible. Specific guidelines determine the system of asking a *talmid chacham* for a halachic ruling. Great care should be taken to eulogize a *talmid chacham* properly.

"The wisdom of a talmid chacham exceeds the vision of a navi" (Baba Basra 12a).

"Of the talmid chacham it is said, 'And those who love Him are like the rising sun in its glory'" (ibid. 8b).

34

וקדשתו – כבוד כהנים
Honoring Kohanim

First Place — In It was not every day that the Ahavas Achim shul hosted
Every Place such a well-known guest — the mayor of the town, Mr.
Dave Snyder. Snyder's great-nephew, Yaakov Schneider,
was making a bar mitzvah for his son that Shabbos in the shul. Shmuel
Schneider, Yaakov's father, had long been considered the black sheep of his
family — he had begun to wear a black hat and suit, chosen *yeshivah* over
university, and opted for a full Torah life as opposed to the tepid Jewish
home where he had grown up. When Yaakov reached bar-mitzvah age,
Shmuel's father, Allan, suggested that it would be a nice gesture to invite
his brother, the honorable great-uncle, to join them for Shabbos — and to
everyone's great surprise, the mayor accepted.

Mr. Snyder, in deference to the memory of his father, had remained
somewhat traditional. He wouldn't drive on Shabbos, or do any shopping,
and he even made *Kiddush* and *Havdalah*. He wasn't much of a shul-goer,
though, and he wasn't overly familiar with shul procedures. Nevertheless,
he got along fine in Shmuel's shul, managing to retrieve his knowledge
from his Hebrew-school days and follow the *davening*.

The first problem arose when they got to *krias haTorah*. "Oh, do they
read from the Torah now? I remember that from my own bar mitzvah!" The
mayor waited eagerly to be called up to the Torah. He had no doubt that

465

a VIP such as himself would be first to get such an honor; he was used to being treated royally.

"The nerve of that fellow," Snyder muttered under his breath when, to his dismay, someone else was given an *aliyah* before he was. When the *gabbai* summoned a timid young man for the second *aliyah*, passing him by once more, the offended mayor whispered indignantly to his host, "What's going on here? Don't the directors here have any sense of propriety?"

Shmuel motioned politely to his uncle to have patience. Indeed, the *gabbai* awarded him a different honor. After the *davening*, as they walked toward the room where the *kiddush* would be held, Shmuel explained to his less-knowledgeable relative that in every shul around the globe, regardless of which prominent individuals are present at the *minyan*, the first honor is always accorded to a *kohen*, the one who is in the special service of Hashem, followed by the *levi*, his worthy assistant. "Please don't take it personally, Uncle Dave…"

THE *KOHANIM* WERE invested with the privilege of serving Hashem by performing the sacred tasks in the *Beis Hamikdash* on behalf of all of *Klal Yisrael*. An explicit *mitzvah* in the Torah obligates us to sanctify the *kohanim*, even in our times, when the *Beis Hamikdash* is not standing, simply because they are descendants of Aharon Hakohen, as the *passuk* states, "*vekidashto* … — You shall sanctify him, for he offers the food of Hashem" (*Vayikra* 21:8). We are expected to treat a *kohen* with the utmost respect, giving him precedence in all *devarim shebikdushah* — such as calling him up for the first *aliyah* of *krias haTorah* (the Torah reading) and choosing him to lead the *bentching*. The *kohen* is also given the first choice of a portion. Similarly, we should respect the *kohen* in our thoughts and in our speech. If there is no *kohen* present, however, we are not obligated to seek one out in order to honor him.

The honor we accord the *kohen* is actually a show of honor for Hashem, Who took the *kohanim* aside and hand-picked them to be His special servants. Conversely, refraining from giving the *kohen* the respect that is his due is more than a personal affront; it is a desecration of Hashem's honor.

This *mitzvah* applies in all places: even outside of Eretz Yisrael, the place of the *Beis Hamikdash*, and at all times, even when the *Beis Hamikdash* is not standing. The *halachos* are incumbent on men and women;

everyone is equally obligated to honor the descendants of Aharon.

Children should be trained in this *mitzvah* from a young age. For example, even in classes of young preschool children, the boys who are *kohanim* can be given first chance at "leading the *davening*" and can be put at the head of the line for washing *netilas yadayim*. (*Mishpetei Hashalom* 23:1, 19)

| 24 Av | 24 Kislev | 24 Nisan |

Which Kohanim Are Included? EVEN THOUGH *KOHANIM* who suffer from certain physical defects are exempt from serving in the *Beis Hamikdash*, these blemishes do not exempt us from our obligation to honor them. Opinions differ regarding the obligation to honor *kohanim* who are under the age of bar-mitzvah; the preferred approach is to follow the stringent view on this matter.

If a *kohen* marries a woman who is forbidden to him halachically, such as a divorcee, the laws of honoring *kohanim* do not apply to him. Only after he has promised to divorce the woman, has taken an oath not to gain benefit from her or from any woman forbidden to him, and has fully repented is the obligation to honor him reinstated. The same applies to a *kohen* who deliberately makes himself *tamei*, ritually impure, in disregard of the *halachah*, by coming into contact with a *niftar* who is not one of his seven immediate relatives and not a *meis mitzvah* — a deceased person who has no one to bury him.

Some opinions maintain that a *kohen* whose daughter converted to a different religion or performed immoral acts is not accorded honor, "*ki aviha hi mechalleles* — she has desecrated [the sanctity of] her father" (*Vayikra* 21:9). However, the prevalent *minhag* nowadays is not to nullify the status of a *kohen* because of his children's misdeeds. Nevertheless, according to some authorities the *kohen*'s own misdeeds would be reason to nullify our obligation to honor him, since we are enjoined to respect only *kohanim* who are worthy of that respect, not *baalei aveiros*.

A *chalal* — someone who is born of a union between a *kohen* and a woman who is forbidden to him — is considered a regular member of *Klal Yisrael* and is not accorded any special honors at all. (*Mishpetei Hashalom* 23:2–3)

First in Shul Honors and Other Mitzvos — DURING *KRIAS HATORAH*, a *kohen* is always called up for the first *aliyah*, a *levi* for the second and a *Yisrael* for subsequent *aliyos*. This arrangement was established by *Chazal* in order to preserve peace.

The prevalent *minhag* is to give precedence in *aliyos* to an ignorant *kohen* (as long as he can follow the reader's Torah reading word for word) over even a great *talmid chacham* who is a *Yisrael*. However, when there is a different *kohen* present who is a *talmid chacham*, the ignorant *kohen* should not be called up before the learned *Yisrael*. There are many subtle nuances in these *halachos*, which are discussed at length in *Shulchan Aruch* (*Orach Chaim* 135) and in the relevant commentaries.

Precedence in regard to various *mitzvos*, such as returning a lost object, redeeming from captivity and allocating *tzedakah* funds, also follow the same pattern: The *kohen* precedes the *levi*, the *levi* precedes the *Yisrael*, and the kosher *Yisrael* precedes the *mamzer* — but only as long as they are all equal in Torah scholarship. However, in these situations, when the *mamzer* is a *talmid chacham* and the *kohen* an ignoramus, then the *talmid chacham*, even though he is a *mamzer*, takes precedence over the ignoramus, even if he is the *kohen gadol*.

We learn this from the *passuk* (*Mishlei* 3), "Yekarah hi mipninim — It [the Torah] is more precious than pearls." The word "peninim," *Chazal* explain, is an allusion to the *kohen gadol*, who would enter *lifnai velifnim* — into the innermost chamber of the *Beis Hamikdash*; nevertheless, the *talmid chacham*, even if he is a *mamzer*, towers above him.

Likewise, when there are two *chazzanim* of equal ability available to lead the *davening*, the *kohen* generally takes precedence over the *levi*, and the *levi* over the *Yisrael*, but a *talmid chacham* comes before an ignorant person who is a *levi* or even a *kohen*. In a shul where only one person says *Kaddish* rather than several people reciting it simultaneously, some say that the same rule of precedence would apply. A number of authorities say that when choosing a *mohel* to perform a *bris milah* as well, a *kohen* takes precedence over a *levi* and a *levi* over a *Yisrael*, when both are equally qualified. (*Mishpetei Hashalom* 23:4–5, 9)

First in Honors WHEN THERE ARE many people present at a meal,
at a Meal there are detailed *halachos* that govern the distribution of honors that arise in the course of the *seudah*.
For example, when there is a large loaf of bread or challah to be shared
among everyone, the honors of making the *birkas hamotzi*, slicing the
bread and taking first from each of the foods served, are doled out as
follows:

- When there is a *gadol baTorah* present, he says the *brachah* on
  everyone's behalf and slices the loaf.
- If those present are equal to one another in Torah scholarship,
  and one of them is a *kohen*, it is a *mitzvah* to give the honor to
  the *kohen*.
- If the *kohen* is an ignoramus, a *Yisrael talmid chacham* precedes
  him.
- If the *kohen* is also a *talmid chacham*, but of a lower level than the
  Yisrael, then it is preferable but not obligatory to give the *kohen*
  precedence.
- If there is no *kohen* present, but there is a *levi*, it is preferable to
  give the *levi* precedence, as long as he is equal to the others in
  Torah knowledge.
- The host of the meal, and a *chassan* at his own wedding, each take
  precedence over all the others.
- In each of these cases, anyone is permitted to forgo the honor
  in favor of someone else. Further details are discussed in the
  Shulchan Aruch (*Orach Chaim* 167).

Likewise, in choosing the one to lead the *bentching*, there is a formal
order of precedence; however, here too one can forgo the honor, with
one stipulation: If a *Yisrael talmid chacham* chooses to forgo his honor
in favor of an ignorant *kohen*, he should be careful not to imply in any
way that he is doing so because he has an obligation because of the other
person's position as *kohen*; this would constitute a disgrace to the Torah.
Rather, he can informally pass the honor to the *kohen* as he would to
anyone else present — even a *levi* or *Yisrael*.

For *bentching*, as for *birkas hamotzi*, when there is no *kohen* present, but there are a *levi* and a *Yisrael* who are equal to each other in Torah knowledge, precedence should be given to the *levi*. *Chazal* write that in the merit of observing this protocol we will be rewarded with long life. When the host is present, however, he may lead the *bentching* himself and need not give over the honors to the *kohen* or *levi*.

On Shabbos, the *kohen* should be offered the honor of making Kiddush on behalf of all of those present.

Even though the *kohen* has "rights" to the *kibbud* of reciting the *birkas hamotzi* or leading the *bentching*, it is still appropriate for him to humbly preface his *zimun* with the words, "*Birshus morai verabosai* — With the permission of my teachers and Rabbis." On the other hand, if someone else is given these honors when a *kohen* is present, it is not sufficient for him to say, "*Birshus hakohen*"; he must first actually ask the *kohen*'s permission. (*Mishpetei Hashalom* 23:6–8)

27 Av	27 Kislev	27 Nisan

First in Other Situations

"Look what a long list of Rabbanim there is, all lined up to speak at the *siyum* tonight," Tal commented as he glanced at the brochure in his hand. "I wonder how the organizers decide who should speak first. Maybe they flip a coin," he joked. Then he caught himself — perhaps such a light remark was irreverent…

"I will now demonstrate to you my powers of prophecy," replied his friend who was sitting next to him. "I predict that Rabbi Yehoshua Katz will be the first on the agenda."

Moments later, to Tal's amazement, the prediction was proven true. "Were you involved in planning the evening?" he asked suspiciously.

"Not at all," his seatmate answered. "I'll reveal to you my secret. Since all the people on the dais are considered equally great *talmidei chachamim*, the one who will always be chosen to speak first is the *kohen* among them. In this case, the only *kohen* is Rabbi Katz. Most people named Katz are *kohanim*; the name **Katz** is a shortened version of '**k**ohen **tz**edek.' So, next time you can also be a prophet…"

THE *POSKIM* SAY that another area included in the general rule of *kohanim* going first is in public speaking. At any public gathering, the *kohen* should be honored with making the first speech. Likewise, he should be the first one asked to voice his opinion at a meeting. These gestures demonstrate that we respect and elevate him above the others.

When two people approach a Rav at the same time to ask a question, there is a set order of precedence, as we discussed in the previous chapter. For example, a great *chacham* precedes an ordinary *talmid chacham*, and a *talmid chacham* precedes an ignoramus. When the nature of the questions differs, a practical question comes before a theoretical one, and so on, as we have explained in detail in chapter 33. When both questioners are of equal scholarship and one is a *kohen*, the *kohen* is given the honor of posing his question first, but when the other person is a greater *talmid chacham*, he is given precedence, even if he is a *Yisrael mamzer*. Some authorities apply the same rule when two cases come before a *dayan*, stating that we should move the case of the *kohen* ahead of the others, just as we do for a *talmid chacham*, but other *poskim* disagree on this point.

As we discussed regarding a *talmid chacham*, when a *kohen* is walking with two *Yisraels*, the *kohen* should be honored with walking between them. Similarly, when a *kohen* is walking with a *Yisrael* and they reach a doorway, the *kohen* should be respectfully allowed to enter first.

In a case where giving the *kohen* honor would cause a monetary loss, we are not obligated to do so, just as we are not obligated to absorb a loss in order to honor a *talmid chacham*.

28 Av	28 Kislev	28 Nisan

Another general principle we mentioned regarding the honor of a *kohen* is that he is given "first choice of a good portion." In other words, in any situation where something has to be split up between a *kohen* and a *Yisrael*, the item should be divided in half, and then the *kohen* should be given the opportunity to choose the portion he prefers.

Some opinions limit this prerogative specifically to *tzedakah* or *maaser ani* — the portion of produce allotted to the poor — in the case of an impoverished *kohen*, and to splitting a portion of food at a social meal. However, when a *kohen* is one of the partners dividing things up in a financial partnership, this rule does not apply, because in such cases, *Chazal* warn that someone who "has his eye on the choice portion of a partnership will never see a blessing in his endeavors." Other authorities disagree and include this area in the obligation to give the *kohen* precedence. Since it is actually the obligation of the *Yisrael* to allow the *kohen* first choice, they explain, the *kohen* has an inherent right to that portion and would not be considered as "having his eye on it"; hence, he would not forfeit any blessing. (*Mishpetei Hashalom* 23:10–12)

Forgoing the Honors SINCE THE PRIVILEGES allotted to the *kohanim* are meant to be for their benefit, a *kohen* may choose to forgo one or all of those privileges — for example, if he wishes to honor his rebbe or someone of greater stature than himself with leading the *bentching,* or other such honors. The only exception is in the rules of being called up to *krias haTorah*; these were instituted by *Chazal* in order to prevent *machlokes* from arising regarding these honors, and therefore neither the *kohen* nor the *levi* is entitled to relinquish his privilege of precedence in order to honor someone else.

Some authorities maintain that in any public meal, such as a *seudas bris milah* or a wedding banquet, where there are many participants, the same rule that applies to *krias haTorah* would apply there, and the *kohen* would not be permitted to forgo his privileges. However, most *poskim* imply that in these situations the *kohen* may give a *Yisrael* permission to lead the *bentching* in his presence.

A *kohen* who chooses to forgo all or some of his honors can reverse his decision at any time and reclaim his privileges. (*Mishpetei Hashalom* 23:13–14)

| 29 Av | 29 Kislev | 29 Nisan |

Using the Services of a Kohen "Ahreleh, do me a favor and help me pick up all these wrappers in the schoolyard," Binyamin called out to his friend Ahreleh Cohen. "The janitor asked me to give him a hand."

"Here, I'll do it," Moishie Israelowitz volunteered, jabbing Binyamin with his elbow.

"Hey, what's the matter? Why did you just poke me in the ribs?" Binyamin asked in annoyance. "And why are you suddenly so eager to help? Ahreleh could have done it just as well."

"Maybe he would have agreed, but I don't know if it was right to ask him in the first place," Moishie explained. "He's a *kohen*, you know, and collecting trash is not exactly the greatest of honors. I don't mind doing it. Let's get to work."

SINCE THE *KOHEN* was set aside to be in the service of Hashem, utilizing the *kohen* for our own personal service without his expressly having waived his honor is considered *me'ilah* — the misappropriation of sacred resources, an *issur* that applies even when there is no *Beis Hamikdash*. As this may be considered a Torah violation, we should avoid calling on the services of even a child who is a *kohen*.

Some authorities maintain that even if the *kohen* expressly waives his honor, we are still not entitled to avail ourselves of his services, unless the *kohen* has a personal benefit to gain from doing the favor, for example, if he is doing it for pay, or if he has a particular interest in serving the person who asked for the favor. It is preferable to be stringent in this matter. Certainly, under no circumstances should we ask a *kohen* to do a task that is lowly and unrespectable — like sweeping a public area.

There are opinions that are lenient and allow us to utilize the services of a *kohen am ha'aretz* — an ignorant *kohen*. Even in such a case, however, we would not be permitted to engage him in a lowly task. Some authorities permit one *kohen* to use the services of another *kohen*.

30 Av	30 Kislev	30 Nisan

Degrading a Kohen ANYONE WHO DEGRADES or shames a *kohen* violates the mitzvah of *vekidashto*. The Rema ruled that the scale of compensation paid to a *kohen* who has been shamed publicly is higher than that of a *Yisrael*.

Therefore, when we speak or accept *lashon hara* or *rechilus* about a *kohen*, hurt him with our words or enter a *machlokes* with him, and certainly if we strike, curse or shame him, then in addition to the other *issurim* we are guilty of transgressing, we also violate the positive

mitzvah of *vekidashto*. According to the Chofetz Chaim, this would be the case even if the *kohen* was not present when the violation was done. (*Mishpetei Hashalom* 23:15–17)

Honor to a Levi   EVEN THOUGH WE find that in certain *halachos* we have discussed — *krias haTorah*, retrieving a lost item, *tzedakah*, redeeming captives, reciting the *brachah* of *hamotzi* and leading the *bentching* or *davening* — a degree of precedence is allotted to the *levi*, nevertheless, the major focus of the *mitzvah* of *vekidashto* is for *kohanim*.

The *levi* himself is obligated to honor *kohanim*, and even a *levi* who is a *talmid chacham* does the service of washing an ignorant *kohen*'s hands for the purpose of *nesias kapayim* — raising the hands to bless the congregation with the *birkas kohanim*. (*Mishpetei Hashalom* 23:18)

In summary: It is a positive *mitzvah* to sanctify and honor *kohanim*, the descendants of Aharon Hakohen, who were chosen by Hashem to perform the service in the *Beis Hamikdash*. This *mitzvah* applies today, even though the *Beis Hamikdash* is not standing. Demonstrations of this honor include giving the *kohen* precedence in *aliyos laTorah*, honors at a meal, such as reciting the *brachah* of *ha'motzi* and leading the *bentching*, and more. The *kohen* is also given precedence when waiting in line to ask the Rav a question, or when speaking at a public gathering. We may not utilize a *kohen*'s services for our personal benefit, unless he has some personal benefit to gain from it as well. A *kohen* may forgo all his honors except for his position in the order of *aliyos laTorah*. Degrading a *kohen* is a violation of this *mitzvah*. A *levi* is also given a degree of precedence over a *Yisrael*; however, he too is obligated, just as a *Yisrael* is, in honoring the *kohen*.

Glossary

All terms are in Lashon Hakodesh unless otherwise noted. The spellings and explanations reflect the way the specific word is used herein. Often, there are alternate spellings and meanings for the words.

ACHICHA: your brother

AGGADOS: homiletic passages in the Mishnah, Gemara and other early sources

AHAVAS YISRAEL: love of fellow Jews

AISHES CHAVEIR: the wife of a *talmid chacham*

AISHES CHAYIL: "Woman of Valor"; the last chapter in *sefer Mishlei*, customarily sung at the Shabbos table on Friday nights

AKUM: acronym for "*Ovdei Kochavim UMazalos*"; worshippers of stars and constellations (In times when Jewish writings were censored this term was often used as a "code word" to refer to any non-Jew. In this work, in most cases, we retained the language as it appears in the sources. See Volume I, chapter 18 for details.)

ALIYAH LATORAH, ALIYOS (PL.): being called up to the Torah

ALMANAH: widow

AM HA'ARETZ: ignoramus

AMIRAH LE'AKUM: telling a non-Jew to do an action on Shabbos that is forbidden to Jews

AMISECHA: a member of your nation

AMOS: cubits

AMUD: the cantor's stand in shul

ANI HAMEHAPEICH BECHARARAH: literally, "a poor person examining a loaf"; this refers to the *halachah* that one must not usurp another's opportunity to purchase something while he is contemplating purchasing it himself

ANOOS: one who has no control over a situation

APEI MAREI (ARAMAIC): in the presence of the person being spoken about

APEI TELASA (ARAMAIC): in the presence of three people

APIKORUS, APIKORSIM (PL.): nonbelievers in Torah, prophecy, etc. (see Volume I, chapter 18)

ARBAAS HAMININ: four "species" of plants used for the *mitzvah* of shaking the *lulav* on Sukkos

ARKA'OS: a secular court

ARON: coffin

ARON KODESH: holy ark in shul: a closet used to store a *sefer Torah*

ARUR: cursed

ARVUS: collective responsibility, guarantee

ASERES HADIBROS: the Ten Commandments

ASHEIRAH: a tree used as *avodah zarah*

ASSUR: prohibited

AVAK LASHON HARA OR AVAK RECHILUS: words, hints, motions or actions that imply a derogatory statement or that will stir up resentment

AVEIL, AVEILUS: mourning, mourner

AVEIRAH, AVEIROS (PL.): transgression(s)

AVI MORI: my father, my teacher

AVODAH ZARAH: idolatry

AZUS: brazen arrogance

BAAL AVEIRAH: sinner

BAAL DIN: litigant

BAAL HABAYIS: master of the house

BAAL HASIMCHAH: host of a joyous occasion

BAAL KOREI: the cantor who reads the Torah

BAAL MAASIM: someone who is known for his extensive good deeds

BAAL NEFESH: a person with spiritual aspirations

BAAL TESHUVAH: repentant, newly observant Jew

BACHUR: young man

BADEKEN (YIDDISH): covering the *kallah's* face prior to the *chuppah*

BAISHANUS: bashfulness

BAL TASHCHIS: wasteful destruction of property

BARUCH HASHEM: "Blessed is G-d"; thank G-d

BAS KOL: Heavenly Voice

BECHEZKAS KASHRUS: presumed to be an upstanding person

BEIS DIN: court of Jewish law

BEIS DIN MUSMACH: a court of Rabbis who were ordained by other ordained Rabbis, from the time of Moshe Rabbeinu, through the time of the *Amora'im,* around the fourth century C.E.

BEIS DIN SHEL MAALAH: the Heavenly Tribunal

BEIS HAMIKDASH: the Holy Temple

BEIS MEDRASH, BATEI MIDRASH (PL.): study hall(s)

BEN TORAH: a person who is steeped in Torah

BENTCHING (YIDDISH): blessing; reciting the Grace after Meals

BRACHAH, BRACHOS (PL.): blessing(s)

BRACHAH ACHARONAH: blessing recited after eating

BIKKURIM: first fruits brought to a *kohen* in the *Beis Hamikdash*

BIKUR CHOLIM: visiting the sick

BIMAH: platform in shul on which the Torah is opened and read

BIRKAS HAMAZON: blessing after meals

BITACHON: faith and reliance on Hashem

BLATT (YIDDISH): page or leaf

BLI NEDER: without promising

BNOS YISRAEL: Jewish girls and women

BRACHAH LEVATALAH: blessing uttered in vain

BRIS: circumcision

CHALAL: someone who is born of the union of a *kohen* and a woman who is forbidden to him

Glossary

CHAMETZ: leavened bread, or any food containing leavened grain

CHANUFAH: flattery

CHAS VESHALOM: Heaven forbid

CHASSAN: groom

CHAVRUSA (ARAMAIC): learning partner

CHAYECHA KODMIN: your life (or needs) takes precedence

CHAZZAN: cantor; prayer leader

CHEMDAH: coveting

CHENEK: execution through strangulation

CHEREM: a ban or level of excommunication

CHESRONOS ATZUMIM: serious deficiencies

CHESSED: act of kindness

CHEVRA KADISHA (ARAMAIC): the group in a community that tends to the burial of the deceased

CHILLUL HASHEM: desecration of Hashem's Name

CHILLUL SHABBOS: violation of Shabbos

CHINUCH: education, training, starting a child off in *mitzvah* observance

CHOL HAMO'ED: intermediate days of the festivals

CHOLEH: one who is ill

CHOSHED BIKSHEIRIM: suspecting a person who is innocent of guilt

CHOTEH: sinner

CHUMRAH, CHUMROS (PL.): stringency

CHUPPAH: literally, wedding canopy; figuratively, marriage ceremony

DALET AMOS: four cubits; a distance of about six feet

DAS MOSHE; DAS YEHUDIS: accepted Jewish conduct

DAVEN (YIDDISH): pray

DAYAN, DAYANIM (PL.): judge(s) in a *beis din*

DERECH: path

DERECH ERETZ: proper conduct

DEVARIM HANIKARIM: clear circumstantial evidence

DEVARIM SHEBIKDUSHAH: words of Torah and prayer, acts related to *mitzvos*

DIN, DINIM (PL.): detail(s) of *halachah*

DIN SHAMAYIM: Heavenly justice

DIN TORAH: according to Torah law; a court case in a *beis din*

DIVREI AGGADAH: homiletic passages in the Mishnah, Gemara and other early sources

DIVREI KABBALAH: the text of the Prophets and Writings

DIVREI TORAH: words of Torah

EIRUV CHATZEIROS: an arrangement to permit carrying from one location to another on Shabbos

EIVER MIN HACHAI: meat severed from an animal while it is still alive

EMES: truth

EMUNAH: belief in Hashem

EREV YOM TOV; EREV SHABBOS: day before *Yom Tov*; day before Shabbos (Friday)

ESROG: citron; one of the four species taken on Sukkos

EVED IVRI: a Jew who has sold himself, or who has been sold by *beis din*, as a slave

EZRAS NASHIM: the ladies' section in a synagogue

FARGIN (YIDDISH): to take joy in others' success

GAAVAH: arrogance; haughtiness; showing off

GABBAI: sexton; manager of a shul or of a *tzedakah* fund

GADOL HADOR, GEDOLEI HADOR (PL.), GEDOLIM: great Torah leader(s) of the generation

GAZLAN: thief

GEBROKTZ (YIDDISH): matzah moistened with any liquid or liquidy substance

GEMACH: free-loan fund

GEMILAS CHESSED: acts of loving-kindness

GENEIVAS DAAS: deceit

GER TZEDEK, GEIRIM (PL.): convert(s) to Judaism

GET: certificate of divorce

GEULAH: redemption

GEZEIRAH: decree; restrictive law

GEZEIRAH SHAVAH: principle of deducing a law of the Torah through different citations of similar language

GEZEL; GEZEILAH: theft; a stolen item

GID HANASHEH: the sciatic nerve of an animal

GILGUL: reincarnation

GILUI ARAYOS: a forbidden intimate relationsihp

GOSEIS: a person on the verge of death

GUZMA: exaggeration

HACHNASAS KALLAH: literally, escorting the bride to the *chuppah*; it also means giving a poor bride funds in order to set up her new home

HACHNASAS ORCHIM: tending to the needs of guests

HADAS: myrtle bush

HAGOMEL: blessing recited after going through danger, illness, etc., safely

HAKARAS HATOV: gratitude

HAKHEL: *mitzvah* for the entire Jewish nation to gather in Yerushalayim once every seven years, when the king would recite *sefer Devarim* to them

HALACHAH, HALACHOS (PL.): Jewish law(s)

HALBANAS PANIM: shaming another person

HALVAYAS HAMEIS: funeral

HAMOTZI: blessing recited on bread

HANHALAH: administration

"HAREINI KAPPARAS MISHKAVO": "I take upon myself any punishment that my parent might be liable for in the afterlife"

HASAGAS GEVUL: encroachment

HASHAVAS AVEIDAH: *mitzvah* of returning a lost object to its owner or of saving people from loss

HASHEM: G-d

HASHGACHAH: Divine Providence

HASHKAFAH, HASHKAFOS (PL.): moral outlook

HASMADAH: diligence in learning

HATOV VEHAMEITIV: blessing recited on specific occasions, e.g., when a finer wine is brought to the table

HATZLACHAH: success

HAVDALAH: prayer and blessings recited over wine at the end of Shabbos or a festival

HECHSHER: kosher certification

HEFKER: ownerless, free for all to take

HESPED: eulogy

HETER, HETERIM (PL.): thing(s) permitted according to *halachah*

HIDDUR, HIDDURIM (PL.): enhancement(s) in observance of *mitzvos*

HIN TZEDEK: literally, honest measures; also used to mean keeping one's word

HOTZAAS HAMEIS: attending the funeral and seeing to all the needs of the deceased

IMAHOS: the four Matriarchs

IMI MORASI: my mother, my teacher

INUI HADIN: keeping people waiting unnecessarily when they have come for judgment or to receive a rabbinical decision

ISSUR, ISSURIM (PL.): prohibition

KADDISH: prayer sanctifying Hashem's Name, recited by the leader of the prayer services, or by men whose parents are deceased

KALLAH: bride or daughter-in-law

KAPPARAH: atonement

KARMELIS: a place where carrying on Shabbos is forbidden only by Rabbinical injunction

KAVANAH: conscious intent

KAVOD: honor

Glossary

KAVOD HABRIOS: human dignity

KAVOD HATORAH: honor of the Torah

KEDEI SEVIAH: enough to satisfy

KEDUSHAH: holiness

KEHILLAH: community

KEVOD SHAMAYIM: honor of Hashem

KEZAYIS: halachic measure, equal to about the volume of an olive

KIBBUD AV VA'EIM, KIBBUD HORIM: honor of parents

KIDDUSH: blessing recited over wine at the first two meals of Shabbos

KIDDUSH HASHEM: sanctification of Hashem's Name

KIDDUSHIN: the act of acquiring a woman's hand in marriage

KIM LEI BEGAVEI (ARAMAIC): a person about whom we are absolutely confident that he would never lie or exaggerate on any matter

KINAH: envy

KINUI: a substitute name (as of Hashem)

KINYANIM: acts of acquisition

KIRUV RECHOKIM: enlightening nonobservant Jews and helping them to return to their traditions

KITNIYOS: legumes (eaten by many among the Sefardic communities, though not by Ashkenazim, on Pesach)

KIYUM: fulfillment

KLAL: the entire community

KODSHIM: section of the Mishnah/Gemara that deals mainly with the offerings in the *Beis Hamikdash*

KOFER, KOFRIM (PL.): atheist(s); one who denies the origin of the Torah or the existence of Hashem

KOHEN, KOHANIM (PL.), KEHUNAH: one of priestly descent; the priesthood

KORBAN; KORBAN TODAH; KORBAN TAMID: sacrificial offering; sacrificial offering of thanks; daily sacrificial offering

KRIAH: tearing of a garment in mourning

KRIAS HATORAH: Torah reading

KRIAS SHEMA: reading of the Shema

LAMDAN: erudite scholar

LASHON HAKODESH: the Holy Language (Torah Hebrew)

LASHON HARA: derogatory speech about someone, even if the remark is true

LASHON HARA BETZINAH: *lashon hara* in which the hurtful remarks are cleverly concealed, or any *lashon hara* said in secret

LASHON SAGI NAHOR: euphemistic expression

LECHATCHILAH (ARAMAIC): the preferable manner of doing something; *a priori*

LEHACHIS: for no reason other than to anger one's Creator

LEHACHMIR: to act stringently

LEHAVDIL: in stark contrast to something either sacred or profane

LE'ILUI NISHMAS: in memory of someone, to elevate the soul of

LESHEIM SHAMAYIM: for the sake of Heaven

LETEI'AVON: something (as a sin) done to satisfy one's physical desire

LETO'ELES: for a constructive purpose

LEVAYAH: funeral

LEVI: Levite, descended from the tribe of Levi

LIFNIM MISHURAS HADIN: voluntary act beyond the letter of the law

LIMUDEI KODESH: Torah studies

LO'EIG LARASH: mocking a person who is incapable of helping himself, thus disgracing him; e.g., flaunting *tzitzis* or other *mitzvos* in the presence of the deceased, who can no longer perform *mitzvos*

LULAV: immature palm frond; one of the four species taken on Sukkos

MAARIV: evening prayer

MAASER ANI: the tithe of produce allotted to the poor

MAAVIR AL MIDOSAV: ignoring insults, letting offenses pass and forgiving the offender

MACHLOKES: discord, argument (for full definition, see Volume I, chapter 5)

MACHRIA: to choose a side in a halachic dispute, or to outbalance one side, determining that this side is right

MALACH(IM): angel(s)

MALACH HAMAVES: angel of death

MALKOS: the punishment of being whipped, given 39 lashes by *beis din*

MALSHINIM: Jews who inform *akum*, or violent or dishonest people, about others' activities or assets, so that they will come to harm

MAMZER: a child born of a forbidden relationship involving *gilui arayos*

MARIS AYIN: doing something that will appear to others to be sinful

MASECHTA, MASECHTOS (PL.): tractate(s)

MASHAL: a parable

MASHGIACH: staff member of a yeshivah assigned to raising the students' spiritual level

MATAN TORAH: the event at Mt. Sinai when we were given the Torah

MATNOS KEHUNAH: the special gifts Jews must give to the *kohanim*

MAZIKIN: evil spirits, demons

MECHALLEL SHABBOS: violator of Shabbos

MECHILAH: forgiveness

MECHITZAH: a halachic partition

MECHUSAR AMANA: one who lacks personal integrity

MECHUTANIM: parents of one's son-/daughter-in-law

MEFARSHIM: commentaries

MEGILLAH: scroll read on Purim

MEHEIMAN LEI KEVEI TREI (ARAMAIC): a person whose word can be trusted as well as the testimony of two witnesses

ME'ILAH: the sin of using the property of the *Beis Hamikdash* for personal benefit

MEIS: deceased; corpse

MEISI'ACH LEFI TUMO: one who gives information without realizing its significance

Glossary

MEISIS (UMEIDI'ACH): someone who attempts to persuade other Jews to worship idols

MEIZID: intentional sin, sinner

MEKABEL: one who accepts and believes *lashon hara*

MEKACH TA'US: a mistaken acquisition, made based on false information, which could lead to annulment

MEKADEISH: a man performing the act of acquiring a woman's hand in marriage

MESAPER LASHON HARA: the speaker of *lashon hara*

MESHUMADIM: apostates, Jews who embrace other religions

MEZUMAN: quorum of three for communal blessing after meals

MI SHEPARA: a curse that is given to someone who backs out on a business deal after payment was made

MIBESARECHA LO SISALEM: "Do not ignore your own flesh"; the halachic principle that one's relatives take precedence over strangers in charitable acts

MIDBAR: wilderness

MIDDAH, MIDDOS (PL.): character trait(s)

MIDDAS CHASSIDUS: a commendable approach, beyond the minimum requirement

MIDDAS SEDOM: senseless selfishness

MIDE'ORAISA: required by the Torah

MIDERABBANAN: a Rabbinical injunction

MIKVEH: ritual bath

MILEI DEBEDICHUSA (ARAMAIC): humorous words

MIN, MINIM (PL.): heretic(s), or Jewish apostate(s), who has adopted another religion

MIN HATORAH: required by the Torah

MINCHAH: afternoon prayer

MINHAG: custom

MINHAG HAMAKOM: local custom

Glossary

MINYAN: quorum of ten for prayer

MIPNEI TIKUN HA'OLAM: to ensure social order

MISHLO'ACH MANOS: Purim food-gift

MISHNAH, MISHNAYOS: outline of the Oral Law, written down and organized into six sections, in the year 200 C.E.

MITZVAH, MITZVOS (PL.): commandment(s)

MITZVAS ASEI: positive commandment

MITZVOS BEIN ADAM LAMAKOM: *mitzvos* between man and Hashem

MITZVOS BEIN ADAM LECHAVEIRO: *mitzvos* between man and his fellow

MITZVOS HATELUYOS BA'ARETZ: *mitzvos* that can be done only in Eretz Yisrael

MITZVOS LO SAASEH: negative commandment

MIZBEI'ACH: Altar in the *Beis Hamikdash*

MOCHEL; MOCHEL ONE'S RESPECT: to forgo; one who forgoes one's honor

MOCHIACH, MOCHICHIM (PL.): one who gives rebuke

MODAAH: a statement made to invalidate future statements

MOHEL: one who performs a circumcision

MORA: reverence; fear

MOREH HETER: giving oneself a dubious halachic dispensation

MOSHAV LEITZIM: a gathering of scorners

MOTZAEI SHABBOS: the night following Shabbos

MOTZI SHEIM RA: saying derogatory things about someone that are untrue

MOTZI SHEIM SHAMAYIM LEVATALAH: pronouncing Hashem's Name in vain

MUKTZEH: items that may generally not be moved on Shabbos

MUMAR LEDAVAR ECHAD: someone who wantonly disobeys one particular *mitzvah*

MUMAR LEHACHIS: someone who sins out of spite, just in order to anger his Creator or other Jews

MUMAR LETEI'AVON: a person who sins to satisfy his desires

MUSMACH: "ordained"

MUSSAF: additional prayer recited after *Shacharis* on Shabbos, Rosh Chodesh and Yom Tov

MUSSAR: personal discipline

NASI: the head of the *Sanhedrin*

NAVI, NEVI'IM (PL.): prophet(s)

NEDARIM: vows

NEFEL, NEFALIM (PL.): a miscarried fetus

NEFESH: spirit

NEGA'IM: skin afflictions, loosely translated as leprosy

NEKIMAH: revenge

NESHAMAH: soul

NETILAS YADAYIM: ritual hand-washing

NETIRAH: bearing a grudge

NEVEILAH, NEVEILOS (PL.): an animal that died without being halachically *shechted*

NEZEK: damage; amount by which the value of a person was reduced (were he to be sold as a slave)

NICHUM AVEILIM: comforting mourners

NIDDAH: a woman in a state of ritual uncleanliness

NIDUI: ban; a level of excommunication

NIFTAR: deceased person, corpse

NIMSHAL: the implied meaning of a parable

NIRDAF: one who is persecuted, who is being pursued and is in danger

NOSEI BE'OL: sharing the burden, empathizing

NUSACH: formula, version

OLAM HABA: the World to Come

ONA'AS DEVARIM: hurting someone with words

ONA'AS MAMON: monetary fraud

ONES: an incident completely out of a person's control

PARNASSAH: livelihood

PARSAH, PARSA'OS (PL.): measure of distance (about 4 kilometers)

PASSUK: verse in Scriptures

PASSUL: disqualified

PERISHUS: abstaining from certain permitted pleasures

PERITZUS: immodest behavior

PERUTAH: a coin of the smallest monetary value

PESAK: halachic ruling

PETIRAH: death

PIDYON HABEN: redemption of the firstborn

PIDYON SHEVUYIM: redeeming captives

PILPUL: Torah debate

PIRKEI AVOS: Mishnah of Ethics of the Fathers

POREK OL: one who has thrown off the yoke of Heaven

POSKIM: halachic authorities of the last 1,000 years

RASHA, RESHA'IM (PL.): wicked person

RAV, RABBANIM (PL.): Rabbi(s)

REBBE MUVHAK: primary Torah teacher

RECHILUS: peddling gossip

REFUAH SHELEIMAH: a full and speedy recovery

REI'ACHA: your friend or colleague

RESHUS: a halachically separate area

RISHONIM: early commentators (from about the year 1,000 C.E. to 1,500 C.E.)

RODEF: pursuer

ROSH CHODESH: first day of the Jewish (lunar) month

RUCHNIYUS: spirituality

SAFEK: a doubt

SEFER, SEFARIM (PL.): book(s

SEFER TORAH: Torah scroll

SEIVER PANIM YAFOS: a pleasant countenance

SEKILAH: execution by stoning

SEMICHAH: in earlier times, authorization to judge cases of corporal and capital punishment and to assign monetary fines; nowadays, used to indicate a much more limited rabbinical ordination

SEUDAH: (festive) meal

SEUDAH SHELISHIS: third meal of Shabbos, eaten on Shabbos afternoon

SEUDAS HAVRAAH: the first meal after a funeral for the *aveilim*

SHAATNEZ: garment made of a combination of wool and linen threads

SHABBOS: seventh day of the week, Sabbath

SHACHARIS: morning prayer

SHADCHAN: matchmaker

SHAKRAN: liar

SHALIACH: messenger

SHALIACH TZIBBUR: leader of the prayers, cantor

SHALOM: peace

SHALOM ALEICHEM: "Peace be upon you"; a greeting

SHALOM BAYIS: marital harmony

SHALOSH REGALIM: three festivals of Sukkos, Pesach and Shavuos

SHAMAYIM: the Heavens

SHECHINAH: the Divine Presence

SHECHT (YIDDISH): ritual slaughter

SHE'EILAH, SHE'EILAS CHACHAM: question posed to a Rabbi

SHE'EILAS SHALOM: inquiry after someone's welfare; greeting with "*shalom*"

SHEFICHUS DAMIM: murder

SHEITEL (YIDDISH): wig

SHEKER: falsehood

SHEKER LETO'ELES: a lie told for a constructive, justified reason

SHELOSHIM: thirty days of mourning following the death of a relative

SHEMIRAS HALASHON: guarding one's tongue from prohibited speech

SHEMITTAH: sabbatical year

SHEVA BRACHOS: seven blessings recited under the *chuppah*, at the wedding meal, and at meals conducted during the week following the wedding

SHEVUOS: oaths

SHIDDUCH, SHIDDUCHIM (PL.): proposed suitor(s) for marriage

SHITUF: the belief in there being other gods besides the Supreme Creator, as in Christianity or some forms of polytheism

SHIUR: lecture, class

SHIVAH: seven days of mourning

SHIVAH TOVEI HA'IR: a halachically elected committee in charge of a Jewish community

SHMATTEH (YIDDISH): rag

SHOFAR: ram's horn made into an instrument

SHOMEI'A LASHON HARA: the one who intentionally listens to *lashon hara*

SHOMER SHABBOS: Shabbos-observant

SHTAR: a legally binding document

SHTUKI: a child whose father's identity is not known

SHUL (YIDDISH): synagogue

SIDDUR: prayer book

SIMCHAS CHASSAN VEKALLAH: gladdening the groom and bride

SIMCHAS MITZVAH: joy in doing a *mitzvah*

SINAH: hatred

SINAS CHINAM: unwarranted hatred

SIYUM HASHAS: completion of the study of the entire Talmud

SOFER: scribe

SONEI: enemy

SOTAH: a woman suspected of adultery

SUKKAH: booth erected for the holiday of Sukkos

TAAVAH: desire

TACHRICHIM: shrouds

TAHARAS HAMEIS: cleansing the body before it is buried

TAHAROS: section of Mishnah/Gemara that deals with ritual purity

TAKANAH, TAKANOS (PL.): Rabbinical regulation(s)

TALLIS: prayer shawl

TALLIS KATAN: garment with *tzitziyos* — fringes — attached and worn throughout the day

TALMID: student

TALMID CHACHAM, TALMIDEI CHACHAMIM (PL.): Torah scholar(s)

TALMUD TORAH: Torah learning

TALMUD TORAH DERABBIM: public Torah learning

TAMEI: ritually impure

TANACH: twenty-four books of the Torah (Bible)

TANCHUMIM: comforting words

TAR'OMES: a legitimate complaint

TASHMISHEI KEDUSHAH: sacred objects

TECHUM SHABBOS: a distance of 2,000 *amos* outside the city

TEFILLAH: prayer

TEFILLAH BETZIBBUR: communal prayer

TEFILLIN: phylacteries

TEKIOS: sounds of the shofar

TENNA'IM: setting down of conditions for an engagement

TERUMOS UMA'ASROS: tithes

TESHUVAH: repentance

TINOK SHENISHBA: someone who was taken captive by *akum* as a small child and grew up knowing nothing of Judaism; used at times to denote any Jew who was denied a Jewish education (See Volume I, chapter 18.)

TOCHACHAH: rebuke

TO'ELES: for a constructive purpose

TORAH SHEBE'AL PEH: Oral Law

TORASO UMANUSO: one whose sole occupation is Torah study

TREIFE: meat that is not kosher, used as a general term for nonkosher food

TUMAS KOHANIM: defilement of *kohen's* purity (through contact with a deceased person)

TUMAS MEIS: defilement through contact with a deceased person

TZAAR: pain; compensation for the pain suffered

TZAAR BAALEI CHAIM: unnecessary pain caused to animals

TZADDIK, TZADDIKIM (PL.): righteous person(s)

TZEDAKAH: charity

TZARAAS: spiritual disease; punishment for *lashon hara* and other sins; see *nega'im*

TZIBBUR: congregation

TZIDDUK HADIN: formula said after a funeral

TZITZIYOS: fringes on a *tallis*

TZNIUS: modesty

VATRANUS: the trait of yielding to another's position for the sake of peace, or forgoing one's rights for any other reason

VIDUY: personal confession of sins to Hashem

YAHRTZEIT (YIDDISH): anniversary of someone's death

YASOM, YESOMIM (PL.): orphan(s)

YAYIN NESECH: the wine of a non-Jew

YEIHAREIG VE'AL YAAVOR: the specific sins regarding which one must allow oneself to be killed rather than to trangress them

YETZER, YETZER HARA: evil inclination

YETZIAS MITZRAYIM: the exodus from Egypt

YICHUD: seclusion of a man with a woman

YICHUS: family lineage

Glossary

YIDDISHKEIT (YIDDISH): Jewish way of life

YIRAS SHAMAYIM: fear of Heaven

YIREI HASHEM: G-d-fearing people

YOM KIPPUR: Day of Atonement

YOM TOV: festival

ZECHUS: merit

ZERIZUS: alacrity

ZICHRONO LIVRACHAH: of blessed memory

Glossary

In loving memory of
Nissi and Ella Dzialowski, *a"h*
who personified *Ahavas Habriyos*
in their lifetime

לעילוי נשמות

דודנו היקרים

ר' **ניסן** בן זכריה חיים ז"ל

נלב"ע כ"ז אלול תשנ"א

וזוגתו

מרת **צרטל** בת החבר ר' שמעון ע"ה

נלב"ע כ"א אדר תשס"ה

לעילוי נשמת

דודנו היקר

ראובן שמואל מרדכי

בן ר' חיים יצחק ז"ל

נלב"ע ה' תשרי תשס"ו

לעילוי נשמות

אבינו היקר

ר' **אברהם** ז"ל בן החבר ר' יו"ט ז"ל

נלב"ע ט"ז חשון תשנ"ג

ואמנו היקירה

מרת **רייזל** ע"ה בת ר' בנימין זאב ז"ל

נלב"ע כ"ז סיון תשל"ח

לעילוי נשמות

משפחת בית חמי

הסבא הרה"ג שמואל אברהם ב"ר משה ז"ל מלצר

נלב"ע א' דר"ח תמוז תשמ"ז

וזוגתו מרת **יחנא** בת ר' שמריהו ע"ה

נלב"ע י"ג כסלו תשנ"ג

◆

סבא הר"ר חיים זלמן ב"ר חעוול גרשון ז"ל פרנק

נלב"ע ז"ך מרחשון תשמ"ח

◆

סבא רבא הר"ר משה ב"ר יוסף ז"ל מיליצער

נלב"ע י"ב תשרי תר"צ

וזוגתו מרת **שיינא מרים** בת ר' יעקב ע"ה

נלב"ע כ"ה מרחשון תרצ"ה

◆

סבא רבא הר"ר שמריהו ב"ר ישעיהו נתן ז"ל סטמפניצקי

נלב"ע כ"א אדר

וזוגתו **שרה וועלא** בת ר' אברהם בנימין ע"ה

נרצחה ע"י הצוררים ימ"ש הי"ד

◆

סבא רבא הר"ר חעוול גרשון ב"ר שמואל שמחה ז"ל פרנק

נלב"ע כ"ה אדר תש"ב

וזוגתו **ליבא** בת ר' יוסף ע"ה

נלב"ע כ"ד שבט

◆

סבא רבא הר"ר אליעזר ב"ר יעקב ז"ל קוולוואסער

נלב"ע י"ג אדר א' תשל"ו

וזוגתו **רחל** בת ר' יעקב הכהן ע"ה

נלב"ע ל' תשרי א' דר"ח מרחשון תשמ"ו

לעילוי נשמות

משפחת בית אבי

סבא רבא ר' מנחם מנלי ב"ר זאב ז"ל	סבא רבא ר' משה ב"ר יצחק אייזיק ז"ל
נלב"ע כ"ג טבת	נלב"ע י"ח ניסן

וזוגתו מרת בינה ב"ר יהודה יונה ע"ה	וזוגתו מרת יוטא רבקה ע"ה
נלב"ע ב' אלול	נלב"ע י"ח או י"ט תמוז

◆   ◆

סבא ר' עקיבא משה ב"ר מנחם מנלי ז"ל	סבתא מרת רחל דבורה ב"ר משה ע"ה
נלב"ע כ"ח אדר ב'	נלב"ע כ"ד אלול

משפחת אבי אמי

ר' דוד ב"ר שמעיה, ר' שמעיה ב"ר דוד

ר' מאיר ב"ר יוסף, מרת חנה ב"ר משה

ר' אברהם ב"ר שמעיה ומרת אסתר ב"ר מאיר

◆

סבא רבא ר' אליעזר ב"ר אברהם ז"ל

וזוגתו מרת צרטיל ב"ר יצחק אייזיק ע"ה

סבא החבר ר' שמעון ב"ר אליעזר ז"ל

נלב"ע כ"ה אייר

משפחת אם אמי

ר' יהודה ב"ר זאנוויל ובתו חנה ובתה גיטל

ר' שלמה ב"ר משה חיים

ואשתו ליבא ב"ר ליפמן יואל

ר' יצחק אייזיק ב"ר שלמה הירש

וזוגתו מרת שיינא ב"ר שלמה

סבא רבא שמואל ב"ר אשר ז"ל

וזוגתו מרת יוטא בת ר' יצחק אייזיק ע"ה

נלב"ע י"ז ניסן

סבתא מרת שרה ב"ר שמואל ע"ה

נלב"ע י"א אלול